D1602437

TEACHING THAT TRANSFORMS

TEACHING THAT TRANSFORMS

FACILITATING LIFE CHANGE THROUGH ADULT BIBLE TEACHING

RICK & SHERA MELICK

B&H
ACADEMIC
NASHVILLE, TENNESSEE

Teaching That Transforms:
Facilitating Life Change Through Adult Bible Teaching

Copyright © 2010 by Shera and Rick Melick

ISBN: 978-0-8054-4856-6

Published by B&H Publishing Group
Nashville, Tennessee

Dewey Decimal Classification: 268.434
Subject Heading: Bible—Study and Teaching \ Teaching \ Religious

Printed in the United States of America
3 4 5 6 7 8 9 10 • 18 17 16 15 14
SB

To Our Children and Their Spouses,

All are Bible teachers:

Rick and Joy Melick;
Kristi and Michael Ent;
Karen and Darren Draeger.

And to Our Grandchildren,

Each of whom love the Bible,
in expectation that they, too, will teach it to others:

Richard and Nathan Melick;
Anna, Michael David, and Abigail Ent;
Rachael and Madeline Draeger.

Contents

PREFACE

TODAY MANY TEXTBOOKS ADDRESS the various aspects of teaching the Bible, and even more on teaching in general. Each volume promises something distinctive: a simple method, an aspect of teaching/learning, or descriptions of this generation. In light of that, the question may appropriately be "why another?" The obvious question begs an answer. This book incorporates both the traditional and the contemporary. Evangelical Christians affirm the authority of the Bible, and that is the traditional. We also affirm the need to make the Bible relevant to every generation in its cultural and educational context. That is the contemporary.

This book differs from others in several ways. First, we focus on adult education. Some may think that too narrow. Yet in the past 50 years in particular this emerging specialization has carved a lasting niche of its own. We now recognize as never before that adults learn differently and their learning needs and interests differ from other age groups.

Second, this book integrates. We as authors bring together two disciplines that naturally should be joined in Christian education. Together we have many years of teaching in biblical studies and education/educational leadership. Our observations reveal that sometimes books are strong in one or the other, but Christian education by definition must be strong in both.

We have consciously sought to integrate. Both disciplines we represent have sharpened focus in the past few years. Today we possess more resources, and more understanding of the skillful communication of them, than ever before. We have given serious attention to the nuances of the Bible and hermeneutics, interpreting the Bible. This consists of almost one-third of the book. We have also given serious attention to the fast-emerging field of adult education. No one can hope to keep abreast of everything in both fields. Nevertheless, at the time of writing, we believe we were current and we consciously attempted to address the best of both fields, putting them into a unified whole.

Third, the book provides a straightforward way of understanding the teaching processes. Again, we have relied on biblical and educational resources. Especially in part 3, we present our conclusions in the Star Model of Transformactional Teaching. The model covers the teacher, the teaching process, and the learners. Students may follow the steps in the Star Model and know their responsibilities to God, themselves, their material, their students, and to Christianity as they seek to promote the age-old message of the gospel.

God has called us to teach the Bible. We have taught generations of students in universities and graduates schools, and at the undergraduate and postgraduate levels, including Ph.D. Rick is currently Professor of New Testament and director of the Academic Graduate Programs (Th.M. and Ph.D.) at Golden Gate Baptist Theological Seminary. Shera is currently associate professor of Educational Leadership and chairperson of the Educational Leadership Department at Golden Gate Baptist Theological Seminary. Through the years of teaching students how to teach and preach, we have observed that most students, like most teachers, teach according to their own inclinations or their past successes. Many fail to understand or implement the principles that will make them more effective. This book was written in part to address that concern.

Our concerns are threefold. First, we hope and pray that both teachers and learners will grow into the maturity that God expects of all Christians. We hope they will be like Christ. Second, we hope they will have a firm confidence in the Bible. Confidence in Scripture comes, in part, from understanding its nature and how to interpret it correctly. Finally, we hope teachers will be attuned to the principles of effective teaching.

THE FORMAT OF THE BOOK

In writing the book, we determined the need for three elements. They are represented in the three sections of the book. The first two are foundational and, at times, theoretical. Part 1 is about the Bible. Part 2 reviews recent contributions to adult education. Part 3 is very practical, yet each chapter has additional theory that supports the points made. We have tried to link each principle to biblical guidelines and what seems to be applicable from adult theory. In that light, we have identified 14 principles from parts 1 and 2. They are listed in the introduction of part 3. Readers could, conceivably, read only part 3 and do so with profit. They would miss out, however, on much of the rationale and support for what we are saying.

ACKNOWLEDGMENTS

No book is produced in isolation. A team of persons cooperates to reach the goal of publication. We are conscious of our indebtedness to others and wish to thank some of them by acknowledging their contributions.

First, it has been a joy to coauthor a book. Ostensibly the task presents multiple challenges. First and foremost, we are husband and wife. Our decades of marriage have brought us closer together, and the writing of the book has accomplished the same. Second, we are both professors. Professors have convictions, and sometimes those convictions form through the academic disciplines in which professors engage. We both have strong convictions about our disciplines. In writing the book, we were pleased to see how we shared the deepest convictions about life, family, spirituality, Christian commitment, and teaching the Bible. Third, there are potential challenges integrating the two disciplines. Sometimes biblical studies and education can be quite disparate, even though they have the same goals. New Testament studies can be a world of its own, though it should never be isolated from any facet of life. Education and educational leadership can be focused on the practical in a way that sometimes simplifies complex issues. We have discovered what we thought. The two can blend and do, in fact, interrelate. We have grown in our appreciation of each other and our separate disciplines. It seems appropriate to acknowledge the multilevel contributions from each other in many more ways than can be identified objectively.

We are grateful for the opportunity to write afforded to us by the leadership of the B&H Publishing Group. Our primary association has been with Dr. Terry Wilder, acquisitions editor for Academic Books. His support and suggestions have encouraged us. Along with Terry, our longtime friend Dr. Ray Clendenen, senior editor for Academic Books, and Mr. Jim Baird, director of Academic Publishing, also participated in the process. B&H Publishing Group is our denominational press, and we have enjoyed our associations with its personnel through the years.

One of our students, Hyea Jin Yoon, did original graphic work as well as polished the graphs, tables, and charts. She spent many hours. We appreciate her readiness to work and her sticking with the project to its end. She is a talented Christian lady.

The leadership and staff of Golden Gate Baptist Theological Seminary provided invaluable assistance. Dr. Jeff Iorg, president, and the Board of Trustees granted us a semester sabbatical together to work on the project. Dr. Mike Martin, vice president of Academic Affairs, supported us along with his staff. Our two administrative assistants, David Busch and Josh Mathews, helped carry the load in our absence and enthusiastically sought ways to be of service and assisted in research. Finally, the library staff provided professional help in securing resources and other services. We especially thank Kelly Campbell, Director of Library Services; Dr. Fred Youngs, research librarian; and Janet Reese, collection development assistant.

Our family always encourages and supports, and they are the joys of our life. We thank our children, Rick III and Joy Melick, Kristen and Michael Ent, and Karen and Darren Draeger, along with our seven grandchildren: Richard and Nathan Melick; Anna, Michael David, and Abigail Ent; and Rachael and Madeline Draeger. Our mom, and mother-in-law, Irene Smith, who lives with us, prayed for us and encouraged us daily. Our friends Jim and Jewell Troxel provided a quiet place for us to study and write in the early stages.

We have approached this task responsibly and earnestly. We hope it is a contribution to those who have the amazing privilege of teaching the Bible to adults. At the deepest level, however, we have written this as a contribution to our Lord's service. If any good comes from it, it has come from Him. The weaknesses are our own.

Through the centuries the church has advanced through teaching. We hope our contribution will encourage teachers today. May our Lord be glorified in all we are, do, and say as we seek to honor and represent Him to those around us.

INTRODUCTION

FOR 2,000 YEARS THE church has advanced by teaching. Each generation has taken seriously the command to pass the faith on to faithful disciples who will be able to teach others also (Matt 28:18–20; 2 Tim 2:2). Teaching may seem second nature to the church. Teaching adults may seem even more intuitive. After all, adults have been taught all their lives. Christian adults should understand the church's theology, and they should be able to pass it on. The key word is *should*.

This generation, however, is leaving the church in droves. If they ever attended church or Sunday school, many do not now. Furthermore, they do not take or send their children to church. How do we reach them? One concern is the way we teach. People will participate in what is meaningful to them.

In the past 100 years, adult education has emerged as its own discipline. Educators now realize that adults learn differently from other age groups. They are not simply "larger children." They have their own distinctive characteristics, and they need to be taught in ways that enable them to learn in their own way.

One concern of this book is that many who teach adults have little or no exposure to the distinctive characteristics of adult learners. There are many reasons for this. Often adults teach as they were taught. Too many adults grew up in classrooms that contained only lecture. Consequently, now they lecture when they have opportunity to teach because for them this is teaching. This produces an ongoing generational cycle, and changing teaching methods may take generations. Others do not want to take the time to understand education. They assume the Bible is best taught by a teacher who "talks" through the lesson. If they employ other methods, it is often the time-honored practice of asking students to read verses consecutively, one verse per student in order, until the entire passage is read. Of course this practice is not only archaic and simplistic; it can also make some students very uncomfortable. Some portions of the Bible are extremely difficult to read, given ancient Near Eastern names and places.

Other reasons may be noted. Teachers often assume that every student learns the same way—like they do. In the last few decades serious attention has been given to different learning modalities and styles. It surprises some to find out that educational research demonstrates that relatively few students actually learn well through lecture only classes. Yet churches seldom reveal an understanding of the different learning modalities and learning styles theories.

Adult learners are often bored. The more committed Christians will attend Bible classes in order to support the church. Some will come because they know they need Bible study—it has been ingrained in them through the years. More, however, are simply leaving church. Church has no challenge to them. In a world of media, activity, resources, and frantic schedules, everything has to be worth their time for adults to give even an hour a week. They will not make that sacrifice for something that has little appeal or relevance.

This book is written to address this concern. The failure of those who teach adults is often a failure to understand how adults learn. The archaic or ineffective methods employed often do not accomplish their intended purpose of stimulating greater interest simply because they are inconsistent with the learning needs and interests of today's adults.

Adult learning can be defined as the acquiring and processing of information that affirms or changes the learner's perceptions, resulting in personal life choices. The choices may be physical, mental, spiritual, social, or cultural. Since the mid-twentieth century, the topic of adult learning has been a topic of significant interest. Educators have studied differences between learning in children and learning in adults, and adult learning emerged as its own area of study. Along with research in adult learning, research in psychology, educational psychology, physiology, and sociology continually contributes new understanding and promotes changes in the teaching process. Most recently, and largely because of technological advances with medical imaging, brain research has impacted our ability to understand adult learning.

The purpose of this book is to present an easily understood method for study and teaching the Bible. There are three parts. First, we address the nature of the Bible and some basic principles of how to understand it.

We have included this because the book is not only about education, it is about teaching the Bible. Secular educational theories contribute to our understanding, but Scripture is the content of our teaching. Therefore, we present information about what the Bible is as well as how to study it. This section is foundational. It contains more than how to study the Bible. It also contains information to equip teachers to handle some of the questions students often ask about the Bible. Teachers need to understand what the Bible is—the nature of its inspiration and authority. We also need to know something about the various translations of the Bible and the implications of confessing the authority of Scripture.

This book is dedicated to presenting proper methods. We do not deny the work of the Holy Spirit. In fact, without the supervision of the Holy Spirit the entire process from study to presentation will be powerless and uninformed. The Spirit has an affinity for an educated mind.[1] On the human side, we must do our part earnestly. Yet with all we can do, it is not enough. The Holy Spirit must enable and empower. We hope, therefore, that teachers will understand the need for serious study as well as the need to rely on the Holy Spirit.

In the second section, we present a survey of the primary contributions to adult learning theory in the past 60 years. In the mid- to late-twentieth century, the developing discipline of adult education had three major contributing theories: Andragogy, Self-Directed Learning Theory, and Transformative Learning Theory.[2] Each foundational contribution was accepted as another piece of the adult learning mosaic. Each piece gave birth to new knowledge and methodology; no contribution was viewed as terminal—completing the final picture. Thus many considered that the significance of Andragogy was its emphasis on Self-Directed Learning Theory. As educators explored Self-Directed Learning Theory, the core emphasis produced Transformative Learning Theory. There were multiple aspects of Transformative Learning Theory, but among them educators began to inquire about the physiological nature of adult transformation. Medical imaging produced maps of the physiological changes as adults learned, and brain research has emerged as perhaps the most significant recent advance in adult education. Recent interaction (twenty-first century) with critical and postmodern perspectives on adult learning and recent discoveries in brain research play a part in expanding the knowledge base and challenging adult educators to redefine teaching practices.

Although adult education theory often has secular presuppositions and theorists may or may not be considered "Christian," the Christian educator can glean helpful teaching principles that will enhance adult learning. Many of the "discovered principles" parallel models of teaching demonstrated in

---

[1] Though we cannot find the reference for this statement, it was passed to us as from the great Baptist preacher Charles Haddon Spurgeon.

[2] Andragogy is used ambiguously. Sometimes it refers to anything related to adult learning. Sometimes it refers to a specific theory. Most commonly in the United States, it refers to one theory of adult learning, and that is the way it will be used in this book.

Scripture. Why then do Christian teachers spend week after week in a "lecture only" style of teaching? Why should the secular world maximize adult learning for math or science while the Christian world refuses to review research and expand methodologies for Bible teaching?

The third section of the book consists of a specific philosophy of teaching, including a step-by-step method of developing lesson plans and presenting them in the classroom. It was born of years of personal study and teaching adult education. The method is eclectic. Every step of the method is informed by both educational theory and important biblical principles. We call it the Star Method of Transformactional Teaching. Our hope is that readers will find it a helpful way of going about teaching.

TRANSFORMACTIONAL

This book includes the use of a strange word: "transformactional." The word is derived from a combination of educational and biblical principles. One of the later theories of adult education was transformative teaching. It had many different nuances, but all had one common theme: the learner must be "transformed" if learning takes place. In a real sense, transformation theory gave rise to much of the modern discussion of adult education. That will be developed later in the book. At this point, it is helpful to understand that transformation is indeed the goal of education, and transformation learning must result in positive action. Responsible action both confirms and seals the learning process.

Some may say that action is the obvious end of education. However, this has not always been the case. Some have seen action as an "add on" to learning. In other words, what is learned must be "put into action." Separating these two elements is the point. Learning is more than mental. It is emotional. It is volitional. It is active. Transformation is indeed mental, but transformation also produces better living through informed action. In using the word "transformactional," we hope to stress two important aspects of learning. First, real learning includes action. Second, the process of learning is active. It actively seeks, embraces, and applies knowledge. In the case of Christian education, the learner actively seeks, embraces, and applies the truths of Scripture so that the learner develops Christlike character and lifestyle.

The word "transformactional" is also rooted in Scripture. It therefore is a word that relates to both education and the Bible: it is integrative. Many have studied spiritual growth in the Bible with different emphases. Some have approached it from a discipleship/mentorship model. Others have studied from a purely spiritual dimension, highlighting the spiritual principles that produce growth. Still others have studied from a psychological perspective, with scholars attempting to determine a "biblical psychology" of living. No doubt the list could go on. One thing all have in common: effective learning changes behavior. Thus action is the normal and desired end of knowledge.

A few biblical texts demonstrate the point, though many texts could be chosen. Later we will discuss how spiritual growth takes place and its essential elements. Here it will suffice to give some indication of a general theme of Scripture. One core passage is Rom 12:1–2. We will refer to it throughout the book. There the apostle Paul speaks of transformation, using the exact Greek word.[3] He says change comes "by the transformation of your mind." Without doubt this has a focus on the mental processes necessary for growth. Yet the passage clearly affirms the necessity of action. Paul introduced this command by saying, "stop being conformed to this world" and "keep being transformed."[4] Conformity indicates a pattern of action that comes from an inner disposition. The action and the attitude blend into one key element, not two. Paul continues the passage by saying the goal is to "approve excellent things." Though there are various translations of the word "approve," the basic Greek word means to put to the test to find the pure substance.[5] This is not exclusively a mental activity. In fact, such testing cannot be done as a quest for knowledge only. "Testing" implies living out the reality described and, in the process of life, burning away the impurities to find what is pure and lasting.

Paul also spoke of conversion as learning and doing. In Eph 4:20–24 he stated that the church had learned to take off the old man and to "put on the new man." This was something they knew from "learning Christ." That is, at the time of conversion they understood that a change of behavior accompanied Christianity.[6] It is not simply a change of mind; God expects a change of conduct. In that context, and its parallel in Col 3:9–10, the subject is how to live the Christian life. It is about acting the Christian life, not just knowing about it. As Colossians says you put off the old self "with its practices" (activities). Clearly Paul expected knowledge to result in action.

Action as essential to knowledge is also part of Christian living, not just conversion. When corrections are needed, or when new phases of growth are anticipated, action is both the proof that truth has been learned and the final component of gaining knowledge. This may be illustrated from 2 Cor 7:10–13

---

[3] The Greek word translated "transformed" contains the root word for "metamorphosis," a change of form.

[4] Significantly, both verbs highlighted here are present tense in the Greek text, indicating action that is ongoing. That suggests that transformation is a process.

[5] It was used of refining gold or other metals. The refining furnace "tested" by melting away impurities so that only the pure metal remained. The word *dokimazō* occurs frequently in Scripture, attesting to the point that action is part of education.

[6] These verbs are not continuous. The "taking off . . . putting on . . . learning Christ" are viewed as past actions that are simultaneous with conversion.

where Paul addressed the thorny problem of immorality at Corinth. It was his fourth time to speak to the specific issue, and this time he could speak with joy because of the change of heart in the failing brother.[7] Our point is that they finally learned. An essential part of their learning was the change of attitude and action toward the man and his sin after his repentance. They may have known about the principles of church discipline and restoration, but in exercising them in a concrete action their knowledge was brought to completion. Action was not simply an add-on.

It is almost impossible to find a place in Scripture where either conversion or Christian growth is only a change in mind. It is always a change in action. The action, of course, comes from an enlightened mind—one changed to understand and accept the ways of God. The educational patterns found in Scripture all suggest that the normal growth process is knowledge and change—action.

To capture this nuance, we have used the word "transformactional." It includes the reality that the transformation expected in learning is action. It involves the will and the emotion. Modern educational theory and biblical patterns both suggest this. God expects us to be transformed. He expects action as an essential part of that transformation. It is not an optional add-on. It is not the next logical step. It is a part of the learning. It is transformactional.

THE PLAN OF THE BOOK

The book is a combination of adult learning theory and biblical examples. The two are integrated into a unified approach to the educational process. You will profit most from the book by understanding the following information:

1. Since the book is about teaching the Bible to adults, it contains both biblical content and educational theory. Major sections of the book are devoted to each separately, and then they are brought together into an integrated procedure.
2. The biblical portions have multiple purposes. First, there are foundational presentations about the nature of the Bible: its revelation and inspiration and their implications. The point is that the Bible is both ultimate truth and the final authority for understanding all truth.

    Second, much of the material in the biblical sections is provided as a guide to answering questions students ask. We have observed these

---

[7] Paul addressed the problem of a man living in a publically known sexual relationship with his stepmother (1) prior to 1 Corinthians (see 1 Cor 5:9—a letter previous to 1 Corinthians), (2) in 1 Corinthians (see 5:3–5), (3) in a now lost additional correspondence with them (2 Cor 5:5–9), and (4) in 2 Cor 5:10–13.

questions in both the academic classroom and the church. One such example is the brief presentation of the theory of Bible translations. No teacher can expect that all students will use only one version of the Bible or the same version as the others. The issue is complex and the average person does not understand the nature and philosophies of Bible translation. We think it is helpful to let the adult teacher know some of the basic issues academicians deal with in producing a Bible translation. The discussion is basic, providing some instruction but hopefully whetting the appetite for further study. We can guarantee that virtually every Bible teacher will be asked two questions: "Why are there so many translations?" and "Which Bible is the best?" Hopefully these discussions will be helpful.

Third, there are illustrations from Scripture in many of the discussions. These also have two points: (1) they often illustrate how a principle may be put into practice, and (2) they are supportive of the educational theories we are affirming. They are not exactly "biblical proof" of educational theory. They rather demonstrate a consistency between the Bible and various aspects of current education practices.

3. There is a significant section on recent educational theories of adult education and adult learning. This section is not intended to be exhaustive, nor will it necessarily satisfy the interests of professional educators. We hope that the overviews are received as fair, and that they are appreciated for what they are: surveys. They are intended to enable the Bible teacher to have a grasp of the nature of adult learners and the need to craft Bible lessons in ways that correspond to this data. As might be expected, in the passing of time, theories are tested and refined. Not every part of any theory has permanence. On the other hand, there are core truths in almost every viable theory that educators should preserve and use. In that spirit, we have sought to present an overview of the theory, to identify the elements that have the most lasting value, and finally to incorporate what has lasting value into the adult Bible teacher's lesson plans. In attempting to accomplish this, we recognize we are stepping into a fast-flowing stream of educational thinking. New resources come available regularly. We have tried to be current at the time of publication, but know that new discoveries will have value. Hopefully the adult Bible teacher will at least understand the need to teach on an adult level.

4. The third section of the book is functional. New material is included, but the primary purpose is to take an adult teacher through a point-by-point checklist approach of incorporating educational theory into teaching and the lesson plan. The five major points are called the Star Method. Each point of the star is presented with sensitivity to the supporting educational and biblical materials, and each point is eclectic, reflecting the values of recent educational theory.

5. The order of the book is logical. We believe it is important to have both a procedure for constructing lesson plans and a solid rationale for each point. A teacher could read any of the three sections independently. Those who care little about the foundational support may read only the section on the Star Method and have benefit. As stated above, however, the method is the product of both educational and biblical study for many years, and each section has its own value and contribution to understanding the learning patterns of adult learners.

The book reflects many years of teaching in higher education, mostly in postgraduate programs. At the time of publication, the authors combined have had over four decades of teaching higher education. In our academic programs we have sought to teach fairly and honestly, interacting with a broad spectrum of issues and positions. Our primary concern, however, has been the effective communication of God's truth, found in the Bible, through teaching and preaching. The book is thus the product of live teaching experiences and serious interaction with well-prepared and motivated students.

Finally, we believe in the church. It is God's primary way of working in the world, and it is the fellowship where most people find spiritual challenge, enrichment, and wholesome relationships. In our day there are serious questions about the nature and organization of churches. We have never before seen such proliferation of theories and models. Most of these theories have come because people were disenchanted with the traditional church. Some have too quickly discarded it. Others have refused to change where it is needed, and therefore face the charge of irrelevance. No matter what church model one follows, the church will be only as strong as its teaching ministry, and the church-sustaining teaching ministry will be largely to adults. Churches that teach the Bible effectively will be effective. This book has value both within and outside of the structured church, but our concern is that the people of God move forward with maturity, sensitivity, and relevance. The Bible is the primary diet of those who desire spiritual growth. May we all learn to teach it with more accuracy, authority, and relevance as each generation answers God's call to faithfulness.

PART ONE

UNDERSTANDING THE BIBLE AND HERMENEUTICS

CHAPTER ONE

THE BIBLE

CHRISTIAN EDUCATION MUST BE CHRISTIAN. That means the educator works from a Christian perspective by conviction. Everything the Christian teacher considers true must have a biblical foundation.

Christianity is both biblically based and historically developed. What we know and believe as Christians depends on both. For centuries Christians have thought about the doctrines of Scripture and applied them to each generation. All modern Christians in one way or another depend on the work of those who went before. The creeds and confessions, catechisms, Bible study curricula, and myriads of sermons have a contribution to make in formulating Christian understanding.

In light of that, it is helpful for Christian educators to understand the particular distinctives of their denominations or other Christian affiliations. Thus, for example, there are distinctive emphases of Baptists, Methodists, Episcopalians, and Catholics. The concern of this book, however, is more ideological than denominational. It is written convictionally from a conservative, Evangelical perspective.

While the denominational perspective of the Christian educator is important, having a truly biblical perspective is more so. This means that the Bible stands at the core of Christian education. The primary concern of the Christian educator is to be informed by Scripture and to measure all content by the limits Scripture imposes. The Bible is primary; other materials are secondary.

For this reason, it is imperative that Christian teachers understand their core authority. The Bible must be more than a springboard into a separate discussion. Teaching the Bible requires that the teacher understand the nature of the Bible as well as the extent of its authority. This has become even more crucial in modern times. Adults are better informed and better educated than at any other time in history. Most have expertise in areas other than theology, and their commitment to their disciplines may subtly shift the locus of authority from the Bible to their own preferences.

Books have been written on the subject. This book is not about how to integrate the truth, nor is it a textbook of theology. Nevertheless, a book on teaching the Bible must address some of the issues that concern both adult teachers and students. We believe God has spoken to us. He may speak in many ways and through many persons and events, but primarily He has spoken in the Bible.

In addition to understanding the nature of the Bible, it is helpful to understand a few other matters related to the Bible. For example, why are there multiple translations of the Bible, and what is their value? How do we study correctly so that we are confident we teach what the Bible says and not what we want it to say? How do we apply the Bible to cultural issues that were unknown when it was written? Both teachers and students have questions in these areas. In the course of this book, we will provide some basic guidelines that will help teachers as they prepare to teach other adults.

REVELATION

The Bible is revelation. Revelation by definition is a disclosure of what is otherwise unknown. Common misunderstandings of the Bible, many prevalent today, suggest that the Bible is simply a record of human attempts to define truth. According to that, the Bible is placed on the same moral level as the religious and moral writings of other spiritual movements. Most Christians would agree that the Bible contains more and qualitatively different spiritual and moral truth. But that is not enough. The Bible is unique. Its uniqueness begins with the fact that it is a unique revelation from God.

GENERAL REVELATION

God chose to reveal Himself in two primary ways: general and special revelation. The first is sometimes called natural revelation. General revelation is truth that is available to all normal people by virtue of their humanness. It is God's way of bringing moral and spiritual truth to every person alive. General revelation accounts for the fact that people of all cultures, and all ages, have some understanding of the truth, though the truth may be obscured by harmful cultural, spiritual, and moral practices. General revelation is generally understood as available through two primary vehicles.

CREATION   General revelation comes through creation. As people view the created world, they view God's handiwork. They are able to draw correct conclusions from their observations, though they are equally likely to draw incorrect conclusions. For example, many remark that they feel closer to God in nature than in church. However, the closeness they feel to God in nature usually means they enjoy the peace and quiet of nature. They enjoy being in "God's creation."

Yet nature reveals more than peace. Nature has a hard side, a side not often identified with God. Animals eat other animals, sometimes subjecting them to painful and slow torture before death. Hurricanes, tornados, earthquakes, famine, and drought cause pain and suffering. This, too, is nature, but few speak of being close to God while witnessing a lion attack a young wildebeest. Often hunters express a closeness they feel to God while hunting out "in nature," though ironically, they may somewhat disrupt its serenity.

Even in its ambivalence, creation does reveal God. It is God's handiwork, and people are responsible to draw logical spiritual conclusions from observing nature. Nature reveals that God exists and that He is eternally powerful (Rom 1:20ff). Knowing these basic truths about the God, we should deduce that we have a responsibility to worship the God who created all things. On the other hand, our observations of nature should also include that nature's serenity is disturbed by sin, the hard side of nature. Something is wrong even in the best of natural environments.

In other words, observing nature should bring a true theology. The apostle Paul spoke to our responsibility in observing nature in an extended passage of Scripture. In Rom 1:18 and following he described our responsibilities along with what happens when people fail to keep them. First, creation reveals the presence of God the creator. The order observed in nature's rituals, seasons, and eras point to the order of a creator. The varieties of plant, animal, and marine life point to God as being greater than His creatures. Second, creation reveals that God is eternally powerful. With all the discoveries of modern science, the forces of nature remain untamed. The power of the sea, wind, and fire point us beyond ourselves to One more powerful than these natural forces. The cycles of nature, including life and death, reveal One who survives these cycles, who is somehow above them, and whose existence is not confined to them. All of these observations should lead us to worship and praise. Some people observe creation and arrive at legitimate conclusions about God. Others fail to do so and end in error. Thus there is a need for something beyond creation to enlighten the mind and put things in proper perspective by correcting nature's mixed message.

One of the fascinating aspects of modern life is the unprecedented capacity to observe nature. It is true that people spend less time in the out-of-doors because of the conveniences of modern life. Even so, more knowledge is available to understand "natural processes" through modern science and technology. Movies, documentaries, and even entire cable channels now describe how nature functions. With this knowledge available to us in our homes, we have no excuse. Now we do not have to be in nature to observe nature. Commentators, narrators, and scientists give us the benefit of their extensive studies and observations. Their commentary may not always be consistent with a biblical perspective on the origins and operations of natural processes, but the accumulation of materials they present should encourage people to think about God, and in their thoughts to worship Him.

THE IMAGE OF GOD   General revelation comes to us through our being created in the image of God. Being created in God's image means that in some respects we are like God. While people are not divine, we approximate and reflect divine characteristics in the way we think and act.

The apostle Paul spoke to this point in several texts. One of the most insightful occurred when he was in dialogue with philosophers on Mars Hill, Athens (Acts 17:16–31). Observing the idols that surrounded this intellectual center, Paul observed that we should not expect idols to reveal God's true nature (17:24). In contrast to them, people rise above idols in their ability to think, act, and express personality. Surely God, by definition, surpasses the idols. The conclusion is clear. People are God's offspring. God, therefore, is more like us than He is like inanimate objects or animal life. Indeed, we should look to our humanness to discover God (17:28–29). In other texts Paul makes it clear that his argument is based on the fact that we are made in the image of God (Rom 2:14–15).

The image of God manifests itself in multiple ways. At the core, it manifests itself in rationality (orderly communication), love (satisfying relationships), and morality (positive choices). First, God communicates in an orderly and organized fashion. Perfect communication exists within the Trinity, among the Father, Son, and Spirit. As an extension of His communicative ability,

God created in an orderly fashion, and creation functions in an orderly way.[1] The highest of creation, human beings, reflect God's order most in rationality: the ability to think and organize. Orderly creation and human rationality allow people to observe, analyze, organize, and, in some cases, reproduce the natural processes of creation. Thus as an extension of orderly communication and creation, people observe and communicate with each other. Rationality enables us to understand and communicate to each other the wonders of natural science as well as to ask questions about the origin and purpose of creation. Human godlikeness brings capacities still unexplored as discovery feeds discovery. All this is possible because people are created in the image of God.

The principle of rationality coming from the image of God impacts us in all we do. Most particularly, natural revelation enables us to discover, refine, and teach many subjects not found in the Bible, including science, philosophy, psychology, as well as education. Christians should be thankful for these disciplines and the people who work within them. We should always remember, however, that they come largely from natural revelation and, since natural revelation is incomplete and partial, the conclusions drawn from human logic and observation must be evaluated outside themselves.

Second, the image of God brings capacity for love. God loves perfectly. God expresses His love perfectly among the Father, Son, and Spirit. They find satisfaction in loving each other. They also receive love perfectly in their threefold reciprocal relationships. Each loves the other, enabling each to receive love from the others. In giving and receiving, therefore, each finds both fulfillment and satisfaction.

Capacity for love is at the heart of human relationships. People need love. When we are loved, we find security and significance. When love fails, self-seeking leads to self-destruction. Many are blinded in relationships and they spend their time seeking to be loved, but being loved is the result of initiating love to others.

The capacity for love brings social order. All things are to be done in love for all people. Relationships built on love satisfy; relationships broken by lack of love harm. The world is full of both satisfying and harmful relationships because of the tension between being in the image of God and our rebellion from God, sin. Being in the image of God, combined with the capacity for organized communication, enables us to study the social and behavioral sciences, including political science where leaders seek to promote the common good.

---

[1] Thinking of creation as an outgrowth of orderly communication reinforces the truth that creation itself "communicates" God to us, as described earlier. It is significant that the Bible records creation occurred when "God spoke."

Third, the image of God brings the ability for moral choice. God created us with the capacity for making choices about right and wrong. As the Bible records, Adam and Eve abused this capacity by choosing wrong. The wrong choice tainted every aspect of life with a rebellion against God and His order. Thus people can affirm right living (Rom 2:14), and they can embrace wrong living (Rom 1:18–32).[2] The capacities for self-direction and moral choices come from our being in the image of God.

The Christian teacher must recognize and value natural revelation. Goodness and truth owe their existence to God, wherever they are found. The great themes of literature, music, rhetoric, and drama come to us because of the human capacities endowed by our being in the image of God. Similarly, our ability to arrive at conclusions by observing scientific processes comes from being in the image of God. Unfortunately, the distorted image of God (sin) brings the capacity to use abilities intended for good to express themes contrary to God and His character. Therefore, throughout the history of the world, some who work in the arts and sciences communicate ambivalent themes. Sometimes they affirm the good, as part of affirming the good nature of God, and sometimes they express the bad, the product of destructive thinking and behavior because of sin.

Because of the ambivalence of human life, the Christian teacher must develop critical thinking. Even Christians can easily become tangential and misguided. Similarly, human beings, no matter how distorted, can often appreciate the good that God is and made us to be originally. Natural revelation enables sensitivity to God and, through observation and logic, enables at least a basic knowledge of God as well. Education often speaks of acquiring knowledge. All true knowledge, however, comes from the fact that God reveals both Himself and truth, allowing people to discover Him through the order of His creation.

Natural revelation, therefore, brings both knowledge and confusion. Themes like truth, love, justice, and peace, along with how they are expressed through various media, enable us to live better. At the same time, natural revelation lacks precision. It does not clearly explain the problems of good and evil. It cannot teach clearly the need for repentance and God's gift of grace in Christ. It cannot place ultimate value judgments on how people live nor can it provide the necessary lessons of life transformation. As wonderful as natural revelation is, there is a need for more.

---

[2] This is the concern of Paul in Romans 1–3. Systematically he describes three different possible relationships to God through the various aspects of creation. He then explains how people fail in all three because of sin. The image of God at creation is, then, distorted by rebellion from God.

Before leaving this subject, we should note that adult teachers have literally at their fingertips a world of possibilities for teaching biblical truths. The natural world provides multiple examples of God's nature that can be illustrated through the various media. Almost every human event and activity can become an occasion for pointing out God's magnificence and our responsibility to profit from the available revelation. General revelation also provides multiple opportunities for adults who have expertise in many different areas of life. Adult students can utilize their experiences well as part of the learning process. Teachers, therefore, should develop their own sensitivity to these issues and cultivate the art of thinking biblically about the world in which we live.

SPECIAL REVELATION

The second type of revelation is special revelation. By definition, this is revelation beyond the ordinary. Christian theologians use the phrase special revelation to define how God chooses to reveal Himself in unusual and uncommon ways. Generally, special revelation includes miracles, the incarnation of Jesus, and the Bible.

MIRACLES Defining miracles challenges Christian thinkers. On the one hand, some call ordinary events miracles, so that on occasion good fortune is considered miraculous. On the other hand, some are skeptical that miracles can occur, at least today, so no matter how unusual the event, they look for natural explanations.

Theologians have defined miracles in two primary ways. Some see them as God inserting higher laws (from the "higher" domain in which He exists) into a world of lower laws (the world in which we live). Thus miracles follow patterns of law, but not necessarily the laws we normally see on earth. Others define miracles as the interruption of law by God's spontaneous intervention. From this perspective, miracles are a matter of God's choice, His will in any given situation, rather than His laws.

Regardless of definition, one function of miracles is that they reveal. They reveal the nature of God and His desire for order in a broken and chaotic world. They are, therefore, normally positive and restorative. Miracles point people to God, but they also bring God to people! Since by definition they are not the norm, and are not available to everyone, they are classified as special revelation.

It should be noted that miracles defy scientific evaluation. They are outside the category of natural revelation and thus receive a mixed review from natural observers. The spectrum of understanding ranges from full acceptance to complete disregard. Some try to build theories of existence on miracles, but they find a major difficulty. Miracles by definition are outside the realm of repeatable observation. When philosophers and scientists operate within their training, they tend to devalue miracles because they cannot be put into the grid of the scientific method. The "one time" nature of miracles makes them impossible to analyze by science, since scientific investigation requires repeatable events. Simply stated, one cannot form a hypothesis about what miracles are and how they function left to observation alone.

Given that understanding, miracles cannot become the basis of theories of behavior. Even if the reality of miracles is accepted, it, and they, cannot be proof of normative principles for conduct. Therefore, if an observer wants to form a set of principles based on personal interpretation of miracles, he or she immediately finds a problem. They do not appear consistently enough to prove the reality of whatever is assumed to be proven by them. They can only be interpreted properly when they fit consistently, and logically, within a worldview that includes them. Thus miracles have value only within a separately and more objectively defined organization of life experiences.

Miracles are, therefore, of limited value in revelation. The writers of the Bible seemed to understand the blessings and limitations of miracles. In the entirety of the Bible, the writers exercise care and caution in recording miracles. In Scripture, miracles are clustered around special transitional times in history: creation, the exodus from Egypt, the conquest of Canaan, the conflict with Baal (and other false gods), the life of Jesus, and the Second Coming. The transitional times required unusual confirmation that God was continuing to work in and for His people. This was acutely necessary when circumstances and situations changed. Furthermore, the writers seemed to realize that miracles only witness to the truth. John quite explicitly writes of them as "signs" (John 20:30–31). Signs point beyond themselves. Miracles point beyond themselves, but to what do they point? They point to God's special intervention into human affairs.

THE INCARNATION OF JESUS   The incarnation of Jesus is the second area of special revelation. It is God's highest revelation, since Jesus is the exact radiance of God's nature (Heb 1:1–3). In the incarnation of Jesus, God revealed the high estate of humanity since God became flesh (Heb 2:8). On the other hand, as God's Son Jesus revealed God to us. Being human, Jesus brought us to God. His life, death, resurrection, and ascension provide unique knowledge of God. Through natural revelation all people should have appreciation for Jesus, but not all understand the special revelation of His presence. Jesus' death reversed the effects of sinful rebellion. It enables those who accept Him to have sins forgiven and a restored image of God within. Those who accept Him recognize that He was more than a human being. He was a divine-human combination, perfectly uniting both God and people. In Him there is divine truth. Jesus is special revelation from God to us.

Although Jesus is the highest form of revelation to us, there are limitations in what we learn from Him. First, in becoming human, Jesus was limited in time and space to one period of time and one geographical place. Thus, unlike natural revelation, Jesus is not available to every person in the way He was to some on earth. A second limitation is the fact that the aspects of His life that are most meaningful to us, His death and resurrection, are extraordinary. They are like miracles in that the uniqueness of these events is not observable to all. Only the people of first-century Palestine had the ability to see these events with physical eyes. In God's wisdom and providence, He entrusted the propagation of the most significant event in history to people who would write about it for posterity.

Like miracles, Jesus' life has little significance to us unless we understand it. We may assume He lived in history, but it is the uniqueness of His life, death, and resurrection that bring us salvation. Like miracles, therefore, we need a more comprehensive framework in which to place Jesus' life for a clear and rational explanation of it.

THE BIBLE   The third form of special revelation is the Bible. After Jesus' death His followers began writing their memories of what Jesus said and did. There were multiple writings (cf. Luke 1:1–4), but God uniquely orchestrated only some of these resources to say exactly what He wanted written. These special writings are the four canonical Gospels, the Acts of the Apostles, the canonical Epistles, and the Revelation. Each has a different function in explaining and applying the gospel to specific circumstances. Over a period of time, the early church recognized the unique nature of these books and affirmed them as Holy Scripture.

The Bible, both Old and New Testaments, provides both a supplement to general revelation and a standard for measuring the truth contained in it. Relying on general revelation, many use logical or other epistemological approaches to arrive at conclusions. Sometimes these conclusions counter what is revealed in the Bible, creating a crisis of confusion in interpreting the data. In this crisis, people rely on one of four epistemologies to provide coherent interpretation. They will revert to logic, empiricism, rationalism, or experience to determine what is true.[3] But each of these epistemologies is the product of

---

[3] There are multiple, complicated definitions of these epistemologies. For our purposes here, we may define them as follows. Logic looks for coherence in all of the available data so that all aspects

human faculties. They are human attempts to arrive at knowledge. The normal human solution to the difficulties in the quest for truth is to debate the relative merits of each epistemology. The hope is to reach some consensus that makes sense of the available data.

Divine revelation speaks to this stalemate of epistemological understanding. Rather than being left to human devices, people now have a word from God. God chose to reveal Himself and His truth in the Bible. Practically, that means that every theory that is considered true must be consistent with, and not contrary to, what the Bible teaches.

Special revelation therefore corrects and supplements general revelation. Where general revelation fails because it is incomplete or inadequate, special revelation provides a proper way of thinking.

Christian education acknowledges both types of revelation. More than that, Christian education incorporates the findings of general revelation into a biblical framework and relates them to life. Much of what we want to know, and a significant amount of what we use daily, comes from natural revelation. Furthermore, natural revelation provides tools and analyses that enable us to know. But ultimately, there is a need for something beyond that to inform us. We have questions about God, eternity, life and death, significance, and morality. They are the important subjects of life. The Bible alone provides the answers.

INSPIRATION

God uniquely inspired the Bible. In fact, its inspiration explains how it is revelation, how it gains its authority, and why it is relevant to every person's life. The Christian teacher should understand both the meaning and significance of the inspiration of the Bible in order to teach from a truly Christian perspective. In addition, understanding the doctrine of inspiration forms a foundation for Christian thinking about all areas of life. We will provide a definition and some of the important implications of the inspiration of the Bible.

DEFINITION OF THE INSPIRATION OF THE BIBLE

We will define the inspiration of the Bible with a simple statement. However, there are significant implications to this definition that must also be explained. The definition is:

---

of the truth support each other and there are no contradictory statements. Empiricism looks to what can be experienced by the senses as ultimately true. Rationalism places the highest value on what the mind can produce in explaining data and the proper use of other epistemologies, such as experience. Experience looks to what happens (experiences) as self-validating and seeks to build a philosophy of life on personal experience.

God so orchestrated the circumstances of the writing of Holy Scripture that every word participates in its context to communicate exactly and accurately what God intended to say. Since every word comes from God, and is inspired, the Bible is inerrant in what it affirms and it is accurate in what it teaches. Because of the many copies of the Bible, this refers to the autographs only.

IMPLICATIONS OF THE INSPIRATION OF THE BIBLE

Several implications may be drawn from this simple statement. It obviously emphasizes the divine origin of Scripture and, more particularly, the words of Scripture. Inspiration reflects God's power to work in history, communicating clearly to and among people. Only God could inspire the Bible in the way He did. Furthermore, the implications of the doctrine of biblical inspiration have certain corollaries that are both essential to understand and important to forming an adequate Christian philosophy within which to teach.

Finally, this section also includes some material that simply informs those who would teach adults. Adults ask many questions. Some come from an attempt to articulate what Scripture is and how to understand it. The following contains many of these implications, corollaries, and answers.

THE BIBLE IS INERRANT.   Since God inspired the words, the Bible is inerrant. Theologians have spoken to this point in various ways. They have done so in order to communicate to the needs of their generations, including the ideas prevalent in them. In the twentieth century there was a need for more precision of thought and the term inerrant became popular. Inerrant captures for us what Christians throughout history had been saying with words appropriate to their times. The word is chosen because of the conviction that God would not reveal Himself in a flawed revelation.[4]

Some have objected to the doctrine of inerrancy. First, some say it is not appropriate to use a term not found in the Bible. Thus we should not say more about the Bible than the Bible says about itself. This sounds like a good argument, but it has its own inadequacies.

For one, the writers of the Bible treat Scripture in a way that reveals their understanding that the Bible does not err. For example, in debate with religious officials, Jesus stated that the "Scripture cannot be broken" (John 10:35). On another occasion, Jesus, speaking with the Sadducees, stated they were in error because they did not know the Scriptures (Matt 22:29). He then proceeded to base His argument with them on the precise wording of Exod 3:6 (Matt 22:32).

---

[4] The word "inerrant" came into theological language about the Bible at the end of the 1800s. It appeared more frequently in the early 1900s, but became a major defining concept of the Bible among Evangelicals from the mid-1900s on.

Peter wrote that the writers of Scripture searched their own writings for the "time and circumstances" when their predictions would be fulfilled (1 Pet 1:11 NIV). Multiple other references suggest that the biblical writers expected the events of Scripture to be fulfilled. They treated the Bible as inerrant.

Second, it is appropriate to use the term "inerrant" for Scripture because it is a theological term that appropriately defines the truth. As the early church sought theological clarification and systematized the Scriptures, they used many terms that are not found in Scripture. We accept many of these terms today. For example, the characteristics of God all orthodox Christians affirm are often described by terms not found in the Bible. These include such terms as omnipresent, omniscient, omnipotent, and aseity. The list could go on. The issue is not whether something is found in the Bible; it is whether or not the word chosen describes the Bible accurately.

An increasing number of scholars today accept the word "inerrant." The most comprehensive statement of biblical inerrancy, and one that is used increasingly in defining inerrancy, is *The Chicago Statement of Biblical Inerrancy*, the product of some of the leading thinkers of our day.[5] Similarly, the *Baptist Faith and Message* states that the Bible is "truth without any mixture of error."[6] Both statements attest to the belief that the Bible does not, and cannot, make mistakes.

The discussions of Scripture are complex. Some prefer the term "infallible" rather than inerrant. The terms are basically synonyms. However, those who prefer infallible rather than inerrant usually use the term to define the message of the Bible rather than the Bible itself. For them, the infallibility of Scripture means that what Scripture teaches is true. They want to stop at that point, however, and not make a general statement that all Scripture is true. The term infallible may be correctly applied to Scripture if it is a synonym for inerrant. If it means that only the message of the Bible is true, it falls short of the Bible's witness to itself. The truthfulness of the Bible includes its message but also includes every aspect of the Bible's presentation of its message. The teacher must think through the authority of the Bible, its inspiration, and develop confidence that it is, indeed, God's word to us.

WORDS DEMAND CONTEXTS. The words of Scripture have meaning only in their contexts. The second implication of the doctrine is the necessity of

---

[5] The International Council on Biblical Inerrancy materials are now housed in the archives of the Dallas Theological Seminary library, Dallas, Texas. The link to the statement is http://library.dts.edu /Pages/TL/Special/ICBI.shtml. It should be noted that Rick participated in constructing this statement and is one of the original signers.

[6] This may be found on the Web site of the Executive Committee of the Southern Baptist Convention, www.sbc.net.

contexts to provide meaning for words. Obviously individual words bring an independent sense to a statement because of their definitions. It is impossible to substitute one word for another and have the exact same meaning in both. The individual words inspired by God have value in and of themselves. Words have *references* (definitions), but contexts provide meaning. The fact is, language needs words and contexts.

This raises the question of how words have meaning. Meaning comes in part from a word's etymology, that is, from its origins. Meaning also comes from tracing the word through the centuries of its use to a current use in a given time (*usus loquendii*). To use an English example, in older English Bibles the Greek word *agapē*, love, is translated by charity. Today charity has a specific meaning, that of helping those in need. The ancient meaning hardly suffices today for the comprehensive nature of love described in 1 Corinthians 13. Good interpretation requires knowing the language well enough to allow for these kinds of changes.

Relating to words, therefore, communication involves understanding two aspects of meaning. Words have a *reference* that may be literal or ideological, such as cat (literal) or love (ideological). This is a definition it brings from the basic way the word is formed. When words are placed in a context, however, the context shapes the meaning of the *reference*.

In approaching Scripture, it is easy to assume that because the words are inspired they have a meaning of their own. They are "god-words." Such is not always the case. Biblical words can be theologically significant, like justification and sanctification. Even they depend on their historical reference points and their local contexts. Thus the words of Scripture are orchestrated by God to participate in their contexts correctly.

This discussion of words has a direct bearing on the interpretation of the Bible. First, it is incorrect to focus on specific words as though they are inspired *without* their contexts. Word study brings rich rewards, but teaching the meaning of the individual words is not teaching the meaning of a Bible text. Second, it is necessary for the teacher to think in terms of logical and defining units of text. Basically, that means we must think *paragraphs*. The context not only helps shape the truth of a statement; it also provides direction for the meaning of individual words.

TEACHING IS CORRECT. What the Bible teaches is true and what it records, it records correctly. The Bible is a library containing many ways of presenting truth. It includes stated *propositions* that are true, and it often illustrates truth through history and biography. Stories are recorded as they occurred. In developing the stories, the statements of some, false prophets for example, are wrong when judged by the standards of Scripture as a whole. Yet their statements are recorded correctly. It is necessary therefore, to determine what the Bible is actually teaching, not just what it is recording. While that is not always an easy matter to determine, once it is determined that the writer affirms something as true, it is true.

On the other hand, much of the Bible content is information the writers recorded that is clearly not true. For example, it contains dialogues that no reader would accept as the truth. Job's friends offered him their wisdom, much of which was indeed spiritually minded wisdom. In other contexts what they said may have been correct. In Job's case, however, they were wrong. Though they may have been generally wise, they misdiagnosed Job's situation. The Bible does not affirm the content of Job's friends. In fact, at the end of the book it is clear that they have been wrong. In these contexts, inerrancy means that the writers of Scripture have accurately recorded the materials they have included. They do not, however, affirm their truthfulness.

Even so, when the Bible records facts or events it records them correctly. One of the greatest tension points regarding biblical authority has been its relationship to science. The Bible does contain scientific statements. Sometimes it teaches what falls into the realm of science. Most of the time, however, the Bible assumes a scientific viewpoint to make another point. That does not mean the Bible is incorrect scientifically. As discussed above, it is essential to determine what the Bible is affirming about science and what it is recording.

Another tension point is in the recording of history. The Bible's message is that God entered history in the incarnation of Jesus. The Bible's story is told on the stage of human history. History is important to the writers. They often teach that history is the locus of God's actions, and they draw significant theological points from the obvious acts of God in history. When the writers interpret history, and when they state events are the result of God's intervention, they are correct. Sometimes scholars debate specifics of the events. Most specifically, these debates take place over events like the fallen walls of Jericho or the dates of certain kings and, therefore, the activities credited to them. We must be careful to study seriously and honestly. But the doctrine of inspiration means that when we are able to determine the correct texts, these texts correctly record history.

The teacher must develop a sense of exegesis and hermeneutics that allows for distinguishing between what is affirmed and what is recorded. Teachers may make the "Job mistake." Because the words *occur* in the Bible it is easy to assume the Bible is teaching them. While we can trust that every part of the Bible is correct in light of its purposes, we can only accept as true what it actually teaches us is true.

GOD USES PERSONALITIES.   God did not violate the personalities of the authors. The Bible is a collection of individual books. The word "Bible" comes from the Latin *biblia* meaning library. In this collection, called the canon, there are 66 different books divided into the Old Testament (39) and the New Testament (27). The first writings were no earlier than 1400 BC and the last were at approximately AD 100. In the 1,500 years of writing the Bible, there were at least 39 authors, three languages (and some Latin words in addition), and several different cultural settings.

The specific texts of the Bible reflect this kind of diversity. Isaiah wrote with the eruditeness of one who walked with kings. Mark wrote with simplicity and quick-moving stories. John used a limited vocabulary and simple imagery, yet produced some of the most profound thought in Scripture. Second Peter is almost hopelessly poor Greek by normal standards. The point is that the writings, like the writers, display many different styles. The vocabulary also demonstrates variety. Writers used words the way they chose, sometimes like other writers and sometimes not. When studied carefully, especially in the original languages, the marks of individualism appear everywhere.

Some assume that God dictated the Bible. If that were the case, the Bible would have less diversity and a far more standardized vocabulary. There are a few places where the Bible claims to be dictated by God (Moses on Sinai for example, Exodus 20), but by in large the writers seem unaware that they were inspired as they wrote. Divine inspiration was recognized by the readers, but not always felt by the writers!

Luke gives the most explicit evidence of this. In his prologue to the Gospel, Luke states that he consulted many oral and written sources to the life of Jesus. Because of the number and variety, Luke said, "it seemed good also to me, . . . most excellent Theophilus" to write in orderly sequence (Luke 1:1–4 NIV). Luke approached his work much like college students do their term papers, researching carefully, evaluating, and then writing.

The process of inspiration coincides with the providence of God. God prepared the writers. He knew their circumstances: birth, growth, language abilities, personalities, and training. He also provided the opportunity for them to write. Then, *while* they were writing what they wanted, God overshadowed them so that all their natural abilities, personalities, and experiences influenced their writing. All the while God guided their thoughts as well as their words, using it all for His purposes.

This divine-human synergy characterizes the Bible. Unlike most other religious books, the Bible contains different genre, the influence of different writers, different circumstances, and different languages. God used each. He did so in such a way that there are common themes and no mistakes. He did not violate individual personality; he used it to the full.

Teachers should appreciate this diversity and work within it. For example, the variety of style means that the teacher should try to understand the particular ways a given writer writes. Vocabulary, themes, and style are intensely personal.[7] From another perspective, two writers may use the same words or phrases in their writing with different meanings. The teacher must develop sensitivity to know *how* the writer uses the words and *what* their meaning is in each context.[8]

ORIGINAL MANUSCRIPT INSPIRED. The inspiration of scripture refers to the special act of god in inspiring the original manuscripts. The process of inspiration involved both the writers and their writings. The primary focus of inspiration is on the writings. God so used the writers that the product, the finished book, was exactly what God wanted written in exactly the way He wished. Thus the books are "God-breathed" (2 Tim 3:16 NIV).[9]

On occasion, however, the Bible affirms the inspiration of the authors. For example Peter states that the Spirit of Christ was in the writers of prophecy (1 Pet 1:21). John quotes Isaiah in a way that singles out the man rather than the writing (John 12:38–40).[10] It is impossible to think of the writings being inspired without the inspiration of the authors. The emphasis of Scripture, however, is on the writings. The locus of inspiration, therefore, is the manuscript that the writer penned. It is the objective and abiding product of inspiration.

A problem arises when we realize that we may not have the original manuscripts. There are thousands of manuscripts containing all or portions of the biblical texts. Some are copies of the various books; others are translations or quotations used in the writings of the church fathers. There are more manuscripts of the Bible, especially the New Testament, than of any other ancient writing. This is due to the energy of Christians who believed it was necessary to have written witnesses to Jesus. The earliest Hebrew manuscripts were found in the Dead Sea Scrolls, written about 200 BC. The earliest Greek

---

[7] Some of the finer distinctions of style are lost in translations. Translations into other languages are, almost by definition, uniform in their style and presentation.

[8] An example of this principle is the difference between Matthew and Paul in using the words "calling" and "chosen" (Matt 22:14 and Rom 8:28–30).

[9] The Greek word translated "inspired" is literally "God exhaled." The result of being "God-breathed" is the texts are "inspired."

[10] It should be noted that in these verses John states "Isaiah spoke" twice and the two are from two different portions of Isaiah. The first quotes Isa 53:1, the section that many call "Deutro-Isaiah" and attribute to a different author; the second is Isa 6:1, the first portion of the book. Thus John attributes the entirety of the book to one Isaiah.

manuscripts we have date from the second century AD. Complete copies of the Bible occur as early as the fourth century AD.

It is quite likely that we do not have the original manuscripts, called the autographs ("self-writings"). Individual manuscripts were sent to specific destinations (in the New Testament most often churches). They were read and circulated. Often copies were made so others who recognized their value could have access to the books. Furthermore, many manuscripts were lost or destroyed. Most were written on papyrus, a plant that Egyptians used to make "paper." Being organic, they only survived in the most arid of climates. The result of all of this is that it is impossible to tell which manuscripts might be original and which are not. The logical assumption is that we do not possess the original.

Why, then, the insistence that inspiration refers only to the original manuscripts? There are two basic reasons. First, it is logical and normal to focus on the original. Even today people focus on the original. We expect signed copies of legal papers, and the original printings of books have more value. We recognize the importance of the original and the high likelihood that changes may take place in later copies.

Second, we know that in the transmission of the books copyists often made mistakes. Since all ancient copies were handwritten, and the product of dictation or laborious comparison of manuscripts, mistakes are inevitable. Scholars refer to these as variants. Variants occur when there are two manuscripts that differ on the same passage. Obviously one is wrong. Through the science of textual criticism we have technical ways of determining which is the original.

Textual criticism reveals two important truths regarding the Bible. We can usually understand why variances occurred. They were normally mistakes of hearing or copying, quite inadvertent and unintended. Sometimes, however, the need to harmonize texts or theologies influenced the writing. Thus we can know with a high degree of accuracy which textual reading is earlier than the others. Furthermore, we know the range of options for any given variant. There are multiple manuscripts, over 5,200 of portions of the New Testament alone. In all of the discoveries, no manuscript contains something outside of those already in our possession. We know what was contained in the original whether we actually possess it or not.

There is one final matter relating to the copies of manuscripts. In all of the copies, there is no doctrine that is changed or questioned because of manuscript readings. In fact, no clear doctrine of Scripture rests on any one text. While there were relatively few changes to clarify or support doctrine, we know where these are, how they arose, and what the original was. Even with them, there are no difficulties with the doctrines of orthodox Christianity.

The average teacher is not equipped to handle the intricacies of textual criticism. It is helpful to know, however, that the multiplicity of manuscripts accounts in part for the variety of modern translations. We will discuss that later. In addition, sometimes students will suggest a reading not found in the teacher's translation of choice. The ultimate question is the reading of the original manuscript as best we can determine it.

BIBLICAL AUTHORITY The Bible's authority is in faith and practice. Any book's authority directly depends on its accuracy. A book may be judged fairly only on what it claims to be teaching. It is wrong to find fault with a science book because it does not teach culinary arts or a psychology book because it does not deal with geology. Obviously the Bible is a book of faith and practice. It was written to instruct us what to believe and how to live out those belief structures in the best possible way. It is wrong to assume the Bible correctly teaches other subjects.

Faith and practice encompass the aspects of life we most need to know for society and ourselves. Volumes of literature exist as testimony to the many attempts to derive meaning in life, resolve evil, and address many perplexing issues we all face. For Christians, when the Bible speaks to these issues, it is the authority. Similarly, modern behavioral sciences speak to the life issues of persons and the societies in which they live. Again, when the Bible speaks to these issues, it is the authority for Christians. The obvious implication is that every Christian has to evaluate subjects like philosophy and psychology, as well as those that come from modern media. The ultimate standard for evaluation is what the Bible teaches.

> *Any claim to truth must be consistent with, and not contrary to, the Bible.*

THE CANON

The Bible was written in three primary languages. The Old Testament was written in ancient Hebrew for the most part, though later portions of it were in Aramaic. The New Testament was written in Greek with a few expressions remaining in Aramaic and Latin. At the time each book was written, the writers wrote in the language of the people who would read it. This became especially clear when in the early 1900s Greek scholars found many papyri documents outside the Bible that read like the Bible. Before that time there were no known documents that read like the Greek New Testament, and many scholars decided the New Testament was written in "Biblical Greek" or "Holy Spirit Greek." We now know that the Bible was written in the common language of the people. The Greek was a simplification of the various dialects of classical Greek to enable the Greek city-states and their armies to communicate for military and economic purposes. Alexander the Great successfully created *koine* (common) Greek.

Koine Greek lasted for about 600 years. It successfully allowed for the necessary communication to form a world empire. The Romans, who conquered the Greeks, kept Greek as the *lingua franca* until slowly Latin eclipsed it after the time of the New Testament. During the years of *koine*, most peoples of the empire spoke a primary language and used Greek for international communication. The Jews of Judea spoke Aramaic as their native tongue. Yet most understood *koine* Greek and the leaders understood Latin, the language of Rome.

The original books of the New Testament were written in *koine* Greek. It was the common trade language and had universal applicability. By the time of the writing of most of the books, Christianity had moved beyond its Judean roots. Much of what we know about its expanse is into Greek-speaking areas, such as Macedonia, Greece, and North Africa.

About 200 BC the Hebrew Old Testament was translated into *koine* Greek. The Egyptian ruler Ptolemy Philadelphus wanted a copy for his library in Alexandria. At the time, many Jewish people lived in Alexandria and were Greek-speaking. They translated and disseminated the Greek Old Testament, called the Septuagint (LXX),[11] into all Greek-speaking territories so Jewish readers could have access to it. By the time of the writing of the New Testament, the church had both the Old Testament and the books written by the apostles in the Greek language they could understand.

The Hebrew Old Testament became the tool of Jewish scholars and conservative Jewish sects, such as the Covenanters of Qumran. By the time of the New Testament, most people could not read Hebrew. They spoke Aramaic. Most Jewish worshippers heard the Old Testament weekly in Aramaic translations of the text. Soon the Greek Old Testament became the standard for both Jews and all Christian readers.

We often consider the Bible as a unit, and well we should, but it is helpful to know that the books were written in different circumstances. Through the process of canonization they were accepted into one collection, the canon.

The process of recognizing the canon is a major study that has been revised and reinvigorated in recent decades. By the time of Jesus' day, the Jews had a fairly fixed canon of 39 books of the Old Testament. They did not officially

---

[11] It is called the Septuagint, Latin for 70, or LXX because of a legend that Ptolemy Philadelphus commissioned 70 Jewish scholars to produce translations from Hebrew to Greek independently, which in the end all agreed word for word. This is surely incorrect.

accept them until later, but there were few who differed with the collection we now have as the Old Testament.

The New Testament canon, however, took longer to recognize and accept. Probably because of the nature of the books and their intended readers, it was more difficult to put them together. The New Testament books are for the most part intended for different readers geographically, and many are directed to specific local problems. By the middle of the second century some Christian writers made comments about the collection of books that all accepted. Virtually all Christians accepted some books immediately. Other books were disputed, primarily because of the question of whether apostles wrote them or not. The earliest collections of books into one book form date from about the fourth century. By that time, all questions about any specific books were resolved and the Bible took the form we now have. It should be noted, however, that most Roman Catholics accept 14 apocryphal books written after the Old Testament was completed and before the New Testament was begun. Also, some eastern churches, such as the Orthodox, accept some early Christian writings not included in the Protestant canon, particularly *The Didache* and *The Apostolic Constitutions*.

For approximately 1,700 years Christian churches had the same canon. In recent decades, however, the question of the nature of the canon has been reopened. Scholars have known of other purportedly Christian writings outside the New Testament for centuries. In fact, the apostolic fathers and the church fathers mention many by name. In 1948 archaeologists discovered a library of Gnostic writings at Nag Hammadi in Egypt. Some of the books claim to be written by Jesus' disciples or apostles. They reflect distinctively Gnostic themes that the early church declared heretical. One of these books, *The Gospel of Thomas*, has received significant attention. Purportedly written by Jesus' disciple (and "twin brother") Thomas, it offers 114 pithy sayings "from Jesus" and bases salvation on knowledge gained by spiritual insight, a typical Gnostic theme. Many liberal scholars today believe *The Gospel of Thomas* should be considered a fifth Gospel and included in the canon. The style and contents of this gospel, however, differ radically from the core teaching of the canonical Gospels. Most importantly, in *Thomas* Jesus offers salvation through knowledge. Nothing is said about His death, burial, and resurrection as essential to providing salvation for all. Conservative scholars have rejected this gospel as part of the Christian canon.[12]

---

[12] The basic differences of style include the fact that there are no contexts to any of the sayings and there is no storyline (plot) in it, both of which characterize the canonical Gospels. The differences in content basically include the way of salvation and Jesus as the provider of salvation. *Thomas* presents salvation by enlightenment, the Gospels as by faith in Jesus based on the events of His life, death, and resurrection.

We now have a more complete knowledge of other writings called Christian in the first three centuries. Most were identified and rejected by the early church. They make for very interesting reading and have some historical and sociological value, but they have been correctly identified as heretical and should not be considered part of the Christian collection of inspired and authoritative books, the Bible.

Because the church fathers discussed and voted their convictions regarding the make up of the canon, many today say that the church determined the canon. The process was a matter of debate and vote involving a few of the questioned books. However, it is better to understand that the church was recognizing the canon. It is obvious that their intent was to understand which books were God inspired and which were not. They used many criteria. In addition to the question of authorship, another primary concern was their content. The books had to be consistent with the faith Jesus and the apostles taught. Thus through their various discussions involving the human aspects of authorship, the church was seeking to recognize divine inspiration.

The teacher can rest assured that the 66 books of our Protestant canon are those God inspired and intended for our use. This has at least two implications. First, the teacher should seek to know the entire canon, all 66 books. They have been continually affirmed because of the work of the early church councils and the consistency of the message they bring. A wise teacher will seek to know and teach the whole council of God as reflected in the entire canon. Second, the canon defines the boundaries for the authority of Scripture. Other reading may be interesting. It also may contain the same message as the canonical books and can, at times, clarify the meaning of a text. Yet the God who inspired the books also providentially led the church to recognize those that were inspired. We can say with confidence that in the 66 books of the Bible, God has uniquely spoken. The uniqueness is in the truthfulness of their message and the abiding relevance the books have to every generation.

Chapter Two

BASIC HERMENEUTICS

THE SUCCESSFUL TEACHER MUST be a good Bible interpreter. Since the Bible is the primary source of instruction, it is necessary to understand its message. That includes knowing what it meant in the day it was written, as well as what it means to readers and listeners today. Many teachers may be legitimately faulted for poor teaching techniques, but these can and should be improved. The teacher without good content, however, has a more serious problem.

The Bible warns teachers about what they teach. Jesus told his followers that it would be better to be cast into the lake with a millstone around the neck than to teach false content (Matt 18:6). Later, James, Jesus' half brother, warned his readers about the responsibility of teaching: "Be not many of you teachers" because of the greater judgment (Jas 3:1 ASV). Unlike most teachers, those who teach spiritual truths answer to God for what they say, and the eternal destiny of their hearers may lie in their hands. God expects us to teach truth in the best way possible. The teacher is responsible for both the content and presenting it in an appropriate and relevant manner.

One of the biggest problems Bible teachers face is the gap of more than 2,000 years between the time the Bible was completed and the present. Most who take the Bible seriously have inherited theological guidelines that keep them on target for the larger matters of doctrine. Conservative teachers are generally clear about personal salvation, heaven and hell, and the work of

Christ on the cross. History has provided us with a stream of orthodoxy that has guarded these truths at all costs. Even when churches or denominations have disagreed, they have generally agreed on the basic tenets of the faith.

Having such a heritage, however, causes a tendency to make every passage speak to these doctrines. It is easy for every lesson to be on how to be right with God, how to love your neighbor, or how to give to the poor. Yet every passage of the Bible is not about these matters. The Bible is complex. Its message comes in various ways, through different authors and situations, to the ears of a complexity of different readers. Intuitively we read the Bible as though it were written for us "this morning." While its message is certainly fresh and relevant, its content comes to us veiled in the clothes of first-century Greek or Roman society or, even more difficult, in the clothes of ancient Near Eastern culture. The 2,000–3,500-year gap requires careful thinking about both the content of the Bible and its relevance for us today.

THE BASIC MODEL FOR COMMUNICATION

The modern age of communications provides us with a simple model for communication. With our technology, we are familiar with radio waves that come in various forms. Radio waves work for us because of three basic elements. The first is a sending device. The sending device is constructed to encode a signal and to broadcast it. Any material may be encoded, and the device can encode in any way demanded to make the broadcast understandable. Second, there is the signal itself. The signal must be appropriate for the device and to carry the encoded message adequately. Third, there is a receptor. The receiving device must be in tune with the sending device and be able to receive and translate the signal. Almost all communication in the modern world depends on this simple model.

If we were working with computers, wireless phones, satellite TV, or military code, we would understand this immediately. Often, however, the reader is not conscious of the same dynamic with the printed page. The same three elements exist. There is an encoder, rather than a sending device. This is a person with a message to share who selects the proper device to send it. This, of course, depends on the audience. Thus the encoder selects the appropriate language, the best form of communication (writing or speaking), and the best style of encoding the message for the intended result.

The second element is the message itself: the text. The text of a message is the single most important part of the process. The message must come in an understandable language. It also must come written in an attractive, interesting, and winsome manner. The most important of messages may be overlooked because it has no interest to its audience. Generally, authors give attention to style, illustrations, vocabulary, and form of writing to make the greatest impact.

The third element is the decoder: the reader. The reader must know the language, appreciate the style and form selected, and have the same vocabulary as the encoder. When the reader has difficulty with the signal, one of several things may happen. There may be a total lack of understanding. There may be disinterest with the assumption that the message does not relate. There may be distortion caused by not discerning figures of speech (style) or not knowing the language or vocabulary. Any of these difficulties cause the reader to misunderstand the message. There may be a total misunderstanding or the failure may be partial due to static.

THE BIBLICAL MODEL

The Bible is literature. Like all forms of literature it contains language, style, structure, and meaning. Like all texts, someone has encoded a message, sent it in such a way that specific readers can understand it, and anticipated a readership that can decode it. The encoder is the author. The message is the Bible text, and the decoder is the reader. One may question why God chose to deliver His message to all people through a specific author, but any other option would be extremely difficult. Alternatively, God would have to deliver His message repeatedly to every person in every generation to be understood. Instead, He chose specific persons in specific situations that have abiding value to all.

THE AUTHOR

For proper interpretation, one must give due consideration to the author of Scripture. The Bible is a library of 66 books. Historically, the church has agreed that there are approximately 39 authors of these books. Most of the books have clear statements or histories that explain the authors. The books span centuries of time. The oldest were approximately 1400 BC and the latest were approximately AD 100, a period of 1,500 years. Furthermore, the authors wrote in different languages, according to the historical time period or setting of the readers. The oldest are in Hebrew, as is the majority of the Old Testament. Some of the later Old Testament books are written in Aramaic, the diplomatic language of Persia, which was forced on Palestine by political conquest. The New Testament is primarily Greek, the common language of the Greeks and the Roman Empire during that time. Even so, there are individual statements that are in Aramaic, and Latin, the official language of Rome. Either Jewish or Christian believers wrote most of the books, but there are many sources that may include unbelievers. First and Second Chronicles list at least 20 other books the chronicler knew and used in compiling his message.

These facts illustrate the complexity of the authorship of Scripture. It is certainly incorrect to assume that all writing occurred in one generation's time, or in one language or culture. The study of almost every biblical author brings unique elements. Even those who wrote within the same time period often wrote in very different circumstances. For example, the Old Testament prophets may be divided according to the countries addressed or the circumstances that prevailed when they wrote. There were prophets to Judah, the southern kingdom; to Israel, the northern kingdom; and to Assyria and Babylon, foreign powers. Proper interpretation begins with knowing the specific situation of the author as he wrote.

From time to time in history, some have objected to the study of the specific authors and their circumstances. Based on the divine inspiration of Scripture, some have argued that the individual author was so eclipsed by God that spiritual principles lead to a proper understanding without having to study historical circumstances. Generally the spiritual principles are that the Holy Spirit overrides differences of time and place to communicate meaning.

Orthodox theologians have always argued the twofold nature of the authorship of Scripture. Often it is paralleled to the person of Jesus: at the same time divine and human. God used the human author to communicate His truth, and He used the Holy Spirit to protect the human author from error. It has always been considered heresy to affirm the human authorship without the divine, or the divine without the human. Affirming the importance of the human author requires studying the human aspects of writing and taking them seriously in the writing process. It means studying their circumstances, language, and style of writing, personalities, and thought patterns.

THE MESSAGE

The message is the most important part of the communication process. The doctrine of inspiration states that it is the Bible that is inspired. While the author is obviously led by the Holy Spirit, the Bible is the product of inspiration, the locus of God's message to us. The interpreter must carefully and prayerfully study the Bible to discover its meaning for us today.

As noted above, the Bible was written over a 1,500-year period of time in at least four languages and to people in various circumstances. The message is always nuanced according to the circumstances of the writer and readers.

That raises an important question. Isn't it enough to read the message in my language, or do I have to read in an ancient language? This is an important question, and it will be discussed later.

The importance of the message is that it carries the meaning. Later we will discuss some of the difficulties when the interpreter does not allow the message to be central. Here it suffices to note that God put into Scripture everything we need to know for life and godliness. He did not tell us everything we would like to know, but only what we need to know. We therefore must study the direct teaching and commands of the Bible, but we also must seek to understand the principles affirmed in the Bible. Often they come without any specific text that clearly annunciates them.

The text of the Bible also points us to what we need to know about the author. Endless hours can be spent studying what might be interesting about the author.[1] What we need to know is what the text suggests that is helpful for interpreting the message. For example, at times there are statements and grammatical constructions that do not communicate clearly to us. It is at those points that we need to investigate the author and his circumstances to see if they help clarify what is otherwise obscure.

THE READERS

The third element in the communication process is the readers. Most of the books of the Bible are addressed to specific readers. Some readers are identified in the titles of the books, like Romans, Colossians, and Corinthians. In other cases, we have to find the readers from the content of the book. For example, in reading the book we learn that Isaiah spoke to Judah, Timothy was in Ephesus, and Peter wrote to Christians scattered around modern Turkey. When specific destinations are known, we should read about the circumstances of those destinations at the time of writing to seek to understand the message given by the writer. Where the destinations are unknown, we should seek to determine from reading the message of the book what the people were like, including the problems they had, and what God said in addressing them.

Interpretation requires that we assume the readers could understand the message. They would know the meanings of illustrations and localized phrases. For example, the Corinthians would understand the meaning of wives having their hair styled a certain way to honor their husbands (1 Cor 11:1–16) or what Amos meant with the "cows of Bashan" (Amos 4:1). It stands to reason that if

---

[1] It is popular in some circles today to psychoanalyze the author or reinterpret him according to modern understandings. Both are, ultimately, impossible and do both the author and the Bible a disservice.

they understood statements like these, we should also seek to put ourselves in their shoes to understand them as well.

Interpretation also requires that we assume the readers were to act and react to the message God delivered to them. Therefore we should note carefully any issues of conduct in the text. We should ask what changes in the readers would satisfy and correct the situations that prompted the author to write. It will then be easier for us to ask how we should react if we find ourselves in a similar situation.

The question of the readers raises another concern for contemporary interpreters. Do I have to understand the text the way they did? Could not the Holy Spirit speak directly to me through the text I read? The answer, of course, is that the Holy Spirit does speak to us regardless of our knowledge of ancient readers and their cultural circumstances. The modern reader must understand, however, that there can only be one interpretation that is correct. Therefore any interpretation derived by modern readers must correspond to the meaning intended by the author and understood by the ancient reader. If today's interpretation differs from theirs, then the modern reader either misunderstands the meaning or fails to understand the original readers' knowledge of the subject.

THE NECESSITY OF SHARABILITY

The model explained above assumes some basic affinities in communication. It assumes that the authors intended to communicate. They chose their mediums of communication carefully, and they expected their readers to understand their communications. There is a major question as to whether they expected modern readers would consult their texts and seek meaning. There is little evidence that the ancient writers wrote with a consciousness that their writings would be preserved for all time and eternity. According to 2 Pet 1:10–12, they did have a sense that God spoke through them in a significant way and that, at times, they did not know the details of the fulfillments of their prophecies.

The communication model works on two levels. First, it is the way all communication works synchronically, that is, at any given slice of time. Communication only takes place when people hold the basics of language in common. Many times imaginations have run wild while thinking about the implications of the instant multiplying of languages at the Tower of Babel (Gen 11:1–9). Effective communication stopped because people were not on the same wavelength.

Second, the communication model works diachronically, that is, throughout the eras of time. People may know there are ancient texts, but they are useless without some translation. This was the case of the Egyptian hieroglyphic script until the discovery and deciphering of the Rosetta stone. Now the contents of the Rosetta stone, and hieroglyphic texts throughout Egypt, are available to all.

In order for clear communication to take place, people have to share. They have to share multiple aspects of being human, but the greater difficulties are cared for by the fact that we are human. Human beings share a sense of order, rationality, capabilities, personality, and responsibility. Beyond these basics, three areas of sharing must take place. They are essential to proper interpretation of the biblical texts.

LANGUAGE

First, we must share a common language. The tower of Babel illustrates the necessity of this (Gen 11:1–9). Also, when Alexander the Great inherited the armies of his father, Phillip of Macedon, the ancient Greek city-states had different dialects of the same language, Greek. They could not all understand each other. The first duty of Alexander was to create *koine* Greek. *Koine* means "common." He created a common, simplified language that all the Greeks could learn and that could be taught in every place he conquered. In doing so, he created the language of an empire.

Modern readers seeking to understand ancient texts must have the same language. We are easily deceived on this point by the many translations of ancient texts. For example, some naively assume that because we can read *The Iliad* in English, we can know its meaning. Classical scholars still debate the finer points of this ancient text.

Ancient texts come into modern times through translations. Translations are always colored by issues of text theory (which textual reading is best) and translation theory (which approach to translation is the best). The modern reader who depends on a translation is no clearer in his understanding of the text than the translator of that text.

The only satisfactory and accurate way to bridge this gap is for modern readers to learn ancient languages. This is done routinely in seminary, but it is not practical for everyone. Commentaries, translations, and Bible dictionaries clarify ancient texts, and the serious student of the Bible should consult them regularly.

The modern reader must understand two important principles. First, without knowledge of the ancient languages, the modern reader is always dependent on someone who knows them. People with knowledge of Greek and Hebrew do Bible translations. People who have studied the ancient languages write commentaries. But the proliferation of translations reveals the diversity of opinion about many of the specific nuances of ancient texts.

Second, the modern reader must take full advantage of resources that enable understanding of the ancient texts. It is imperative to develop a sense of which resources are the more accurate, reliable, and up to date. At times theological, philosophical, and methodological differences cause different opinions about translation. While these occur in very few places, it is best to know and use scholars who hold the same basic theological and philosophical assumptions.

There are multiple implications of this discussion. One of the most important, however, is the necessity of realizing that any modern translation of Scripture is simply a translation. English or other modern translations always accommodate ancient patterns of writing into what is acceptable and understandable in modern cultures. In Bible study it is always appropriate to ask: what does the Greek or Hebrew say?

WORLDVIEW

The second area of sharing is worldview. The word "worldview" means the basic and core values of a specific culture, and the way they view the world growing out of them. Thus to understand any given culture, it is necessary to understand how that culture "puts existence" together. From a synchronic perspective, we know that Chinese, South Africans, Koreans, and Polynesians, for example, do not "see" things the same way Americans do. From a diachronic perspective, it means that it is likely that no modern society will understand the ancients and the way they "thought."

One of the major differences in worldview comes with the division caused by the Copernican Revolution. With the advent of modern science, the world is viewed differently. It is almost impossible for modern minds to embrace the perspectives of prescientific societies.

The question must be raised as to the degree to which science enters one's worldview. Most of the Bible relates to morality and to our relationship to God. The teachings and illustrations often come in historical situations, but a major question exists as to how much of "the ancient" worldview the writers of Scripture displayed. The fallacy of "the unified whole" suggests that everyone back then thought the same way. "They all" believed a certain way. That is hardly a position that can be substantiated now. But even if the writers of Scripture did accept some of the false views of the world, there are very few places where the false views influence the interpretation of Scripture, and these places of question are highly disputed. In other words, God protected the writers of Scripture so that they wrote what was true.

The primary question of worldview relates to the relationships between God and humanity. The questions occur primarily in thinking about sin, creation, humanness, morality, God, the supernatural, and the afterlife. Many today think it is untenable to hold to the biblical explanation of human beings and history. Yet many today do accept the Bible without reservation. The fact is, one cannot understand and properly interpret the Bible without understanding and affirming the important elements of the Bible's worldview. It is different from the natural worldview of any age, but it is expressed through the vehicle of localized cultures. Given the origins of the human story as recorded in the Bible, there is a logical and experiential cohesiveness to creation and existence.

CULTURE

The third shared element is culture. Culture is defined in many ways. For simplicity, we may say culture is the way a society organizes itself in accord with its worldview. Thus the worldview is a platform for action. Society develops with sensitivity to worldview. It develops logically consistent religious practices, life and death rituals, holiday celebrations, and other practices directly out of its core worldview values.

Major differences exist between ancient and modern cultures. Many of the ancient practices reflected primitive ideas about deity. Many ancient cultures organized the seasons of life around pleasing or displeasing the gods. Fertility and economic practices reflected the essentials of worldview, as did the law codes.

Naturally modern societies organize differently. In the west we no longer offer sacrifices to the gods to avert a famine or engage in ritual fertility dances to assure the birth of a child or a season of good crops. Yet if we are to understand ancient texts, we must understand the cultures reflected in them. Since they cannot come to us, we must "go" to them.

Interestingly, much of the Bible is about differences in culture. The Bible speaks consistently against offering children in the sacrificial fires to false gods. It warns Christians about engaging in cultural practices that are, at heart, contrary to their Christian profession. For example, they are not to participate in offering food to idols in the idol ceremonies (1 Cor 10:20–21). The Bible calls Christians to renew and reform all cultures with the lordship of Jesus at the center.

Studying the cultural elements of the Bible requires thinking on several levels. There are at least three levels of difficulty in handling biblical texts that are intertwined with culture. First, there is the need to understand the meaning of the ancient cultural practice. Second, there is a need to understand the biblical point the writer makes with reference to the cultural practice. Third, there is the need to make a proper application to today's cultures consistent with the ancient cultural practice.

Understanding culture is necessary to understand the communicative signal, the text. Without it, the Bible remains a book that is unknowable and irrelevant for people today.

Does this mean that every proper interpreter must go to seminary? If so, some will be discouraged because the circumstances do not allow that luxury for many. Seminary is a catalyst. It accelerates learning by providing classes in the areas of understanding necessary for interpreting the text. It is certainly possible to learn what is needed without seminary. Regardless, it is necessary to study, interpret, derive meaning, and make application in proper ways.

THE TWO DIMENSIONS OF BIBLE STUDY

The student of Scripture must recognize two dimensions of study necessary for arriving at proper conclusions. They were suggested above, but need further discussion. The dimensions relate directly to the twofold authorship of the Bible. The Bible was inspired by God but written by men! Myriads of pages have been written related to this truth and the implications of this dual authorship.

The dual authorship of Scripture may be viewed as two parallel tracks. For illustration, they may be conceived as a railroad with the two rails running parallel. If something happens to either one, the train will derail. The rails represent two sets of laws. Proper interpretation requires following these laws. Laws, of course, can be broken, but they are intended to produce freedom. Like rules of a game, they define the processes and objectives that enable success. In biblical interpretation there are Laws of the Spirit and Laws of Human Communication.[2]

LAWS OF THE SPIRIT

Spiritual principles sometimes defy understanding. By definition they are beyond the objective, legal codes that we often follow. Who can know the

---

[2] I was first introduced to this idea and the terminology in my first hermeneutics class my sophomore year of college by Mr. James M ("Buck") Hatch, longtime professor at Columbia International University. I am indebted to his seminal insights that have blossomed over the years of study and teaching. Before his death, he gave me permission to use his hermeneutics notes in any of my writings.

mind of the Holy Spirit? Who put the Holy Spirit into a theological box for our observation? Yet the Holy Spirit clearly works in certain ways, with common threads of behavior demonstrated in Scripture, and with clearly defined results of the Spirit's activity. The Holy Spirit joins with the human spirit and mind to bring understanding otherwise unachievable.

Relating to interpretation, the Laws of the Holy Spirit are basic and clear. There are three. Following the Laws of the Spirit does not *guarantee* a "right" interpretation, but failure to follow these laws almost certainly brings failure. The failure may be an inability to articulate proper conclusions. It may also be a failure to grasp the entirety and significance of any given truth. The dangers of disregarding the Spirit are great; the advantages of following the Spirit encourage us in the path of proper interpretation.

CONVERSION The most basic Law of the Spirit is conversion. In order to grasp the truths of God, it is necessary for one to be converted, to have moved from the realm of self-domination to the lordship of Jesus Christ. This does not mean that a non-Christian person cannot understand the proper meaning of any given passage. In fact, non-Christians may have better tools for study and, therefore, may articulate the proper meaning well. In many ways the interpreter is like an archaeologist. The meaning of a text is uncovered layer by layer. The textual artifacts are available to all, but they are more likely to be discovered by those who use the proper tools for digging. Non-Christians may have acquired better tools and better methods of using them, but the truth of Scripture goes beyond that.

God's truth is not simply words on a page. It is spiritual reality that transforms those who grasp it, bringing them into a progressively deeper understanding of Christian life. Those who do not seek to follow spiritual truth by becoming disciples of Christ cannot appreciate the full impact of the Bible's message. The message grips the heart as well as the mind.

The apostle Paul expressed this clearly in 1 Cor 2:14–3:3. Here Paul spoke to the Corinthian Christians about their responsibility to accept and understand God's truth. At conversion a new dynamic takes place in one's life. Truth is dispensed from the Holy Spirit and is, therefore, spiritual. In order for us to understand the truth, God has given us His Holy Spirit (2:12). The Holy Spirit communicates this truth to people who have received the Spirit, those who are converted.

In contrast, non-Christians do not have the Holy Spirit operating in the same way in their lives, and they cannot receive spiritual truth. Verse 14 expresses this clearly. First, non-Christians are "soulish." Bible translations normally translate this as "natural," but the Greek words have their own nuance.

The "soul" is one of the ways of identifying all people. Everyone is created with a soul. Later Paul speaks of the Corinthians as "fleshly" (3:3). The word "flesh" connotes the natural way of living. It is a moral term indicating that people live with themselves in the center of their lives. It describes rebellion from God and the desire to put ego first. The terms soul and flesh are in the same semantic fields, describing unsaved people, but they imply two different aspects of life.

The person whose life is characterized by "soul" does not receive things of the Spirit. This passage does not refer to a person having different parts: body, soul, and spirit. There is little justification for such a division into trichotomy or dichotomy here. Paul's point is that a person without the Holy Spirit has a severe and unnecessary limitation.

Paul further describes the problem with his word "receive" in 2:14 (NKJV). The soulish man does not "receive" what comes from God's Spirit. Again Paul puts words in contrast and complement with each other. In 2:12 he explains that Christians have "received" the Holy Spirit and not the "spirit of the world." The word used there is a normal word for accepting a gift (*lambano* in Greek). It is clear that all Christians have received the Holy Spirit, and they do so at conversion (Rom 8:9). In his contrast with the "soulish" person, however, Paul explains that the soulish do "not welcome what comes from God's Spirit" (1 Cor 2:14). Here the word "welcome" is a good translation (*dexomai* in Greek in contrast to *lambano*). It was used for appropriate reception. It implies embracing joyfully, often times with preparation and forethought. For example, people expend great energy preparing for a political leader's visit, and they "welcome" him appropriately.

There is a basic difference between Christians and non-Christians. Non-Christians have the spirit of the world; Christians have received the Holy Spirit. Non-Christians think in a "soulish" way; Christians "welcomely embrace" truth that comes from the Holy Spirit. The result is that things of the Holy Spirit are foolish to the non-Christian. They not only make no sense; they cannot know them.

One other word is important. Non-Christians do not "know." The word "know" is to know experientially or relationally.[3] All persons can know truth at some levels. Non-Christians can even recite doctrine or detailed theological arguments. The difference between non-Christians and Christians is the attitude toward spiritual truths ("welcome") and their ability to embrace them

---

[3] It is from the Greek root *gno*, which speaks either to the process of gaining knowledge or the experience of that knowledge. It is usually contrasted with the Greek root *id*, which speaks either to a factual knowledge or an intellectual grasp of something.

in their experience. For understanding of spiritual truth, therefore, one must be converted.

COMMITMENT   The second Law of the Spirit is commitment to Christ. In 1 Cor 2:15, Paul explains one of the characteristics of the converted: "The spiritual person, however, can evaluate everything, yet he himself cannot be evaluated by anyone." Two ideas come together. The "spiritual person" is the one whose life is characterized by the Holy Spirit. It involves receiving the Spirit (2:12), "welcomely embracing" spiritual truth (2:14), and seeking to live life following the Holy Spirit's direction. Because of this, the converted and committed can know the mind of Christ. The Holy Spirit brings a new way of valuing and thinking. This reflects itself in a deep desire to know and follow the ways of God, to learn the lessons that come from spiritual truth.

CONSECRATION   The third Law of the Spirit is consecration to God's plans. Consecration is a deeper stage than committed. It assumes commitment to Christ, but it also implies the results of following the Holy Spirit. It suggests maturity in the things of God. Maturity comes from embracing truth, seeking to know God's mind, and having your life changed because of the Holy Spirit's working. It thus suggests that the more refined the commitment to Christ, the more consecrated the Christian life.

Paul speaks to this point in 2 Cor 3:3. Paul had fed them milk, not food, because they were unable to receive it. They were "fleshly," living life according to the morality of non-Christians. The evidence of this is that they were still promoting groups, following one of their four previous Christian leaders. The great evidence of the nonconsecrated, and therefore "carnal" mind, is that it tries to do God's work in human ways. Thus in Corinth they were sectarian, gathering together to follow one human leader or another (Paul, Apollos, Cephas, or Christ). This hindered their ability to know God and His ways. They should have moved from "fleshly" to "spiritual" in their lives.

First Corinthians 3 is a classic passage on Christian carnality. The English word "carnal" comes from the Latin translation of the Greek, "fleshly" (*sarkikos*). In Corinth, the carnal Christians were those who acted in "normal" ways, even though they were Christian. They were converted and committed. Some were leaders in the church. Yet because they did not follow the Holy Spirit's direction for the church, and rather divided it, they were carnal believers.

The term "consecration" was chosen because it speaks to that point. Consecrated Christians are converted and committed (dedicated), but they also have

walked in the ways of the Holy Spirit so that they do not lapse into carnal thinking. They do not attempt to do God's work in their own ways.

The Laws of the Spirit are the starting point for good Bible interpretation.
The more one understands spiritual truth and seeks to apply it consistently in
life, the more that person understands. There is no substitute for walking with
the Lord in the light of His word.

LAWS OF HUMAN COMMUNICATION

Some people understand the Laws of the Spirit but fail to understand the
Laws of Human Communication. They may be mystics or spiritualists who
believe that God continues to reveal Himself directly through the Spirit and
there is no need for the study of language and backgrounds.

The dual authorship of Scripture requires us to think differently. God chose
to reveal Himself to human beings through language. Just as in person-to-
person communication, there are principles that allow for clear communication, so also in reading texts the same kinds of principles apply, only the task
is made more difficult since we cannot actually speak to the writers. The texts
cannot accommodate themselves to our ways of thinking, so we have to go
back to theirs.

In biblical interpretation, the Laws of Human Communication are both
general and specific. The general laws were developed primarily by the early
church interpreters who were concerned also with recognizing which books
belong in the Bible, the canon. Some of these will be discussed later.

The specific laws relate to understanding a passage in its context. Later, in
part 3, we will demonstrate many of these principles in the Transformactional
Bible Study method we propose. Here it will suffice to provide a general overview of some basic hermeneutical principles.

First, it is necessary to see the specific text in its *context*. Context covers a
broad area of study, but it may be divided generally into the historical context
and the textual context. Historical context includes knowing about the human
author and readers and their circumstances. These include what in the culture
prompted the author to write when and as he did. The fact is, every book of the
Bible is specific to some context. Sometimes we know the contexts with certainty; sometimes we must make an educated guess. Textual context involves
seeing the specific text in its location within the Bible and, more directly, its
location in the specific Bible book. Each paragraph contributes to a larger
argument. We cannot really understand an individual paragraph unless we understand the larger argument of which it is a part.

Second, it is necessary to understand the *content*. Generally speaking, this means tracing the logic of the paragraph, understanding the meanings of its words, and seeking to know the theological principles that either lie behind it or to which it speaks. Gaining understanding of content will likely be the most demanding and time-consuming part of study, but without it, there is nothing to say!

Third, studying context involves the author's *concern*. The place to start is the author in his historical circumstances. At this point, the issue is "why?" Why did the writer write what he did? Why did the author use the specific words that he did? Why did the writer see a need for change in those who would read his text? Sometimes it is helpful to ask: "What would the readers look like if they actually did what the author intends?"

After understanding why the author wrote what and as he did, the reader must apply the original concern to modern readers. Here the question changes from "Why?" as with the historical investigation—to "What?" What am I to learn from this passage? What makes the passage relevant to me today? What in my culture is equivalent to that culture and needs the same correction? What in the text is specific to that time and location, and what is universal, requiring application for all people in all times and places?

Finding the answers, and understanding the text, requires a combination of both sets of laws. The reader should always begin with a humble request that God the Holy Spirit will illuminate the truth of the passage. That prayer, if genuine, assumes that the reader is willing for a life change in accord with what the passage teaches. In other words, the Laws of the Spirit require a willingness to do in order to learn.[4] Following that prayer, every phase of the study should be conducted with a conscious sense of dependency, asking God for help in the process of study as well as understanding the message.

Along with the Laws of the Spirit, the reader should consciously apply the Laws of Human Communication. This requires serious thinking about the text. It requires using the proper tools for Bible study for both context and content. Applying these human laws successfully is both a science and an art. The scientific aspect is the skill developed in the process of exegesis. Exegetical skills develop over time. The artistic part is in understanding when and where to apply the specific exegetical tools to arrive at proper conclusions. No Bible student will be successful without a clear understanding of these principles and skill in their application to the Bible.

---

[4] It should be noted again that doing the truth is not simply an "add-on" to its meaning. "Doing" is a part of "understanding." This point comes from Jesus' statement in John 7:17.

CHAPTER THREE

UNDERSTANDING LITERATURE

IN ADDITION TO UNDERSTANDING texts, the interpreter should understand biblical literature. Basically that involves the *form* and *genre* of written texts. Sometimes the two combine in the writer's strategy, but often they are separate issues.

UNDERSTANDING FORMS OF WRITING

The form of the text is the way a writer chooses to present his material. In broad terms, form may be either prose or poetry, although both have multiple subcategories. The specific form makes an appropriate impact on the reader, or it may be selected because it is necessary for the writer's purposes. For example, poetry may involve songs, psalms, and other poetic ways of writing. For our purposes here, poetry also includes metaphorical language that may be used within a text. Prose is natural for writing history, letters, and more straightforward materials. As mentioned, it is common for literature primarily composed of prose to have poetic elements within it, and for literature that is primarily poetic to have sections of prose.

Most literature is written in prose. It is the normal and straightforward way of communicating. In prose the words have standardized, clear meanings. Figures of speech are less prevalent, though they may occur. Most of the Bible is written in prose form. It is easier to translate and to interpret prose writing than poetry.

Today scholars recognize that prose is too general a description for the complexities of literature. Therefore it is necessary to identify the kinds of literature that compose various writings. The Bible contains many examples of various literary genres. We will describe the basic elements of each in order to provide interpretive insights to the Bible student.

UNDERSTANDING LITERARY GENRE

Genre studies can be quite complex. Experts in this area of study have developed numerous forms of genre in literature in general and Scripture in particular. They determine the forms of genre by well-developed styles, clues in the text as to what particular genre the writer has employed. Genre may be a classification of the major characteristic of an entire book, such as Gospel, or it may be a classification of relatively minor literary motifs found within a book, such as parable.

There are major interpretive principles to guide study with each genre. The Christian educator should recognize these and incorporate them into the lesson plan. Like the literary forms, genre is particularly useful in teaching the Bible to adults. Adults can quickly catch the significance of literary devices and enter into both the impact and the emotion each brings.

The New Testament books may be divided into basically four genres: gospel, history, epistle, and apocalyptic. Within the books, however, there are several genres that we should discuss. Each has its own characteristics that guide interpretation. Great confusion can occur if an interpreter treats Revelation, the Apocalypse, like the Epistles. They simply do not function in the same way. Thus an overview of genre makes interpreting the New Testament easier. There is some overlap in the genre of the New Testament and the Old Testament. Yet there are also distinct literary styles that occur primarily in the Old Testament. The following discussion follows no particular order, but it does address the primary genre.

POETRY

Poetry occurs in every language, but its specific patterns may vary. Hebrew poetry is different from Greek. It is important that the interpreter recognize poetic forms when they occur. Sometimes entire books are poetry, such as Psalms and Job. Sometimes poetic sections occur within other documents.

The Old Testament contains far more poetry than the New Testament. In the Old Testament, poetry predominates in Psalms, Proverbs, Job, and Song of Songs. The prophets also include many sections that are poetic: Isaiah, Jeremiah, Joel, Amos, Jonah, Nahum, Habakkuk, Zephaniah, and Lamentations. The English reader may not recognize them as poetry since Hebrew poetry differs from English. It is helpful to use a Bible translation that keeps poetry in poetic form so it can be spotted easily.

Hebrew poetry focuses more on meter and less on rhyme. Those who have studied Hebrew poetry have noted its most striking feature is its parallelism. Parallelism occurs when two or more lines follow a statement and are parallel to it. Sometimes the parallel statements are complementary, two or three lines saying the same thing. Sometimes they are antithetic, or opposing lines.[1] We should recognize that the parallel lines are about one subject. Rather than treating them all as separate statements, we should get the main point which may be developed and explained by the second or third lines that are in parallel with it.

One key to understanding poetry is to note its personal nature. It is a part of language that speaks to human experience and the heart. Who can read the Psalms without thinking personally about God and life? Furthermore, the poetry of Scripture often covers the entire spectrum of life: joy and pain, success and failure, blessings and calamity, walking with God and failure to walk with him.

In interpreting poetry, it is necessary to understand that experiential language is the primary point of contact between the writer and the readers. Since poetry has a high frequency of metaphor and figurative language, much of biblical poetry will be set in ancient times, drawing on particular images of that day. We should never diminish the power of the form. Yet the modern reader will appreciate the poems more, and they will have more power in life, if we seek to interpret them in light of the ancient settings.

This is seen most strikingly with the imprecatory psalms. At times the Psalms seem crude and "unchristian" by modern standards. It is helpful to note that the psalmists cried out in pain about the fact that ungodly nations treated their enemies inhumanely, and God seemed not to care. It was natural to plead with God to stop them from their intentions and devices. Furthermore, the language reflects the ancient situations that are uncivilized by modern standards. How could the atrocities they committed go unpunished? It is natural to be emotional and ask God to let others feel how it feels to be mistreated. Moreover, when hurting, one may even question God's presence.

---

[1] Parallelism is quite involved. It is common to speak of the kinds of parallelism such as synonymous, antithetical, synthetic, ascending, and introverted. Many commentaries will present these in particular places of text where they occur.

A second factor about poetry is its use of figures of speech and varied imagery. Reading it in the original language makes this more striking. Figurative language requires an extra step in interpretation. Interpretation requires: (1) understanding the poetic nature of the text, (2) seeking to interpret in light of ancient standards and worldview, and (3) applying the ancient patterns and expressions to modern readers in an appropriate manner.

Poetry is a universal form of expression. When a creative person experiences the greatest joys of life—or its deepest pains—the result is often poetic. We should appreciate both the form and the emotion of poetry.

In recent years scholars have devoted significant study to the poems of the New Testament. The most obvious poetical texts are Christological. Modern scholars normally classify them as hymns, assuming the poems were likely sung in early worship. Scholars first discussed Phil 2:5–11 and Col 1:15–21. Significantly the poems of the New Testament often reflect the deep doctrinal foundations of the faith, rather than personal experience and emotional expressions. They are a way of communicating truth rather than experience.

New Testament poems are noted by several characteristics. Usually the poem interrupts the flow of a text. It is an interpretive and illustrative break in the writing. Furthermore, poems are known by a high element of nonstandard language. That is, the words of the poem are unlike the surrounding text. Sometimes the words occur only one time in Scripture; they are *hapax legomena*. Additionally, poems can be noted by their rhyme.

One other factor makes New Testament poems different. There are major questions as to who wrote them. Because they generally cause a break or change from their surrounding texts, as noted above, they may not be from the same writer. It is quite possible to think that Paul or other writers appealed to preexisting hymns to reinforce and apply their messages. That is tantamount to saying: "even as you sing in your worship services—make the hymn be part of your life."[2]

PARABLES

Jesus is known for His stories, often presented in parables. Parables are stories that everyone understood because they were true to life. They also disclosed truth about God and heaven that call the hearer to spiritual life. The Greek word *parabolē*, translated "parable," means to "cast alongside." That

---

[2] Extended discussion of this is helpful, but at this point it is worth noting that if the "hymns" preexisted the texts around them, we have insight into the worship patterns of the early church. Most of the New Testament hymns are highly Christological, suggesting that the early church celebrated the person of Jesus from a theological perspective, not just a personal one.

has given rise to a well-known definition of parables. They are "earthly stories with heavenly meaning."

Parables in the Gospels require interpretation. It is noteworthy that the first parables in the Gospels occur about halfway through Jesus' ministry. They increase numerically as opposition to Jesus increases. Some of the most famous actually occur the last week of Jesus' life when there was an organized attempt to kill Him. The disciples did not always understand them and, when they asked what they meant, Jesus gave the key. They are stories to bring understanding to those who believe, and thus can understand them. They are, equally, stories to hide the truth from those who do not believe and, thus, cannot understand them (Matt 13:10–15). Parables both reveal and hide truth.

That gives us a clue about interpreting parables. Some elements are obvious in the stories—they are almost self-evident. Some are only understood when a believer, aided by the Holy Spirit, makes correlations between the parable and spiritual truth. Some others, however, will be vague and leave the listener with questions about their meanings. Children appreciate parables like the Good Samaritan and learn the most basic truths from them. Yet adults ponder the parable to determine whether or not they have grasped the message fully.

The qualities of both revealing and concealing truth make us all cautious about interpreting parables. When does the message actually stop? How many points are intended in a parable? One or many? How are we to project the parable's life situation into the next? That is, what does the parable reveal about the afterlife and the kingdom of God? Since parables are fertile ground for teaching truth to adults, it will be helpful to provide principles of interpretation.

The problem of interpreting parables can be traced in the history of the church.[3] Christians have had different approaches to their interpretation. Because they are stories, parables can be milked for all they are worth, stretching the story to speak to multiple aspects of the Christian life. Interpretive mistakes committed in the past are being repeated today.

Parables are basically extended similes. They are often confused with extended metaphors, which are allegories (normally with the use of "like" or "as" for comparisons). Similes have normally one main point of comparison.

The early church normally approached parables like they were allegories. They looked for deeper truths in every part of a parable. Following the prevailing philosophy of neo-Platonism, they believed that all language had multiple dimensions. One early Christian, Origen, taught that Scripture had at least three senses: a literal sense (what the words actually said), a moral sense

---

[3] A brief history of interpretation can be found in G. R. Osborne, *The Hermeneutical Spiral: A Comprehensive Introduction to Biblical Interpretation* (Downer's Grove: InterVarsity, 1991), 249–51.

(the moral truth all could understand), and a spiritual sense (only available to Christians). Words were like human beings: body, soul, and spirit. Naturally they interpreted parables with at least three senses or dimensions. The believer, with spiritual insights, could read into the parable multiple Christian truths. Some of their interpretations are humorous to us, yet many today commit the same mistakes many early interpreters did. They read Christian truths into the story that may not be intended by Jesus. After all, they reasoned, anyone can get the simple main ideas. Surely the Holy Spirit intended more.

This approach prevailed in many circles until the last of the eighteenth century. Not all segments of the church interpreted "mystically," but there were not serious correctives to it. In 1910 a German scholar, Adolf Julicher, wrote convincingly that a parable has only one main point.[4] The twentieth century for the most part was dominated by his thinking: a parable has only one main point. It was a good corrective to somewhat wild interpretations with no resemblance to the text. His contribution helped bring us back to a responsible approach.

In the last portion of the twentieth century some scholars questioned Julicher's principle that parables have only one main point. The stories are very stylized, with each character contributing to the story in a clearly developed way. The characters also are lifelike, and the reader identifies them with modern counterparts. When Jesus explained the parables to His disciples, He provided more than one main point. This can be seen most graphically in the parable of the Sower (or "seeds," or "soils").[5] Readers intuitively "see" more than one truth as they think of a parable. It seems obvious that Jesus intended His hearers to understand more than one simple truth from most parables. The parables were well-conceived and well-developed stories that enable believers and unbelievers to identify with the characters.[6]

One further point impacts parable interpretation. The parables are about the kingdom of God. Despite the search for the actual intended meanings, the "earthly" side of parables can be easily grasped. The "kingdom" side cannot. It is because we do not naturally understand the kingdom that we need parables. Parables symbolize the kingdom, presenting it in terms and images we can appreciate. That causes us problems because we think of the kingdom in earthly pictures and we project theology from earth to heaven. But Jesus

---

[4] A. Julicher, *Die Gleichnisreden Jesu* (Tubingen: J.C.B. Mohr, 1910).

[5] Matt 13:1–23.

[6] Two recent books are helpful in studying parables. C. L. Blomberg, *Interpreting the Parables* (Downer's Grove: InterVarsity, 1990); also the most comprehensive book on parables perhaps ever is K. R. Snodgrass, *Stories with Intent: A Comprehensive Guide to the Parables of Jesus* (Grand Rapids: Wm. B. Eerdman's, 2008).

warned the Sadducees that they erred because they confined God's kingdom to earthly principles (Matt 22:29–30).

Since the days Jesus told the parables, listeners and readers have pondered their meanings. They are a distinct form. Like children who hear "once upon a time" and think of fairy tales, parables have a distinct form that shapes their interpretation. Because we can identify with them, they are popular for teaching and preaching. Even with their popularity, many miss their points because they interpret them in contemporary cultural settings rather than biblical.

MIRACLES

Jesus' life and ministry cannot be separated from the miracles He performed. Since the Enlightenment liberal scholars questioned the reality of miracles. They have tried for 300 years to explain Jesus' life after extracting the miraculous element from the Bible. They tried to understand the "Jesus of History" apart from the Bible's presentation, which many called the "Christ of faith."

In the twentieth century those who question the reality of miracles follow one of two major approaches. First, many seek to "de-myth" them. Assuming the miracles represent mythological literature, and cannot be real events, the interpreter must seek to take the point of the miracle story and apply it today. The point, of course for them, cannot be the actual miracle. Second, many relegate them simply to "religious" history but not "actual history." Actual history is the history of the historian—what can be satisfactorily recovered and explained. Religious history is the history of faith, quite apart from the scientific realities.[7]

Both of these approaches illustrate the necessity of interpreting miracles. Miracles are interwoven into the biblical accounts of God's activities in the world. They demand interpretation. They call for some decision about Jesus' person and work, but they also demand some decision about their importance to understanding spiritual truth. In other words, a serious interpreter and teacher cannot avoid the miracles. They have always been significant in Christianity.

The interpreter must make some choices. Are miracles compatible with a true worldview? Are miracles essential to the message of the Bible and to

---

[7] These two primary approaches to interpretation of miracles come from two giants of New Testament interpretation. R. Bultmann, a German Lutheran New Testament professor, developed the "demythologizing" hermeneutic to make the "irrelevant" Bible relevant to modern readers. K. Barth, a Swiss Reformed pastor, developed the distinction between history and religious history. He was basically a conservative theologian and interpreter, but his division of existence into historical and religious does disservice to the incarnation and the biblical patterns of revelation.

Jesus' life? If so, how are we to interpret them? We may understand miracles as God interfering with natural law according to His will. That means that He replaces normal order with spontaneous corrections to the way the events of history are going. We may also understand miracles as the interjection of a higher set of laws into the lower laws of creation. Thus miracles reveal the kingdom of God that always brings a higher dimension of life than we expect on earth. Either way miracles are interpreted; the fact that God exists and seeks to relate to His creation opens the door to understanding that miracles are completely consistent with God's plan as revealed in Scripture.

It should be noted in passing that the Bible is not "full" of miracles. They may be far less numerous than many expect. Considering biblical history, miracles occur at significant and transitional times. It may be that miracles occurred more regularly than the Bible records, but that raises the question of why the biblical writers only note the miracles at certain times and for certain reasons. They use miracles to substantiate their narrative points explaining what God is doing at a particular time in history.

As noted earlier, miracles are relatively infrequent in the Bible, and they seem to occur in the great transition times. They accompany a change in direction or the need for religious purity. They support the teaching of Scripture. Miracles are evidence of what God does. At the major transitions of biblical history, God both says what He is doing through His credentialed spokespersons, and He demonstrates His ability to affect change through the miracles He works through them. That suggests that miracles witness to the truth of the message. They are not the message themselves.

The Gospel of John presents the clearest hermeneutic for how to handle miracles. Unlike the other Gospel writers, John rests his case for belief in Jesus on seven miracles, apart from Jesus' resurrection. These seven miracles interface with John's presentation of Jesus to produce a woven fabric of support for Jesus' person and His message.

John instructs us as to his purposes in John 20:30–31. There he admittedly selects certain miracles to produce faith that the Christ is Jesus, and that through believing in Jesus one may have eternal life. Significantly John calls miracles signs. The other writers normally refer to miracles as wonders, stressing the reaction of the people who observed them, or powers, stressing the innate ability Jesus had to perform them. John's unique designation, signs, gives us the clue as to how to interpret them.

There is a pattern in John's presentation. In the heated dialogue with the Pharisees and people of Judea, there is a focus on the miracles. It begins with Nicodemus and continues through the arguments of chapter 12. Only believers see signs. Unbelievers see "works." Yet they are observing and discussing the

same event, a miracle. Jewish interpreters focused on works—power and activities that could be debated. John saw the miracles as signs, powerful works
that point people beyond themselves to another, and greater, truth.[8]

Hermeneutically, miracles are significant. They are pointers. They support
and complement something else. Naturally there is a strong tendency to focus
on the miracle as an end to itself. A miracle points to the miracle worker. But
John's careful use of signs informs us that we are to look to a message beyond
them for clear understanding. We must ask, therefore, why did Jesus do a miracle at this time? What was the purpose of the miracle? How does this miracle
help to bring people to faith? How does it help us understand the message?

In some ways, miracles resemble parables, only they are real-life situations.
As discussed earlier, parables have main points that one is to grasp from the
story. Not every part of the story is to be interpreted, but the characters who
have developed profiles and play clearly stylized roles are surely significant.
Miracles have many aspects to them. They are done in many settings, accomplished in various ways, and produce different results. Not every part of a
miracle is significant. We suggest the following principles for interpretation.

1. Observe the primary point of the miracle. This may be obvious, such
    as producing a coin to pay taxes (Matt 17:27), or it may require sig-
    nificant study. One may easily miss the main point. For example, in
    Jesus' first miracle at the wedding in Cana, changing water into wine
    (John 2:1–11), many focus on the reason Jesus helped the young cou-
    ple as they faced the greatest embarrassment of their lives. Yet John
    provides the interpretation in v. 11—it brought the first disciples to
    faith in Christ.
2. Study the cultural and theological backgrounds that enable the miracle
    to communicate its message. For example, some of Jesus' miracles in-
    volve correcting handicaps or sicknesses. While the main point of the
    event may not be the miracle, it is helpful to know of the ingrained
    Jewish theology that sickness only results from sin. Many Jews even
    assumed a person could sin before birth and a handicap was a punish-
    ment for a rebellious prenatal act.[9] For them, healing a handicap or
    sickness implied that spiritual healing had taken place first. This was
    particularly a problem for those who believed that the sickness was

---

[8] This is an important pattern for John. It is interesting, however, that the first to come to Jesus
because of the miracles was Nicodemus. Apparently he was an unbeliever at that time (John 3:2).

[9] John 9:1–2 makes this abundantly clear. Jewish rabbis based this theology on the Old Testament
account of Jacob's "tricking" Esau by having a bodily appendage appear first and then being born
second. Interestingly, even the disciples succumbed to the theory.

evidence of eternal consequences on the victim. The main point of a miracle may be discerned from its relationship to the context of the account, but the significance of the miracle to the observers may be found in background studies.

3. Determine why the biblical writer included it in his writing. This involves knowing his purpose in including it, since there were an abundance of miracles that were legitimate candidates for telling the life of Jesus. This point also includes determining how the miracle builds a case for the ultimate message the writer communicates through his book. Therefore, specific miracles are chosen because they effectively support the story line.

4. Explain what the miracle tells us about how God works in the world. That means we should bring the theology of the miracle and its surrounding and complementing texts to the point of interpretation. Building on the miracles enables us to develop a more consistent profile of Jesus or others who performed miracles.

5. Relate the miracles to the kingdom of God. Miracles are both corrective and revelatory. That is, in restoring health or providing for needs, they correct the ills of the sinful world in which we live. They correct the world by bringing good to a bad situation. That miraculous correction also reveals that the difficulties that call for a corrective miracle will not be present in the kingdom of God. God's work is about correcting wrong and healing from spiritual and physical ills. While we will not understand the kingdom of God fully until we enter it, the miracles give us a glimpse into what heaven will be like. They also point us to the kinds of activities and concerns we should have as representatives of God's kingdom.

6. Apply the miracle's message to life today. How does this help us understand the Bible better? The point is not that we should look for miracles today. The point is we should look to why the Bible records a specific miracle and what the writer wanted us to know from it.

Miracles have a particular function in the Bible. They reveal and correct. They are easily misinterpreted because people tend to focus on the miracle rather than the miracle-worker or his message. They also become the "standard" some people expect in life now, as evidence that one has entered God's kingdom. They say that Christians should be immune to illness, handicaps, needs, or weaknesses. They focus on the spectacular display of power, as God's will breaks into the darkness of earth. But miracles call us to a deeper interpretation. They are not about God's relieving us of difficulties, sicknesses, and hardships. They point us to our responsibility to walk with God and to know that nothing is beyond His power. The Christian teacher should look to the purpose of the miracles as developed in the text.

NARRATIVE

Much of the Bible is written as narrative. It is in story form. This is true of large sections of the Old Testament and the Gospels, but also of Acts as history. Recent narrative criticism has revealed the complexity of narrative evaluations. In a simple way, however, we may make some suggestions about narrative forms that may be helpful.

Narrative is always a device of the writer. It is a way the writer chooses to make a point. He could have simply made a list of propositions, but listeners and readers tend to remember them better when they are in story form.

Narrative literature is known by plot, characters, and setting. The plot is the primary way of making the point. The plot may be involved or simple. Just as reading a novel requires detecting the plot, reading narrative in Scripture requires an understanding of the plot. Understanding the plot is intertwined with the characters and the setting.

The characters are chosen and profiled to carry out the plot. Normally there are contrasting characters, some good and some bad. The characters always reflect the setting of the story and their part in it. Therefore the characters fit naturally into the setting of the narrative.

The settings of narrative vary. They may be essentially tied to the larger historical setting, or they may be located in a specific cultural "location," such as dinner at a Pharisee's house. The setting provides the atmosphere for the narrative as well as the rationale for the actions of the characters. In Scripture, some narratives are biographical, such as the stories of King David; some are legal, such as the "court case" of Malachi; and some are cultural, such as the table talk at a Pharisee's dinner.

At a simple level, we may suggest the following principles for interpreting narrative.

1. Observe carefully the setting. Sometimes the settings are obvious; sometimes they are subtle and known only when serious background, cultural, and lexical studies reveal a context. Scholars may debate the settings of some narratives, so care must be taken here.
2. Note how the characters of the narrative are profiled. The assumption is that the stories were prethought and therefore characterizations are

intentional. Think about each of the characters and what they contribute to the story.

3. From the setting and the interplay of the characters, form your understanding of the plot. Where does it start? What point does it make? How do each of the characters take the plot to the next level?

4. Seek to understand the author and readers. This seems obvious, but at times there are "implied authors" and "implied readers." The narrator tells or writes the story from the standpoint of an (implied) author who may be different from himself. Similarly, the (implied) readers of the story may not be the same as the readers of the book in which the story occurs. For example, some of the accounts of Jesus' actions were told with specific reference to the "readers" in Jesus' life. Yet the readers of the Gospels were a different audience.

5. Interpret the narrative in terms of the plot development, particularly how the plot "suffers" or "succeeds" because of the various characters, and how the plot ends. Some points of the narrative are relatively unimportant; other points are indispensible.

> *Sensitivity to narrative brings new discovery in understanding much of the Bible.*

GOSPEL

At the beginning of the Christian era, gospel became a popular and significant form of writing. We know of no gospels before those of the New Testament. There are, however, many gospels written from the second through the fourth centuries. Gospel became a popular way of writing. Most of the gospels are pseudonymous or anonymous, but there are gospels supposedly written from all the main characters of Jesus' life. Among the most famous spurious gospels are *The Gospel of Thomas* and *The Gospel of Judas*.

The first use of "gospel" to define a Christian writing came from the Gospel of Mark.[10] The New Testament Gospels did not originally have the word "gospel" in their titles. It was added later as scholars began to recognize the unique characteristics of this form of literature and its presentation of the life of Jesus. Though the word does not occur as a title, the Gospel of Mark begins with a statement "the beginning of the gospel of Jesus Christ." The English word "gospel" translates the Greek word *euangellion* that literally means

---

[10] Most scholars today believe that the Gospel of Mark was the first gospel to be written.

"good news." Mark, therefore, intends his readers to know at the start that his message is good news.

The word "gospel" also occurs elsewhere in the Gospels. It describes Jesus' preaching: "The gospel of the kingdom." Following that lead, apostolic writers began to speak of the message of Jesus' life and death as "good news," the *euangellion*. Thus there is a tension as we correlate the use of these terms. The gospel is a message that encapsulates the life and death of Jesus; the Gospel is also a book describing His life, teaching, death and resurrection (and we capitalize it when referring to any of those four books). Consciously, the apostles wanted hearers and readers to know that the gospel message was an abridgment of the gospel story.

Scholars have debated the specific genre of Gospel. Three basic ideas have drawn most of the attention: they are history, biography, and proclamation. None of these completely describes a Gospel, but each has strong elements of truth.

The Gospels are primarily *witnesses*. They are unashamedly clear in their allegiance to Jesus, and their writers have been impacted positively by His life. They attribute their changed character to Jesus' death and their worldview to Jesus' resurrection. They have shaped the data of the Gospels to bring people to a realization of what they found in their own lives. Every part of the Gospels reinforces their convictions. They witness to Jesus.

Earlier we considered the purpose of John's Gospel (20:30–31). Turning to it again helps us understand the witness element of the Gospels. John begins by stating that Jesus did "many other signs" that he did not include. He included the seven he did so that people would believe. The first witness element is that the Gospels are *selective*. The writers had an abundance of material and made choices as to what would carry their readers along.

John continues that the signs he chose to include have the capability of bringing readers to faith. The Gospels are consciously *perspectival*. The events are more than randomly selected; they are faith-building events. The writers write from their own changed lives.

John's third point comes from his statement that "Jesus is the Christ." Faith has an object. The events selected point to Jesus. In this, the Gospel is purposefully *theological*. John has a primarily Jewish readership. Who is the Messiah? John's Gospel answers this theological question.

Finally, John's Gospel is *purposeful*. The ultimate purpose is to bring people to eternal life. Events carefully chosen, supporting a unique perspective, with a deeply theological point, provide a new level of living: the life of Christ. Of course it is necessary to follow through the entire process to have life. John carefully describes and shapes events, dialogues, and debates to address each of these four concerns.

Other Gospel writers followed the same process. It is necessary to find the purpose of each one and follow it through from beginning to end. A good discipline is to take each pericope (logical unit) and relate it to the purpose for writing. This is easier to see with John, but it can be done with the other three as well. The key to finding the purpose of the Synoptics is to compare them with each other, determining how they handle the events they hold in common with the other(s). That includes the words they use, the order they employ, and the events they include that the others do not. In so doing, the careful observer will begin to understand the target audience, the distinctive characteristics of Jesus they wish to include, and any theological nuances each writer may have.

The Gospels clearly bear witness to Jesus' life. That, in part, explains why there are four of them. Two factors were primary influencers in the need to write multiple accounts. First, Christianity was advancing into new territories. The church faced cultural, linguistic, and personality differences within its constituency. Not every culture appreciated the same characteristics that others did. Jews were Messianic. Greeks looked to the perfect man in body and mind. The Romans prized action and authority. The Gospel writers responded quite willingly and of necessity. Matthew wrote to Jews. Mark wrote to Romans. Luke wrote to Greeks. John wrote to Rabbinic Jews and, possibly, Ebionites. Because of the eternal significance of the Gospel message, these writers wrote so that the various ethnic and cultural groups could connect with Jesus.

The second factor was the passing of time. The ancient world relied on oral transmission, and the integrity of the events rehearsed depended on the integrity of the one telling them. As time passed, there were fewer eyewitnesses. The stories were promoted by second generation Christians. This was especially true as the apostles aged and died. There was a need, therefore, to have authoritative eyewitness accounts available for all to read or hear. The passing of time and the encounter with other cultures encouraged the writing of the Gospels.

The teacher of adults has options in how to teach Jesus' life. One Gospel or another will suit the learning and personality styles of every reader. It is sometimes very helpful to take time to compare multiple accounts from the different Gospels, even in the classroom. In the Gospels we see God accommodating Himself to the diversity of the people He created.

HISTORY

Having dismissed the Gospels from being in the genre of history, where do we find history in the New Testament? There is one book, the Acts of the apostles. Acts continues the story of the Gospel of Luke, having been written by the same author, Luke. In fact, Luke introduces Acts by saying he is writing what Jesus continued to do through the apostles. Yet Acts is not like the Gospel of Luke. In Acts, there is a presentation of sequential events with little commentary. The events are self-evident. Only God could do what happened in the first three decades. Thus Acts is the closest book we have to history writing in the New Testament.

The hermeneutical issues of interpreting history can be simply stated. What is *descriptive* and what is *prescriptive?* Descriptive writing tells what happened. Prescriptive writing informs as to what should happen. Many confuse these two. It is very difficult to say something *should* happen just because it happened.

From a genre perspective, all history is descriptive. Many people, for example, impressed with the power and wonder of the events at Pentecost (Acts 2), urge people to ask God for the same experience. Sometimes they want it repeatedly. Yet Acts never suggests that Pentecost is repeatable. It was the birth of the church. It was the inauguration of the Holy Spirit's visible ministry, continuing what God had begun in Jesus. In order for Pentecost to be repeated as recorded in Acts, we would have to be in an identical situation as they were and expect the same results. Obviously that is impossible.

Most often, those who pray for another Pentecost experience focus on the Holy Spirit's manifest power. Rightly, they realize the key to God's working in the world is the Holy Spirit acting through those who willingly follow His lead. Yet even in Acts the event was not repeated. The gift of tongues only occurs two other times, once to a proselyte in Judea (Acts 10) and once to a Gentile in Ephesus (Acts 18). None of the messages or evangelistic efforts focused on the gift of tongues. The gift of tongues and the powerful display of the Holy Spirit's power are *descriptive* in Acts. Taking them to a more normative level requires other hermeneutical principles that may or may not be appropriate.

Another example approaches this from the other direction. Late in Acts the apostle Paul was shipwrecked on the island of Melita. Luke describes the event in the same way that he does the events of Pentecost, from a genre perspective. Why not make the shipwreck normative? Why not pray that we will be shipwrecked like Paul, assuming people will be amazed and turn to Christ? Since the two events are described in the same historical manner, what makes one *prescriptive* and the other *descriptive?* The shipwreck is relatively insignificant to most people, relegated to times when we teach the life of Paul. Many other events have more interest to modern readers. Some of these include: Should the church today meet in houses rather than purchased buildings? Should the deacon's job description come from Acts 6? Should the church focus on healing as part of its ministry? Are the repeated characteristics of the early church the marks of a healthy church in every age of history? Should we evangelize by teams as they did or by individuals as we tend to do? The list can go on.

We easily understand the *descriptive* aspect of history. Yet it seems too confining to think that history sections of Scripture have no *prescriptive* elements, since all Scripture is inspired by God for our profit (2 Tim 3:15–16). Intuitively Christians look for lessons, abiding truths, and theologies from history as well as the other genre. The fact is, the quest for *prescription* is legitimate, but only in a limited way.

Discerning the *prescriptive* elements requires the interpreter to see the whole. It is necessary to think through the entire document, noting its characteristic themes and how they are presented. By putting the various events together into a communicative whole with one major reason for writing, we can formulate a thesis statement for history writings as well as Gospel writings.

Once we understand the whole, the author's purpose in writing, we can make the pieces fit into it. The same methodology employed in the Gospels applies to Acts. Every writer weaves the sometimes seemingly isolated events into a product he hopes will impact people with the truth.

The primary key to understanding which elements are normative is repetition. For example, in Acts, Luke presents the advance of the gospel to the uttermost parts of the world. One constant in this, because of its repetition, is that the church finds opposition. Furthermore, God continues His work in spite of that opposition. While it would be foolish to take any given conflict as what should happen to everyone, it is clearly true that God's work advances through the church in spite of opposition. Some people will side with Christ; others will not. Yet God's work goes on. Surely Luke wanted us to understand those points. Repetition also occurs in other similar events.

A second important point for interpretation is to understand how individual stories included relate to the plot, the central point. History normally tells a story. It revolves around a central theme developed sequentially through time. The plot develops with alternating contrasts of supportive and challenging events. Throughout, the hero of the plot emerges as the clear hero. In Acts, the hero may seem to be the apostles, it may be the church, or it may be the gospel. Confusion may result because of the closeness of each to the central plot of the story. Taking the beginning statement as indicative of the point of the writing, we may say that Acts is the story of the continued work of Jesus in the world. It is accomplished through the gospel message, proclaimed by the apostles, and fostered by the church. Normative principles can be derived from these three because of their crucial role in plot development.

A third important evidence that something is *prescriptive* rather than *descriptive* only is the clear affirmation of a practice in nonhistory texts. For example, if there are places in Scripture that clearly command or exhort that a practice be done, it is likely the writer chose the events he did for teaching purposes. The commands or exhortations may be in Acts, but they are recorded in speeches or teaching passages. It is always questionable to make principles of a specific practice when it is only found in the recording of events.

There are other interpretive principles that aid in this distinction, but these are the primary ones. They apply to the history of both the Old and New Testaments. The crucial interpretive element in understanding and applying history writings is distinguishing what is expected of all ages and all cultures, and what is simply a record of what God did at one specific time.

EPISTLE

Over half the books of the New Testament are epistles. Considerable study has been done on epistolary writing since the early 1900s. Scholars have found an abundance of epistles in *koine* Greek and determined that the New Testament does reflect its culture.

Epistles are basically letters. At the most general level we may say that there are both *formal* epistles and *informal.* Formal epistles are those that seem to be prethought. They represent organized responses or developed argumentation. Formal epistles include such letters as Romans, Hebrews, and 1 Peter. In these kinds of letters there seems to be no urgent issue requiring immediate response from the writer. Each epistle is set against a background of theological concern, but some of the concerns are more general. The formal letters address these concerns in a systematic way.

Informal letters are generally those that reflect a personal or immediate response to specific issues. They include letters like Philippians, Colossians, 2 Timothy, and 2 Corinthians. They read with a spontaneity that suggests the writer sat down and penned a response to some localized issue that concerned him.

Practically, the difference is inconsequential. The primary concern with letters is to realize they are letters. They are partial responses to specific concerns that require a context to understand. The epistles may be characterized as "answers" to "questions." The primary data needed for interpretation comes from within the letter itself, but it is very helpful, and sometimes necessary, to understand the context to which the letter is being written. It is very difficult to understand the "answer" if we do not understand the "question."

An example of this is 1 Corinthians. Paul clearly is responding to a series of questions and concerns that come from the local church (1 Cor 1:11). The evidence of this is Paul's frequent statement "now concerning" (ASV) that he uses to introduce a new direction in his writing (e.g., 1 Cor 7:1). Reading 1 Corinthians is like following an agenda. By contrast, 2 Corinthians appears to be far more spontaneous as Paul answers the criticisms of his enemies.

When reading epistles, there are some basic questions to ask and answer. First, what is the writer actually saying? The piecemeal and immediate responses often produced a partial message. The author wrote only what was necessary for the immediate concern. Second, what is the "question" (issue) that demands this "answer" (response)? The answer comes primarily from the writing itself, but there is a serious need to research background information. For example, what was happening in Corinth? What is the situation of the churches? Who are the people, and do we know anything else about them? Do the language and style of the epistle give us a clue as to the issue? We must realize that the message of the epistles is often incomplete, issue oriented, and local rather than universal.

APOCALYPTIC

Apocalyptic literature appears in the Old Testament, the intertestamental literature, and the New Testament. Multiple examples of it exist in other Jewish and Christian literature. It is likely that the Old Testament writers who employed it coined a new genre that is distinctively Judeo-Christian, though after the first century it is found in Gnostic circles as well as others.[11] The primary apocalyptic texts are Revelation, the "Little Apocalypses" of the Gospels (Matt 24; Mark 13; Luke 21), the Old Testament books of Ezekiel, Daniel, Joel, and others. Some scholars have expanded apocalyptic to include any statements about the kingdom of God or eschatology, thus including passages like 1 Thess 4:13–5:18, but it is most helpful to confine apocalyptic genre to the major portions written in that style.

The basic issue is its closeness to prophecy. Since both apocalyptic and prophecy generally deal with the future, and most focus on the end times, many interpreters treat them alike. Yet it is erroneous to assume apocalyptic is prophecy.

Some primary characteristics define apocalyptic. It may be defined generally as "a revelation of a particular kind, through visions."[12] The vision is the central defining element, but frequently other characteristics give it shape.

---

[11] It is true that some apocalyptic writings appear in Egypt and other Ancient Near Eastern literature (Akkadian and Persian), but the apocalyptic form generally found in Scripture dates from about the fourth century BC.

[12] W. F. Arndt and F. W. Gingrich, *A Greek-English Lexicon of the New Testament* (Chicago: University of Chicago Press, 1957).

1. It is *cosmic.* The characters in the vision are in the realm of the natural and supernatural. They blend together in one great drama.
2. It is *dualistic.* It always presents a dualistic perspective, pitting God and good against Satan and evil.
3. It is *eschatological.* It focuses on the end of the world and God's triumph over evil.
4. It is *symbolic.* It utilizes bizarre, otherworldly creatures and/or mutated creatures of earth.
5. It is *stylized.* The reader immediately senses the drama and easily follows the plot.

Prophecy, on the other hand, is eschatological, but the other features are not prevalent.

Using these characteristics, apocalyptic generally clusters the events within it around the end of the world. On occasion it provides a drama leading to the end.[13] The events are dramatic, violent, and descriptive presentations of God's triumph. While prophecy predicts *earthly* events in normal ways that readers can understand, apocalyptic takes us to the heavens to present truths in ways we can see unencumbered by the normal conventions of earth.[14]

The crucial question is how to treat apocalyptic. When interpreters assume apocalyptic is prophecy, they look for correlations between contemporary events and the symbols of apocalyptic. Thus, in Revelation every new vision is taken as a prediction of the future. Yet there is no agreement as to how the visions correlate to events.

When modern readers read Revelation, the natural tendency is to take it as literally future.[15] People do look for event correlations. Perhaps they do so because they have read prophecy and everything future is considered literal. Furthermore, the first portion of Revelation is epistolary with prophetic elements within the letters to the churches (Rev 1–4). There have also been myriads of attempts to interpret the book prophetically. Without doubt, Revelation is prophetic apocalyptic or apocalyptic prophecy, a combination of the two.

We offer some suggestions as to how to interpret apocalyptic.

---

[13] One might argue that both Daniel and Revelation have sequences of time and events leading to and including the end.

[14] In this sense, it *functions* like science fiction. The drama is clear, but the story is told in a way that draws the readers or watchers into it so they can "return to earth" with renewed commitment to God's plan.

[15] Revelation has been approached in four major ways: preterist, all events except the Second Coming happened in the first century; idealist, that these are purely spiritual (ideal) and not literal; historicist, that Revelation presents a forecast of what will happen throughout history from the first century until the end; and futurist, that Revelation presents a future description of the end of the world.

1. *Enter the world of apocalyptic.* Appreciating and interpreting apocalyptic depends on understanding the genre. There are common themes, common kinds of figures, and common expectations. They are repetitive enough to be interpretively significant.
2. *Consider the impact of the whole.* Probably more than any other genre, apocalyptic makes a dramatic point that requires holistic thinking.
3. *Approach apocalyptic like parable.* In parables there is a climactic point supported by clear movements within the text. Yet there are many interesting points that do not have a direct bearing on the climax. Some points are necessary to tell the story.
4. *Interpret biblically.* Canonical apocalyptic takes place within the canon of Scripture. It illustrates what is otherwise presented with clarity in other places of Scripture.
5. *Be Christological.* Apocalyptic focuses on Jesus as the initiator of God's kingdom and He is the conquering King. The ultimate apocalyptic book is a "Revelation of Jesus Christ" (Rev 1:1–2).
6. *Be doxological.* Doxology is worship. The vivid descriptive images of apocalyptic facilitate clarity even in their obscurity. They enhance worship. While many become ecstatic about finding what the secretive elements mean, the point is to trust the theology and find hope in worshipping God.[16]

PROVERBS

Another prevalent genre is the proverb. Proverbs occur throughout Scripture, but they are most obvious in the Old Testament book that bears their name: Proverbs. Proverbs are pithy, sharp, easily remembered statements of what is generally true. They become proverbs because of the high percentage that what they say happens. Proverbs may be simple statements, like "Do not muzzle an ox while it treads out the grain" (1 Cor 9:9). This comes from the law of Moses, but through time it became proverbial. Proverbs may also be more extended depictions of life, such as the warning about the immoral woman in Proverbs 7.

The confusion about proverbs is how reliable are they? Because they occur in the Bible, many confuse them with promises. They count on the outcome if the circumstances that shape their fulfillment are the same. For example, how many parents have counted on the proverb "train up a child in the way he

---

[16] These suggestions first appeared in a chapter by Rick on preaching apocalyptic. See R. R. Melick Jr., "Preaching and Apocalyptic Literature" in M. Duduit, *Handbook of Contemporary Preaching* (Nashville: Broadman, 1992), 378–92.

should go, and when he is old he will not depart from it" (Prov 22:6 NKJV)? They question what it means to train, when is a child considered old, and what does it mean to depart? Sometimes in desperation their misunderstanding of proverbs leads them to question their faith.

The truth is, proverbs are axioms. They are pithy statements that help people remember what is likely to happen. They do not carry a guarantee that they will always work. The simple proverbs recall truisms about life to remind readers how to make a decision when facing difficult life situations. The more extended collections of proverbs help shape life in a proper direction by remembering the discipline they teach. The genre presents likelihoods, not guarantees.

In recent decades scholars studied genre carefully. There are many different sources that are helpful in acknowledging the impact of a specific genre. One of the most helpful and simple, written for laymen, by Gordon Fee and Douglas Stuart, is *How to Read the Bible for All Its Worth*.[17] The book describes the various genre of the Bible and gives valuable pointers about how to interpret them accurately. We also recommend Gordon Fee and Douglas Stuart's *How to Read the Bible Book by Book: A Guided Tour*.[18]

This brief and simple survey of genre is intended to help sensitize readers and teachers to the distinctive contributions of the variety of styles presented in Scripture. In some senses, that makes the Bible unique. Few other religious books have such variety, but God trusted the personalities of the writers He selected to do it their way. In so doing, they also did it His way.[19]

UNDERSTANDING THE PRINCIPLES FROM HISTORY

One final area of preparation for Bible study should be mentioned: principles handed down through Christian history. We have multiple examples of good and bad approaches to the Bible in Christian history. It has often been stated that awareness of history brings a better likelihood that we will not repeat its mistakes.

This section is not about the history of interpretation. There are good books on that for those who are interested.[20] Here we want to describe some of the

---

[17] G. D. Fee and D. Stuart, *How to Read the Bible for All Its Worth* (Grand Rapids: Zondervan, 2005).

[18] G. D. Fee and D. Stuart, *How to Read the Bible Book by Book: A Guided Tour* (Grand Rapids: Zondervan, 2002).

[19] We also recommend several other books that survey the issues of hermeneutics with an inclusion of genre. B. Corley, S. W. Lempke, and G. I. Lovejoy, *Biblical Hermeneutics: A Comprehensive Introduction to Interpreting Scripture* (Nashville: Broadman and Holman, 2002); W. C. Kaiser and M. Silva, *An Introduction to Biblical Hermeneutics: The Search for Meaning,* revised and expanded (Grand Rapids: Zondervan, 2007); and G. Osborne, *The Hermeneutical Spiral* (Downers Grove, IL: InterVarsity, 2006).

[20] We recommend W. Yarchin, *History of Biblical Interpretation: A Reader* (Peabody:

guiding hermeneutical principles the early church developed to help interpreters, teachers, and preachers remain true to the text. Most of these relate
to broad, overarching principles that Christian orthodoxy has affirmed. They
are indispensible, given the awareness that each of the individual books was
accepted as canonical based on divine inspiration. People needed criteria for
seeing the whole and trusting God's revelation in the Bible.

THE CLARITY OF SCRIPTURE

From the earliest days of Christianity common people have read and followed the Bible.[21] While scholars debated issues and theologies, most Christians simply wanted to follow their Lord. Scripture was written with a view to
the fact that the oral impact would be the greatest. The greater point, however,
is that all Christians can understand the Bible.

The Bible has a self-correcting nature. Not all who read come to the Bible
with the same presuppositions or principles of interpretation. Some read correctly; some are seriously misguided; others are naïve. Even those who want
to understand have the human problem of perceiving divine truth. For a time,
the priesthood claimed the prerogative of interpreting the Bible for people.
With the Reformation, Martin Luther broke the hold of the Roman Catholic Church's approach to indoctrination. He believed in the priesthood of the
common believer, and its corollary that the Bible could be safely translated
into the language of the people.

Luther was correct. People without proper training can understand. Reading the Bible as a whole corrects its parts even if the parts are misunderstood.
Trusting the Holy Spirit as the teacher brings new vistas of understanding that
open our eyes to the truth. Thus the Bible can be clearly understood by all, and
it corrects the lives of all believers.

Before leaving this point, care must be taken. The clarity of Scripture does
not excuse the use of improper methods, and it certainly cannot be taken to
mean that readers do not need a cultural understanding of the world of the
Bible. The truth is, the better we understand proper methodologies, and the
more we apply proper hermeneutical principles, the more likely we are to
understand correctly. Proper principles should shorten the process of finding
a proper interpretation.

, 2004); and D. S. Dockery, *Biblical Interpretation Then and Now: Contemporary Hermeneutics in
Light of the Early Church* (Grand Rapids: Baker Academic, 1992).

[21] It should also be noted that until modern times the majority of people, including Christians, were
illiterate. Their acquaintance with Scripture was in hearing it read or in being told what it says. That
brings a special importance to the reading of the text.

THE ANALOGY OF FAITH

Christianity has always had various movements and emphases within it. In the early church they recognized that not all who claimed to be Christian were true to the faith. Shortly, heretical groups also claimed a heritage in Christianity, causing distortion of the faith. Even within orthodox Christianity,[22] questions were raised about theology. At the same time, there were discussions about which books God inspired. For many reasons, there was a need to define apostolic Christianity.

This need resulted in the *analogy of faith*. The analogy of faith rested on theology. That is, the early church systematized the basic theology of the church that they traced back through the apostle Paul to Jesus. This basic theology was used as a test of true Christianity and of virtually any doctrinal position. Later, Martin Luther emphasized the *analogy of Scripture*, partly in reaction to the theological heavy-handedness of the Roman Catholic Church of his time. The analogy of faith and the analogy of Scripture call us to root our interpretations in the Bible itself as historically interpreted.

The analogy basically means that nothing in Scripture can differ with Scripture as a whole. All Scripture supports the basic doctrines. No text interpreted correctly will counter or contradict these doctrines. This was later taken to mean that no individual passage of Scripture could reverse the meaning of the whole. Thus a doctrinal test provided consistency and shape to Christianity.

The hermeneutical value of the analogy of faith is twofold. First, since God inspired the writings, and He could not contradict Himself, the writings have the unity produced by inspiration. The interpreter should expect that unity. Second, texts that seem counter to the unity of doctrine must be restudied in light of the expected unity. Thus the doctrine provides a guideline for the overall integrity of Scripture.

THE UNITY AND DIVERSITY OF SCRIPTURE

At first this may seem contradictory to the analogy of faith. However, it builds on the unity of the doctrine and affirms it, but it recognizes that the various authors may—and do—express themselves differently from each other. We should not expect Matthew to "speak the same theological language" as Paul, for example. The Bible's unity is deeper than the words of Scripture.

---

[22] Now it is more fashionable to refer to pre-Constantine orthodoxy (pre-AD 317) as proto-orthodoxy. It is impossible to distinguish between the proto-orthodox theologies and the orthodoxy that survived. We prefer however to speak of both as orthodoxy.

Hermeneutically, this means that we must expect the writers to agree in basic doctrines. They may have a nuanced understanding and may be burdened to express themselves in light of their own situations. But they do not disagree.

We may illustrate this with two different levels of interpretation. First, the writers are free to use words for what they wish. Most likely the core of Christianity was passed from person to person and generation to generation. Naturally there would be similarity of language for some foundational truths. Further, the Old Testament, especially the LXX, brought its own theological jargon. Nevertheless, the writers had freedom. Matthew told a parable of the kingdom (Wedding Feast) and ended it with "many are called, but few are chosen" (Matt 22:14 NKJV). Paul, however, in discussing the doctrine of the security of the believer says "those whom he called he also justified" (Rom 8:30 ESV). These are not two different theologies. Matthew used "called" as invited; Paul used "called" as included.

At the second level, this impacts doctrinal formulations. For example, Paul speaks of those who come to Christ as the elect. God chose them for His purposes (Rom 8:28–30). Yet in order to understand God's nature, calling, and selection processes, we cannot disregard Peter's statement that God is "not willing that any should perish" (2 Pet 3:9 NKJV). The two cannot characterize God in opposite ways. Finding the unifying truth requires serious and sometimes lengthy study. Nevertheless, the expectation that they ultimately do not contradict guides the interpreter.

THE PROGRESS OF REVELATION

Part of the Bible's diversity is seen in that it was written over a 1,500-year period. At each stage of writing, the individual books had relevance to their culture and were written in ways the culture could understand. At the same time, God chose to reveal truth progressively culminating in the life, death, and resurrection of Jesus. Thus there is a need to see the developmental aspect of revelation.

We may illustrate this by the sacrifices presented in the Bible. The first sacrifice was one God officiated for Adam and Eve. It consisted of animal skins to cover their nakedness. Later, Abraham offered his son Isaac to God knowing that God will provide the lamb, which He did (Gen 22:8). Centuries later Moses officiated in ritual sacrifices commanded by God as activities of worship revealing their repentant hearts. Each of these gives us information about God's plan, and each points us to the ultimate sacrifice, Jesus. From Adam we learn that God cares enough to provide salvation even in our failure. From Abraham we learn that God will provide what we do not have on our own and thus cannot give to Him. From Moses we learn that the sacrifices accompany a request for forgiveness for those who break the law.

It would be a grave mistake to assume that Adam knew what John did, or that Abraham knew what Paul did. The latter illustration is instructive. Paul develops the Abraham sacrifice more than any other writer. He uses the event and text as an opportunity to describe Abraham as a man of faith, which he was. Paul, however, never alludes to the fact that Abraham had any personal knowledge of Jesus. That is only attained by reading into the text a much later developed truth.[23]

The perspective of history provides the teacher with reasonable expectations of Scripture. Generations of Christian thinkers developed, agreed on, and followed the principles. The principles helped them resolve seeming conflicts as well as provided a way to evaluate pure Christianity.

Hermeneutically, they had one other function. They forced interpreters to search until they found satisfactory answers. When disparities occur, it is all too easy to dismiss them by having a predisposition to the fact that there is no unity. Throughout history that has impeded serious exegesis and research. When scholars are predisposed to a unity, they continue to study to find how that unity is expressed, even in a seemingly contradictory text. No readers or scholars want to force various texts into harmonies that cannot be supported, but too quickly dismissing possible resolutions can also lead to wrong exegesis.

This section of interpreting the Scripture has focused on principles preparing one to read, interpret, and teach the Bible. The issues are significant, but even the most uninformed reader can understand them. We must begin with a good translation—a more complicated matter today than ever in history. We must have knowledge of the available tools—and there are more available in more languages today than ever in history. We must be sensitive to how literature "works" to inform and move the reader—and there is almost every form of genre represented in Scripture.

If it seems overwhelming, take heart. As you begin to use the tools and follow the guidelines provided, they shape your study. There is an increasing return on the investment. In a sense, however, regardless of how one feels about these matters, it is necessary to turn to the text itself. What do you do to get started? To that we turn.

---

[23] Some may recall that Hebrews states that Moses esteemed the afflictions of Christ as of more value than the treasures of Egypt (Heb 11:26). It should be noted that Hebrews states literally "the Christ." Moses was aware of a Messianic movement and wanted to be a part of it.

CHAPTER FOUR

PREPARING TO STUDY

EVERYONE NEEDS THE RIGHT set of tools. How many times have we attempted to perform a task only to find we were not prepared? Perhaps we did not have the correct wrench, or proper pen or pencil, or adequate knowledge about the task at hand. When this happens, frustration comes. First we attempt to do the job with makeshift instruments—those not made for the task. If that fails, we spend the extra time and money involved to get the proper tool or do the necessary research. Extra time, extra money, extra frustration—all because we were not prepared.

It may seem odd to talk about Bible study and tools. After all, isn't the Bible to be read with open heart and mind, and God will direct us to the truth? Hopefully by now the reader understands our commitment to the Holy Spirit and His ability to work in a devout heart. Furthermore, we are convinced that the Holy Spirit has an affinity for the biblically educated mind. All other things being equal, which they seldom are, God will do more with those prepared than with those who are not.

This section of the book speaks to that point. Today there are available tools. The tools are in public bookstores, in libraries, and on the Internet. No one is left to personal imagination or creativity in approaching the text of Scripture.

This chapter identifies several indispensible tools. Gathering them around makes the study go quicker and the product better. We expect that most students of the Bible have a toolbox ready. Nevertheless, it is wise to identify some of the basics and their values.

A GOOD BIBLE TRANSLATION

In a real sense, your understanding of the Bible will only be as accurate as the translation you are using. Today there are many options. Choosing a translation can be bewildering simply because there are so many, and more are becoming available. One of the blessings of living in the twenty-first century is precisely this: there are translations of the Bible for almost every situation and every age, gender, or interest group. Some are very good reading, but in the desire for readability they have lost precision in expressing the meaning. Others are quite good technically, but are far too cumbersome for the average reader. The Christian teacher needs the best translation available.

Most people choose and use a translation because someone told them it was good. Perhaps the church leaders have selected the version they wish for the church, and therefore the attendees use it. Frequently professors are asked: "What is the best Bible translation?" The answer is somewhat complicated, but many students simply take the word of a trusted professional. Publishers market their translations with bookstore or electronic displays that usually commend the translation for being the best representative of the Greek and Hebrew originals. The choice can be overwhelming and bewildering. Thus the most basic tool—the choice of Bible—becomes one of the most difficult issues for the teacher.

It is necessary to speak to the issue of translations. They are too prevalent to overlook. In fact, one of the common "methods" of Bible study is to have each participant bring a different translation so the group can compare them and arrive at the meaning of the Bible by "consensus." This can be helpful if the teacher understands Bible translations, but it often becomes nothing more than "pooling ignorance." Bible translation is a complicated and technical process, an academic discipline of its own. Nevertheless, a few helpful insights will guide the teacher in selecting an appropriate Bible to use.

The reasons choosing a Bible translation is difficult are because of two basic issues that are highly debated: text theory and translation theory. There is more to a translation than what someone thought was the best way to communicate in English. The beginning point is what determines which Greek and Hebrew manuscripts you use. This is text theory. Following that, the question is what theory of translation should you use. This is translation theory. We will make some general comments about each in the hopes that the teacher will at least be conversant with the process.

TEXT THEORY

Text theory is the philosophy of how and why you choose certain Greek and Hebrew manuscripts in your translation. The individual books of the Bible circulated independently. We have more knowledge of the New Testament books than the Old Testament, so the illustrations provided will involve the New Testament. The Epistles and Gospels had specific destinations for the most part. It was natural for Christians, and certainly churches, to want their own copies. So the books were copied early. Furthermore, they were translated into other languages very early, especially Latin, Coptic, and Syriac. The result is that there are over 5,200 manuscripts or pieces of manuscripts of the New Testament books. In addition, the early church fathers often included quotations in their writings or sermons. Altogether, we have multiple manuscripts in Greek, other early languages, and documents from the church fathers.

All were hand-copied. Generally scribes took great care in copying the manuscripts. Inevitably, however, variant reading began to appear. Some variations in manuscripts can be easily explained. For example, a copyist may have mistaken one Greek letter for another. A scribe may have thought he remembered what he was copying and wrote out of his memory rather than from the page. On a few occasions scribes thought they found mistakes and tried to correct them.

The result of this activity is that there are multiple manuscripts of every book of the New Testament and they do not all agree in every point. Nearly all the variants are insignificant, and no doctrine depends on any textual variant. The differences, however, raise a serious question about which reading is the original. The original manuscript, called the autograph, is the most significant and, as we stated in the section on the Bible, the one inspired by God.

Scholars have divided into two basic camps in seeking to determine the original reading of any given variant: the Majority Text advocates and the Critical Text advocates. First, there are the Majority Text advocates. Building on the fact that most of the manuscripts agree on any given passage, they claim the majority of manuscripts contain the better reading, even though most of the supporting manuscripts are relatively late (AD 900–1400). Majority Text scholars also see the "majority" reading in the earliest manuscripts and make their case that the majority readings are quite early.

The majority text in Greek is the basis of many modern translations. It was the Greek text of the earliest English translations and, indeed, most modern language translations globally. It is the theory behind the King James Versions and the many modern translations that agree with the King James.

The majority of scholars today do not accept the Majority Text theory. They are Critical Text advocates. They basically state that the number of texts is not as crucial as the age and purity of the various manuscripts. They have developed and applied to the manuscripts a series of criteria to determine the correct reading. In doing so, they divided the many Greek texts into families of texts, with each family containing the same basic variants.

Most of the early manuscripts have been discovered in the last 300 years. Many of them differ with the majority texts and therefore following them leads to some differences in the translations. The two largest sections of the Bible in question are Mark 16:9–20 and John 7:52–8:11. Critical text advocates indicate that these do not belong in the original. Majority Text advocates accept them. The result is that some translations today include these sections and others do not.

Even casual Bible readers notice these passages. Many English translations indicate the textual questions that exist. The issue is textual theory: what procedure is best in determining the reading of the original manuscript. It is not likely that the average Christian teacher will have the skills or interest to enter this discussion at a technical level, but it is important that the teacher have an understanding of the processes so that explanations can be made to the learners where genuine questions arise. Thus the first issue in choosing a translation is textual theory.[1]

TRANSLATION THEORY

Once Bible translators agree on a textual theory, they must consider how best to translate. This is an issue of translation theory. There are basically three approaches in dealing with how to make Hebrew/Aramaic and Greek manuscripts understandable to modern readers.

First, there are paraphrases. Bibles like *The Living Bible*[2] and *The Message*[3] are paraphrases. They may depend on the Hebrew and Greek texts, but

---

[1] For those interested in further study, we recommend: for the layman, J. H. Greenlee, *The Text of the New Testament: From Manuscript to Modern Edition* (Hendrickson, 2008); for a more academic approach see B. M. Metzger and B. D. Ehrman, *The Text of the New Testament: Its transmission, Corruption, and Restoration* (Oxford University Press, 2005); K. Aland and B. Aland, *The Text of the New Testament: an Introduction to the Critical Editions and to the Theory and Practice of Modern Textual Criticism* (Grand Rapids: Eerdmans, 1995).

[2] *The Living Bible Paraphrased* (Guideposts Associates, 1971).

[3] E. H. Peterson, *The Message: The Bible in Contemporary Language* (Colorado Springs: NavPress, 2007). There are many editions of this due to its popularity in interpreting the meaning of the Bible.

the goal of the editors/translators is to make the *meaning* understandable in modern idiom. Paraphrases take great liberties with the text and with the definitions of words. They sacrifice technical precision to gain readability and understanding. Most modern readers enjoy paraphrases. Some remark that the Bible makes sense for the first time through paraphrases. They have value, but they are not good tools for the serious Bible teacher simply because of the liberties they take with the text. Paraphrases often reflect the interpretation of their producers. They are, therefore, "second hand" in that they reproduce the interpretations of others.

Second, there are literal translations. They stand at the opposite end of the spectrum from paraphrases. A literal translation attempts to be as close as possible to the words and structure of the original writer. The goal is to produce a careful translation true to the text (rather than true to the interpretation of the text) so that the reader has the tools to make a personal interpretation. Literal translations sometimes suffer from a pedantic repetition of word definitions and from a style that is awkward for most English readers. Literal translations are best for those whose goal is a serious understanding of the text, but many complain about the lack of readability.

Third, there are dynamic translations (dynamic equivalents). About 60 years ago scholars began to produce dynamic translations rather than literal. They followed contemporary linguistic theory in this. These scholars claimed correctly the impossibility of being literal in translation because the languages (e.g., English and Greek, for example) are too different in structure, and English readers have difficulty with the grammatical and syntactical constructions of the classical languages. In order to communicate effectively, meaning, grammar, syntax, and, sometimes, semantics have to be viewed differently. Dynamic translators take the difficult expressions and concepts in the source language, look for the kernel truth they communicate, and then seek to communicate that kernel truth in the receptor language. At first many Christians harshly criticized the dynamic translations, but in the past 60 years they have become the more common translations, and the fastest selling English Bibles today are basically dynamic.[4]

The three types of modern language Bibles discussed here all have value. On a scale of technical accuracy to interpretation the order is literal, dynamic, and paraphrase. Teachers should only consult paraphrases after their personal study is complete and they wish to read another interpretation for their own understanding. Literal and dynamic translations are acceptable to teachers

---

[4] These include *The New Living Translation* (Carol Stream, IL: Tyndale House Publishers, 2004)— we recommend the second edition—and *The Holy Bible: The New International Version* (Grand Rapids, Zondervan, 1987).

because they both attempt to translate. For the most part, teachers will do better to have a literal version closest to the original languages.

Thus choosing a Bible can be a confusing task. For example, those who understand and follow a Critical Text theory still must decide whether to use a literal or dynamic translation. Those who prefer a Majority Text theory still must make the same decision. As noted earlier, often the decision is made already by church leaders or the general availability of a specific version.

HEBREW AND GREEK REFERENCE WORKS

Since the Bible was written originally in Hebrew and Greek, today's teacher should have some knowledge of the words and grammar of these ancient languages. Formerly, these languages were taught in all seminary programs so that the pastor and other Christian workers have a firsthand knowledge of them. Learning the original languages is laborious and time intensive. Most laypersons will not have sufficient time, if they have interest, to devote to mastery of the languages. Yet gaining the fruit of what they offer is essential.

In the past few years there have been significant advances in making the original languages accessible to laypersons without knowledge of Hebrew and Greek. One of the oldest and easy-to-use tools is *Strong's Concordance of the Bible.*[5] The advantage of *Strong's* is that every Hebrew and Greek word is given a number. That number refers the reader to a Hebrew or Greek word and an English translation so that the reader can know exactly what original word is being translated. The numbers are correlated with a basic dictionary of the Greek and Hebrew meanings. This approach was so well accepted that a number of other reference and study works have appeared that use *Strong's* numbers. Thus the English words are tagged, and the reader has access to the definition of the original language word and where it occurs in the text.[6]

Interlinear Bibles also include both original and modern languages. Most interlinear Bibles work from the original languages and have the English words under them. They were designed for Hebrew and Greek students who need definitions in English to facilitate their reading.

---

[5] J. Strong, *Strong's Exhaustive Concordance of the Bible with CD* (Peabody: Hendrickson, 2007). Strong's Concordance has been in publication since the late 1800s. This CD edition is one of the latest.

[6] *Young's Analytical Concordance* does much the same thing by arranging the English according to the Hebrew and Greek word, but there is no numbering system that allows for other works to key to it. J. Young, *Young's Analytical Concordance to the Bible* (Peabody: Hendrickson, 1984). Like *Strong's*, *Young's* concordance has been reprinted multiple times.

Recently, however, the *English Standard Version* has been produced with a "Reverse English Interlinear."[7] This literal version of the Bible has the English text with the Greek text underneath and is keyed to *Strong's* numbers. The advantage of this text is it reveals the exact Greek word used when any English word occurs. It also gives quick access to definitions. For example, the English word "love" actually stands for at least two Greek words. This makes it difficult to translate passages like John 21:15–18 where Jesus asked Peter "do you love Me?" three times. It is important to note in interpretation that the Greek text uses two different words for love (*philos* and *agapē*). Is there progress from one to the other? Without knowing the Greek words, the interpreter does not have the same options for discussing what the author may have meant in distinguishing the two words in one context. Although most translators try to make a distinction, there is no adequate synonym for love that effectively captures the nuance intended by John. The *ESV Reverse Interlinear* enables one to see these fine distinctions quickly.

With the availability of exceptional tools, teachers have a wealth of information at their disposal. There is still a need to consult experts on the meaning of grammar, syntax, and other functions, but teachers should learn how to use the English tools to the best level of their ability.

BACKGROUND INFORMATION

Much of the Bible assumes the readers know geography, politics, living and social conditions, and other cultural issues. Since times and circumstances have changed, it is imperative that we consult background helps to try to understand the message better.

ATLAS

Every interpreter should read the Bible with an atlas in hand. It is so basic that most printed copies of Bibles have a section of maps in them. Geographical and topographical data help bring the Bible to life. For example, the Old Testament writing prophets ministered to specific nations, kings, and people. Most ministered in a time when Israel was divided into the northern kingdom called Israel and the southern kingdom called Judah. Israel and Judah were very different. Israel rebelled from everything God intended for His people. According to the Scriptures, they never had a king who "walked in the ways of

---

[7] *The English Standard Version* (Wheaton: Crossway/Good News, 2003). The Reverse Interlinear was produced by Standard Bible Society and *Logos Bible Software* (Bellingham, WA).

his father, David.'"[8] They waffled politically, usually selling out to the powerful political leaders who threatened them. They had alternate places of worship so the unifying effect of the temple would no longer be an influence. They brought in other gods, built them temples, and married women who followed alien religions. There were some devout people who lived in the north, but the nation as a whole departed from the ways of God. It is necessary to know which prophets brought God's word to them. Their vivid applications of truth spoke to the heart of the insensitive nation, but they make little sense if their applications are applied to Judah, the southern kingdom. An atlas provides the boundary lines of the nations, timelines of governmental leaders, and what part of the Old Testament relates to each.

In the New Testament, geography helps interpret. We learn significantly about Jesus and His ministry as we try to plot His journeys and correlate them with events in the Gospels. On occasion He traveled outside Jewish territory and sometimes to Jerusalem, but most journeys were in the common places of Galilee. Rather significantly, there is no reference to any activity of Jesus in the Greco-Roman cities even though they dotted the terrain of Galilee, one being only four air miles from Jesus' home in Nazareth.[9] Why did the biblical writers omit any of Jesus' ministries to these? It would seem the Gospel writers, seeking to attract Gentiles to Christianity, would have chronicled His contact with them.

It is almost impossible to understand the Pauline Epistles without seeing their locations and the sequential nature of Paul's encounters with them. Knowledge of Roman roads and the locations of specific cities often afford the interpreter a better understanding of Paul's strategies and the unique nature of the churches he addressed. Good Bible atlases provide a myriad of helpful information that makes the Bible more understandable.[10]

BIBLE DICTIONARY OR ENCYCLOPEDIA

In addition to a good atlas, every teacher should have a good Bible dictionary or encyclopedia close at hand. There is some overlap in the information provided by Bible dictionaries and atlases, but dictionaries provide more information.

---

[8] This is the common rule by which the kings are judged in the historical books of the Bible, Kings and Chronicles.

[9] There were 10 famous Roman cities in Judea called the Decapolis, and Sephoris was closest to Nazareth.

[10] We recommend T. V. Brisco, ed., *Holman Bible Atlas: A Complete Guide to the Expansive Geography of Biblical History* (Nashville: B & H, 1999).

Bible dictionaries have individual articles on virtually every aspect of life identified in the Scriptures. One may consult theological themes (such as "righteousness"), develop profiles of the major figures in Scripture (such as John or Paul), reconstruct living conditions in houses (helpful for understanding early Christian meeting places), and understand economic and political situations, and many other matters. It also helps to have specific monographs on background issues, but at a minimum the teacher needs a multipurpose Bible dictionary.[11]

TEXT COMMENTARIES

Commentaries interpret the text of Scripture. Some are condensed and function like handbooks. Others are sets with multiple volumes. Some are basic, commenting paragraph by paragraph. Others are detailed, using the original languages and commenting on technical matters of interest primarily to scholars. Generally speaking, a commentary in the middle, one that comments seriously on the text but with less technical analysis, is most helpful to the average teacher. One helpful commentary is the *New American Commentary*.[12]

COMPUTER RESOURCES

Computer software is revolutionizing biblical studies, as it is other areas. Now data is immediately at hand, and information that formerly took weeks or months to gather is available in less than a second.

The Internet is a bottomless pit of information for any subject or any text. There are articles, sermons, lesson plans, and text details that provide more helpful information than can be accommodated in any lesson plan. The difficulty with the Internet is that no one regulates the quality, accuracy, or applicability of the material on it. Teachers should measure information gained there by comparison with trusted sources, such as written commentaries, and be careful in using information that "no one else has." It may well be wrong.

Other software packages are invaluable. Many companies offer search software that contains multiple copies of Scripture in various translations and helpful background information as well. The three most popular are

---

[11] There are many good Bible dictionaries and encyclopedias with varying degrees of information provided. We recommend *Holman Illustrated Bible Dictionary,* ed. T. C. Butler, C. Brand, C. Draper, and A. England (Nashville: B & H, 2003).

[12] *The New American Commentary: An Exegetical and Theological Exposition of Holy Scripture* (Nashville: Broadman). This is a 42-volume set on the entire Bible from a conservative perspective. It is about three-fourths completed at this time. Rick is a consulting editor of the set and author of one of its volumes.

BibleWorks, Accordance, and *Logos Bible Software.*[13] *BibleWorks* is a comprehensive software package that focuses on texts. It has multiple versions of the Bible in Greek and Hebrew and many modern languages. It also contains early Christian texts, Qumran and other background texts. There are few helpful reference books, but there are Greek and Hebrew grammars and lexicons. Relatively inexpensive, this is one of the best pure search and text packages available. Users find it a regular companion providing information.

Accordance is a search and data program built for the Apple Mac. Like *BibleWorks*, it has multiple texts of Scripture and early Jewish and Christian literature. It is more costly than *BibleWorks*, but for those using a Mac it is an excellent program.

Logos Bible Software is more comprehensive software than the others and operates on both PC and Mac. *Logos* provides an entire library available at all times. The library includes multiple texts of original languages, translations, background, and early Christian writings. It also includes commentaries, Bible dictionaries and theologies, monographs, and virtually everything needed to study a topic or a text. The advantage of the software is its ability to search everything in its database immediately. It has multiple pricing depending on the extent of the package, but is the best package to have for a ready resource of "all you need to know." *Logos* also allows for keeping notes, lesson plans, and other information in the program itself so that personal notes are always available through its search engine. Finally, it includes prayer guides and devotional reading for those who wish them.

These and other software packages continue to improve their holdings and their search capacities. They are the way of the future and are worthwhile investments for anyone serious about Bible study and teaching.

RESOURCE LIST FOR BIBLE STUDY

There are many good resources for Bible study today. The following is a very brief list of our recommendations to help get one started. It assumes no knowledge of Hebrew and Greek.

BIBLE TRANSLATIONS

How to Choose a Translation for All Its Worth: A Guide to Understanding and Using Bible Versions. Gordon D. Fee and Mark L. Strauss. Grand Rapids: Zondervan Publishing House, 2007.

---

[13] *BibleWorks LLC* (Norfolk, VA), *www.bibleworks.com; Accordance* (Altamonte Springs, FL), *www.accordancebible.com;* and *Logos Bible Software* (Bellingham, WA), www.logos.com.

Holman Christian Standard Bible. Nashville: B & H Publishing Group.
Holy Bible: The New International Version. Grand Rapids: Zondervan
Publishing Co.
The New Living Translation. Carol Stream, IL: Tyndale House Publishers.
The English Standard Version. Wheaton: Crossway Books/Good News
Publishers, 2001. The Reverse Interlinear was produced by Standard Bible
Society and *Logos Bible Software* (Bellingham, WA*).*

BACKGROUNDS

*Holman Bible Atlas: A Complete Guide to the Expansive Geography of Biblical
History.* Edited by Thomas V. Brisco. Nashville: B & H Publishing Group,
1999.
Holman Illustrated Bible Dictionary. Edited by Trent C. Butler, Chad Brand,
Charles Draper, and Archie England. Nashville: B & H Publishing Group,
2003.

BIBLE CONCORDANCE

Strong's Exhaustive Concordance of the Bible with CD. James Strong. Peabody:
Hendrickson Publishers, 2007. Strong's Concordance has been in publication
since the late 1800s. This CD edition is one of the latest.
Young's Analytical Concordance. James Young. Peabody: Hendrickson
Publishers, 1984, reprint of earlier edition. Good, but not as helpful as
Strong's.

COMMENTARIES

*The New American Commentary: An Exegetical and Theological Exposition of
Holy Scripture.* Nashville: Broadman Press..
Baker Exegetical Commentary on the New Testament. Grand Rapids: Baker
Publishing Group.
New International Commentary on the New Testament. Grand Rapids:
Eerdmans.
New International Commentary on the Old Testament. Grand Rapids: Eerdmans.
New International Greek Commentary on the New Testament. Grand Rapids:
Eerdmans.
Holman New Testament Commentary. Nashville: B & H Publishing Group.
Holman Old Testament Commentary. Nashville: B & H Publishing Group.
Zondervan Exegetical Commentary on the New Testament. Grand Rapids:
Zondervan Publishing.

COMPUTER SOFTWARE

BibleWorks LLC (Norfolk, VA), www.bibleworks.com
Accordance (Altamonte Springs, FL), www.accordancebible.com (MAC only)
Logos Bible Software (Bellingham, WA), www.logos.com.

GENERAL BOOKS ON REFERENCE TOOLS

An Annotated Guide to Biblical Resources for Ministry. David R. Bauer.
    Peabody, MA: Hendrickson, 2003.
New Testament Commentary Survey, 6th ed. D. A. Carson. Grand Rapids: Baker,
    2007.
Commentary and Reference Survey, 9th ed. John Glynn. Grand Rapids: Kregel
    Publishers. 2003.
Old Testament Commentary Survey, 4th ed. Tremper Longman, III. Grand
    Rapids: Baker, 2007.

CHAPTER FIVE

UNDERSTANDING SPIRITUAL GROWTH

THUS FAR, WE HAVE discussed several foundational issues related to the Bible. As stated earlier, these provide information about the Bible to equip the Bible teacher to understand the nature of the Bible and its interpretation. One final subject should be covered before we turn to adult education theory. It is helpful to gain an understanding of the patterns of spiritual growth from a biblical perspective. This chapter provides that overview so that the Bible teacher will understand what God intends for every believer.

THE GOAL OF GROWTH: HOLINESS

The most fundamental principle in the entire universe is "God is holy!" God's holiness causes some to rejoice, others to fear. It is His holiness that enables Him to "see" things as He does. He sees them correctly. Furthermore, it is His holiness that provides the moral power to change things into the perfection He desires. Because God is holy, He is also just. His holiness is the part of His nature that demands punishment of wrong and reward for what is right. It is, therefore, God's nature that keeps all of creation on an even keel.

The biblical words for holiness basically mean "separateness."[1] They describe God as being different, "separate," from everything created. People and things devoted to God are also separated to Him. God's separateness also involves His perfect character, wisdom, and "sight." That means that God sees and knows better than His creation does, He sees and knows perfectly. His wisdom relates to His ability to direct His creation into a way that is better for them, based on His perfectness, His holiness.

God expects His creatures to be holy. The foundation for this occurs in the Old Testament. God created people in His image (Gen 1:26), innocent and holy, but endowed with the capacity for moral choice. In their world of innocence, Adam and Eve had a satisfying relationship with God. God urged them to seal their innocence by choosing God; Satan urged them to choose against God. As Satan hoped, they rebelled, a decision that introduced sin into the world. Holiness was lost. From that time, God began the plan of redemption to enable people to regain the holiness they lost.[2] With the loss of holiness came the loss of personhood. With the regaining of holiness, people regain a sense of personhood, satisfaction, joy, and significance.

Part of redemption is the need to explain what was lost, holiness, as well as how to regain it. This is both taught in the Old Testament and pictured there symbolically. For example, the pictures include the standards for those who serve God (Leviticus), the standards for the sacrificial animals brought to God (Lev 1:3; 3:1), and the rituals of sacrifice that included purification and purity. Thus the Old Testament consistently develops the themes that (1) God is holy, (2) people are sinful, and (3) God cares and will provide an ultimate sacrifice pictured by the sacrifices of the Old Testament.

These themes are repeated in the New Testament, but there is a major difference in the use of "holiness." The New Testament calls God's people "holy." Even with all the problems of inconsistency, as in Corinth, Christian people are still called "sanctified" (1 Cor 1:2). The New Testament pictures of holiness equate Christians with the true, spiritual temple (2 Cor 6:16). Further, Christians are the true, spiritual sacrifice (Rom 12:1–2), and we are the true, spiritual priesthood (1 Pet 2:5,9).

The New Testament also clarifies the goal of holiness. In Colossians, Paul wrote "Do not lie to each other, since you have taken off your old self with its practices and have put on the new self, which is being renewed in knowledge in the image of its Creator" (3:9–10 NIV). Clearly the early church recog-

---

[1] The Hebrew word most often used is *qadosh*. The most frequent Greek word is *hagios*.

[2] This is immediately explained in Gen 3:15, often called the *protoevangeliorium*, the "beginning of the Gospel."

nized Jesus as the Creator,[3] and the Christian's goal is to be like Him. This is more explicit in Ephesians, where Paul describes the functions of both church leadership and membership as "until we all reach unity in the faith and in the knowledge of the Son of God and become mature, attaining to the whole measure of the fullness of Christ" (4:13 NIV).

The goal of transformation, then, is holiness, which is equated to becoming like Jesus. Jesus is God come to earth to reveal God's nature and to sacrifice Himself to enable us to be holy. Jesus' incarnation provides a model for us, demonstrating perfect humanity in a way that we as human beings can see and appreciate it. Rather than leaving us with only an abstract idea of holiness, God chose to give us a concrete model. Therefore our goal is to live like Jesus did, with holiness.

The Christian teacher has a clear model to present. Both the Old Testament and the New Testament present Jesus, though in two different ways. Ultimately, the teacher must clearly describe Jesus, present His work accurately, and call students to be like Him.

THE BEGINNING OF TRANSFORMATION: CONVERSION

Christian teachers must acknowledge a major difference between their work and that of secularists. While both have a concern to change behavior, the starting point and the end differ. Secularists believe the basic problem in human nature stems from either a bad environmental background or poor educational opportunities. The answer, of course, is to correct background inadequacies by cleaning up neighborhoods and/or moving a person out of the negative environment. In addition, it is necessary to provide proper instruction so that people can improve themselves and create new opportunities. Either way, the solution to human transformation comes as an add-on to the basic person. People are basically good, that is, capable in themselves as long as they have appropriate help.

The Bible presents the person differently. The basic problem to overcome is that people need a change of heart. However benevolent, compassionate, and self-fulfilled they are, everything revolves around them. We are selfish at heart. That is the essence of sin, the ego-centricity that says "I do not need God." Unless that changes, a person will never become holy as God desires. Holiness comes as a result of God's changing a person's attitude and ways of living.

The necessary change of heart is described variously in Scripture. Sometimes it is called being "born again."[4] Paul seems to prefer the idea of adoption

---

[3] This is generally presented in the New Testament. Specific references include John 1:1–4; Heb 1:1–3; Col 1:16.

[4] This occurs in John's writings and has particular reference to the Jewish pride of genealogy.

into a different family, God's family.[5] Several writers use the word "saved," but being saved is used for the beginning, the process, and the culmination of the Christian's life. Another descriptive term is "regeneration," a word that implies a remaking of the old into the new. All of these can be encapsulated in the word "conversion."

Conversion is a change. It brings the "new heart" prophesied by Jeremiah,[6] and represents the change from the "natural person" to the person led by the Holy Spirit.[7] The character change God expects comes from God and brings a new perspective. It is a perspective of dependence on God for transformation. It recognizes that at the heart, all successful change of character and behavior is spiritual. The teacher's task is to help provide the proper environment in which conversion can take place.

Conversion brings two complementary truths related to personal transformation. First, at conversion God sees a person as complete in character and behavior. This comes from the forgiveness of sins and restoration to righteousness. From the moment of conversion, God considers a person as already perfect and "in heaven" because of what Jesus did. Sometimes this is called a "positional" or "legal" sanctification: that in God's mind everything is already done. Paul can speak of Christians as already "seated in the heavenlies" with Christ because of this.[8]

The second truth is that we live in a developmental sphere of life where progressive change makes us what we should be. While we are complete from the perspective of what God has done for us, providing everything on the cross, we are incomplete as we live our life on earth. It is necessary to grow into the holiness that God desires. Therefore transformation is a necessary experience for all Christians.

One more factor about conversion should be mentioned. How does conversion relate to the make-up of individuals? Often we hear Christian people speak about the fact that they have two natures struggling within. They assume conversion brings a new nature that coexists with the old nature. This is based on observing experiences where there is ambivalence in desires and action.[9] That position is wrong both experientially and biblically.

Interestingly, the description does not occur in other writers. Jesus used the phrase in John 3:3 to the Jewish leader Nicodemus.

  [5] This communicates more directly to non-Jewish hearers for whom birth status was less significant than adult statue. Adoption was not practiced in the same way in Jewish circles. See Paul's use in Gal 3:27–4:7.

  [6] Jer 31:31–34

  [7] 1 Cor 2:14ff

  [8] Eph 2:3–7

  [9] This receives some support from a misinterpretation of Rom 7:13–25, which assumes the conflict language is synonymous with natures. Yet this is foreign to biblical descriptions in general.

The Bible speaks of conversion as moving from the "old self" to the "new self."[10] These words describe the contrasts in three passages: Rom 6:1–14; Eph 4:25; and Col 3:5. In each of these passages, it is clear that Paul states people are either unconverted, the "old self," or converted, the "new self." The Bible never describes a person as in both of these situations. "Old self" and "new self" are historical, not psychological, designations.[11]

A second matter of definition is important. There is no evidence that the terms "old self" and "new self" mean "old nature" and "new nature." "Nature" does describe the non-Christian in Eph 2:1, and it describes the Christian in 2 Peter 1:4, we are "partakers of the divine nature" (NKJV). A nature is a characteristic way of thinking and acting. There cannot be two characteristic ways simultaneously. Christians have only one nature.[12] It is a nature defiled by ego-centricity before conversion and capable of restoration to the image of God after conversion. The process of that transformation comes largely through accurate learning. Most of the time, learning implies a teacher who understands and facilitates the learning process.

THE PROCESS OF TRANSFORMATION

Personal transformation is a process. The process begins at conversion and ends at the resurrection of the body after the believer enters heaven.[13] The Bible clearly speaks to this fact. Romans 12:1–3 says "be transformed by the renewing of your mind."

THE PRACTICAL CHANGE AT CONVERSION

At conversion the Christian has a new heart and the prospect of a new life. The new heart comes from the forgiveness of sins and the impartation of Jesus' righteousness. As a partial manifestation of this, there are specific values and ambitions God gives. They evidence the regeneration that has taken place. The heart clouded by self-orientation is regenerated to a God-orientation. The

---

[10] Literally the language is "old man" and "new man." Because of political correctness, however, many translations change the language that also requires an interpretation of the terms.

[11] "Historical" means they describe two stages of a Christian's existence. The old person died at conversion, and the new self emerged. The "psychological" interpretation seeks to use the terminology to explain motivations for behavior. The terms are never used that way in Scripture.

[12] There are multiple, serious problems with assuming a person has "two natures." Two of the most crucial are soteriological and eschatological. The soteriology issue refers to what exactly is regenerated at conversion? It must be something already in existence or regeneration has no meaning. The eschatological issue is what goes to heaven? Is there some part of us that does not enter heaven because it is unchanged? That is hardly the way the Bible describes the Christian's ultimate destination.

[13] There is one exception to this. Those alive at the rapture of the church will have their bodies changed into the new body immediately.

new values and ambitions are embryonic at conversion, and they need maturity through the process of growth, but they are very real.

NEW VALUES   From a practical perspective, God changes a person by inserting new values in life. They are core and radical. Living in and for God's kingdom involves cultivating these values and the implications that come with them.

First, *God is more important than I am.* While almost everyone would acknowledge this fact intellectually, the new Christian begins to realize it in experience. The change is from a universe where the "I," the ego, is central, to a world where we recognize God is more important. It is only in living out this value that significance and purpose replace frustration and insecurity.

Having a God more important than ourselves changes our outlook. It brings a consciousness that we are God's servants as well as His children. It allows us to think in terms of honoring Him in all we do which, in turn, brings us all we need for satisfaction and happiness (Matt 6:33). It brings significance as there is a growing realization of God's purposes in history, and that each generation of God-honoring people have contributed to them. The Christian begins to realize that the purpose of life is to glorify God and enjoy Him forever.[14] Christians realize the eternal nature of life, that death is not the end, and that it is possible to live for God in time as well as eternity.

On the surface, putting God above self seems foolish. For Christian growth, however, it is necessary to understand this part of God's plan. The Christian learns to trust God with life, based on the realization that God's holiness means God is able to "see" what is best and lead His people into it. Christian maturity means we seek to honor God in every aspect of life.

Second, *eternity is more important than time.* Growing out of the first value, Christians begin to realize that time is only a small portion of human existence. Eternity matters more. Therefore the wise person lives with a consciousness of the reality of eternity. Furthermore, wisdom consists of using the resources and opportunities of time to contribute to eternity. This is more than simply choosing to avoid eternal punishment, and it is certainly not "buying" heaven. It is recognizing the truth of Jesus' words "lay up for yourselves treasures in heaven" (NKJV).[15] It is foolish to limit life and perspective to earthly existence when time is only a part—a small part— of our existence.

Some may misconstrue this value. Recognizing the importance of eternity leads Christians to work for "heaven on earth" as Jesus requested in His

---

[14] *The Westminster Shorter Catechism,* 1674. Article 1 of 107 articles: "Q. 1. What is the chief end of man? A. Man's chief end is to glorify God, and to enjoy him forever." *Center for Reformed Theology and Apologetics* Web site: www.reformed.org

[15] Jesus stated this in Matt 6:19–20.

prayer.[16] Christians are often accused of not caring for others and/or failing to work for justice in this life since they are so focused on life after death. Nothing could be further from God's plan. It is precisely because we value eternity that we engage in the affairs of this life.[17]

Involvement in life is more than seeking to win people to Christ and thus securing their eternal happiness. Valuing eternity, when coupled with putting God over self, brings the realization that Christians are God's representatives on earth. We must, therefore, live our lives as God would were He physically on earth. Therefore we represent and work for true compassion, love, justice, truth, and positive perspectives.

Third, *people are more important than things.* People and things present the core of the struggle we face in time. Many without Christ seek to gain things as the ultimate good, and will use people to get things. This is not confined to physical things; it also relates to positions of prominence. Things and positions occupy the natural mind until God changes the perspective.

Christian teachers should spend time thinking about these values. The Bible reinforces these in various ways and instructs us how to live. Rather than teaching a list of "dos and don'ts," each with its own independent contribution to life, the wise teacher sees the whole, the core values that change at conversion. Regeneration means a Christian has the capability of living as God intends. This capability comes because of the regeneration of our nature and because of the new outlook and resources emerging after conversion. It is helpful for all Christians to seek actively to integrate all of life around these values.

NEW AMBITIONS Values produce ambitions. At conversion God also gives the believer new ambitions. Some Christian values overlap with the desires of all people, since we are created in the image of God and share many common aspirations. The difference is, however, that as regenerated persons we have the ability to achieve the things that satisfy the heart. There are five new ambitions. They encompass all of life and, as such, are stated in general categories.

First, Christians desire to *worship.* Worshipping God is one of the core changes in a Christian. Before conversion, some people may acknowledge that God exists, and even at times pray for His blessings, but the unbeliever's

---

[16] Matt 6:10

[17] Christians have a stellar record of helping those in need on earth, including founding educational institutions, hospitals, orphanages, rescue missions, and other social ministries. One interesting book that affirms this in part is written by A. C. Brooks, Louis A. Bantle Professor of Business and Government Policy at Syracuse University's Maxwell School of Citizenship and Public Affairs; see A. C. Brooks, *Who Really Cares?* (New York: Basic), 2006.

life can hardly be characterized as loving genuine worship. Worship as an ambition means that the believer studies worship, enjoys it, and spends time doing it. Life revolves around worship. It includes designated times of worship corporately and individually, as well as making every part of life honoring to God.

Second, Christians desire a *Christian lifestyle.* Christian lifestyle is living in a way that represents God well. It is a mistake to think of Christianity as a list of things to do or not do. It cannot be measured by doing without being. Christians confess Jesus as Lord and live according to the lordship of Christ. The first thought should be "does this honor the Lord, or is it going to detract so that other people are not conscious of Him?"

Third, Christians desire *stewardship.* Stewardship is the responsible administration of all things. The word is often used in financial areas, which is certainly a proper use, but Christian stewardship cannot be limited to money. It is an attitude toward all of life: that God owns everything and gives to us as He will. He holds us accountable for how we honor Him with everything we have and are. True stewardship goes beyond oversight of things. It includes opportunities, relationships, and experiences. Further, it extends to the earth, calling for a proper understanding of ecology. Stewardship is comprehensive.

Fourth, Christians desire *effective ministry.* Ministry is an awareness of and engagement in the privilege of service. Those who have truly accepted God's love want to respond to Him by service. This cannot be confined to professional or vocational ministry. Every Christian has spiritual gifts, a personality, talents, experiences, and opportunity to serve.

Fifth, Christians desire good *family relationships.* Good family relationships are those that follow God's patterns for the family as revealed in Scripture. God ordained the family, and it is His most available and effective institution for revealing Him to others in our world. Christians must be committed to God's principles. Though we live in a sinful world, and even family members fall prey to sinful attitudes and actions, Christian people seek to involve themselves in their families in ways that honor God as revealed in the Bible.

These five new ambitions are outgrowths of the three new values. They are changes God puts in the hearts and minds of all Christians. In a sense, Christians "find" they want these things as they experience God's working in their lives. The effective teacher recognizes that spiritual success means growth in these areas.

NEW PLEASURES As a natural outworking of the values and ambitions, there are new *pleasures.* Pleasures come from events and behaviors that line up well with values and ambitions. That is, as we affirm the new values and embrace the new ambitions, there are changed pleasures. We find we enjoy life with the consistency this brings. It is impossible to identify the specific new pleasures, since every part of life is affected. It is possible to say with certainty that Christian joy results from the changes brought at conversion and that joy is deepened to the degree that we live consistently with our new values and ambitions.

THE FACILITATORS OF CHANGE

Christian growth comes from three basic elements. They are presented repeatedly in Scripture, and without any one of the three, growth will not take place.

KNOWLEDGE   The first, and most basic, element in effecting change is knowledge. Generally speaking, God works in the mind first; then He enables us to live consistently with the new way of thinking. This is seen in the clearest text on change, Rom 12:1–2: we are "transformed by the renewing of your mind." While the word "mind" used here describes more than just mental processes, knowledge is crucial to change. We must know truth in order to grow into it.

Knowledge as the foundation for new life occurs repeatedly in Scripture. It is also evidenced by the continual emphasis on "information" imparted by Jesus, the apostles, and the other biblical writers. The very fact of writing to correct behavior, as we find in the Bible, is based on the importance of knowledge to effecting change.

Christian educators, therefore, have a significant role to play in the growth of their students. The time spent in presenting the Word of God and applying it to life is crucial to the change God intends. It is imperative that teachers know and teach in accord with accurate knowledge that comes from knowing God's Word.

Knowledge comes in some basic, primary ways. First, *propositional truth* reveals knowledge. We learn from statements that are true. Jesus focused on this in His dialogues with the people of His day. Repeatedly He explained that He was telling them the truth. Furthermore, the apostles spoke to issues in the churches, basing their arguments on theology received from or implied by the words of Jesus and the Old Testament. The early church asked first: "What does God say?"[18] Paul and others clearly based their commands to the

---

[18] See Acts of the Apostles where the repeated characteristics of the church include "the Apostles' teaching." (e.g., Acts 2:41–42).

churches on propositional truths.[19] The very common use of the Old Testament in the New Testament speaks to this point: they sought to base their
understanding on the Bible, the Word of God.

Second, knowledge comes from *other Christians who model the truth*. This
may be seen in the statements to "follow me,"[20] follow the example of other
Christians,[21] and follow the leaders who have gone before.[22] Those who live
the truth in the presence of others make knowledge tangible and relevant for
those who observe their lives.

Third, *knowledge comes from envisioning* the truth. Envisioning is the
product of meditation and imagination. It comes from thinking about what
is known and seeking ways to apply it to life. For example, Paul said we
"see through a glass, darkly" but that vision transforms us into the image of
Christ.[23] The "dark glass" suggests an imperfect grasp of the truth, but even
though partial and blurred, the truth is able to change lives. Thus Christians
are encouraged to think about what they have read, seen, and heard. Visualizing the truth helps to shape the mind and to prepare the life for embracing
it personally.[24]

Fourth, *Christian experience* can teach the truth. Experience is a good
teacher, but only when experience is evaluated as to its positive or negative
outcome in life. Ultimately all experiences must be evaluated in light of their
consistency to what God revealed in the Bible. Experiences of the past witness to success and failure. Success encourages further success; failure can
also encourage success as one analyzes the causes in accord with scriptural
principles.

All truth must be measured by Scripture, but not all truth is found in Scripture. As was discussed in the section on the nature of the Bible, all truth must
be in accord with and not contrary to Scripture. There are many sources of
help in understanding and implementing proper changes in behavior. Generally, the help one gains outside of the Bible is in clarifying or applying the
truth.

It often helps to study psychology, for example, to understand human behavior. Psychology also helps people implement changes by explaining the

[19] For example, in 1 Thess 4:15 Paul said "For we say this to you by a revelation from the Lord." A
similar distinction occurs in 1 Cor 7:10 and elsewhere.

[20] Phil 3:14–15.

[21] Timothy, for example, in Phil 2:20–21

[22] Hebrews 13:7.

[23] 1 Cor 13:12

[24] It should be noted that *envisioning* is not to be confused with *visions*. Visions are the product
of the human experience. They may have value, in specific circumstances, but they are always to be
evaluated in light of God's objective standard, the Bible. Envisioning is taking what is objectively clear
and trying to incarnate it so that understanding takes place.

personal or environmental factors that influence behavior. In the final analysis, however, what one affirms as truth must be consistent with and not contrary to the Bible. There is no substitute for knowing the Bible in order to live successfully. God works through the biblically enlightened mind.

CHOICES   The second element encouraging transforming growth is choice. Acting on the truth enables living the truth. The Bible is full of commands. They are both positive and negative, and they occur in both the Old Testament and the New Testament. The commands are not intended to be lists of actions; they are guidelines to shape life. Both testaments clearly affirm the fact that knowing God and living appropriately are relational. Commands help provide boundaries and measurements for relationships. Furthermore, they are only effective when they enhance already established relationships.

The Bible encourages positive choices to every area of life. Beginning a relationship with God is a choice. Joshua called the people to choose God in Josh 24:15: "choose you this day whom ye will serve." Living according to God's kingdom values involves choice. Jesus said, "seek first the kingdom of God and His righteousness" (Matt 6:33).

Overcoming personal sin and learning patterns of obedience call for choices. Paul affirmed this in Rom 6:12–13. There three commands sum up responsibility in this area: "do not let sin reign in your mortal body, so that you obey its desires. And do not offer any parts of it to sin as weapons for unrighteousness. But as those who are alive from the dead, offer yourselves to God, and, all the parts of yourselves to God as weapons for righteousness."[25] There is no growth progress without making good choices.

Proper choices are not simply "additions" to knowledge. Complete knowledge takes place in action. Knowledge is the foundation; choices are the superstructure. Actions reveal the presence of the truth. This may be seen in Paul's relationship to the Corinthian church. The church had a long-term problem with immorality: a man was in an affair with his stepmother. The entire church knew about it but refused to do anything to censure the man's conduct. After repeatedly addressing this, Paul was able to write complimenting them for their repentance. In 2 Cor 7:9–11 he said,

---

[25] Literally, the first two commands are presented as stopping an action already in progress. Therefore "stop letting sin reign . . . and stop offering any parts." There are many other texts that could be quoted, such as: Col 3:5, "put to death . . . whatever belongs to your earthly nature" (NIV) Putting to death means to keep these things from expressing themselves as they did before conversion. In Colossians 3:9 and 12, Paul used the imagery of changing clothes. He said, "you have put off the old man" (3:9). The metaphor is completed in 3:12 where he says, "clothe yourselves . . . " with the good qualities that accompany Christian living.

> Now I am rejoicing, not because you were grieved, but because your grief led to repentance. For you were grieved as God willed, so that you didn't experience any loss from us. For godly grief produces a repentance not to be regretted and leading to salvation, but worldly grief produces death. For consider how much diligence this very thing—this grieving as God wills—has produced in you: what a desire to clear yourselves, what indignation, what fear, what deep longing, what zeal, what justice! In every way you have commended yourselves to be pure in this matter.

In this passage the actions describe growth: grief to repentance; repentance to a desire to clear themselves; and clearing to indignation, fear, deep longing, zeal, and justice. The combination of these strong words of affirmation indicates the reality of their godly sorrow for their sin. In fact, Paul concludes with the statement that they "commended" themselves "to be pure in this matter." We could quote many other texts and writers, such as John the Baptist who implored his hearers to "produce fruit consistent with repentance" (Luke 3:8). Actions reveal knowledge.

It is imperative that the adult teacher recognizes this. Teaching adults requires that teachers point out the ways knowledge must be fulfilled by actions. While the specifics of action may vary according to circumstances, the fact that action is necessary does not vary. Knowledge without implementation is not simply failure to make application; it is failure to know accurately and completely.

Choices associated with spiritual truth are not neutral. They are not purely matters of choice without consequences. Spiritual choices are moral. They are always matters of right and wrong; good and evil. One either chooses to walk with God and His will, or chooses to go against God and His purposes. There is no neutrality.

The choices take place on a spiritual battlefield. There are influences available to help make correct choices, and there are influences aligned to keep you from doing what is right. The Bible identifies three external influences committed to keeping people from making correct choices: the world, the flesh, and the devil.

The Bible warns repeatedly about the world. The Greek word world, "cosmos," may refer to the material world, but usually refers to the world's systems: political, economic, and cultural. The systems are contrary to God.[26]

---

[26] John warned about the power the world exerts against Christians and the dangers of following it. He says, "Do not love the world or anything in the world. If anyone loves the world, the love of the Father is not in him" (1 John 2:15 NIV). James issued a similar warning. Speaking like an Old Testament prophet, "You adulterous people, don't you know that friendship with the world is hatred toward God? Anyone who chooses to be a friend of the world becomes an enemy of God" (Jas 4:4 NIV). These statements echo what both writers may have heard from Jesus Himself. Jesus knew that His followers would be persecuted, and told them that they should expect it. He said, "If the world hates you, keep in mind that it hated me first. If you belonged to the world, it would love you as its

They, along with those who promote them, keep us from God. Choices have to be made to counter the world and its influence on all Christians.[27] Christians will have to make difficult choices to be separate from the world and to become like Christ.

Equally, the Bible warns about listening to and following the patterns of "the flesh." The Greek word "flesh" may refer to the physical body, but in this sense it has a metaphorical meaning with moral connotations.[28] "The flesh" is the natural way of thinking and acting, unaided by the Holy Spirit. While the world is an environment, a system constructed by people, the flesh is the natural way people in the worldly environment look at life. Like the world, the flesh is contrary to God.[29]

When Christians think and act like those without the Holy Spirit, they are living like the flesh (1 Cor 3:1–3). The task of transformation is to learn and implement the patterns of life taught by the Holy Spirit. With enlightened minds, Christians live differently from those motivated by "the flesh."

Finally, Scripture attributes significant opposition to "the devil." His more personal name is Satan, a slanderer and deceiver. He is a personality who is the antithesis of God and good. Satan deceives people, blinding them to the truth and to proper choices. He and his cohorts, demons, actively seek to oppose proper choices, amassing his own following.[30] Like the world and the flesh, the devil seeks to counter the choices God's people should make.

The world, the flesh, and the devil manifest themselves in many ways. Since they are the natural way of thinking, they work their deception through uncritical people who follow their own inclinations. Soon their "systems"

---

own. As it is, you do not belong to the world, but I have chosen you out of the world. That is why the world hates you" (John 15:18–19 NIV).

[27] John warns, "The world and its desires pass away, but the man who does the will of God lives forever" (1 John 2:17 NIV). The natural environment is a dead-end street.

[28] It literally means "meat" and is used that way in Scripture. When it is "nonliteral," which is very common, it refers to people's actions.

[29] Paul warned about the dangers of following the flesh because of the personal and corporate destruction it causes (Gal 5:19, literally the "works of the flesh"). The way of thinking of the flesh also brings death (Rom 8:6), it is preoccupied with wrong desires (Rom 8:5), and it is hostile to God and cannot please Him (Rom 8:7–8). The natural way of thinking formulates value systems that are contrary to God's way (2 Cor 5:16).

[30] The devil opposes God, has from the beginning, and encourages others to sin as well. John says of him "He who does what is sinful is of the devil, because the devil has been sinning from the beginning. The reason the Son of God appeared was to destroy the devil's work" (1 John 3:8 NIV). Peter issued the same warning, "Your enemy the devil prowls around like a roaring lion looking for someone to devour" (1 Pet 5:8 NIV). Again these warnings echo Jesus' own explanation of Satan's activity. When Peter questioned Jesus He said of Peter "Get behind me, Satan! You are a stumbling block to me; you do not have in mind the things of God, but the things of men" (Matt 16:23 NIV). His followers realized that Satan could motivate people as well (John 13:27).

become the normal, natural way most people think and act. Anyone who acts differently is odd, including Christians who stand against the norm.

In addition to these external forces, there is also an internal issue. The Bible consistently warns of the dangers of "lust." The common word for lust means "strong desire." Normally it is for something harmful and, therefore, is a wrong desire. It is the clearest evidence of the distortion of the image of God through sin. Lust is a movement toward something we should not have. It is for something outside of God's will and, therefore, outside of God's plan for satisfying a person's desires.

Lust cooperates with lure. James 1:13–14 states that we are tempted when we are enticed, the lure. Enticements are outside, part of the environment. They activate inside desires, however, and lust embraces them. James further warns that we must stop the harmful process of sinning at the lust stage or actions will follow that are more hurtful. Using the analogy of birth, marriage, and birth, he states that "lust can conceive" and the baby born is "sin." When sin grows to maturity, it gives birth to death.

Christian teachers have two responsibilities in this regard. First, they must think biblically about life and culture. They must seek to impart sensitivity to the opposition as well as how it works. Alerting people to proper choices requires recognition of the deception of the world around and our sensitivities to it. Second, teachers must offer an alternative way. That requires knowing Scripture and having Christian maturity and wisdom. No one can make choices for another, but providing information for proper choices is essential. Proper choices are not made out of neutrality. They are made from a background of opposition to God, the result of every person's sinfulness. There is no need for fanaticism at this point, but naïveté is counterproductive. Without adequate awareness of these issues, people may naively make the wrong choices, those of the world, in the name of seeking to do what is natural and right. Personal and corporate sinfulness blind people individually and collectively so that they do not always understand God's truth.

The point is simple. People will not become what they want to become; they become what they choose to become. Knowledge is completed by action! It is necessary for people to choose, and all choices are based on knowledge. Usually the knowledge we have is conflicting information. In our minds there is information on both, or all, sides of an issue and the individual chooses consistently with some information and contrary to other information. Actions usually make sense to the person who chooses them. The role of the Christian teacher is to make sure an individual understands the importance of Christian choices.

POWER   The combination of knowledge and choices produces patterns of behavior. The choice to follow one type of information against another, and the resulting life changes, produces deeply ingrained ways of thinking and acting. Choices form habits. Often people have adequate knowledge to encourage change, and they decide to act on it. Yet they cannot successfully break the old mental and behavioral habits. There is a need for power.

The Holy Spirit empowers the believer. He enables a Christian to think and act differently from before, to break the power of the past habits. There is no ability to grow as a Christian without the power of the Holy Spirit. In Rom 8:2 Paul explained that the "the law of the Spirit of life set me free from the law of sin and death" (NIV). Here the word for "set free" is "liberates." It means enjoying the actual experience of freedom.[31] What Jesus accomplished on the cross, which we come to know at conversion, is applied to us directly by the Holy Spirit.

One of the most helpful passages in this regard is Gal 5:16–26. In describing the Holy Spirit's work in the believer,[32] Paul set the "works of the flesh" against the "fruit of the Spirit." It is the Spirit who keeps us from completing the works of the flesh. Thus while we may make choices to do what is right, it is only through the Holy Spirit that we can actually live out those choices. Success comes from walking with the Spirit.

Walking with the Spirit requires balance. Some people exert no personal effort to change. They expect the Holy Spirit to override their inclinations and actions so that they are carried along by a power higher than they know. Others believe the Holy Spirit only points the way. It is up to them to walk the road indicated by the Spirit. Both are wrong. The Holy Spirit seldom does what a person will not do, and He seldom supplies power to those who do not think they need Him. Instead, there must be a conscious sense of trust in the Holy Spirit's power. At the same time, it is necessary to act in order to put the process into motion. Trust and actively attempting to do the truth cooperate in

---

[31] This word, "liberates," is often confused with the word "justifies," which also occurs in this larger context (Rom 6:7). In Romans 6 the believer is said to be "justified" from sin; in 8:2 there is "liberation."

[32] Paul used three verbs to describe the Spirit's enabling. The first occurs in 5:16. The NIV translates it "live" (the Greek is literally "walk around" [*peripateo*]. The believer is to conduct all of life in the sphere of the Spirit. That is, we are to invite the Spirit into all aspects of life, and seek to please Him at all times. The second verb occurs in 5:18. The NIV correctly translates it as "led." If the Holy Spirit leads believers, they are not under law. The Holy Spirit brings freedom from the law, replacing external standards (law) with internal (relationships), and brings God's power to replace self-effort. The final verb is "keep in step with the Spirit" (5:25: the Greek word is *stoicheo*). This rare word means to place our feet exactly in the place the Spirit leads. It was appropriately used of the military who marched "in step."

revealing the need for the Holy Spirit. The Holy Spirit's power is available to those who want to live in obedience to God.

These three elements—knowledge, choices, and power—combine to allow for Christian growth. If any of these is missing, spiritual growth is stunted. Without knowledge there is no certainty that the changes are genuinely what God intends. People then become the victims of their own experiences and desires, not necessarily conforming to the patterns described in Scripture. Without choices, knowledge remains purely theoretical. God gives knowledge so that people will change. In fact, the willingness to do what God instructs is prerequisite to God's instruction (John 7:17). Finally, without power even Christians are no more able to accomplish God's plan than unbelievers are. The self, left to itself, is inadequate. When proper knowledge, choices, and power work together, knowledge is brought to completion: theoretical becomes actual experience.

HELPS FOR CHRISTIAN GROWTH

Those who choose to change have help. We have already discussed the work of Christ in forgiveness and regeneration, and we have indicated the necessity of the Holy Spirit's power. There are additional helps that Christians have found encourage and enable the positive choices necessary for holiness.

THE BIBLE   By far the most important help for Christians is the Bible. We have discussed the nature of the Bible and its value as a revelation from God to us. It is the most accurate information we have about God, sin, life, and death. It is also the clarifier and monitor of truth not disclosed in the Bible. All truth must be consistent with and not contrary to the Bible.

Christians must not only affirm the nature of the Bible, they must live according to its teachings. Many fail at this point. History provides many examples of people, churches, and governments who pridefully confessed their faith in the Bible, only to live contrary to the Bible's teachings. Paul spoke to his Jewish friends in Romans 3, warning them that possession of the Scriptures was not enough. They also had to practice them.

There is no substitute for regular Bible study. It should be done daily. The Bible should be applied to the everyday experiences, pressures, and opportunities of life. Christian teachers can lead the way in teaching and living the truth.

PRAYER   A second help in Christian growth is prayer. Throughout the Bible there are both injunctions to pray and instructions in how to pray. Jesus, Paul, and James, among others, wrote that we do not have what we really want because we do not pray. Prayer is an antidote for discord, materialism, and wrongful ambition. It focuses us on God and His will, rather than our own concerns.

Mature Christians pray. They pray daily, even many times during the day. They pray about their world, their friends, their ministries, their opportunities, and their own personal needs and wants. While our minds may be cluttered with personal concerns, the instructional prayer of Jesus informs us that we are to ask for "your kingdom to come, your will to be done on earth as it is in heaven." The cumulative evidence from Christians through the years is that prayerful people are peaceful people, and that prayerful people are powerful people. We cannot neglect prayer.

THE CHURCH   Another vital lifeline for growth is the church. God's people are instructed to meet together for fellowship, teaching, encouragement, and general Christian growth. The church is pictured as a body, needing each of its members, whose head is Christ Himself.

Growing Christians know there is no substitute for the church. Christian teachers should make church as relevant and relational as possible so their learners learn the value of being in the church. The church's concern, prayer, help, and support in times of need are legendary. Equally, the church provides a place for people to give of themselves, an even greater need in God's economy. People neglect church at great peril to their spiritual lives.

CHRISTIAN SERVICE   God called each of us to serve. He gave us gifts useful to the building of the body and reaching the world for Christ. He expects every Christian to participate in promoting His interests in the world.

Christians should be involved in service. Christian teachers can provide the model, but they can also provide opportunities for service with a supportive group. It is important for all Christians to share their faith. We need to take a stand for God and Christ in a world that increasingly misunderstands who Christians are. Many have reported with joy the way they grew through mission activities and service projects.

As noted above in the New Ambitions section (p. 89), Christians will intuitively want to reach out. Love instills love, and love by nature gives. God's love for us motivates us to love others as He does. The proper outlet for that is through the church and with other Christians.

SUFFERING   The final way God provides for growth for us is through suffering. We must exercise care here. God does not need suffering or persecution to effect holiness in His people. If He did, there would be a flaw in His person and character. Yet we live, by God's permission, in an evil world. Everyone suffers. Christians are persecuted. The question is not "if" I suffer, but when.

Suffering provides opportunity for growth when we respond correctly to it. Romans 5:1–5 indicates that tribulation brings patience, patience brings character, and character brings hope. James provides the same pattern in 1:2–4. Christians may fail to trust, assuming God has turned against them, or they may trust, determining that nothing will stop their commitment to Christ.

Going through suffering helps in at least two ways. First, a proper response to suffering brings humility and trust. Suffering people cast themselves on God's mercy, asking Him to do what they cannot. Suffering refines and focuses our commitment. Thus it brings a greater sense of dependency. Second, a proper response to suffering brings greater sensitivity to others who suffer. After suffering, there is a greater sense that the world is evil and people are not always the cause of their difficulties. Furthermore, it brings opportunity to offer assistance through prayer and tangible help. It makes us more godlike because we see people realistically and are moved to help them.

This chapter is about the biblical pattern for Christian growth. We have discussed the goal: holiness. We surveyed the process: knowledge, choices, power. We observed the biblical theme that we live in an evil world, anxious to derail us in our quest to be like Christ. Finally, we considered some of the helps God has provided to encourage us along the way.[33]

The biblical patterns for growth coincide with the Transformactional Bible Study. The two words "transform" and "action" fit God's desire that we progressively change. Regeneration provides the new way of thinking and acting. It enables us to see the goal clearly and to trust God's grace. The bottom line, however, is that God wants us to gain knowledge and act on it. Action is essential to transformation.

We will now turn from the biblical section to the educational. First, we will survey adult learning theory from the past 50 years. Then, in part 3, we will offer the Star Method of Transformactional Teaching. It seeks to incorporate both the biblical principles and the best of adult learning theory into a workable tool for preparation and delivery of Bible study.

---

[33] Much of the material in this chapter first occurred in a book by Rick; Richard R. Melick, *Called to Be Holy* (Nashville: LifeWay Press, 2001).

PART TWO

FOUNDATIONAL THEORIES OF ADULT LEARNING

PART I EMPHASIZED THE importance of understanding the nature of the Bible and studying it properly. Parts 2 and 3 turn attention to adult learning theory specifically. Part 2 provides the reader with a brief survey of the most significant contributions to adult learning theory since the middle of the twentieth century. Although the descriptions are brief, the discussion and bibliography should serve to orient the reader to this dynamic field of education. Furthermore, it should provide enough information to serve as a foundation for part 3.

Foundational theories of adult learning were originally and are currently influenced by the contributions of other academic disciplines. Using research in physical science, psychology, educational psychology, and sociology, scholars from the emerging discipline of adult education formulated three major foundational theories of adult learning: Andragogy, Self-Directed Learning Theory, and Transformative Learning Theory. Current theories of adult learning and the resulting models of teaching are still influenced by the powerful implications of other academic disciplines.

With the development of each learning theory, the separation between childhood education and adult education became more defined, and the discipline of adult education became professionalized. The clarity of other adult learning issues, however, has not been as precise. Although adult educators now have much more information available, many unanswered questions remain. Twenty-first century theorists are addressing some of these questions through studying critical and postmodern ideology and recent brain research.

Part 2 consists of two chapters. The two should be considered as one, since they both speak to the point of modern adult learning theory. In order to help the reader, however, we have chosen to make a chapter break after self-directed learning. This is a logical point because of the influence of transformative learning theory and its many facets.

EXTERNAL INFLUENCES ON THE DEVELOPMENT
OF ADULT LEARNING THEORY

ALONG WITH OTHER DISCIPLINES, psychology, educational psychology, sociology, and physical science have had an osmotic influence on the
development of learning theory and teaching practice. Research and theories
of one discipline filter into the theories of another. Additionally, it should
be noted that early learning theory primarily focused on children. As adult
learning theory emerged in the mid-twentieth century, it was influenced by
children's learning theory and the multi-disciplines that impacted both. It
is necessary, therefore, to address these influences. Examples include Sig-
mund Freud (1856–1939), a Viennese physician, whose psychosexual theory
helped educators to understand the importance of early parent-child relationships on the development of the child. Erik Erikson (1902–94), artist and
teacher, blended Freudian psychology with the principle of epigenesis (an
embryological model from science) and profoundly affected the field of education with his eight stages of psychosocial development.[1] Konrad Lorenz
(1903–89), a European zoologist, studied animals, observing behaviors that
promoted survival. His research lead to the concept of critical period: "a limited time span during which the individual is biologically prepared to acquire
certain adaptive behaviors but needs the support of an appropriately stimulating environment."[2] The concept of *critical period* became influential in the
understanding that there is a period of time for optimal learning in humans.
Russian psychologist Lev Vygotsky (1896–1934) studied the importance of
children having social interaction with more acculturated members of society
in order to acquire culturally appropriate behavior. His studies captured the
attention of educators and raised their level of awareness as to the importance
of social interaction in all learning.

BEHAVIORISTS

The major contributions from external academic disciplines generally fall
into two categories: behaviorism and constructivism.[3] Behaviorists believe that
learning occurs through observation, and behaviors form through the developing of habits. Behaviorism is studied through experiments with both classical
conditioning and operant conditioning. Classical conditioning is association

---

[1] N. J. Salkind, *Second Edition: Theories of Human Development* (New York: John Wiley & Sons, 1985), 107–11.

[2] L. E. Berk, *Exploring Lifespan Development* (San Francisco, CA: Allyn and Bacon, 2008), 18.

[3] L. M. Baumgartner, "Adult Learning Theory: The Basics" in L. M. Baumgartner, Ming-Yeh Lee, S. Birden, and D. Flowers, *Adult Learning Theory: A Primer* (Center on Education and Training for Employment, College of Education, The Ohio State University, Information Series No. 392), 8–9.

between stimulus and stimulus. Examples are Pavlov's experiment with dogs salivating[4] and Watson's experiments with little Albert.[5] Trainers work to associate a natural autonomic response to a stimulus with another stimulus that would not ordinarily bring a response. Through the associated link, the new stimulus attains a similar response. We all experience classical conditioning when we associate the pleasure of academic achievement with an A on a piece of paper. The A in itself means nothing unless association and classical conditioning has occurred.

Thorndike and Skinner made significant contributions in understanding human learning by associating behavior and consequence—operant conditioning. Thorndike's "Law of Exercise" encouraged teachers to use drill exercises and repetition. His "Law of Effect" emphasized the importance of rewarding (reinforcing) success in learning.[6] Skinner, using operant conditioning, promoted the reinforcing of positive behavior with rewards (such as praise, tokens, candy, and gifts), thus increasing the probability of that behavior being repeated. By associating behavior with consequence, both positive and negative behaviors can be "operantly" conditioned. For example, when a driver exceeds the speed limit and the policeman immediately gives a ticket, the policeman is using operant conditioning. When an adult student gives a correct answer in your classroom and you immediately praise the student, you are using operant conditioning.

Criticizing the premises of behaviorism and the work of Skinner, Albert Bandura proposed social learning theory.[7] Bandura noted that people sometimes alter or acquire behavior simply by imitating. The person they imitate may be totally random or carefully selected. Imitated behavior is not specific to any time frame, and it is not necessarily associated with reinforcement. Reinforcement can occur, however, by observing consequences instead of personally experiencing them. "From watching others engage in self-praise and self-blame and through feedback about the worth of their own actions, children develop *personal standards* for behavior and a sense of *self-efficacy*—the belief that their own abilities and characteristics will help them succeed."[8]

The advertising industry uses social learning theory when they promote commercials that associate a perfume with passion and beauty. People imitate the model using the perfume because they are drawn to passion and beauty.

---

[4] Berk, *Exploring Lifespan,* 14.

[5] J. B. Watson, *Behaviorism* (New York: W. W. Norton & Company, Inc., 1930), 159.

[6] D. L. Edwards, "6. An Evaluation of Contemporary Learning Theories," found in *The Christian Educator's Handbook on Teaching: A Comprehensive Resource on the Distinctiveness of True Christian Teaching,* ed. K. O. Gangel and H. G. Hendricks (Grand Rapids: Baker, 1988), 89.

[7] A. Bandura, *Social Learning Theory* (Englewood Cliffs, NJ: Prentice-Hall, 1977).

[8] Berk, *Exploring Lifespan,* 15.

You use social learning theory when you say to an employee or a student, "I love your work ethic! You are such a hard worker," and the work of all who hear rises to a higher intensity. Although Bandura's work grew out of behaviorism, he emphasized cognition and recognized that people have control over their learning.

Exercise 6.1

---

1. In your usual teaching practice, how much time is devoted to drill and practice, creating habits, memorizing, reinforcing desired behavior by rewards, and diminishing negative behaviors by punishment or disapproval?

   10%   20%   35%   50%   75%   100%

2. On the Behaviorism continuum, where do you rate your teaching?

   Not very behaviorist   1   2   3   4   5   very behaviorist

3. What is it about you, or the people you praise, that your students are imitating?

CONSTRUCTIVIST

Constructivists emphasize thinking rather than behavior. They believe that thoughtful learning occurs through active interaction with one's environment. A student constructs new learning by absorbing new information and attaching it to a growing internal structure of knowledge and experience. Based on perception, the student organizes and reorganizes these mental constructs.

Wolfgang Kohler (1887–1940) studied the problem-solving processes of apes and applied the term insight for "grasping relationships."[9] When the apes connected a word with a behavior, they "grasped the relationship" ("insight") between the two. His work contributed to Gestalt psychology, and Gestalt psychology influenced constructivism. Gestalt theory emphasizes that learning involves the brain's processing complex data. Multisensory perceptions and insights can be stored by the brain and later retrieved. These retrievals can either enhance or inhibit future perception and understanding. Gestalt thinking forced educators to open themselves to the possibility that some learning is neither conditioned nor programmed.

Jerome Bruner made significant contributions toward understanding the learning process from a social learning perspective.[10] With a background in psychology, he did research on children in classrooms and came to the conclusion that regurgitating information through memorization was not enough. Memorization was only developing a learning habit through conditioning.

[9] W. R. Yount, *Created to Learn* (Nashville, TN: Broadman & Holman, 1996), 195.
[10] J. S. Bruner, J. J. Goodnow, and G. A. Austin, *A Study of Thinking* (New York: John Wiley & Sons, 1956).

Bruner believed that learning required understanding. He wanted teachers to help students form global concepts, build generalizations, create cognitive networks, and understand the relationships between ideas.[11] He proposed that students should learn through individual or group discovery. For him, understanding, retention, and creative thinking were heightened by exploration and manipulation. His book *The Process of Education*,[12] published in 1962, marked a departure from behaviorism and made "discovery learning" a term that challenged educators in the late twentieth century.

Perhaps the most important contributor to the constructivist view is Jean Piaget (1896–1980), a Swiss cognitive theorist. "According to his cognitive-developmental theory, children actively construct knowledge as they manipulate and explore their world."[13] Based on his background in biology and personal research conducted on his own children, Piaget formulated a theory including stages of cognitive development that addresses the sequence of learning. Learning comes through the process of *assimilation* and *accommodation*. According to Piaget, children form mental *schema* as they construct knowledge by experiencing their environments. They also expand the quantity of information within the *schema* through *assimilation*. If they experience new information that does not fit within the *schema,* the quality of the mental construct is reorganized and refined through *accommodation*.

For example, a baby learns that the liquid in the bathtub is "water" (*assimilation*), and he forms a *schema* for "water." He learns that the liquid that mother pours from the tap in the kitchen is also "water" (*assimilation*). He then learns that the liquid in a Coke bottle is not "water." His *schema* for "water" is not adequate for the new information. His *schema* for "water," therefore, is reorganized to exclude some liquids (*accommodation*). As a child resolves each such dilemma, or *disequilibrium,* through the process of *assimilation* and *accommodation*, he reaches a state of *equilibrium. Equilibrium* lasts until an experience brings new information that does not fit the existing *schema.*

Piaget's stages of development roughly follow biological age, and they describe the sequential steps toward cognitive maturity.[14] Piaget's ideas became popular during the mid-twentieth century and, although the validity of his research was criticized, his contribution still offers valuable insight into the process of learning. Though he worked primarily with children, he greatly influenced theories of adult learning.

---

[11] Yount, *Created to Learn,* 196–97.
[12] J. Bruner, *The Process of Education* (Boston: Harvard University Press, 1962).
[13] Berk, *Exploring Lifespan,* 15.
[14] Edwards, "An Evaluation," 94. See appendix A.

Exercise 6.2

In my teaching practice, how much time do I give to "hands on" student exploration of learning materials?
10%   20%   35%   50%   75%   100%
I believe that my students learn more from me imparting knowledge than from discovering truth for themselves.   True   False

BLENDED INFLUENCE

Educators today view learning as a combination of the behaviorist and constructivist perspectives. Teaching method may be defined by the behaviorist as the drilling of information so that the learner observes and collects habits. It is defined by the constructivists as facilitating the assimilation and accommodation of information so that the learner analyzes facts and expands existing cognitive structure.[15] If the teacher embraces behaviorist views, the classroom will be teacher-centered. The teacher distributes information followed by drill and practice. To the behaviorist teacher, the measurement of learning is whether or not the student acquires a new habit. If the teacher embraces the constructivist view, the classroom will be student-oriented. The student will explore new ideology, engage in critical thought, and formulate opinions based upon discovery and discussion. Learning is measured by changes in mental constructs and worldview because of new knowledge.

Behaviorist   Constructivist
BLENDED INFLUENCE

All educators are influenced by both of these orientations. Adult learning theory and education practice reflect a combination of each influence. The blended influence of behaviorism and constructivism becomes the tinted lens through which the teacher views learning theory as well as the spawning bed for teaching practices. Practically, most disciplines of learning require memorizing content or vocabulary (behaviorism) as a rite of passage that enables the learner to function within the new discipline. For example, one would be hard pressed to experience the discipline of chemistry without a basic understanding of its primary concepts and vocabulary. It can be dangerous for a learner to experiment in order to create a new product (constructivism) before understanding the basics. Thus, the habits of behaviorism and the experiences of constructivism work together to enable the learner to be changed by an understanding of chemistry.

---

[15] Baumgartner, "Adult Learning Theory," 8–9.

Teachers have different educational experiences and individual propensities for learning. Some teachers value a focus on memorization and drill (behaviorist) while others may skip the minutia and emphasize experience or discussion (constructivist). The wise teacher of adults recognizes the value of both and rejects extremes on the behaviorist/constructivist continuum. Setting aside personal inclination, the teacher will use a combination of methods that embraces both views at the appropriate time. This maximizes learning and retention.

Exercise 6.3

My natural inclination in teaching is: (put an X on the continuum)

Teacher-centered) . . . . Student-centered
    (behaviorism)   (constructivism)

Where do you think you should be in order to maximize learning? (Draw a bull's-eye.)

CHAPTER SIX

ANDRAGOGY/SELF-DIRECTED LEARNING THEORY

ANDRAGOGY

The term andragogy is regionally defined. Merriam explores various definitions and includes the following: (1) pedagogy means the discipline of education and andragogy is used as a subsidiary of pedagogy, (2) both andragogy and pedagogy are subsidiaries of the scientific discipline of education, (3) andragogy is considered its own independent scientific discipline, (4) andragogy is a term used synonymously with adult education, and (5) adult education is a professional discipline and andragogy is one of its components or theories. Educators in the United States generally use the term "andragogy" to refer to one of the theories/components of adult education.[1]

American educators explored adult learning and in the twentieth century proclaimed three major theories: andragogy, self-directed, and transformative. They based their work on eclectic theorists. Andragogy, the oldest of the adult learning theories, is traced to Eduard C. Lindeman's "The Meaning of Adult

---

[1] S. B. Merriam, *The New Update on Adult Learning Theory,* New Directions for Adult and Continuing Education, no. 89, Spring 2001 (San Francisco: Jossey-Bass, 2001), 7.

Education" published in 1926.[2] The term andragogy, however, "originally used by Alexander Kapp (a German educator) in 1833, was developed into a theory of adult education by the American educator Malcolm Knowles (1913–1997)."[3] The term andragogy literally means "man-leading" in contrast to pedagogy, which means "child-leading."[4] Knowles, a humanist, originally defined andragogy as "the art and science of helping adults learn."[5] He introduced his ideas in an article he wrote in 1968, "Andragogy, not Pedagogy."[6] Knowles continued refining his ideas while writing books and articles throughout the 1970s and 1980s. He struggled with his definition of helping adults learn and eventually proposed that andragogy consists of the idea of a continuum between teacher directed and self-directed learning.[7]

> *As I rounded the corner, I could hear the buzzing of busy conversation even before I entered the adult Bible study class. Adults were grouped around round tables sharing their experiences. On the wall was a sign "What scares you?" This was an introductory activity (based on the principles of andragogy) that introduced the Bible lesson for the day.*

KNOWLES' MODEL OF ANDRAGOGY

Knowles' model of andragogy was an attempt to identify characteristics that were observable in adult learning. Andragogy gave adult education an identity separate from other fields of education, particularly pedagogy (teaching children), and was a springboard for further study. Knowles' concept of andragogy led to six assumptions that provided the andragogical foundation for building teaching strategies for adult learners.

Knowles originally advanced the following four assumptions:

1. As a person matures, his or her self-concept moves from that of a dependent personality toward one of a self-directing human being.
2. An adult accumulates a growing reservoir of experience, which is a rich resource for learning.

---

[2] M. K. Smith, "Eduard Lindeman and the Meaning of Adult Education" (1997, 2004), *The Encyclopaedia of Informal Education,* http://www.infed.org/thinkers/et-lind.htm (accessed February 9, 2009).

[3] *Wikipedia,* January 18, 2009, "Andragogy," http://en.wikipedia.org/wiki/Andragogy/ (accessed February 11, 2009).

[4] Ibid.

[5] M. S. Knowles, *The Modern Practice of Adult Education* (Chicago: Association Press, 1980), 43.

[6] M. S. Knowles, "Andragogy, not Pedagogy," *Adult Leadership* 16(10): 350–52, 386.

[7] S. B. Merriam, R. S. Caffarella, and L. M. Baumgartner, *Learning in Adulthood: A Comprehensive Guide,* 3rd ed. (San Francisco: Jossey-Bass, 2007), 87.

3. The readiness of an adult to learn is closely related to the developmental tasks of his or her social role.
4. There is a change in time perspective as people mature—from future application of knowledge to immediacy of application. Thus, an adult is more problem centered than subject centered in learning.[8]

In later publications, Knowles also referred to a fifth and a sixth assumption:

5. The most potent motivations are internal rather than external.[9]
6. Adults need to know why they need to learn something.[10]

Knowles understood that teaching adults was different from teaching children because adults approach learning differently. Children may be comfortable depending on a teacher to direct a learning experience. However, although adults may enter a learning situation with a dependent attitude, they expect not to be treated like children. They have a need to be seen as capable and self-directed.[11]

Knowles emphasized the importance of acknowledging experience in adults. He recognized that adult experiences differ from children's both in quantity and quality. In any group of adult learners there is a large pool of experience from which to fish. The richest resources for learning may be in that heterogeneous pool of adult experiences. "To children, experience is something that happens to them; to adults, their experience is *who they are.*"[12]

Knowles's assumption regarding adult readiness to learn refers to the observation that there is a relationship between motivation to learn and real-life need. When a need becomes apparent in an adult's life, there is an instant lure to learn. That moment of need may arise when adults move through developmental changes or when they encounter new social expectations: a new job, a death or birth in the family, or a new location.

Readiness is accompanied by a problem-centered rather than topic-centered approach to learning. Adults perceive a problem and are motivated to look for a solution. They want to apply new knowledge to a problem in real life so that they feel the new knowledge is relevant. They want to know why they need to know. "While adults are responsive to some external motivators (better jobs, promotions, higher salaries, and the like), the most potent motivators are internal pressures (the desire for increased job satisfaction, self-esteem, quality

---

[8] Ibid., 84.
[9] Ibid.
[10] Ibid.
[11] M. S. Knowles, *The Adult Learner: A Neglected Species,* 4th ed. (Houston: Gulf Publishing, 1990), 58–59.
[12] Ibid., 60.

Table 6.1

Conditions of Learning	Principles of Teaching
The learners feel a need to learn.	1. The teacher exposes students to new possibilities of self-fulfillment.
	2. The teacher helps each student clarify personal aspirations for improved behavior.
	3. The teacher helps each student diagnose the gap between his aspiration and his present level of performance.
	4. The teacher helps the students identify the life problems they experience because of the gaps in their personal equipment.
The learning environment is characterized by physical comfort, mutual trust and respect, mutual helpfulness, freedom of expression, and acceptance of differences:	5. The teacher provides physical conditions that are comfortable (as to seating, temperature, ventilation, lighting, decoration) and conducive to interaction (preferably, no person sitting behind another person).
	6. The teacher accepts each student as a person of worth and respects his feelings and ideas.
	7. The teacher seeks to build relationships of mutual trust and helpfulness among the students by encouraging cooperative activities and refraining from inducing competitiveness and judgmentalness.
	8. The teacher exposes his own feelings and contributes his resources as a co-learner in the spirit of mutual inquiry.
The learners perceive the goals of a learning experience to be their goals.	9. The teacher involves the students in a mutual process of formulating learning objectives in which the needs of the students, of the institution, of the teacher, of the subject matter, and of the society are taken into account.
The learners accept a share of the responsibility for planning and operating a learning experience, and therefore have a feeling of commitment toward it.	10. The teacher shares his thinking about options available in the designing of learning experiences and the selection of materials and methods, and involves the students in deciding among these options jointly.
The learners participate actively in the learning process.	11. The teacher helps the students to organize themselves (project groups, learning-teaching teams, independent study, etc.) to share responsibility in the process of mutual inquiry.
The learning process is related to and makes use of the experience of the learners.	12. The teacher helps the students exploit their own experiences as resources for learning through the use of such techniques as discussion, role-playing, case method, etc.
	13. The teacher gears the presentation of his own resources to the levels of experience of his particular students.
	14. The teacher helps the students to apply new learning to their experience, and thus to make the learning more meaningful and integrated.
The learners have a sense of progress toward their goals.	15. The teacher involves the students in developing mutually acceptable criteria and methods for measuring progress toward the learning objectives.
	16. The teacher helps the students develop and apply procedures for self-evaluation according to these criteria.

of life, and the like)."[13] Self-motivation erupting from internal goals engages adult learners.

Knowles designed principles of teaching (see table on p. 111) that apply his assumptions to adult education. These teaching principles are linked to what Knowles called "conditions of learning." The teaching principles of Knowles' andragogy continue to have a profound influence on adult education today. They emphasize the importance of the learner rather than the teacher, and demonstrate respect for the individual's experience, needs, and internal motivation. Andragogical teaching principles recognize the importance of an appropriate learning environment. Most educators of adults recognize the components of andragogy and practice at least some of the proposed methods. (See Table 6.1 on preceding page.)

CRITICISMS OF ANDRAGOGY

Two main criticisms have plagued andragogy since popularized by Knowles in 1984: an ambiguous definition, and a failure to attend to cultural and contextual issues. The problem of definition has been the basis for complaints that andragogy is a set of assumptions rather than a theory. Rachal reviewed 19 research studies on andragogy between 1984 and 2001 and concluded:

> Due to the elasticity of meanings of andragogy and the consequent variability of interpretations, empirical examinations of andragogy—its science, one might say—have tended to be inconclusive, contradictory, and few. This fate is likely to persist as long as an operational, researchable definition of andragogy eludes researchers.[14]

Educators argue over whether andragogy is a theory or a set of assumptions.[15] Knowles himself offers the opinion that he prefers to think of andragogy as a model of assumptions foundational to future theory.[16] Whether theory or assumption, all agree that it is a body of organized information that has had a profound effect upon teaching practice. In the twentieth century, andragogy was a springboard to launch new thinking and new research about adult learning. In the twenty-first century, many educators have turned their focus to revisions of the practice of andragogy and the development of other theories.

The second criticism pinpoints andragogy's lack of attention to culture and context. Baumgartner, Lee, Birden, and Flowers express the opinion:

---

[13] Ibid., 63.

[14] J. R. Rachal, "Andragogy's Detectives: A Critique of the Present and a Proposal for the Future," *Adult Education Quarterly* 52, no. 3 (May 2002): 211.

[15] J. Davenport and J. Davenport, "A Chronology and Analysis of the Andragogy Debate," *Adult Education Quarterly* 35, no. 3 (1985): 152–59, esp. 157–58.

[16] M. S. Knowles, *The Making of an Adult Educator: An Autobiographical Journey* (San Francisco, CA: Jossey-Bass, 1989), 112.

"Scholars believe that Knowles focuses on the individual learner and ignores the impact of socio-cultural factors on learners."[17] This accusation is generally interpreted by educators to mean that Knowles built his andragogical assumptions on individual learners characterized by the attributes of a "normative" segment of the population rather than a cross-section. A survey of the literature demonstrates that most adult learners in the United States since the 1980s are predominately employed, middle-class Caucasians with past educational experience that serves as a base for additional learning.[18] If educators view all adult learners as "the predominate learner," they may view andragogy as adequate. If, however, educators seek to recognize the "at risk" learner and explore the impact of cultural context, andragogy will be viewed as inadequate.

Who is the "at risk" adult learner? If one defines cultural context as the influence of environment and experiences, the educator's focus must broaden to include learners marginalized by such things as gender, geography, ethnicity, socioeconomic circumstances, immigration, and physical challenges. When viewed through cultural context, the brilliance of andragogy fades. The question becomes: How does andragogy address the issues of cultural context?

Education is not for the "normative adult" only. The purpose of teaching is to expose the secrets and share the tools so that the learner is equipped for personal success. The privilege of learning is to uncover truth and acquire skills resulting in life-change that leads to the fulfillment of personal goals. The teacher must adjust teaching strategies to consider cultural perspectives and societal impact.

Andragogy, therefore, is criticized for its definition as well as its lack of attention to cultural context. The affect has been a struggle to produce replicative research and universal application. The criticisms are valid and must be acknowledged. Perhaps the most serious charge is cultural. American culture is diverse by definition, and the Christian community is diverse by design. God deliberately embraced variety while expressing the multiplicity of his own image in his created humanity. We are created in God's image.[19] As we look into the "individual" faces of our peers, we catch a glimpse of God's enormity.

Not only are we individual in creation, we are also individual in our cultures. There is no truly homogenous group (not even within a family) because every individual is the product of unique cultural experiences. The adult

---

[17] L. M. Baumgartner, "Andragogy: A Foundational Theory/Set of Assumptions," in L. and M-Y. L. Baumgartner, S. Birden, D. Flowers, *Adult Learning Theory: A Primer,* Information Series (Washington, DC: ERIC Clearinghouse on Adult, Career, and Vocational Education, Office of Educational Research and Improvement [ED], 2003), 14.

[18] S. B. Merriam and R. S. Caffarella, *Learning in Adulthood: A Comprehensive Guide,* 2nd ed. (San Francisco: Jossey-Bass, 1998), 71.

[19] Gen 1:2

learner has individuality and cannot be lumped into one approach that works for all. All teachers, then, must consider andragogical teaching principles only as some of the tools on the tool belt: helpful in some situations but incomplete. The Christian educator must recognize the limitations imposed by the cultural differences of adult learners, while at the same time allowing the assumptions and teaching principles of andragogy to rattle personal comfort zones and challenge old paradigms.

ANDRAGOGY AND CHRISTIAN EDUCATION

In addition to the secular criticisms of andragogy, the Christian educator must also acknowledge that andragogy has humanistic underpinnings. Humanism is a broad term with several definitions.[20] On hearing that something has humanistic origins, Christians immediately recoil and think of secular humanism as deifying man and excluding God. While it is true, however, that humanism emphasizes the goodness of man and excludes God, it is also true that, "Humanistic learning theory emphasizes the values and attitudes of students rather than their behavior or thinking."[21] As Christians, we emphasize God and acknowledge man as his creation, *and* we focus on change in our values and attitudes (humanistic learning theory). Although our goal in Christian education is to change behaviors, we are interested in intrinsic value and attitude changes that transform daily living. We do not want mere extrinsic molding to a stereotypical image. As Christian educators, therefore, we evaluate all research and every theory in the light of God's Word, selecting from secularists the truths that are synchronous with the Bible.

Several andragogical ideas are helpful to the Christian educator. First, the goal of learning in the andragogical model is for adults to establish a lifelong pattern of self-directed learning. Likewise, the goal of the Bible teacher is to help the student establish a lifelong pattern of personal Bible Study and life response. Andragogical learning moves the adult student from teacher-directed to self-directed learning. The Bible teacher must make a conscious effort not simply to lecture, but also to facilitate and support adult self-directed learning. The Bible teacher must not just share facts, but must also share tools for acquiring knowledge by stimulating the appetite of the learner. These essential ingredients motivate the Bible student to crave the nourishment of the Word of God[22] and to devour it constantly.

Second, andragogy recognizes that adults are both capable and possess valuable experiences. In the classroom, adults should bring this knowledge

---

[20] For a more complete discussion of humanism, see Yount, *Created to Learn*, 231–48.
[21] Ibid., 231.
[22] 1 Pet 2:2

into their own learning. The teacher must acknowledge adult competency, value adult capabilities, and provide opportunities for adult interaction in the learning process. One goal for the Bible teacher is to encourage the habit of personal Bible study. The learner should bring to the classroom questions and interests from individual Bible study and life experience. These can influence the direction of the group study and contribute to a deeper level of application.

Third, andragogy assumes that an adult learner should have a physical and psychological environment that supports adult learning. Allowing for different cultural perspectives, the physical environment may include such things as food, flexible seating, and comfortable temperature. In addition to the physical environment, the psychologically safe learning environment provides mutual respect and support. Teachers acknowledge the experience and intelligence of the learners and speak both to them and of them respectfully. Students are expected to treat each other and the teacher with the same courtesy. Maintaining a nonthreatening environment encourages students to agree or disagree with each other, discussing controversial issues without personal attacks. The Christian educator understands that the issue is dissected, not the contributor.

Fourth, according to andragogical assumptions, the learner must know the purpose for learning. If the learner is motivated by a real-life problem that can be solved by new information, he is more likely to learn. Seeing personal relevance provides motivation and increases attention to the learning task. As the teacher introduces the lesson by connecting the learning to personal relevance, the learner responds with eager interest. If the teacher applies the new information by posing a problem and facilitating synthesis, the learner can visualize personal change through problem-solving.

The adult Bible teacher analyzes the premises of andragogy in the light of God's Word. The sacred cows of personal teaching preferences are sacrificed on the altar of the learner's needs. New tools are sharpened and new methods practiced. The biblical educator must be flexible and adaptive in order to maximize adult learning and retention.

ANDRAGOGY SUMMARY

Perhaps the most significant contribution of Knowles' theory of andragogy is that he changed the direction of adult education from teacher-directed to student-directed. In so doing he inspired student-based methods of teaching adults. He also differentiated between teaching children and teaching adults by giving attention to the unique needs of adult learners. Still, most andragogical educators would like to see a more researchable definition of andragogy. That would enable future studies specifically designed to evaluate the benefits of using andragogical methods in teaching adults. Differences in culture and context must also be acknowledged in adult learners, and the Christian educator must address these differences. They are imperative in all learning theories. Even with the criticisms in mind, most would agree that andragogy has been foundational for more recent learning theories and for current practice in adult education.

TEACHING TOOLS FROM ANDRAGOGY

1. Adult learners must move from teacher-directed to self-directed.
2. Adult learners need a comfortable and safe learning environment both physically and emotionally.
3. Adults are internally motivated and need to know the purpose for learning and the reason the content is relevant to them.
4. Adult learners need to have their experiences recognized and tied in to new learning.
5. Adult learners use problem-solving as a way to understand new information.

ANDRAGOGY APPLIED

Exercise 6.4
(Rate yourself, 1 being poor and 5 being terrific)

1. My goal in teaching is to facilitate self-directed learning	1	2	3	4	5
2. I provide a comfortable adult environment for adult learners.	1	2	3	4	5
3. My students can express their opinions without fear.	1	2	3	4	5
4. I am comfortable with my students eating or drinking while learning.	1	2	3	4	5
5. I consistently tell my students why the content of my lesson is relevant.	1	2	3	4	5
6. I frequently ask my students to share their experiences.	1	2	3	4	5
7. I help my students draw connections between old experience and present learning.	1	2	3	4	5
8. I frequently use case studies with real life problems or ask a student to share a problem so that my students can apply the scripture passage to a contemporary scenario..	1	2	3	4	5

SELF-DIRECTED LEARNING

The basic idea of directing one's own learning has been around for centuries. Current self-directed learning theory, however, was popularized in the 1960s about the same time Malcolm Knowles introduced andragogy. Although one of Knowles' andragogical assumptions was to develop self-directed learning in adults, Allen Tough, building on the work of C. O. Houle,[23] provided the first comprehensive description of self-directed learning. Tough's "Adult Learning Projects"[24] describes adult learners who want to assume responsibility for their own learning, and who plan and direct their own learning activities.

Personal, theoretical perspectives drastically affect the interpretation of self-directed learning. For example, the humanist approaches self-directed learning from the basic belief that human nature is good, people have unlimited possibilities for growth, and people have a responsibility to take control of personal learning. The behaviorist presupposes that self-directed learning occurs when new information results in the positive or negative reinforcement of new behavior. Constructivists value self-directed opportunities for the development of new mental constructs as the individual explores personal interests. Critical theorists value the self-directed learner's interacting with culture and creating social change. Educators view learning theory from biased perspectives. Even the most open mind is influenced by beliefs, values, and experiences.

> *Our third child loved music. Though she had excellent skills and an ear for it, she did not enjoy piano recitals or clarinet competitions. We encouraged her in every way we could, but she was reluctant. One day she told us at dinner she wanted to try out for field commander of her high school band. We were shocked. She was always happy to be in the group, not leading it. We gave her all the support we could but, as a ninth grader, it seemed unlikely. She worked hard and after the try-outs was named field commander for her tenth-grade year. She won the try-outs for field commander for three years, and in every band competition, including the state, she received an excellent rating, the highest award. Though she was a teenager, she demonstrated that once self-directed, amazing things can happen.*

AIMS OF SELF-DIRECTED LEARNING

Merriam, Caffarella, and Baumgartner define the aims of self-directed learning: "(1) to enhance the ability of adult learners to become self-directed in their learning, (2) to foster transformational learning as central to self-directed

---

[23] C. O. Houle, *The Inquiring Mind* (Madison, WI: University of Wisconsin Press, 1961).

[24] A. Tough, *The Adult's Learning Projects: A Fresh Approach to Theory and Practice in Adult Learning,* 2nd ed., Research in Education Series No. 1, (Toronto, Canada: The Ontario Institute for Studies in Education, 1979).

learning, and (3) to promote emancipatory learning and social action as an integral part of self-directed learning."[25] The work of Allen Tough supports the first aim: a progression toward becoming more and more self-directed in the learning process.[26] Both personal choice and independence are vital to this aim. Jack Mezirow promoted the second aim in the 1980s: the connection of self-directed learning to transformational learning. He emphasized that the reflective discourse of transformative theory must be based upon both self-understanding and cultural understanding.

Of the three aims of self-directed learning, the most difficult to attain is the third, emancipatory learning and social action. Brookfield challenges educators to create an environment for learning that enables social awareness and action. He argues that learners having control over the elements of learning is consistent with the self-directed learning theory, and that all learners, regardless of economic status or cultural prejudice, should be given appropriate resources to exercise control over their own learning. Brookfield's argument requires total student control over learning content, process, and evaluation.[27] Total student control causes problems for many educational institutions and has been met with considerable resistance.

LINEAR/SEQUENTIAL MODELS OF SELF-DIRECTED LEARNING

The numerous models of self-directed learning generally fall into three categories: sequential, interwoven, and instructional. This book presents sample(s) in each category. Sequential models define steps to the self-directed learning process. An example of this is Tough's 13-step model of self-directed learning. "Tough provided the first comprehensive description of self-directed learning as a form of study that he termed *self-planned learning*."[28] Tough's model describes a sequential, linear way to orchestrate self-directed learning.[29] Learners followed a self-directed sequence of steps to reach personal learning goals.

---

[25] Merriam, Caffarella, and Baumgartner, *Learning in Adulthood,* 3rd ed., 107.

[26] Tough, *Adult Learning Projects,* 2.

[27] S. Brookfield, "Self-Directed Learning, Political Clarity, and the Critical Practice of Adult Education," *Adult Education Quarterly* 43, no. 4 (Summer 1993).

[28] Merriam, Caffarella, and Baumgartner, *Learning in Adulthood,* 3rd ed., 105.

[29] Tough, *Adult Learning Project,* 95.

Table 6.2

Tough's 13-Step Model of Self-Directed Learning[30]

1. Deciding what detailed knowledge and skill to learn . . . .
2. Deciding the specific activities, methods, resources, or equipment for learning . . . .
3. Deciding where to learn . . . .
4. Setting specific deadlines or intermediate targets.
5. Deciding when to begin a learning episode.
6. Deciding the pace at which to proceed during a learning episode.
7. Estimating the current level of his knowledge and skill or his progress in gaining the desired knowledge and skill.
8. Detecting any factor that has been hindering learning or discovering inefficient aspects of the current procedures.
9. Obtaining the desired resources or equipment or reaching the desired place or resource . . . .
10. Preparing or adapting a room (or certain resources, furniture, or equipment) for learning or arranging certain other physical conditions in preparation for learning . . . .
11. Saving or obtaining the money necessary for the use of certain human or nonhuman resources . . . .
12. Finding time for the learning . . . .
13. Taking steps to increase the motivation for certain learning episodes . . . .

Tough's method presents self-directed learning in 13 decisions or choices with subsequent actions. The goal of this method is for the learner to develop in the capacity to be self-directed. It assumes that adult learners have the capacity and motivation to be self-directed.

INTERWOVEN/ INTERACTIVE MODELS OF SELF-DIRECTED LEARNING

Interwoven or interactive models do not view self-directed learning as linear. The interwoven model views learning as the coming together of personal characteristics, opportunity, circumstances, cognitive process, and a myriad of other factors that converge to catalyze an episode of self-directed learning. Here are three samples of interwoven models. The first is George E. Spear's model. For Spear, the learner's control is most prominent when arranging the

---

[30] Ibid., 95–96.

elements in order of importance. He also proposes that the past success or failure is an important contributor to the present learning environment.

Table 6.3

Spear's Model of Self-Directed Learning[31]

Knowledge
1. Residual knowledge: knowledge the learner brings to the project as a residue from prior knowledge
2. Acquired knowledge: knowledge acquired as part of the learning project

Action
1. Directed action: action directed toward a known or specific end
2. Exploratory: action that the learner chooses without knowing what the outcomes may be or with certainty that any useful outcome will ensure
3. Fortuitous action: action that the learner takes for reasons not related to the learning project

Environment
1. Consistent environment: includes both human and material elements that are regularly in place and generally accessible
2. Fortuitous environment: provides for chance encounters that could not be expected or foreseen and yet affect the learner and the project.

The second interwoven model is the Personal Responsibility Orientation (PRO) model from Brockett and Hiemstra:[32]

> By proposing the Personal Responsibility Orientation model, we are suggesting that in order to understand the complexity of self-direction in adult learning, it is essential to recognize differences between self-directed learning as an instructional method and learner self-direction as a personality characteristic. These two dimensions are linked through the recognition that each emphasizes the importance of learners assuming personal responsibility for their thoughts and actions. Finally, the PRO model is designed to advance understanding of self-direction by recognizing the vital role played by the social context in which learning takes place.[33]

In addition to the personal responsibility and social context emphasized in Spear's model, the PRO model adds emphasis on the element of "personality."

---

[31]G. E. Spear, "Beyond the Organizing Circumstance: A Search for Methodology for the Study of Self-Directed Learning" in H. B. Long et al., *Self Directed Learning: Application and Theory*. (Athens, GA: Department of Adult Education, University of Georgia, 1988), pp. 199–221, 213.

[32] R. G. Brockett and R. Hiemstra, *Self-Direction in Adult Learning: Perspectives on Theory, Research, and Practice* (New York: Routledge, 1991), 26.

[33] Ibid., 33.

Self-direction is seen as both a personality construct and a learning process. Personality is identified as the internal motivation of the learner to learn in addition to the external self-directed instructional process.

Figure 6.1

Brockett and Hiemstra's "Personal Responsibility Orientation" (PRO) Model[34]

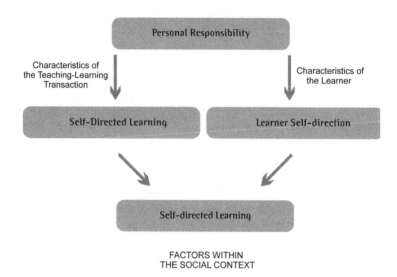

The third interwoven model is from Randy Garrison, who integrates control of the learning process, cognitive responsibility, and self-motivation. The individual is responsible for personal learning while embracing the collaboration and affirmation of others in constructing new knowledge —self-directed learning from a collaborative constructivist perspective.[35] This model acknowledges the previously identified elements of self-directed learning and emphasizes the importance of both the personal and the social aspect of learning.

---

[34] Ibid., 25.
[35] Merriam, Caffarella, and Baumgartner, *Learning in Adulthood*, 114.

Figure 6.2

Garrison's Model: Dimensions of Self-Directed Learning[36]

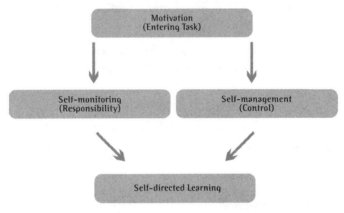

Garrison's concept of "self-management" focuses on external control of the learning environment. Many models of self-directed learning theory emphasize the teacher-structured learning environment. In the Garrison model, instead of teacher-directed external controls alone, the student and teacher collaboratively construct the learning environment. The adult learner's input shapes both learning goals and activities, and the teacher's input provides confirmation of worth and knowledge.[37]

Garrison's use of the concept of "self-monitoring" refers to cognition and meta-cognition—thinking about one's own thinking.[38] The ability to engage in cognition and meta-cognition requires the ability to construct meaning from one's environment, and to associate the new constructs with old constructs and/or to change old mental constructs to accommodate the new information (assimilation and accommodation). As the learner engages in this process and reflects on its meaning, the teacher provides external feedback that the learner must integrate with his internal assessment.

In the Garrison Model, "motivation" includes what he further defines as "entering motivation" and "task motivation." Garrison makes the point that a learner must be motivated both to enter the learning experience and persist

---

[36] D. R. Garrison, "Self-Directed Learning: Toward a Comprehensive Model," Adult Education Quarterly 48, no.1 (Fall 1997): 22. Available online at Education Research Complete (http://www.ebscohost.com/), accessed February 24, 2009.

[37] Ibid., 4–6.

[38] Ibid., 6–7.

to the completion of the task.[39] Motivation can be extrinsic, intrinsic, or both. The teacher or the environment externally imposes extrinsic motivation. Intrinsic motivation is internal, coming from the student. The more effective self-directed learning is, the more intrinsic the motivation. Internal motivation is affected by many factors, such as self-esteem, past experience, and values.

Interwoven or interactive models combine the following: emphasis of learning as a personal responsibility, opportunities that facilitate self-learning, character traits conducive to self-directed learning; the match of need and opportunity for self-directed learning, and a social context which facilitates self-directed learning.[40] Interwoven or interactive models may differ in emphasizing these elements.

INSTRUCTIONAL MODELS OF SELF-DIRECTED LEARNING

In addition to linear models and interwoven/interactive models, self-directed learning includes instructional models. Instructional models approach self-directed learning from the perspective of stages of development, and they provide instructors a tool for implementing self-directed learning in their classrooms. Gerald Grow's instructional model of staged self-directed learning is an example.

In Grow's model, the stages progress from heavy teacher dependence to high self-direction with little teacher influence. The instructor moves from being the authority to motivator, to facilitator, and to delegator. Simultaneously, the learner moves from being dependent to interested, to involved, to self-directed. The teacher matches the learner's stage with an appropriate teaching response while maintaining the goal of encouraging the learner to the next stage of self-direction. As seen in the example of Grow's model, instructional models of self-directed learning theory focus on the practical application of self-directed learning.

---

[39] Ibid., 7–10.
[40] L. M. Baumgartner, "Self-Directed Learning," 31–32.

Table 6.4

Grow's Staged Self-Directed Learning Model[41]

	Student	Teacher	Examples
Stage 1	Dependent	Authority, Coach	Coaching with immediate feedback. Drill. Informational lecture. Overcoming deficiencies and resistance.
Stage 2	Interested	Motivator, guide	Inspiring lecture plus guided discussion. Goal-setting and learning strategies.
Stage 3	Involved	Facilitator	Discussion facilitated by teacher who participates as equal. Seminar. Group projects.
Stage 4	Self-directed	Consultant, delegator	Internship, dissertation, individual work or self-directed study-group.

CRITICISM OF SELF-DIRECTED LEARNING

Self-directed learning theory, like andragogy, receives criticism for assuming homogenous values in addressing adult education. Although both learning approaches seem to demonstrate awareness of individual differences, both fail to address adequately the problem of a heterogeneous group of learners with different cultural experiences and expectations for the education process. The basic criticism of both andragogy and self-directed learning is that they are focused on white Western values of independence and autonomy.[42] The more eclectic the group of learners, the more the educator must consider the limitations of these approaches; however, the educator must also acknowledge the research-validated success of these different approaches for many learners. Teaching tools based on self-directed learning theory should be thoughtfully added to the biblical educator's resources.

SELF-DIRECTED LEARNING IN CHRISTIAN EDUCATION

The degree of appreciation for self-directed learning is shaped by one's theoretical and theological perspective. Unlike humanists, Christians believe that the impetus for learning does not come from the goodness of people. Christians acknowledge that all people are born with a sinful nature. All are

---

[41] G. Grow, "Teaching Learners to Be Self-Directed," *Adult Education Quarterly* 41, no. 3 (Spring 1991): 129.

[42] L. M. Baumgartner, "Self-Directed Learning," 33.

in need of redemption from sin through personally receiving the sacrifice of Christ's death as payment for sin. At conversion, the new believer receives the Holy Spirit who takes the role of internal motivator.

In some church settings, external peer pressure molds the new believer into conformity. It calls for the new believer to look, act, and talk like everyone else. This behavioristic view of discipleship often overwhelms the new believer and stunts Christian growth. It is true that extrinsic motivation does have a role in helping the new believer form habits of studying God's Word and praying. Role models who practice the presence of Jesus draw the new believer toward the Savior. Christians, however, cannot mature toward Christlikeness if they are stuck in dependency on external motivators. The internal motivator, the Holy Spirit, must be primary. The role of both the church and of Christian educators is to be facilitators, encouragers, and role models.

As Christians discover the vastness of God's love, their hunger to know more of God grows dynamically in a cyclical process. Understanding even some measure of God's love motivates the new believer to look for a deeper knowledge of God and His direction for life. The desire for God is followed by obedience to whatever God reveals, which is then followed by understanding more of God's love.

The cyclical nature of Christian growth increases in power and dynamic. It is never static. God's love produces tremendous internal motivation for knowledge and Christlikeness. Adrian Rogers once said, "If you obey what you understand, God will give you more understanding."[43] The growth cycle spirals upward—the learner becoming more and more like Christ. The ascending spiral does not become increasingly distant from the

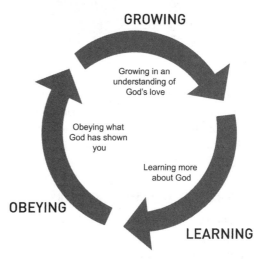

hurting world around it. Rather, the momentum of its centripetal force impacts people trapped in the inertia of the world. It draws them toward the Savior.

---

[43] From an undocumented church service from Adrian Pierce Rogers (1931–2005), three-term president of the Southern Baptist Convention, 1979–80, 1986–88, pastor of Bellevue Baptist Church, Memphis TN, 1972–2005; online http://en.wikipedia.org/wiki/Adrian_Rogers (accessed April 2, 2009).

How then does self-directed learning theory help the Christian educator? From the linear models, we learn that it is helpful to plan proactive steps supporting self-directed learning of Scripture. In the planning process, we need to allow for student choices, to provide adequate resources, to insure an appropriate learning environment, and to support motivation.

From interwoven models of self-directed learning we understand that Christian educators should emphasize personal responsibility for self-directed learning. We do so by providing learning opportunities. We should help students identify the prompting of the Holy Spirit and encourage obedience. The adult Bible teacher should facilitate matching need with opportunity and provide a supportive social context for learning. Finally, from the instructional models, the Bible teacher should understand the dynamic between teacher and learner—intentionally moving from teacher-directed to student-directed education.

Self-directed learning theory is helpful to the Christian educator. It enables the conception of an instructional model that pictures the instructor moving from authority, to facilitator, to consultant, as the new Christian learner moves from being hand-fed baby food to a self-directed meat eater. The task of the Christian educator is to view self-directed learning theory as another addition to the tool belt for teaching.

SUMMARY OF SELF-DIRECTED LEARNING

The main contribution of self-directed learning theory is the emphasis on adults taking the responsibility for their own learning for a lifelong experience. As was true of andragogy, criticism mainly focuses on cultural neglect: assuming homogeneity rather than celebrating diversity. Self-directed learning theory developed in a parallel time frame with andragogy, and both theories have maintained an active following. Ralph Brockett, from the University of Tennessee, conducted a review of 122 self-directed learning articles published between 1980 and 1998 and found a decline in the interest in this theory.[44] The decline in research interest, however, does not negate the significant permanent changes in adult education because of the influence of self-directed learning theory. As the interest in self-directed learning waned, a new interest, transformative learning, took the lead.

Table 6.5

Teaching Tools from Self-Directed Learning

1. Use pro-active steps to plan opportunities and support self-directed learning.
2. Give students choices in what they learn and how they learn it.
3. Provide learners with available resources.
4. Provide an environment conducive to adult learning.
5. Emphasize personal responsibility for learning.
6. Help students identify their internal motivator and character traits related to learning
7. Match student need with learning opportunity.
8. Provide a stimulating, safe, social context for learning.
9. Keep in view the teacher/learning dynamic: the teacher decreasing as the learner increases in the self-directed learning process.

Exercise 6.5

Self-Directed Learning Applied

(Rate yourself, 1 being poor and 5 being terrific)

1. I regularly provide opportunity for students to make choices about what they learn and how they learn.	1	2	3	4	5
2. Rather than expect new Christians to conform to the church "norm" I expect new Christians to exhibit the way Christ would look in the world if he had their personality and circumstances.	1	2	3	4	5
3. I help my students understand the role of the Holy Spirit in interpreting the meaning of scripture and convicting them of life change.	1	2	3	4	5
4. I learn to know my students personally so that I am sensitive to their personal needs and can match learning opportunities to needs.	1	2	3	4	5
5. In my adult teaching experiences, I find myself making significant progress toward helping my students move from teacher-directed to self-directed learning.	1	2	3	4	5
6. I do not use self-directed learning in the place of thorough lesson preparation.	1	2	3	4	5
7. I help my students to understand that it is not the teacher's responsibility to make them learn; rather, it is the learner's responsibility to learn.	1	2	3	4	5

---

[44] R. Brockett, et al., "Two decades of literature on SDL: A content analysis" (Boynton Beach, FL: International SDL Symposium, 2000).

CHAPTER SEVEN

TRANSFORMATIVE LEARNING THEORY

ATTEMPTING TO ANSWER THE criticisms of andragogy and self-directed learning theory, Jack Mezirow developed his concept of transformative learning. According to Mezirow, transformative learning theory is:

> ... the process of becoming critically aware of how and why our assumptions have come to constrain the way we perceive, understand, and feel about our world; changing these structures of habitual expectation to make possible a more inclusive, discriminating, and integrating perspective; and finally, making choices or otherwise acting upon these new understandings.[1]

Transformative learning theory can be divided into four categories: cognitive-rational approach, emancipatory approach, developmental approach, and the spiritual approach.[2] Each category is worthy of definition and description. Jack Mezirow is clearly the main contributor to the transformative theory, and his constructivist cognitive-rational approach is foundational for other contri-

---

[1] J. Mezirow, *Transformative Learning: Theory to Practice* (San Francisco, CA: Jossey-Bass, 1991), 167.

[2] J. Dirkx, "Transformative Learning Theory in the Practice of Adult Education: An Overview," *PAACE Journal of Lifelong Learning* (1998) 7: 1–14 .

butions. The subsequent approaches to transformative theory similarly have their own champions. The most recent approach is the spiritual.

COGNITIVE RATIONAL APPROACH TO TRANSFORMATIVE LEARNING

Jack Mezirow, emeritus professor of Adult and Continuing Education, Teachers College at Columbia University, developed transformative learning theory over the past several decades. Mezirow began in 1978, in response to a research project involving women students returning to community college. His theory became popular through the momentum of the women's liberty movement. Mezirow defines learning as: "the process of using a prior interpretation to construe a new or a revised interpretation of the meaning of one's experience in order to guide future action."[3] As do andragogy and self-directed learning theory, transformative learning theory reflects a student (rather than teacher) orientation. The theme that consistently emerges from Mezirow's writing is that, along with socialization, the ultimate goal for the student is acceptance and inclusiveness. Transformative learning theory is the student-centered negotiation of new understanding and changing circumstances. Mezirow believed that all truth and knowledge is relative. In his own words, "As there are no fixed truths or totally definitive knowledge, and because circumstances change, the

Susan, a bright young woman, had the personal goal of having a large house, a new car, and a million dollars in the bank by age 35. Her life was totally focused on these values and goals. Then Susan visited the doctor and discovered that her frequent headaches were caused by an inoperable malignant brain tumor. As she explores her options and realizes that she has less than a year to live (informational learning), her values change. She is no longer interested in the house, car, or a million dollars. Now Susan wants to know about God, forgiveness, and heaven. Her friends and family have become more important than any material possessions. She has experienced transformative learning. The information she learned became personally life changing—transforming her values and goals. Informational learning resulted in transformational learning—life change.

---

[3] J. Mezirow, "Contemporary Paradigms of Learning," *Adult Education Quarterly* 46, no. 3 (1996): 162.

human condition may be best understood as a continuous effort to negotiate contested meanings."[4]

Mezirow does not describe transformative learning as a frequent experience. He acknowledges that adults create meaning structures through the daily experiences of cognition (computation, memorizing, reading and comprehending) and meta-cognition (self-awareness and self-evaluation). Mezirow assigns transformative learning theory to the area of epistemic cognition. "Epistemic cognition has to do with reflection on the limits of knowledge, the certainty of knowledge, and the criteria for knowing."[5] Constructs from cognition and meta-cognition develop slowly and become the basis for the adult's values and actions. Mezirow describes transformational learning, the realm of epistemic cognition, as occurring only periodically and leading to new or revised constructs of meaning followed by new patterns of action.

Mezirow suggests that transformations often occur in some variation of the following stages:

1. A disorienting dilemma
2. Self-examination with feelings of fear, anger, guilt, or shame
3. A critical assessment of assumptions
4. Recognition that one's discontent and the process of transformation are shared
5. Exploration of options for new roles, relationships, and actions
6. Planning a course of action
7. Acquiring knowledge and skills for implementing one's plans
8. Provisional trying of new roles
9. Building competence and self-confidence in new roles and relationships
10. A reintegration into one's life on the basis of conditions dictated by one's new perspective.[6]

Regardless of the sequence of events, or the elimination of some of his stages, reflective discourse stands out as one ultimate ingredient to the success of accomplishing transformative learning.

Reflective discourse involves the ability to understand one's own perspective and that of others, and to communicate relationally toward deeper understanding and acceptance. Goleman explores this quality as "emotional

---

[4] J. Mezirow et al., *Learning as Transformation: Critical Perspectives on a Theory in Progress* (San Francisco: Jossey-Bass, 2000), 3. Hereafter, *Learning as Tramsformation.*

[5] K. Kitchener, "Cognition, Metacognition and Epistemic Cognition," *Human Development*, no. 26 (1983): 230.

[6] Mezirow et al., *Learning as Transformation*, 22.

intelligence." Goleman defines the five elements of emotional intelligence as, "self-awareness, motivation, self-regulation, empathy, and adeptness in relationships."[7] These five elements characterize learners who not only have the ability to engage in meta-cognition but also can interact in reflective discourse—successfully negotiating the circumstance of life.

In addition to displaying these elements that comprise emotional intelligence, the student must be willing to identify real-life problems rather than ignore physical, emotional, and philosophical dilemmas. In reflective discourse, the student must identify the problem, select which facts, formulas, and theories are relevant to the problem,[8] synthesize the resource information, and generate potential solutions. Finally, the student must be willing to conduct this process in concert with community. Reflective discourse requires not only understanding one's own perspective, but also embracing dialog with others to influence, modify, or expand one's perspective.

Reflective discourse is not seen as universal in concept. America consists of many ethnicities and cultural groups. For some Americans, the negotiation of reflective discourse is problematic due to the prevailing emotional emphasis on entitlement and debate. Americans with this orientation must consider the destructive impact of argument over understanding, self-interest over relationship, and litigation over constructive discourse. Students who struggle with these dichotomies will require a supportive environment that facilitates a change of perspective. In order to accomplish a safe environment conducive to discourse, Mezirow created the following guidelines for learners:

- More accurate and complete information
- Freedom from coercion and distorting self-deception
- Openness to alternative points of view—empathy and concern about how others think and feel
- The ability to weigh evidence and assess arguments objectively
- Greater awareness of the context of ideas and, more critically, reflectiveness of assumptions, including their own
- An equal opportunity to participate in the various roles of discourse
- Willingness to seek understanding and agreement and to accept a resulting best judgment as a test of validity until new perspectives, evidence, or arguments are encountered and validated through discourse as yielding a better judgment.[9]

---

[7] Ibid., 24.

[8] P. M. King and K. S. Kitchener, *Developing Reflective Judgment: Understanding and Promoting Intellectual Growth and Critical Thinking in Adolescents and Adults* (San Francisco: Jossey-Bass, 1994), 7. See appendix B.

[9] Mezirow et al., *Learning as Transformation*, 13–14.

Mezirow proposes that a comfortable and safe environment supports reflective discourse and empowers students so that the teacher can facilitate effective transformation.

EMANCIPATORY APPROACH TO TRANSFORMATIVE LEARNING

A second constructivist approach is Paulo Freire's emancipatory transformative learning. From a social context of oppression and the need for social reform emerged the emancipatory approach to transformative learning. The emancipatory approach focuses on education leading to empowerment. Paulo Freire (1921–97), a Brazilian educator, developed a method including three phases: identifying the problem, analyzing the cause of the problem, creating solutions for the problem.[10] In phase 1 of this model, students identify the problem through social interaction within the proposed setting. In phase 2, the analyzing phase, the educator encourages reflective discussion and describes the cause through interaction with the students. In the final phase solutions are created through collaboration between students and educator. Students are empowered as they discover agencies and opportunities for change. Students and educator are interdependent as the process goes forward, and the resulting solution is a confirmation that circumstances are not to be passively accepted, but rather resolved in a collaborative manner. "Its goal is social transformation by demythicizing reality, where the oppressed develop a critical consciousness (that is, conscientization)."[11]

In both Mezirow's cognitive rational approach and Freire's emancipatory approach, students construct new knowledge from interpretations of new and old experiences. Knowledge is not just out there somewhere waiting to be discovered. "While Freire's focus is social-justice, Mezirow concentrates on the importance of rational thought and reflection in the transformative learning process."[12]

---

[10] D. Solorzano, "Teaching and Social Change," in *Education Is Politics: Critical Teaching across Differences, Postsecondary*, eds. I. Shor and C. Pari (Portsmouth, NH: Boynton/Cook Publishers, Inc., 2000), 16.

[11] E. W. Taylor, "Transformative Learning Theory," in *Third Update on Adult Learning Theory*, ed. S. B. Merriam, New Directions for Adult and Continuing Education, no. 119, Fall 2008 (San Francisco: Jossey-Bass, 2008), 8.

[12] L. M. Baumgartner, "An Update on Transformational Learning," in *The New Update on Adult Learning Theory*, ed. S. B. Merriam, New Directions for Adult and Continuing Education, no. 89, Spring 2001 (San Francisco: Jossey-Bass, 2001), 17.

DEVELOPMENTAL APPROACH TO TRANSFORMATIVE LEARNING

Laurent Daloz led the movement to understand and promote the developmental approach to transformative learning. In his book *Effective Teaching and Mentoring: Realizing the Transformational Power of Adult Learning Experiences,* Daloz offers three "maps" of adult development—each picturing how adults progressively change.[13] Daloz believed that adult students function in various stages of development due to their individual circumstances, and they look to education for answers to life issues. Although he focuses on an educational response to promote adult development, Daloz embraced the transformative process of learning, through understanding and acting on experience with an emphasis on mentoring. Developmental transformative learning is intuitive and contextual.

SPIRITUAL APPROACH TO TRANSFORMATIVE LEARNING

The secular adult educator embracing the spiritual approach to transformative learning makes a distinction between spirituality and religion. Tisdell explains the terms as follows: "spirituality is about an individual's personal experience or journey toward wholeness, whereas religion is about an organized community of faith."[14] The spiritual transformative model is connected to experiential learning. Although one may have a spiritual experience at a particular moment, the journey of growing in the knowledge of that experience and its resulting life change takes place as a process over time. The spiritual model of transformative learning describes the spiritual experience as one that lifts us from the mundane to see the possible: a shining moment that brings hope, healing, or affirmation.

John Dirkx[15] and Mike Healy[16] promote a connection between spirituality and adult learning. Dirkx focuses on imagination affecting learning through the soul. Healy found that students participating in meditation had a greater self-awareness that contributed to the progression of the transformative

---

[13] L. Daloz, *Effective Teaching and Mentoring: Realizing the Transformational Power of Adult Learning Experiences* (San Francisco: Jossey-Bass, 1986), 43–88.

[14] E. J. Tisdell, "Spirituality and Adult Learning," in *Third Update on Adult Learning Theory,* ed. S. B. Merriam, New Directions for Adult and Continuing Education, no. 119, Fall 2008 (San Francisco, CA: Jossey-Bass, 2008), 28.

[15] Dirkx, "Transformative Learning Theory," 1–14.

[16] M. Healy, "East Meets West: Transformational Learning and Buddhist Meditation," in *AERC 2000, An International Conference: Proceedings from the 41st Annual Adult Education Research Conference,* ed. Sork, T. V. Lee, and R. St. Claire (Vancouver, Canada: University of British Columbia, 2000).

learning process. The spiritual approach to transformative learning involves the extrarational knowledge of self that affects transformation.

Tisdell, in her 2003 study of 31 adult educators and their spiritual lives,[17] reported the following divisions of response: (1) cross-cultural universal experiences such as witnessing birth or giving birth, witnessing death or having a near-death experience; (2) night dreams that coincide with day-time incidents; (3) experiences in nature, meditation, or prayer and exercising a habit of looking for extraordinary in the ordinary process of life; (4) developing a sense of identity as an ongoing process, deconstructing cultural spirituality that had been imposed and reconstructing meaningful spirituality or reframing earlier life experience.

James Fowler, known for "Stages of Faith,"[18] taught at Boston College and Harvard University and currently leads the Center for Ethics in Public Policy and the Professions at Emory University. Using the works of Piaget and Kohlberg, he contributed a synthesis of religious experience and psychology. His "Stages of Faith" model has been recognized by spiritual transformative theorists and has made a significant impact on Christian education. These stages articulate the usual progression of a person's experiences while learning to know God. Although the sample for his study was 359 mostly white people from the Judeo-Christian tradition, his work is significant for both the secular and Christian worlds because he highlights the way people construct knowledge through image and symbol. According to Fowler, the research base for these stages is inclusive of general evidences of faith across religions.[19] A description of Fowler's stages can be found in appendix C. The brief list of Fowler's stages includes the following:

---

[17] E. J. Tisdell, *Exploring Spirituality and Culture in Adult and Higher Education* (San Francisco: Jossey-Bass, 2003).

[18] J. W. Fowler, *Stages of Faith: The Psychology of Human Development and the Quest for Meaning* (San Francisco: Harper & Row, 1981).

[19] J. W. Fowler, *Becoming Adult: Adult Development & Christian Faith, Becoming Christian* (San Francisco: Jossey-Bass Publishers, 2000), 40.

Table 7.1

Fowler's Stages of Faith and Human Becoming[20]

Stage 1	Birth to 2	Primal Faith
Stage 2	2-7	Intuitive-Projective Faith
Stage 3	7-13	Mythic-Literal Faith
Stage 4	Early adolescence	Synthetic-Conventional Faith
Stage 5	20s and 30s	Individuative-Reflective Faith
Stage 6	Mid-life	Conjunctive Faith
Stage 7	Late mid-life to older	Universalizing Faith

In secular adult education, theorists who embrace spiritual transformative learning challenge adult educators to create a space in learning for their students to share spiritual experiences. They further remind educators that the construction of knowledge through spiritual experience is powerful and has the ability to lead the learner to further development. Finally, spiritual transformative learning expresses openness to the possibility of teaching spirituality as part of course content.

Table 7.2

Summary of Major Transformative Learning Theories

COGNITIVE-RATIONAL	EMANCIPATORY	DEVELOPMENTAL	SPIRITUAL
Mezirow	Freire	Daloz	Dirkx
*Constructivist *rational thought *critical reflection *discussion	*Constructivist *empowerment *social justice *champions liberation	*negotiating developmental transitions * need for mentors	*soul-based learning that emphasizes feelings and images *extra-rational

ADDITIONAL APPROACHES TO TRANSFORMATIVE LEARNING

Edward Taylor, in a review of recent research related to transformative learning, says the "focus has shifted somewhat away from the possibility of a transformation in relationship to a particular life event, toward greater interest in factors that shape the transformative experience (critical reflection, holistic approaches, and relationships)."[21] First, transformation has been found to be not only an epistemological change, but also an ontological change. For

---

[20] Fowler, *Stages of Faith*, 119–211, 290.

[21] E. W. Taylor, "Transformative Learning Theory," *Third Update on Adult Learning Theory*, ed. S. B. Merriam, New Directions for Adult and Continuing Education, no. 119, Fall 2008 (San Francisco: Jossey-Bass, 2008), 10. Hereafter "Transformative Learning Theory."

example, Lange's[22] studies suggest that learners must have opportunity to act on new knowledge in order for true transformation to take place. As Christian educators we recognize that action is necessary for true transformation.

Second, more research is being done on the reflection and dialog process. Being reflective is now seen as a developmental process that takes time and experience. Researchers encourage educators to assist learners in developing critical thought processes and rational discourse. This could include the addition of reflective journaling, classroom dialogue, and critical questioning.[23]

Third, there is a new emphasis on a holistic approach involving feelings, intuition, and relationships. Dirkx[24] has encouraged educators to invite the whole person into the learning experience, including personal affect. This means engaging the feelings of the learner throughout the learning process. Internal motivation and impetus for life change does not come without engaging the emotions. Viewing transformative learning holistically also includes attention to the characteristics of relationships needed for critical and reflective dialog. Carter[25] listed the types of relationships found to be most significant for transformation as love relationships (defined as enhanced self-image, friendship), memory relationships (former and deceased individuals), and imaginative relationships (inner-dialogue, meditation).

Fourth, there has been recent interest in why in some instances transformational learning does not take place. What barriers inhibit transformation? One finding was that the learning group might not ask critical questions of one another. Another finding is learning preferences vary. Some learners engage critical reflection through journaling while others seem to need dialogue. This cautions educators to use a variety of approaches to learning, recognizing the variety of individual learning preferences present in any group. In the online setting, studies have found that life experience is particularly significant in giving the learner resources from which to contribute to discussion and respond to questions. "Greater life experience seems to constitute a 'deeper well' from which to draw and react to discussion that emerged among online participants."[26]

---

[22] E. A. Lange, " Transformative and Restorative Learning: A Vital Dialectic for Sustainable Societies," *Adult Education Quarterly* 54, no. 2 (2004) , 121–39.

[23] Taylor, "Transformative Learning Theory," 11.

[24] J. M. Dirkx, "Engaging Emotions in Adult Learning: A Jungian Perspective on Emotion and Transformative Learning," in *Teaching for Change: Fostering Transformative Learning in the Classroom,* ed. E. W. Taylor, New Directions for Adult and Continuing Education, no. 109, Spring 2006 (San Francisco: Jossey-Bass, 2006), 15–26. Available online at Education Research Complete (http://www.ebscohost.com/), accessed January 20, 2009.

[25] T. J. Carter, "The Importance of Talk to Midcareer Women's Development: A Collaborative Inquiry," *Journal of Business Communication* (2002), 39, 55–91.

[26] Taylor, "Transformative Learning Theory," 12.

Fifth, there is an exploration of a cultural-spiritual view of transformative learning[27] that is concerned with "connections between individuals and social structures . . . and notions of intersecting positionalities."[28] Culturally relevant and spiritually grounded transformation takes place through narrative storytelling facilitated by a teacher/collaborator in a supportive group setting. Cross-cultural relationships and spiritual awareness are valued.

Sixth, there is ongoing interest in the intersection of transformative learning and cultural perspective. A race-centric view[29] studies a non-Eurocentric transformative learning—most often African American women.[30] This is similar to Friere's emancipatory transformative learning with the emphasis on social and political ramifications, but different in that the race-centric perspective specifically considers race as the predominate component of analysis. It considers the African consciousness of connectedness with the self, the community, and the universe.[31] This view has three key concepts that foster transformation: "promoting inclusion (giving voice to the historically silenced), promoting empowerment (not self-actualization but belongingness and equity as a cultural member), and learning to negotiate effectively between and across cultures."[32]

Seventh, the planetary view of transformative learning looks at the reorganization of the political, social, and educational systems. "This view recognizes the interconnectedness among universe, planet, natural environment, human community, and personal world. . . . Transformation is not only about how we view our human counterparts; it explores how we, as humans, relate with the physical world."[33]

CRITICAL AND POSTMODERN TRANSFORMATIVE LEARNING

Critical and postmodern perspectives are important to our consideration of transformative learning theory. Both views propose that knowledge is socially and individually constructed rather than knowledge that is a separate entity. Both perspectives focus on the interaction between power and learning.

---

[27] Ibid., 8–9.

[28] E. J. Tisdell, "Feminism," in *International Encyclopedia of Adult Education,* ed. L. M. English (London: Palgrave, 2005), 256.

[29] Taylor, "Transformative Learning Theory," 9.

[30] S. H. Williams, "Black Mama Sauce: Integrating the Theatre of the Oppressed and Afrocentricity in Transformative Learning," ed. C. A. Wiessner, S. R. Meyer, N. L. Pfhal, and P. G. Neaman, *Proceedings of the Fifth International Conference on Transformative Learning* (2003).

[31] Ibid., 463.

[32] Taylor, "Transformative Learning Theory," 9.

[33] Ibid., 9–10.

In spite of these similarities, important differences between the views exist. Critical theorists believe that adult learning is the logical result of combining adult interests with opportunity. A person will know when various aspects of life intersect personal interests. Critical theorists are concerned that both the teacher and peers utilize power to move adult learners to serve the interests of those who are empowered.

Postmodern theorists tend to see "knowledge" as pieces of incomplete information that is not necessarily rational. Different people have different views of the same information. Postmodern theorists feel that power exists in the relationships between learners. Power can be exercised but not possessed. The following table clarifies some of the differences between the two views:

Table 7.3

Comparison of Critical and Postmodern Worldviews[34]

Critical Theory	Postmodernism
Knowledge is a rational product of human interests	Knowledge is tentative, multifaceted, not necessarily rational
Power is possessed by subjects, repressive	Power is expressed by subjects, productive
Knowledge frees subjects from power	Knowledge is an expression of power
Learning is achieved through critical reflection, consciousness raising	Learning is achieved through deconstruction, play, eclecticism

One invaluable contribution of both the critical and postmodern theorists is our understanding of the diversity of the adult learner. Learning is not a generic journey that one takes from point A to point Z; it is the interaction of many different cultures, experiences, and circumstances and is intertwined with power and politics.

NEUROSCIENCE TRANSFORMATIVE LEARNING

Neuroscience is the last of the new transformative trends we will discuss. For many years scholars have known that the physiological and psychological well-being of the very young child is linked to learning capability. Scientist have demonstrated that the brain develops rapidly from prenatal to two years of age and that healthy brain development requires good nutrition, adequate sleep, a positive emotional environment, and sensory stimulation. In light of this, the current trend is for educators to get information out to parents so that they will know how to care for young children and support their brain development. Educators and social service organizations have also provided early

---

[34] D. Kilgore, "Critical and Postmodern Perspectives on Adult Learning," in *The New Update on Adult Learning Theory,* ed. S. B. Merriam, New Directions for Adult and Continuing Education, no. 89, Spring 2001 (San Francisco: Jossey-Bass, 2001), 59.

intervention programs for impoverished children who may not have access to appropriate support.

BRAIN CELL STRUCTURE New developments in the field of medicine, particularly in the area of medical imaging, have allowed researchers to discover what actually happens in the brain. They can trace brain activity not only in young children, but also in adult brains. "The human brain has 100 to 200 billion neurons, or nerve cells that store and transmit information, many of which have thousands of connections with other neurons."[35] Most body cells are tightly packed together, but neurons have spaces between them called synapses. In these synapses, fibers from different neurons reach for one another but do not touch. Most cells in the body live, die, and get replaced. Brain cells (neurons) change rather than get replaced—especially during learning.[36] When stimulated by learning experiences, neurons release chemicals that carry the messages from one neuron to the next. By observing (through imaging) the chemical changes taking place in the brain during the learning process, scientists understand more about the structure of the brain and the function of the different sections of the brain during the actual process of learning.

NEURON NETWORKING In addition, scientists have learned that the density of the fiber network between neurons is the direct result of a healthy environment. Imaging of an infant's brain at one month shows there is little density. If the infant is nurtured, given good nutrition, and stimulated through language and experiences, that same infant's brain will show a much increased neuron density at six months. Although changes do not occur as rapidly, adult brains do respond as they experience new learning. The more complex the learning experiences, the more interconnected the neurons and the stronger the connections between the neurons.[37] Follow-up learning experiences increase the number of dendrites. Dendrites are the hair-like projections from the cell body that receive information from other cells. The network of

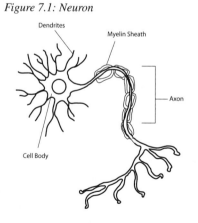

Figure 7.1: Neuron

Dendrites

Myelin Sheath

Axon

Cell Body

---

[35] L. E. Berk, *Exploring Lifespan Development* (San Francisco: Allyn and Bacon, 2008), 93.

[36] Taylor and A. Lamoreaux, "Teaching with the Brain in Mind," In *Third Update on Adult Learning Theory* 119 (San Francisco: Jossey-Bass, 2008), 50.

[37] Ibid.

dendrites becomes thicker, which shortens the synapse between neurons, tightening the connections. If, however, the learning experiences decrease or stop, the dendrites widen.

For example, if you conducted brain imaging on twin adult pharmacy graduates, the density of the cellular structure of their brains may look similar. Over time, however, they may differ. Suppose 10 years pass and the first pharmacist has been working in a large hospital pharmacy where she constantly handles new drugs and receives new information. The second pharmacist had a motorcycle accident the month after leaving pharmacy school and has spent the 10 years incapacitated in a care facility. After again conducting brain imaging, you would discover that the first pharmacist has expanded and thickened the complexity of her original dendrite network, while the second pharmacist's neuron network has thinned.

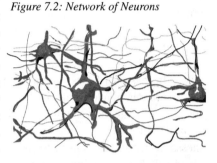

Figure 7.2: Network of Neurons

THE AGING BRAIN   The aging adult brain has also been studied at different decades of life. For many years researchers believed that as the adult brain aged, it became less flexible and lost neurons without the capability of replacing them so that all people eventually lost their brain functions as they aged. Scientists have now come to understand that the quality of function in the aging brain is not linked as much to the number of neurons (except in the case of severe trauma) as it is to the density of the connections between neurons. The adult brain is capable of continuing to create new connections and to strengthen networks within groups of neurons even as it ages.

The old adage "If you don't use it, you lose it" is true of the adult brain. When adult brains were examined postmortem, researchers confirmed that education increases the complexity of the neuron networks, but the networks diminish unless new learning experiences continue. We now understand that the aging brain not only needs stimulation, but it needs quality stimulation— new learning.

For example, an elderly person who does interlocking picture puzzles has a developed competency with a matching neuron density. He may increase the density of the neuron network as he becomes more and more competent with increased puzzle-solving experience. If the puzzle-solving becomes easy and "old hat," however, the density may no longer thicken. It may even decrease. On the other hand, if the elderly puzzler continues to challenge himself by learning to solve new types of puzzles—perhaps Sudoku or crossword—his brain will respond with changes and new networks. Clearly, if we desire to preserve mental function throughout the aging process, we must continually challenge the brain to learn something new.

In senior brains, continuous learning is not the only factor in brain performance. Like the infant brain, adult brains need general physical and psychological health. Brain research with the elderly has demonstrated these "four factors help to retain mental agility: (1) education, (2) strenuous activity, (3) adequate lung function, and (4) the absence of chronic disease."[38] Health and learning therefore, rather than age, are more important factors in retaining quality brain function. Mental agility depends on a healthy, active, disease-free body that is constantly learning new things. Seniors need to be challenged to leave the rocking chair behind and to continue engaging the world around them. Learning new concepts supports a healthy brain.

THE LEARNING PROCESS   As scientists viewed the chemical changes in the brain during adult learning, it became apparent that different parts of the brain are used during the different stages of learning. The configuration of brain structure is important to learning. The neocortex of the brain uses a directional process for handling external signals. A person receives environmental signals through the senses (hearing, seeing, tasting, touching, smelling) from changes in the physical environment. The back area of the neocortex of the brain is responsible for associating multiple sensory input and grouping it with memories of old sensory input. These associations are often slow and may occur during periods of reflection or sleep. The associated clumps of sensory information then travels to the front portion of the brain. The front portion of the brain is responsible for conscious associations, manipulation of sensory and memory experiences, creativity, and problem-solving. This front portion of the brain then sends signals to the motor areas of the body, thus initiating and controlling movement.

---

[38] L. H. Hill, "The Brain and Consciousness: Sources of Information for Understanding Adult Learning," in *The New Update on Adult Learning Theory*, ed. S. B. Merriam, New Directions for Adult and Continuing Education, no. 89, Spring 2001 (San Francisco: Jossey-Bass, 2001), 76.

Figure 7.2

Directionality in the neocortex [39]

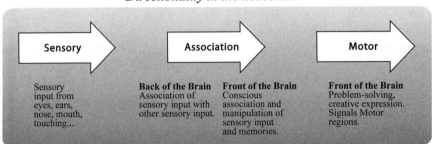

Sensory	Association		Motor
Sensory input from eyes, ears, nose, mouth, touching...	**Back of the Brain** Association of sensory input with other sensory input.	**Front of the Brain** Conscious association and manipulation of sensory input and memories.	**Front of the Brain** Problem-solving, creative expression. Signals Motor regions.

When the brain receives sensory input, it records the input as experience. New experience can create new brain constructs, can retrieve old constructs, or can reconstruct existing constructs within the brain. When storing new learning experiences, the brain looks for similar earlier experiences (constructs/ memories) in order to connect the new to what already exists. Retention is increased if a suitable link to earlier information is found, and retention is more difficult if there are no connections. It is therefore important that educators consciously create connections to the life experiences of adults in order to build current connections to existing neuron complexes.

According to Zull, "learning experiences should be designed to use the four major areas of the neocortex (sensory, back-integrative, front-integrative, and motor). This leads to identification of four fundamental pillars of learning: gathering, reflecting, creating, and testing."[40] These phases of learning seem familiar as one compares them to other models of transformative learning. "Gathering" is the assimilation of data through sensory experiences. "Reflecting" occurs in the back of the brain where the sensory data is merged into larger more meaningful images. This merging involves attaching value to people and experiences. It also involves the association of new experiences with old. "Creating" happens when the front of the brain receives the associated data from the back of the brain, retrieves the relevant concepts, facts, or meanings, and inserts them into "working memory."[41] This becomes the basis for conscious thought and planning. "Testing" occurs when an individual acts upon the new information. The front of the neocortex gives signals to the motor receivers and actions result.

---

[39] J. E. Zull, "Key Aspects of How the Brain Learns," in *The Neuroscience of Adult Learning*, ed. S. Johnson & K. Taylor, New Directions for Adult and Continuing Education, no. 110, Summer 2006 (San Francisco: Jossey-Bass, 2006), 3.

[40] Ibid., 5.

[41] Ibid., 6.

LEARNING AND EMOTIONS   Emotion affects all stages of learning. The regions of the neocortex are enmeshed in networks of special neurons that come from the brain stem and deliver chemicals that are linked to emotions. The emotion chemicals directly affect the signaling systems.[42]

> A moderate level of arousal—where the learner is attentive and motivated to learn— maximizes the biochemical processes that drive the protein synthesis necessary for modifying neural structures. Though they can be disconnected by fear and anxiety, activation of both affective and cognitive circuits allows executive brain systems to coordinate their activity in support of learning.[43]

The learner needs to be motivated and attentive to learning throughout the learning process. The learner must both think and feel. Opportunity should be given for reflection and association so that students can process data and make the associations while attaching appropriate emotions. Support and encouragement must come from the educator as the learner builds confidence in the learning processes.

Negative emotions inhibit the learning process. Such emotions as fear, stress, and anxiety can emerge from a stressful learning environment or from memories of past experiences. Educators, who pressure students to learn, motivate students by the threat of negative consequences, or use humiliation tactics produce long-term negative effects on students. The brain holds negative emotions in memory and resists releasing them.

> As an individual feels threatened, he or she moves along the arousal continuum from left to right. The further along he or she is on this continuum, the less capable he or she will be of learning or retrieving cognitive content; in essence, fear destroys the capacity to learn.[44]

A person with a background of education failure or humiliation will move along this continuum much faster than a person who has a secure self-image and happens to be in a negative learning environment. As the student's feelings of fear increase, the "fight or flight" impulse takes over. Students may respond by becoming angry, leaving the premises, or they may shut down and dissociate from the learning environment. Students who exhibit poor behavior or inattentiveness may really be dissociated because of past or present fear.

---

[42] Ibid., 7.

[43] L. Cozolino & S. Sprokay, "Neuroscience and Adult Learning," in *The Neuroscience of Adult Learning,* ed. S. Johnson and K. Taylor, New Directions for Adult and Continuing Education, no. 110, Summer 2006 (San Francisco: Jossey-Bass, 2006), 12–13.

[44] B. D. Perry, "Fear and Learning: Trauma-Related Factors in the Adult Education Process," in *The Neuroscience of Adult Learning,* ed S. Johnson and K. Taylor, New Directions for Adult and Continuing Education, no. 110, Summer 2006 (San Francisco: Jossey-Bass, 2006), 23.

Figure 7.4

Fear and the Capacity for Learning

The first priority for all educators is to create trust and safety in the learning environment. Teachers may help students deal with negative emotions from the past by reflective narration and journaling, which enable them to retell their stories and work through their negative emotions.[45] Many neuroscientists suggest that mentoring helps to reduce the fear factor and maximize learning.

MENTORS AND LEARNING   As educators, many of us are more comfortable with the classroom expectations of teacher/student than with the relationship of mentor/student. However, we know from multiple theorists, including Janik's study of traumatic learning, that mentoring is an important component of transformative learning. Mentoring involves vulnerability on the part of the educator as "a mentor shows students how he or she is learning and demonstrates trust in both his or her own and the student's learning process."[46]

Classroom learning can become easier for both the learner and the teacher as the teacher masters the course content and the students become dependent on the teacher to impart knowledge. With mentoring, learning does not become easier.

> Mentorship directly supports independent, critical listening, reading, writing, and thinking. The mentor doesn't get in the way; his or her ideas simply become irrelevant. Learners learn, through observing mentors in the act of learning, that the disquieting feelings that arise before making discovery are "normal" and not a sign of weakness, inexperience, lack of effort, or incompetence.[47]

Unlike many teachers, a good mentor measures effectiveness by the richness of the learning environment not by great teaching skills. The goal is for the student to acquire personal critical thinking skills.

---

[45] For additional information on how to do this, see Cozolino and Sprokay, "Neuroscience," 16.

[46] D. S. Janik, *Unlock the Genius Within: Neurobiological Trauma, Teaching, and Transformative Learning* (Lanham, MD: Rowman & Littlefield Education, 2005), 51.

[47] Ibid., 52.

CONCLUSIONS FOR NEUROSCIENCE AND ADULT LEARNING   The brain research now available demonstrates that adults are very capable learners. We suggest, therefore, the following conclusions: (1) the experiences of adults are different from other age learners, and, therefore, the construction of their brain connections are different; (2) age does not diminish the healthy adult's ability to learn; (3) adults learn best through contextually related learning; (4) positive emotions and relationships are linked to effective recall; (5) multisensory learning increases both short-term and long-term memory; (6) connecting new learning experiences to past or present experiences brings relevance and increases learning; (7) successful adult learning experiences connect them to the world around them through new values and new relationships; and (8) the potential for learning and brain growth is life-long.[48]

Although we as Christian educators can find some value in most of the approaches to adult learning theory, the physiological information about learning discovered in the neuroscience transformative theory is perhaps the most helpful. Our scientific discovery confirms biblical truth as we remember the stories of Jesus. He mentored/taught His disciples as they wandered Palestine. Together they experienced lessons from life and acted on their newfound knowledge.

TRANSFORMATIVE LEARNING IN CHRISTIAN EDUCATION

The concepts of transformative learning theory are important for the adult Bible teacher. Its major emphasis is teaching for change, and change is the point of Bible teaching. Yet there are differences between transformative learning theory and Christian education. These differences must be discussed lest instructional ideas are blindly embraced.

There are three major differences between the general premises of most transformative learning and Christian thought: (1) Transformative theorists generally believe that all truth and knowledge is relative. We, as Christians, understand that our lives are based on the absolute truth of Jesus Christ and Scripture. (2) Most transformative theorists put great value on inclusiveness and acceptance. The moral aspects of right and wrong are less significant. While Christians believe in loving and accepting others, we cannot accept the sin of others. That is, we love the person but not always their ideas and actions. Christians believe that God loves people unconditionally. He accepts us for the flawed creatures we are and offers his son Jesus as our redemption. God, however, never loves or accepts our sin. He sent Jesus to die in our place to pay the penalty for sin so that we could enter His heaven without sin. He

---

[48] Hill, "The Brain and Consciousness," in Merriam, *New Directions,* 79.

calls us to love others in the same way. We are to love people unconditionally but to hate their sin. Indeed, we are to love ourselves but hate our own sin as well. (3) Transformative theorists generally believe that a major purpose of dialog is to merge ideas into the greater truth. Students are to dialogue in order to morph their personal understanding of truth with that of others. The Christian engages in dialogue, hoping to influence others through a clear understanding of Scripture, positive Christian experience, and genuine compassion for all in need. Christians may learn significantly through dialogue, but in the end, commitment to the lordship of Jesus Christ and the authority of the Bible shape our understanding of truth. We cannot negotiate on those points.

In the third part of the book we will develop a model for transformactional teaching. It is a model informed by adult education learning theory where it is consistent with principles found in Scripture. Transformactional teaching seeks to integrate the two. No Bible teacher can teach without knowledge of the Bible, which we discussed in part 1. Similarly, no teacher of adults can be successful without the knowledge of recent adult learning theory, which we discussed in part 2.

SUMMARY OF TRANSFORMATIVE LEARNING THEORY

The strength of transformational learning theory is its emphasis on change. The transformational views that emphasize changes in the individual are: cognitive-rational, developmental, spiritual, and neurobiological. These models are psychologically centered, and each model views learning as a more universal concept. The models of transformational learning theory that are culturally centered look for change to occur within society. They are emancipatory, race-centered, planetary, and cultural-spiritual. These models emphasize the individual's position within a cultural context. They stress that transformative learning not only changes the view of one's "self," but it also addresses needed changes in the larger cultural and societal context. As an extension of learning into the natural world, planetary learning occurs within and is directed toward improving ecology.

Transformative teaching methodology emphasizes a safe learning environment free from the coercion of power and influence. Each learner is responsible to be prepared, to contribute to discussion, and to maintain respect for other participants. The educator focuses on collaborative learning, defined as moving the student from teacher dependence to peer interaction. Both educator and students understand that each learner brings to every learning experience a frame of reference shaped by culture and personal experience.

For transformative learning to take place, reflective discourse occurs through mutual acceptance and genuine attempts to understand individual frames of reference. The learners explore both personal ideas and the ideas of others. Together and interactively they reshape the frames of reference of the entire group. Ultimately, they explore, embrace, and act out these redefined frames of reference.

Originally, Mezirow defined transformative learning theory as linear. He understood that a single dramatic event moves the learner toward transformation. As the concepts of transformative learning multiply, transformative learning is both fluid and cumulative. Additionally, transformation is relational, built on trust, and is inextricably intertwined with culture and context. It presents the challenge that the educator must be willing to both facilitate transformation and be personally transformed in the process. It is a willingness to change together.

TEACHING TOOLS FROM TRANSFORMATIVE LEARNING

1. Teachers must not exert power and control over the adult learner.
2. Teachers must empower learners by providing learning tools and inspiring confidence.
3. Teachers understand that retention is enhanced when learning is accompanied by positive emotion and they provide a supportive emotional environment for learning.
4. Teachers should use multi-sensory methods for sharing new information and should create a multi-sensory environment for students to experience new knowledge.
5. Teachers must create opportunities for learners to connect new learning with previous learning experiences.
6. Teachers provide adults with opportunity for reflection and dialog.
7. Teachers provide students with opportunities for collaboration.
8. Teachers provide students with opportunities to connect learning to problem-solving.
9. Learning results in life-change.

Exercise 7.1
(rate yourself, 1 being poor and 5 being terrific)

1. I empower my students by providing tools for learning and emotional support.	1	2	3	4	5
2. I provide a loving and safe environment for my students.	1	2	3	4	5
3. I use multi-sensory experiences to share new material with students.	1	2	3	4	5
4. I create a multi-sensory environment for discovery learning.	1	2	3	4	5
5. I give students opportunity to connect new information with previous learning experiences.	1	2	3	4	5
6. I give students opportunity for reflection.	1	2	3	4	5
7. I give students opportunity for collaboration.	1	2	3	4	5
8. I teach for life-change.	1	2	3	4	5

PART THREE

THE STAR METHOD OF TRANSFORMACTIONAL TEACHING

THE PAST 50 YEARS have seen significant progress in adult learning research and theories. The information proves invaluable in both secular and biblical education with one major distinction: the view of absolute knowledge and truth. Many secular educational theorists view all knowledge as relative: learning is viewed as a negotiation of changing and emerging truth. Truth is embraced as the product of the observations and experiences of the learners. In contrast, Evangelical Christians believe that "all truth is God's truth."[1] Christians understand that truth is absolute. All truth must be consistent with and not contrary to the inerrant Word of God: "the supreme standard by which all human conducts, creeds, and religious opinions should be tried."[2] The question then becomes: "What does the Christian educator do with learning theory?"

Adult learning theory has much to say to those who teach Bible to adults. Even a cursory reading of part 2 of this book reveals the multiple points of contact between adult learning theory and Christian education. In part 3 we explore many of these points of contact with reference to their essential nature in teaching. Some of the principles evident in adult learning theory seem to come almost directly from biblical principles, if not biblical texts.

Many of the principles from adult learning theory are demonstrated in Scripture by the Master Teacher Jesus, and by His apostles. In his chapter in the book *The Teaching Ministry of the Church*, Rick Yount explains in detail

---

[1] D. Dockery, "The Divine-Human Authorship of Inspired Scripture," in *Authority and Interpretation: A Baptist Perspective*, eds. D. Garrett and R. Melick (Grand Rapids: Baker Book House, 1987), 13.

[2] Southern Baptist Convention, *The Baptist Faith and Message* (Nashville: LifeWay Christian Resources, 2000).

the role of Jesus the teacher.[3] When viewed in light of Scripture, principles of adult learning theory can help the Christian educator maximize adult learning. When we acknowledge that Jesus, the Master Teacher, did not merely lecture, we should be challenged as pastors and Bible teachers to strive for more effective avenues of communication.

The following table is a list of 14 principles for biblical adult learning. Some of the principles are found in Scripture. Others are found in adult learning theory and are modeled in Scripture. The former come from the Bible, special revelation. Other helpful principles come from natural revelation as serious thinkers have observed the way God's world operates. We believe both sources of truth have value to the Christian educator.

These principles are used in the Star Method of Transformactional Bible Teaching. In the table, we have identified the 14 major principles gleaned from adult learning theory and correlated them with Scripture passages that either teach or demonstrate each principle. These 14 foundational principles are identified at the beginning of each of the chapters of the Star Method Transformactional Teaching that follow.

The Star Method uses the image of a star. The center of the star is the goal of a Christian's life and that of Christian education: Christlikeness. The five points of the star represent the five parts of the transformactional teaching model. The points of the model include information about the Christian teacher, the teaching/learning process, and a guide for effective lesson plans. All of the information included is based on the 14 principles from adult learning theory and Scripture. The points of the star are: relationship, relevance, revelation, responsibility, and results.

The five sections of the model do not operate in isolation. Though they represent different subjects, they also interconnect. Thus they move from the center of the star outward. To indicate the interconnectedness of these five, we have called each chapter "Connecting" in relationship to the points of the star. This is additionally reinforced visually by the fact that a chain connects the points. Thus the interconnectedness comes from the "inside," from the essence of the star as well as the points relating to each other as they move outward.

As part of the last four points of the Star Method, the lesson plan is presented. While the lesson plan is only a part of the philosophy of teaching and learning, it is an important part. We have provided examples of biblical passages and teaching methods that could well be used to engage the adult

---

[3] R. Yount, "Jesus the Master Teacher," in *The Teaching Ministry of the Church: Integrating Biblical Truth with Contemporary Application*, ed. D. Eldridge (Nashville: Broadman & Holman, 1995), 21–42.

Adult Learning Theory and Scripture

Principle	Adult Learning Theory	Bible Reference
1. The Bible teacher demonstrates a consistent pattern of commitment to Christ and Christlike life choices.		Running the race like those before. Heb 12:1-2. The heroes of the faith were faithful. We should be too.
2. Both Bible teacher and learner grow in their understanding of Scripture and in obedient life choices as they respond to a growing knowledge of God through Scripture.	Neuroscience Learning Theory	Paul's humility. 1 Cor. 3:18-23. Paul warns the church that they, and their leaders, stand together under God's judgment.
3. Scripture is absolute truth and is the standard for life.		Jesus' rebuke of Sadduccees. Mstt 22:29-32. They erred in their understanding of life because they did not know the Scriptures.
4. The teacher must not exert power over the learner or impose any agenda, but rather empower the learner with tools and confidence in his own learning.	Transformative Learning Theory Critical Learning Theory Neuroscience Learning Theory	Paul's conduct, 1 Thess. 2:2-12. Paul came "gentle among them," allowing them to derive the truth of the message.
5. Learning is enhanced when the learning takes place in a loving, safe environment of acceptance and mutual respect.	Andragogy Learning Theory Neuroscience Learning Theory	All parts of the body of Christ honored and respected. 1 Cor 12:12-26.
6. Adults are treated like adults and are responsible for their own learning.	Andragogy Learning Theory	Paul's exhortation to Corinth. 1 Cor 11:13-16. After providing theological instruction, Paul urged them to "judge for themselves" about the matter.
7. Motivation to learn is enhanced when adult learners know the purpose for learning.	Andragogy Learning Theory	Lazarus died at Bethany. John 11:4 Jesus gave the purpose for Lazarus' death so he could teach them about death and resurrection.
8. Retention of learning increases when learners have multisensory experiences gathering new information through discovery and experience.	Neuroscience LearningTheory	Serving others. John 13:1-17. Jesus gives a visual and kinesthetic learning experience (washing feet) so they would learn the lesson of service. (also Matt. 17:24-27)
9.Retention of learning increases when, through reflection, the learner connects new learning to memories of previous experience.	Transformative Learning Theory Neuroscience Learning Theory	Parable of the Lost Sheep, Luke 15:3-7. Jesus used a familiar vocation (shepherding) to help them understand. (Also Col. 2:6).
10. Bible learning is a lifelong process that should move from teacher-directed to self-directed as the teacher changes roles to match the learner's needs.	Andragogy Learning Theory Self-Directed Learning Theory Transformative Learning Theory	Immaturity. Hebrews 5:13. Christians are not to stay students but to mature to deeper truth and to share it. (also 1 Cor. 4:26; Luke 9:10-14).
11. Retention of learning increases when learning is accompanied by emotion.	Neuroscience Learning Theory	Obedience will bring greater mutual joy. I John 1:1-4. Joy is deeper than emotion, but involves emotions.
12. Retention of learning increases through collaboration and reflective dialogue.	Self-Directed Learning Theory Transformative Learning Theory	The Jerusalem Council. Acts 15:6-7. Apostles and elders debated the issue together before resolution.
13. Learning and retention is enhanced when problem-solving is employed.	Andragogy Learning Theory Neuroscience Learning Theory	Jesus' question to the Pharisees "Whose son is the Messiah?" Matt 22:41-46. Jesus pointed to a "problem text" of the Old Testament and asked them to solve it.
14.Learning is the negotiation of one's reality in light of new insight, resulting in change.	Transformative Learning Theory	Peter's confession and Jesus' challenge to him for future ministry. Matt 16:13-20.

learner. Methodology can become quite complex with the variety of methods and their relationship to learning preferences. For that reason, we present many methods in an appendix, along with suggestions as to which part of the lesson plan they may have most relevance.

Part 3 is where the "rubber meets the road." It integrates adult learning theory and biblical truths. It suggests methods and means of communicating, understanding, and implementing the teaching/learning processes. It is a practical section, intended to guide the adult Bible teacher in a step-by-step understanding of the wonderful privilege of teaching.

CHAPTER EIGHT

CONNECTING RELATIONSHIP: TO GOD AND SCRIPTURE

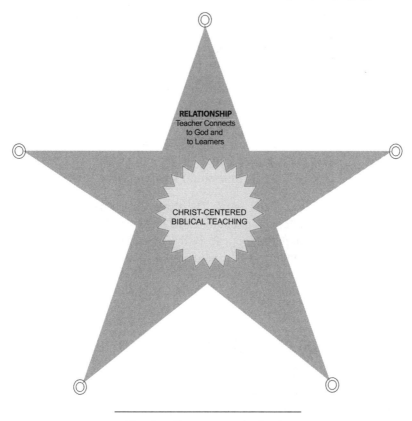

RELATIONSHIP
Teacher Connects
to God and
to Learners

CHRIST-CENTERED
BIBLICAL TEACHING

Teacher Connects to Authority

THE FIRST POINT OF the Star Method of Transformactional Teaching is about connecting relationships. It is the longest of the Star points because it includes one's relationship to God, Scripture, and the learners. For that reason, Star Point 1 takes two chapters. The first is "Connecting to God and Scripture." The second is "Connecting to the Learner."

This Chapter Covers

1. *The teacher's relationship to God.* The teacher's spiritual life seriously impacts the teaching/learning environment and relationships. We discussed this at length in part 1, "Understanding the Bible and Hermeneutics," as well as elsewhere. If the teacher does not seek to live according to biblical patterns, the learners will likely suffer in their lives as well.
2. *The teacher's relationship to the Bible.* This chapter contains the Star Model of Transformactional Bible Study that demonstrates how to approach Scripture with a view to knowing the passage accurately. In chapters 10–13, we will present how to construct an effective lesson plan, point by point. This chapter is preparation. Without good content, there is no point to teaching. This is one of the most important of the Star points.

This Chapter Includes the Following
Transformactional Principles

- *Transformactional Principle 1:* The Bible teacher demonstrates a consistent pattern of commitment to Christ and Christlike life choices.
- *Transformactional Principle 2:* Both Bible teacher and learner grow in their understanding of Scripture and in obedient life choices as they respond to a growing knowledge of God through Scripture.
- *Transformactional Principle 3:* Scripture is absolute truth and is the standard for life.

CONNECTING RELATIONSHIP WITH GOD

Throughout the remainder of this book we will describe what we call the Star Method of Transformactional Teaching. The method builds on the principles of the first two parts of the book, "Understanding the Bible and Hermeneutics" and "Foundational Theories of Adult Learning."

Being connected to God means, first of all, being saved. Salvation is the genesis, the process, and the end of becoming Christlike. At conversion, we receive the indwelling presence of the Holy Spirit, who has already opened the eyes of the seeker's soul to the truth of salvation. Now resident within the believer, the Holy Spirit connects the believer to God the Father through interpreting the truth of Scripture and urging obedience. As the believer responds to God in prayer and obedience, God continues to reveal more of Himself through the Bible and the Holy Spirit.

Through this growth process believers become more knowledgeable of themselves as Christians. They find intuitively the desire to follow Christ consistently as well as the desire to serve within the body of believers. Serving God is not an option; it is the obedient response to knowing God (2 Cor 5:15). The growing believer begins to exercise spiritual gifts (1 Corinthians 12) as part of the body of believers. Salvation, both an event and a process, dynamically transforms believers until we reach the perfection that comes at the final resurrection.

Learners tend to imitate the lives of their teachers whether we desire it or not. Modeling a mature faith is essential. Hebrews 13:7 says, "Remember your leaders who have spoken God's word to you. As you carefully observe the outcome of their lives, imitate their faith." Modeling a mature faith includes practicing God's presence in the daily fluctuations of life. The teacher's growing and maturing faith becomes the pattern for the learner to imitate. God takes an interest in process. Are you more like Christ today than yesterday? Can the learners see your faith growing and permeating every life choice? Exemplary living can only be accomplished through the supernatural power of God operating through submission and total commitment.

Teaching Scripture should bring an overwhelming sense of humility. God warns teachers about the seriousness of their task. James 3:1 says, "Not many should become teachers, my brothers, knowing that we will receive a stricter judgment." The Bible teacher stands before God—responsible to teach and affirm the truth of Scripture. A personal relationship with Jesus Christ in salvation, a life of obedience to Scripture as revealed by the Holy Spirit, and a consistency of life characterized by personal holiness enhance and enable proper understanding of Scripture.

Growing in Christlikeness includes modeling right relationships in marriage and family. A survey of the New Testament reveals the importance of the family in God's economy. As noted in the first section of chapter 5, "Understanding Spiritual Growth," the desire for proper family relationships is one of the new ambitions God implants at conversion. God's model for marriage is the relationship of Jesus to the church. This is explicitly stated in Eph 5:22–33, the most extended analogy between marriage and Jesus and the church.

Clearly, each member of the family has a role to play in the successful family. The husband is to love and nurture his wife as Christ loves and nurtures the church. The wife is to respect and submit to her husband, as the church is to respect and submit to Christ. The apostle Paul expected that maintaining proper marriage relationships was a prerequisite to leadership in the church.

In 1 Cor 11:2–16 he addressed a problem of the women not honoring their husbands. His advice was that such women could not pray nor prophesy in the church until they corrected their errant attitudes. Similarly, no man was qualified to be bishop or deacon unless he related well to his family (1 Tim 3:4–5,12; Titus 1:5–6). These Bible texts indicate the importance of both husband and wife living in proper relationship to each other as an act of obedience to God.

God expects Christians to demonstrate proper relationships with others for whom they are responsible. They are to respect and understand their children, being godly examples for them to follow (Eph 6:4; Col 3:21). In the first century slaves were also considered a part of the extended family, and, therefore, Christians had explicit responsibility to honor and respect them as well (Eph 6:9; Col 4:1). Though Christians should never participate in or promote slavery, the principle rings clear: Christians are to maintain proper relationships with all for whom they are responsible in their family circles and elsewhere.

The family is the best available picture of God. It is also the model of God most easily observed by the world around us. Christian families should model the Trinity: each seeking maturity in Christ and each relating to the other properly. It should be an easy step for observers of the Christian family to accept the loving fatherhood of God and respectful submission to Christ because they see it modeled effectively in the Christian home. The person seeking to establish and maintain relationships as God outlined them in Scripture is powerful. Improper relationships interfere with the work of the Holy Spirit in teaching. When teachers fail to live according to biblical standards, the Holy Spirit has to work *in spite of* instead of *in harmony with* them.

CONNECTING RELATIONSHIP TO SCRIPTURE

THE NATURE OF THE BIBLE

In part 1 of the book we discussed the nature and authority of Scripture. As with the teacher's relationship with God, the teacher's relationship to the Bible is foundational. For that reason, some of the basic principles bear brief repetition here.[1]

The Bible teacher must first know and affirm that the Bible is true. Teachers must know the content of the passage selected for teaching and submit their study of the text to the interpretation and leadership of the Holy Spirit. The

---

[1] The reader is reminded of the content of part 1, "Understanding the Bible and Hermeneutics." This brief restatement intends to recall the heart of that discussion.

Bible teacher must place the Bible in its proper setting. That includes understanding the content and cultural background of the Scripture passage. It also includes the textual context: how the passage fits into the whole of Scripture, the book in which it was written, and the immediate context of the surrounding passages. The biblical educator accumulates this knowledge by engaging in serious study of the passage.

At the core of our Christian faith is the knowledge that God chose to reveal Himself to us and that His revelation is true. The Bible is one important way God has provided for us to know Him. A person's view of Scripture, therefore, is of the utmost importance. It influences both knowledge and practice. A correct view of Scripture involves at least four components: revelation, inspiration, inerrancy, and authority.

REVELATION Scripture is a special revelation of God to us—second only to Jesus who is revealed in Scripture. The written Word bears witness to the Living Word. Scripture speaks propositionally. Although special revelation does not require a response to justify its validity, special revelation challenges us to action. A correct view of Scripture includes obedience to revealed Truth (John 7:17).

Revelation is also progressive: "later revelation builds upon earlier revelation. It is complementary and supplementary to it, not contradictory."[2] New Testament truth builds on Old Testament truth. Jesus often quoted the Old Testament as truth (Matt 5:27–29). Scripture, as a special revelation of God, allows us to know about God, to grow in our knowledge and practice, and to share the knowledge of God with others.

INSPIRATION Scripture is not only revealed Truth; it is also inspired Truth. Inspiration indicates that the Holy Spirit superintended the writing of the original documents of the 66 books of the Old and New Testament, resulting in accurate revelation—the Word of God. "All Scripture is breathed out by God" (2 Tim 3:16 ESV). Plenary verbal inspiration indicates that God inspired both the individual words and the entirety of the original text. Although God allowed the writings to be influenced by the personalities and backgrounds of the authors, He protected His revelation from error.

INERRANCY The inerrancy of Scripture means that God-inspired revelation is truth without any mixture of error and is reliable for faith and practice. Scripture is the standard of truth for every area of the believer's life:

---

[2] M. Erickson, *Christian Theology*, vol. 1 (Grand Rapids: Baker, 1983), 197.

"inerrancy applies to all areas of knowledge, since all truth is God's truth."[3] It also extends to miracles and historical recordings such as Genesis 1–3. The principles for faith and practice apply to all people in all periods of history. Most important, Jesus, God's plan for the salvation of mankind, embodies essential Truth—the foundation of our Christian beliefs.

AUTHORITY Finally, Scripture is the ultimate authority for faith and practice. The Bible is the standard of measurement by which we measure all other influences in our cultural context, " the supreme standard by which all human conducts, creeds, and religious opinions should be tried."[4] As the complete authority over Christian practice, the Bible demands action—obedience to its truth (Heb 4:12). The Holy Spirit, operating within believers as they interact with Scripture, illumines the understanding of the believer by bringing comprehension and conviction of truth.

THE ROLE OF THE HOLY SPIRIT

Along with a strong foundational view of Scripture, one must acknowledge the need for the presence of the Holy Spirit in the life of the teacher and the learner. The Holy Spirit operates to convict us of sin and bring us to salvation (Eph 1:17–18). At conversion, the Holy Spirit lives within us and illuminates the truth of Scripture to us so that we can understand and obey God in faith and practice—growing in Christlikeness (John 14:26; 16:13). Refusal to obey God's Word as revealed to us hinders the operation of the Holy Spirit in our lives and stunts our growth as Christians (1 Cor 3:1–3).

In his book *Spirit-Filled Teaching,*[5] Roy Zuck does a comprehensive study of the work of the Holy Spirit and teaching Scripture. He explains that the claim of the Holy Spirit's leadership cannot become a license for tangential interpretation. The Holy Spirit facilitates logical and usual understanding. Zuck gives 14 propositions for evaluating the operation of the Holy Spirit in biblical interpretation (see appendix D). Zuck's eighth proposition explains that the work of the Holy Spirit does not substitute for study of the text. Teachers must study and obey God's Word and lead learners in doing the same.

TRANSFORMACTIONAL BIBLE STUDY

When friends suffer from medical incompetence, it shakes our faith in medical professionals. As consumers, we fear when we realize that our physical

---

[3] Dockery, *Authority and Interpretation,* 13–43.
[4] *The Baptist Faith and Message* (2000).
[5] R. Zuck, *Spirit-Filled Teaching: The Power of the Holy Spirit in Your Ministry,* ed. C. Swindoll (Nashville: Word Publishing, 1998).

lives sometimes lie in incompetent hands. We feel that death from negligence or incompetence cannot be excused. Biblical educators teach the Word of Life to people sick with sin or discouraged with the bruises of life. They are searching for the truth of God's Word to find eternal life and to apply healing to their spiritual illness and wounds.

Teachers of God's Word must be knowledgeable, competent, and diligent. We cannot afford spiritual casualties. Serious Bible study and preparation of lesson plans before you teach Scripture is just as important as knowing how to put in an endotracheal tube before you administer anesthesia. As Jesus gives us power and knowledge through studying His Word, we must faithfully connect seekers to Jesus, the source for healing, through the Word of God. There are many Bible studies available that encourage teachers to shortcut preparation. No matter how wonderful the Bible study curriculum, there is no appropriate shortcut for prayerful thorough Bible study before teaching.

Jim was a healthy young man in his early thirties. He began to have flu-like symptoms, and he went to the doctor. The doctor treated him for the flu, but Jim did not respond to the treatment. Three days later Jim went to the emergency room with high fever and belly pain. He was diagnosed with a ruptured appendix and was admitted to the hospital. I wasn't particularly worried about Jim until I learned that he was in intensive care and on a respiratory ventilator. I knew one of the nurses in the intensive care unit, so I asked her what happened. She relayed that the surgery went well and the ruptured appendix was removed. However, the anesthesiologist punctured Jim's trachea while administering anesthesia. Jim didn't make it.

Properly studying the text is the core of a good Bible lesson. Over the years we have observed in churches and in the classroom that many fail at this point. Too often a text becomes a pretext, a sounding board for some "hobby horse" issue. At other times the words of the text are substituted for the meaning of the text and the lesson becomes simply a time of definition of words rather than exposition of text. Finally, we have observed that many students take the ideas of the text, as they understand them, and build on them. Throughout the lesson the "learners" continue to wait for a connection between the lesson and the Bible, only to wait in vain.

Effective Bible study prevents mishandling the text. The method that follows, the Transformactional Bible Study Method, takes the Bible text seriously. It provides a step-by-step approach to analyzing, understanding, and applying the text to the learners. We do not profess that it contains new methodology. Rather, we hope that teachers will find a simplified and straightforward way of study that will ultimately lead them to writing effective lesson plans and delivering powerful Bible lessons.

Figure 8.1

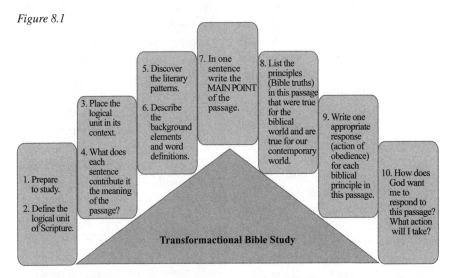

1. Prepare to study.

2. Define the logical unit of Scripture.

3. Place the logical unit in its context.

4. What does each sentence contribute it the meaning of the passage?

5. Discover the literary patterns.

6. Describe the background elements and word definitions.

7. In one sentence write the MAIN POINT of the passage.

8. List the principles (Bible truths) in this passage that were true for the biblical world and are true for our contemporary world.

9. Write one appropriate response (action of obedience) for each biblical principle in this passage.

10. How does God want me to respond to this passage? What action will I take?

Transformactional Bible Study

Preparation for teaching a Bible study begins with an in-depth study of the selected passage. An inductive Bible study starts with the details of the Scripture passage and builds to a general summary of what the passage means. A deductive study begins with the general meaning of the passage and sharpens the focus, becoming more and more specific. The effective Bible teacher needs a method of study that includes both inductive and deductive components.

The Transformactional Bible Study Method begins with an examination of the historical and grammatical components of the passage and builds to a main theme (inductive). It then takes the theme and identifies the principles and truths in the passage that are true to the theme. These principles apply to both the biblical world and the contemporary world. They produce appropriate actions of obedience (deductive). If the teacher studies a passage properly, it will result in life change for the teacher during preparation and teaching and for the learner who engages the material in the lesson presentation.

To help you understand how to use transformactional Bible study, and how to build a lesson plan from your study, we will use Romans 5:1–5 as an example. Read the Bible study on the following pages and refer to it as you come to subsequent chapters that explain the Star Model Lesson Plan. This example will help you observe the continuity between the study and the lesson plan.

Transformational Bible Study

1. Prepare to study.
Collect your tools for studying the Bible.
Assess the needs of your learners.
Pray for God's guidance as you study.

2. Define the logical unit of Scripture.
Decide on the general scriptural topic and define the specific passage by selecting a logical unit (paragraph) of Scripture.

3. Place the logical unit in its context.
What is the theme of the book in which the passage resides?
Who is the author of the book?
Who are the recipients of this book?
What historical, cultural, and geographical features contribute to the text?
What happens immediately before and after your selected passage?

4. What does each sentence contribute to the meaning of the passage?
Put each sentence in the passage into one of the following categories:
-States the main point
-Illustrates the main point
-Explains the main point
-Gives the purpose for the main point

5. Discover the literary patterns.
List any literary patterns that occur in your passage such as:
Cause and effect
Progression of time, event, logic, emotion
Repetitions
Imagery (metaphors, antonyms, synonyms, etc.)

6. Explain background elements and word definitions.
Explain any elements in the passage that have cultural implications or any vocabulary that needs definition.

7. Write the main point of the passage in one sentence.

8. List the principles (biblical truths) in this passage that were true for the biblical world and are true for our contemporary world.

9. Write one appropriate response (action of obedience) for each biblical principle in this passage.

10. How does God want me to respond to this passage? What action will I take? How will my life change?

THE TRANSFORMACTIONAL BIBLE STUDY METHOD APPLIED

Transformactional Bible Study: Rom 5:1–5

1. **Prepare to study**

   To study this portion of Paul's letter to Rome, you will need to have on hand the following tools:

   - A Bible arranged in paragraphs. We are using the HCSB.
   - Good commentaries on Romans; we suggest at least 2–3 exegetical commentaries.[6]
   - Other tools such as a good concordance like Strong's or Young's.
   - It is helpful to approach this with a Bible software package like *Logos* or *BibleWorks.*[7]

2. **Define the logical unit of Scripture.**

   All Bible study should be consistent with the logical units of the Bible. Basically, that means that the teacher should consider the passage which is the text or within which the text was written. A logical unit for developing the lesson plan can be a paragraph, a sentence, or even a part of the sentence. Regardless of how much of the Bible the teacher intends to use for the lesson, it is imperative to define the unit for an understanding of context.

   We have selected Rom 5:1–5 for two reasons. First, it is in accord with the paragraph divisions of the Bible translation we are using, the HCSB. Second, as we conduct a study of this paragraph, there are many indicators that suggest this is a logical unit that Paul intended to be read together. This will become clear as the Bible study progresses.

3. **Place the logical unit in its context.**

   What is the theme of the book in which the passage resides?

   The theme of a book may be discovered in two ways. First, a personal reading of the book will give the reader a sense of the subjects

---

[6] Exegetical commentaries focus on the meaning of the biblical text. They discuss matters of grammar, word definitions, and context. Other kinds of commentaries, like devotional commentaries, focus on the application of the text rather than its explanation. For serious Bible study, teachers should rely on exegetical commentaries.

[7] *BibleWorks* provides multiple translations of the text and vocabulary helps. *Logos* provides everything necessary for Bible study in an integrated package. After entering the passage in *Logos,* the screen displays commentaries, theologies, dictionary articles, and a multitude of other information specifically keyed to that passage.

discussed and, therefore, the theme of the book. In a book like Romans, this is a large task. Second, reference works provide the theme. The teacher should consult the introduction section of the commentaries. It is also helpful to consult Bible handbooks or introductions.

Most Bible scholars consider the Epistle to Romans to have the theme "Justification by Faith."

Who is the author of the book?

The author of Romans is the apostle Paul. First of all, Paul states that he is the author in the first verses of the book (Rom 1:1–6). From these verses we learn not only that Paul wrote the book, but also some important information he wanted to disclose about himself. Paul was (1) a slave of Jesus Christ; (2) an apostle called by God; (3) a man singled out for the gospel (God's good news); (4) a man called by God to promote "the obedience of faith" everywhere, including Jews and Gentiles; and (5) a man particularly concerned about Christians in Rome.

We can find out more about the apostle Paul from the commentaries and reference tools. It is helpful to read about Paul's background, his conversion, his specific ministry, his life, and his death. The reference materials will also point out that Paul had never been to Rome even though he had always wanted to go there. This is his longest letter and his most systematic about justification by faith. Paul wrote to introduce himself to the church and to gain their support as he hoped to continue his missionary work to the west, all the way to Spain (Rom 15:22–24).

Who are the recipients of the book?

Once again, you can find the recipients of the book in two ways. First, the introduction to this epistle names them (Rom 1:7). Second, the introduction section of commentaries and other reference tools reveal this. The reference books also provide more information about these people. Significantly, Paul had never met them all, even though he knew many of the people who were part of the church (see 16:1–15, the longest list of individuals named in any of the epistles).[8]

---

[8] On a deeper level of study, you will find that some scholars think the Roman destination is in error because some of the early manuscripts do not have it. They think it may have been a letter written to many different churches. In all the manuscripts we have of Romans, however, there is no other place mentioned, and most scholars are satisfied that the letter was directed to Rome.

What historical, cultural, and geographical features contribute to the text?

There are many interesting facts about the Epistle to the Romans as well as the people of Rome. It is noteworthy that Rome was the capital of the entire world—the Roman Empire. Ultimately, however, understanding the text we have selected does not depend on these matters.

One of the cultural features derived from both reading and the reference works does help illuminate the passage. In addition to justification by faith, a large portion of the book addresses a problem of unity between Christian Jews and Christian Gentiles. Almost every section of the epistle has some discussion relating to the two cultural and ethnic groups. In Rom 5:1–5 Paul lays a theological foundation for understanding the common access to God both have, a truth that should influence their abilities to relate in harmony to each other.

What happens immediately before and after your selected passage?

Romans 5:1 continues a discussion begun earlier (it begins with "therefore"). There have been two major discussions so far. The first, beginning at 1:18, describes why all people are sinful and in need of a savior. The second, beginning at 3:21, informs the readers that God has provided a universal Savior who is Jesus Christ.

That raises the question of how Jesus is a universal Savior, since He was a Jewish man living in a specific time and place. In Romans 4, the primary discussion about faith, Paul demonstrates faith in the life of Abraham, the father of the Jews. By faith, Abraham is the forefather of all Christians through faith.

Chapter 4 ends with one of the most helpful discussions of what faith means in a person's life. Though many Jews thought that God accepted Abraham because of his obedience, Paul clearly indicates that God honored Abraham's faith. He also states that all people (Jews and Gentiles) can be related to God by having the same faith Abraham did.

In Romans 5:12, Paul begins an extended discussion about Jesus, the universal Savior. He describes the significance of Jesus' life and death, and explains Jesus' qualifications to be the Savior for everyone by comparing Him to Adam and his disobedience that brought the problems of sin and death to everyone.

Our text, therefore, stands in a pivotal and transitional position. Paul stopped discussing Abraham as the father of faith and, in anticipation of his emphasis on Jesus the universal Savior, decided to describe the benefits a life of faith brings to the believer. In our passage, Paul answers the "so what" question about what Jesus has done for us.

4. What does each sentence contribute to the meaning of the passage?

First, we must seek to understand the flow of thought: the "hierarchy of thought" in the writer's expression.[9] The best way involves laying out the paragraph according to the contribution of its sentences. Following the HCSB we find there are four main sentences.

We can further analyze the sentences into what they contribute to the meaning of the passage. We have identified the contribution of each sentence in capital letters after each sentence.

Therefore, since we have been declared righteous by faith, we have peace with God through our Lord Jesus Christ. **INTRODUCES THE MAIN POINT *(the two parts of the sentence perform two different functions)***

Also through Him, we have obtained access by faith into this grace in which we stand, and we rejoice in the hope of the glory of God. **DEVELOPS BY FURTHER EXPLAINING THE MAIN POINT *("And through him . . . and we rejoice")***

And not only that, but we also rejoice in our afflictions, because we know that affliction produces endurance, endurance produces proven character, and proven character produces hope. **DEVELOPS BY FURTHER EXPLAINING THE MAIN POINT IN PARALLEL WITH THE PRECEDING SENTENCE *("And not only that")***

This hope does not disappoint, because God's love has been poured out in our hearts through the Holy Spirit who was given to us. **DEVELOPS BY GIVING A THIRD POINT AND ULTIMATE PURPOSE FOR THE PARAGRAPH *("because")***

The passage develops. First, it takes its starting point with an introductory idea: "since we have been declared righteous by faith." While this statement is not the primary idea, it ties the discussion to

---

[9] This point recognizes that all writers write hierarchically. That is, they have main points, and they support them with secondary points. Not all writers make their points in a "linear" fashion, but they all are hierarchical. It is the task of the reader to discover that hierarchy so as not to violate the author's message.

the previous passage. It also informs the reader that justification by faith is the platform on which this paragraph stands.

Second, the paragraph makes a statement that has two parts, represented by the next two sentences. After reminding the readers of his concerns for faith, Paul introduces the sentences with "also" and "and not only so." This makes the two sentences parallel, an observation that will be confirmed in a later step of the process.

Third, the paragraph ends by pointing to the certainty of Paul's message. Everything points to the fact that faith brings certainty of God's love. Paul adds another reason for certainty: the Holy Spirit confirms the truth as well by disclosing that the Holy Spirit brings a certainty of God's love. The passage ends with an affirmation about what God does for us. Significantly, walking with the Holy Spirit brings confirmation of God's love and hope.

It should be noted that some of the sentences are complex. That is, they have major statement parts and supporting parts. For thorough study, you should observe how the supporting parts of the sentence contribute to the meaning of the sentence as a whole. We will discuss this in the next point as well.

5. Discover the literary patterns.

The discussion of literary patterns opens a wide area of study. Many writers describe various literary patterns, but no one can supply a list of them all. Some are "normal" conventions used in ancient Greek writing;[10] others are created "at the moment" of writing to emphasize the message.[11]

Looking at the passage, we can find several very common patterns that will serve as a model for every passage.

1. *Cause and effect.* The text begins "since," a word basically giving a causal relationship. Thus "we have peace" is "because we have been declared righteous by faith." A second cause-and-effect relationship occurs in 5:3 where Paul states, "Because we know that affliction produces endurance."

2. *Progression* (of time, event, logic, emotion, for example). Even a cursory reading of the passage reveals at least two progressions of logic. First, Paul makes the statement "we have peace" (5:1).

---

[10] The Greek orators used the term "conventions" for the devices they could use in oral or written communication to bring interest and make a stronger impact.

[11] The best single work that describes the kinds of literary devices the writers use is W. L. Liefeld, *New Testament Exposition* (Grand Rapids: Zondervan, 1989).

He then continues with "also through Him" (5:2) and "not only that" (5:3). Obviously each statement adds to the previous.

Second, Paul progresses in a fairly common theme in Scripture about the opportunity to grow through difficulties. The progression is "affliction produces endurance, endurance produces proven character, and proven character produces hope."

3. *Repetition.* Repetition occurs frequently in Scripture as a way of emphasis. When it occurs, it may also indicate a secondary idea, such as the fact that the subject begun earlier (with one word or phrase) continues to the inclusion of the second use of the same expression. Repetition may also tie two or more statements together.

In this text we can see repetition to unite two parts of a basic principle. In 5:2 Paul says, "*we rejoice* in the hope of the glory of God." In 5:3 he repeats the exact verb "*we rejoice* in our afflictions." Though the repetition introduces two separate aspects of joy, each makes one major point: those justified by faith can rejoice. Those who can read the Greek text, or take advantage of a good commentary, can see that the first cause of rejoicing describes the foundation of joy and the second the environment in which joy triumphs.[12]

4. *Imagery.* Imagery is also a large category including word pictures (metaphors, antonyms, synonyms, for example) and visual or symbolic references (such as the temple and sacrifices). In this passage, there is no significant imagery.

5. *Theology.* Theological patterns often emerge in a text and bring added importance. Here Paul included the Trinity: (1) we have peace with **God**, (2) through **Jesus Christ** our Lord, and (3) **the Holy Spirit** brings knowledge of God's love. Each person of the Godhead is involved in our salvation.[13]

6. Describe the background elements and word definitions.

Since this is a relatively straightforward text, it does not require any necessary background research. There are, however, several very important words to study. At least a partial list follows, in order, with

---

[12] The first is a Greek preposition *epi,* which means "our joy is based on." The second uses the Greek preposition *en,* which means "our joy is in the midst of tribulations." They complement and form their own progression.

[13] This occurs commonly in Paul. Theological patterns require experience and thoughtful analysis of the text in order to "spot" them and confirm the writer's intent to use them as the reader "suspects."

the basic meanings included. The meanings come from studying the words by the use of a concordance or other reference tools like commentaries and theological dictionaries.

- *"we have been declared"*—this is a term from the law courts. It means that a judge has pronounced us innocent.
- *"faith"*—the word may refer to "the faith" (Christianity) or the expression of personal trust. A study of the immediate context (Abraham in chap 4) reveals that Paul is talking about the experience of faith, personal trust.
- *"peace with God"*—while not a word, this phrase makes a very important contribution. First, peace may be an emotion or it may be a relationship. We often speak of "having peace" in spite of pain. We can also speak of signing a "peace agreement." The preposition "with" demonstrates this is the peace of relationships, not emotionally experiential. Thus God pronouncing one just by faith establishes a "treaty" between sinful people and God.
- *"grace in which we stand"*—like peace, grace may be the expression of God's attitude of mercy or it may also describe an environment or ideology ("grace" instead of "works"). Here, standing in grace informs us it is an environment, the environment that brings you into faith.
- *"afflictions"*—of the many words for difficulties, this one literally means caught between a rock and a hard place. It is pressure applied by circumstances. It is not persecution.
- *"endurance"*—this word is often translated "patience." It implies the ability to endure difficult circumstances without failure (another Greek word usually refers to patience with people).
- *"proven character"*—the word is the noun of a common word for "tried and purified by fire." In this context, it is the refined character that the fire ("afflictions") produces.

7. In one sentence write the main point of the passage.

This phase of the study is one of the most important, yet one of the most challenging. It is challenging because it takes effort, and most people want to "feel" a point rather than study. All writers express themselves in a hierarchical fashion with words stating and then explaining one main point.

Nothing is more important than finding the main point. The main point is the subject the author wishes to express. Speaking from his passage and not using his subject violates the author's intent.

Furthermore, the main point functions like the backbone to the skeleton in that all other supports tie into it.

The process of finding the main point involves largely observation with trial and error. Building on the data from the previous points, it is necessary to write a simple statement. We are likely to be drawn emotionally to a secondary part of the passage, rather than the primary. This often involves making a statement, thinking about it in light of the various elements of the passage, and testing it to see if all the parts fit into it.

Romans 5:1–5 has the four sentences identified above. It also begins with "therefore," uniting the passage to the previous. "Therefore" must be taken seriously, as well as the four statements of the sentences.

The paragraph makes three main statements: (1) we have peace, (2) we rejoice (two complementary truths with the repetition of the word), and (3) hope does not disappoint. These three all tie into a greater main point.

The main point of this passage should be stated something like this:

Trusting in the salvation God provides in Jesus, the believer experiences the benefits of being right with God.

The benefits are [1] relationship, a proper relationship with God; [2] perspective, joy because of God's ultimate triumph and His ability to work in and through negative circumstances; and [3] confidence, hope that provides confidence and is continually reinforced in our lives by the Holy Spirit.

8. **List the principles (biblical truths) in this passage that were true for the biblical world and are true for our contemporary world.**

Unlike the main point, the principles can come from any section of the passage. A partial list of principles follows:

- *True righteousness is something God gives; not something we earn ("declared righteous," 5:1).*
- *True righteousness alone brings us into the relationship with God that we all desire ("peace," 5:1).*
- *The person and work of Jesus Christ is God's way of granting us righteousness (through Jesus, 5:1).*
- *Once converted, the believer identifies with and longs for God's glory. This has both immediate aspects and refers to the second*

*coming of Christ when God will be glorified before all the earth.
("we rejoice," 5:2–3).*

- *God is able to use difficult circumstances to promote our good
character so that all situations help Him accomplish His work in
us ("afflictions," 5:3).*
- *The presence of a living hope enables us to remain steadfast and
confident regardless of the circumstances of life ("hope," 5:4–5).*
- *The Holy Spirit brings a conscious realization of hope in our lives
by applying to our lives the implications of our relationship with
Christ. ("Holy Spirit," 5:5)*

9. **Write one appropriate response (action of obedience) for each
biblical principle in this passage.**

   We have repeated the principles and made action suggestions below. The response follows the principle.

   1. *True righteousness is something God gives; not something we
   earn (declared righteous).*

      **Since God gives righteousness, I should accept it and encour-
      age others to do so as well.**

   2. *True righteousness alone brings us into the relationship with
   God that we all desire ("peace")*

      **Since I will only be truly happy when I have God's righteous-
      ness, I will consciously trust God and thank Him for His won-
      derful gift.**

   3. *The person and work of Jesus Christ is God's way of granting us
   righteousness.*

      **I will trust Jesus and seek to help others see that He is the only
      Savior of the world.**

   4. *Once converted, the believer identifies with and longs for God to be
   glorified. This has both immediate aspects and refers to the second
   coming of Christ when God will be glorified before all the earth.*

      **I will actively submit myself to the lordship of Jesus and, espe-
      cially in times of difficulty, remember that He is the Lord.**

   5. *God is able to use difficult circumstances to promote our good character so that all situations help Him accomplish His work in us.*

I will trust that God is working in me through the difficult times of life as well as the good. I will read Scripture and seek to see things "His" way.

6. *The presence of a living hope enables us to remain steadfast and confident regardless of the circumstances of life.*

I will start each day in prayer and Bible reading in order to renew my commitment to what God is doing.

7. *The Holy Spirit brings a conscious realization of hope in our lives by applying to our lives the implications of our relationship with Christ.*

I will try to honor the Holy Spirit, living in obedience to Christ, in order to let Him communicate the joys of my relationship with Christ.

10. **How does God want me to respond to this passage? What action will I take? How will my life change?**

In the study of the passage the teacher must respond in obedience to the content of the passage.

Exercise 8.1

I know I am saved.	
I could lead someone else to find a relationship with Jesus.	
I read my Bible and pray daily.	
I am obeying everything God is telling me to do.	
I have selected a passage to teach.	
I have done a complete study of the passage.	

In following these steps the teacher has an abundance of material about the Bible text. It helps to write all observations as you think about them, not assuming you will remember everything later. By now, you have a passage, have observed the structure of the passage, have noted the literary devices of the passage, have found the main and secondary ideas, and have some embryonic idea about principles to apply. The next step is to begin crafting a lesson plan. Before we discuss that step, however, it is helpful to continue the first point of the Star Method of Transformational Teaching: Connecting Relationships. The teacher must connect carefully and realistically with the learner.

CHAPTER NINE

CONNECTING RELATIONSHIP: TO THE LEARNER

RELATIONSHIP
Teacher Connects
to God and
to Learners

CHRIST-CENTERED
BIBLICAL TEACHING

Teacher Relates—Learner Responds

WE HAVE DISCUSSED THE Bible study method; now we must develop competence in relating to the learners. We have observed through the years that many well-prepared lessons either fail or have limited effectiveness because the teacher simply did not understand the needs of the learners. This also meant that they did not really understand their own preferences as both learners and presenters. Effective teaching means the teacher has sensitivity to how people learn.

This Chapter Covers

1. *Individual learning preferences.* Teachers often assume everyone approaches learning the way they do. Therefore they teach to their preferences. A major portion of this chapter covers learning. It includes understanding learning modalities and learning styles.
2. *The Christian teacher has relationships built on genuine love.* Love extends beyond the classroom. Those who know God's love—*agapē*—relate to all people in love wherever they may be. Love is especially important in the classroom, providing the atmosphere in which the teaching is done.

This Chapter Includes the Following Transformactional Principles

- *Transformactional Principle 4:* The teacher must not exert power over the learner, but rather empower the learner with tools and confidence in learning.
- *Transformactional Principle 5:* Learning is enhanced when the learning takes place in a loving, safe environment of acceptance and mutual respect.

CONNECTING THROUGH UNDERSTANDING INDIVIDUAL PREFERENCES

Individuals do things differently—they are individuals. Individuals also see things differently as well as prefer to learn through different media. The teacher often forgets this basic and simple fact. They assume "their way" is "the right way to communicate." Most Bible teachers in church settings tend to imitate the preacher. After all, the preacher draws the greatest crowd on Sunday morning. Imitating him, they lecture, perhaps with a few questions included that students may or may not answer. In many cases the answers to the teacher's questions have little to do with the lesson, so it does not matter much whether they are answered or not.

One way teachers can be competent is to know themselves. Self-knowledge includes self-evaluation by using instruments that shed light on such things as personality, learning preferences, strengths, and weaknesses. The more teachers understand themselves, the more potential they have for accommodating learners. In our many years of observing student teachers, we have noticed that teachers tend to teach the way they learn. If teachers prefer listening to a lecture, they lecture. If they prefer viewing images, they teach with visuals. If they enjoy processing information by talking about it, they teach using collaborative activities. Because humans are creatures of habit, teachers find one comfortable way of communicating and settle into it. We assume that our students have the same comfort level that we do. The problem with this "migration toward comfort" is that people have different learning preferences and learning styles. The wise teacher uses multiple methods and at some point in the lesson teaches to every individual learner's preference.

Pete was a college student. To the frustration of his professor, Pete never seemed to be paying attention. He did not watch the PowerPoint presentation, and he did not take notes. Instead, he worked on the complicated lacing of a leather bag he was making. When the professor asked him why he was not paying attention, Pete explained that working with his hands helped him remember the information that was presented in class. He proved to be an "A" student and a kinesthetic learner.

Learning diversity represented in a normal classroom may result from variety in learning preferences. The preference for the way materials are presented, processed, and received is a discussion of learning styles. That discussion will come later. Students also prefer receiving sensory information through different sensory presentations. This is a difference in learning modalities preference. The capable teacher understands both issues, both in themselves and their students.

LEARNING MODALITIES

Learning modalities are physical preferences for sensory input. Does the learner prefer receiving new information via auditory, visual, or kinesthetic receptors? Does the learner rely most heavily on hearing, seeing, or doing in order to receive and remember new information? Both visual learners and auditory learners may be equally capable of assimilating new information on the battles of King David. Visual learners, however, prefer to see images rather than hear lecture; whereas, auditory learners prefer to hear a lecture rather than see images. We also know that some learners feel they can assimilate information more readily if they can use motion in their learning. These kinesthetic learners like to change body position, take notes or doodle, and participate in learning activities. Some kinesthetic learners feel they can learn better if they can chew gum or sip a cup of coffee. The best teaching practice includes opportunities for all modalities. Students will more readily engage materials when the teacher delivers them in their own learning preferences. Furthermore, retention increases when students engage materials through multiple sensory input.

STAR MODALITY PREFERENCE ACTIVITY   Our interest in sensory input and perceptual modality preference comes because of the connections that current transformative neuroscience research makes between multisensory input and learning retention (memory). Perceptual modality preference (auditory, visual, and kinesthetic) is easily determined. A simple, informal indicator to determine preference follows. Before doing this activity, make a prediction of how you think you will score. As you take the inventory, numerically weigh your answers and place a 1, 2, or 3 in each of the three boxes labeled A, B, and C. Mark 1 as the answer most unlike you and 3 as the answer most like you. (on following page)

To score this modality preference activity, add the columns. The A column is auditory, B is visual, and C is kinesthetic. Your highest score will give your possible modality preference. The higher your score the more you prefer that particular modality. You may find that all of your scores are similar. This indicates that you do not have a strong preference for a particular modality. If you find that your score for one modality is much lower than the other two, you may have more difficulty when teaching students with this modality preference. This activity is not diagnostic. No one passes or fails. Feel free to disagree with the findings. The results can help, however, if you see a pattern of preference that influences the way you communicate with learners.

Although research on the specific percentages for modality preference varies, one research base reported that in a cross-section of American society ages 10 through adults, only 20 percent of learners are auditory, 40 percent are visual, and 40 percent are kinesthetic.[1] In 2006 spring and fall semesters at Golden Gate Baptist Theological Seminary (GGBTS), we gave LeFever's modality preference inventory[2] to seminary students in our Bible teaching classes. (All academic degree-seeking students are required to take this class, and GGBTS is one of the most multicultural campuses in America.) We projected

---

[1] M. LeFever, *Learning Styles: Reaching Everyone God Gave You to Teach* (Colorado Springs: David C. Cook Publishing Co., 1995) 100.

[2] Ibid., 101–2

Exercise 9.1

	A	B	C
1. When talking to others, my friends would say I use A. clear and precise information. B. word pictures and illustrations. C. hand gestures.			
2. If I have something serious to discuss I prefer A. talking on the phone. B. talking face to face. C. talking while doing an activity together.			
3. In a Bible study, I learn best when A. The teacher tells me what the passage says. B. The teacher shows me what the scripture says. C. The teacher lets me discover what the passage says.			
4. When I teach I enjoy A. telling. B. using pictures, charts, and displays. C. facilitating discovery.			
5. To relieve stress I prefer A. to listen to music. B. to watch TV or go to a movie. C. to walk, run, or ride a bike, etc.			
6. I prefer to encourage my friends by A. saying words of praise or encouragement. B. writing them a note. C. taking them somewhere special.			
7. I usually do better studying for a test if I A. tape the lectures and listen to them again. B. re-read the text and my notes. C. participate in a study group.			
8. I most enjoy playing A. password (giving oral word clues). B. pictionary (drawing or interpreting pictures of words or phrases). C. charades (acting out titles or phrases).			
9. When giving directions I prefer to A. tell people how to get there. B. draw a map. C. take the person to the location or have them follow me.			
10. When putting together a complicated new purchase I prefer to A. follow the explanation given by the store assembler. B. follow the diagrams in the box. C. figure it out by trial and error.			
11. When I attend church I prefer a sermon A. with no distractions. B. with Power Point. C. with a study guide and breaks for coffee and visiting.			
12. When I worship I prefer A. to hear music and prayer. B. see God's beautiful world around me. C. to clap my hands and participate.			
13. When learning a Bible verse it helps me to A. hear it over and over. B. see it over and over. C. write it over and over.			
14. When recalling the books of the Bible I A. hear them in my head. B. see them in my head. C. need to write them.			
	Auditory	Visual	Kinesthetic
Column Totals			

that because seminary students already have baccalaureate degrees and have sat through many lectures, they would have a very heavy preference for auditory learning. We were wrong. The expressed preferences were: 27 percent auditory, 50 percent visual, and 23 percent kinesthetic. These findings may not be true of all graduate students. The results are significant only because it helps us, as Christian educators, to realize that we preach and teach to a diversity of learning preferences whether our audience is formally educated or not. If pastors and Bible teachers want to maximize learning for the entire congregation or all of the students in a class, they must incorporate multiple modalities of learning in teaching practice. To be effective, preaching and teaching should not be lecture only (auditory) because lecture only does not maximize learning modality preference and learning retention for most people. Adding PowerPoint (visual) and study sheets with a cup of coffee on the side (kinesthetic) acknowledges all learning modality preferences. With the privilege of knowing one's modality preferences comes the responsibility of teaching beyond individual preference to multiple styles.

LEARNING STYLES

Learning styles can be defined as preferences a learner has for the way learning materials are presented, processed, and received. Although neuroscience tells us that all adult brains basically process information through a similar cyclical physiological process, our many years of teaching experience tells us that each person has unique learning preferences—a style of handling new information that makes the learning process more comfortable for them.

Researchers have defined various learning style paradigms by studying students' preferred processes of learning. Current descriptions of learning style seem to come from research on cognitive styles, personality theory, aptitude, and sensory preference. Therefore, learning styles might be classified as cognitive, affective, and physical/modalities.[3] Generally, cognitive styles describe the way the brain prefers to process information: the way thinking occurs. Affective classifications of learning styles indicate the emotion or lack of emotion connected to processing of information. Physical styles of learning best describe physical and sensory preferences in the learning process.[4]

---

[3] C. Kelley, "A Study of the Relationship Between Anxiety Levels and Perceptual Learning Style Preferences" (Ed.D. diss., Auburn University, Auburn, AL, 2004), 24–35.

[4] J. W. Keefe and B. G. Ferrell, "Developing a Defensible Learning Style Paradigm," *Educational Leadership* 48, no. 2 (October 1990): 57. Available online at Education Research Complete (http://www.ebscohost.com/), accessed March 28, 2009.

UNDERSTANDING THE KOLB LEARNING STYLES INVENTORY (LSI)   One of the cognitive learning styles inventories that still seems particularly relevant is the LSI. The LSI measures experiential learning preference. It is designed to evaluate the way a learner learns. Kolb's LSI is based on a model of experiential learning that goes back to John Dewey. Experiential learning begins with a concrete experience followed by observation and reflection. Principles or patterns are deduced from reflection, and the principles or patterns become the guides for future learning experiences.

Although experiential learning has been around for many decades, and Kolb's original LSI was published in the 1980s, the learning components it measures are similar to the learning process explained in the contemporary neuroscience transformative theory in part 2 of this book. Neuroscientific studies indicate the continuing relevance of Kolb's LSI. The LSI has been published five times; the most recent is the 3.1 version published in 2001.[5]

In the LSI, there are four possible learning styles. Divergers are creative, imaginative, open minded, and emotional. They can generate ideas prolifically and sell everyone on their ideas. Assimilators are good at planning, defining problems, and developing theories. Convergers enjoy problem-solving, deductive reasoning, finding principles, and finding practical uses for theories. Accommodators enjoy taking risks, initiating ideas, and getting things done. This information and more "in depth" interpretation about Kolb's Learning Styles can be found in the LSI manual.[6]

When taking the LSI or a similar learning style indicator, you explore the way you process information—your experiential preference. The scores should not make you feel confined. A high score in one area such as Diverger does not mean that you are not capable of all four of the styles of learning. Many factors (such as education, vocation, and experiences) influence the results of any assessment. Scores, learning styles, learning strengths, and learning weaknesses will change throughout life. The information helps you to understand new ways of thinking about learning, and to explore and analyze yourself for how you prefer to learn and teach. Collect as much information as you can about yourself. Reflect on it and see if it fits your self-concept. Examine your strengths and weaknesses as a learner and as a teacher. Which types of learners are most difficult for you to teach? How can you change your teaching practice to include all learners? Identify one change you could make immediately to make your teaching more inclusive? Commit to make that change.

---

[5] Those interested in choosing a learning styles inventory may want to begin with the LSI. It is available online at http://www.haygroup.com/tl/Questionnaires_Workbooks/Kolb_Learning_Style_Inventory

[6] For an LSI manual, contact: Hay Resources Direct, 116 Huntington Ave., Boston, MA 02116, 800–927–8074, www.hayresourcesdirect.haygroup.com

THE 4MAT MODEL   Bernice McCarthy developed a model based on Kolb's work.[7] Her model became the 4MAT system.[8] The terms in her model (imaginative, analytic, common sense, dynamic) parallel Kolb's terms but are more descriptive and less confusing. McCarthy has spent much time applying her method to education practice. 4MAT has a number of different inventories available. The inventory that measures the way learners learn is the Learning Type Measure (LTM).[9] It was first published in 1994 and is still widely used.

Table 9.1

Comparing Terms for Kolb and McCarthy[10]

KOLB	MCCARTHY
Diverger	Imaginative
Assimilator	Analytic
Converger	Common Sense
Accommodator	Dynamic

McCarthy assigns a question to each of the learning styles. She says the imaginative learner asks "Why?," the analytic learner asks "What?," the common sense learner asks "How does this work?," and the dynamic learner asks "What if?" In the Star Method of Bible study the four components of the Bible study lesson answer similar questions. The components of the lesson and the key questions answered are demonstrated in the chart below.

Table 9.2

Star Bible Study Lesson Plan Questions and Key Words

Diverger/Imaginative	Assimilator/Analytic	Converger/Common Sense	Accommodator/ Dynamic
Introduction	Biblical World Passage Content	Contemporary Application	Obedient Action
Why is this Bible passage relevant to me?	What did God want the original receivers of this passage to know?	What spiritual principles from this passage apply to the contemporary world?	What does God want me to do to obey this passage?
Connect	Content	Principles	Action

STAR LEARNING/TEACHING STYLE ACTIVITY   The learning/teaching style activity below is an informal activity. It provides a general idea of how you might score on an experienced-based indicator[11] Write a number beside each

---

[7] http://www.aboutlearning.com/index.php/what-is-4mat (accessed April 28, 2009).

[8] About Learning, 441 West Bonner Rd., Wauconda, IL 60084 800–822–4MAT, www.aboutlearning.com

[9] Available through About Learning, Inc. 1251 N. Old Rand Rd, Wauconda, IL 60084, 800–822–4628.

[10] LeFever, *Learning Styles,* 35.

[11] Note that this exercise is called an "activity." It is not intended to replace a fully developed

description in each row to designate how much each descriptor is like you. Four is always like you; three is mostly like you; two is occasionally like you; one is never like you. Add the columns and compare your total scores in each column to determine which style is your strength. Read the descriptions and decide if you think your highest score is really similar to your learning preference. (*See Exercise 9.2 on following page.*)

Discerner: If you score the highest as a discerner you are a people person. God may likely have given you the gift of discernment. You are sensitive to peoples' needs and aware of both their sorrows and their joys. Although emotion plays an important role in all adult learning, you are particularly sensitive, and you need a positive happy learning environment where you feel that all learners are valued and treated fairly.

If a fellow student is hurt or misunderstood, it is difficult for you to learn because you are concerned, even preoccupied, with their well-being. When teaching you have a strong concern for your student's happiness. You generate ideas. You can think of many ways to do something and you are imaginative. You do not like lectures so you rarely give them. You hate memorization, competition, and objective tests. You like collaboration, shared projects, brainstorming, drama, simulations, artistic expression, and assignments where students can choose evaluative tools.

When approaching a Bible study, you ask, "What is the purpose of this Bible study? Do I really need to know this Bible passage? Is it relevant to me and to my adult learners?" For you, the introduction (relevance) is extremely important because you need the answers to your questions in order for you to decide whether or not this study is worth your time.

Constructor: If you scored the highest as a constructor, you love to build ideas and theories from the bare and accurate facts. You are logical and sequential. You prefer working alone, and you have difficulty when people are so caught up in their own problems that they don't attend to the task at hand. If there is a job to be done, everyone can depend on you. You consider yourself smart and capable.

If you can have a room full of excellent resources with peace and quiet, by yourself you can accomplish almost anything. You prefer task over people and

---

"experience-based indicator" such as Kolb or 4MAT. For a limited list of professional inventories available online, see Appendix F.

Exercise 9.2

Star Learning/Teaching Style Activity

	Discerner	Constructor	Excavator	Activist
1. I work best:	collaborating	observing facts and constructing theory	experimenting	Inventing
2. My question is:	Is everyone's opinion being considered?	Do we have all the facts?	Did we test it to see if it works?	Is it making a difference?
3. People describe me as a:	Idea generator	Logical thinker	Problem Solver	Risk Taker
4. When I am honest, I see myself as	sensitive and kind	intellectual	industrious	flexible and intuitive
5. When I study the Bible I want	to know why this passage is important	to understand the content of the passage	to understand the principles for Christian living	to know what action I should take.
6. I enjoy	creative expression	knowing facts	doing projects	making new things happen
7. In heaven I want to	find my friends and together enjoy the beauty of God's creation	understand the vastness of knowledge	explore the lists of things I can do.	try something heaven's never seen before
8. I feel like a failure when	people are upset with me	I cannot give the correct answer	I can't make my project work	I can't get people to change.
9. The most fulfilling part of teaching is	using a really creative method that helps everyone participate in and enjoy learning.	getting people to really understand the content of the Bible passage	helping people understand the principles for Christian living that the passage teaches.	seeing people actually act differently because of the Bible studies.
10. I prefer	discussing and sharing ideas	doing things correctly	"hands on" experimenting with my ideas	doing things uniquely
11. I am known for	supporting and encouraging learners	challenging learners to complete the task correctly	facilitating the developing of skills	challenging learners to creative action
12. This is true of me	the more I talk the more I understand	the more I study the more I know	the more I discover the more skills I have	the more I act, the more difference I can make.
13. I could say that I'm	empathetic	competitive	strategic	Adventurous
14. I hate	memorizing facts instead of discussing ideas	having discussions with people who don't know the answers	being told what answers I should know	learning things that do not make a difference.
Total Each Column				

product over process. You love to hear factual content lectures, and when you teach you expect others to receive your factual lectures. How can anyone not be mesmerized by great information?

You love competition, objective tests, and being right. You dislike discussion groups, group projects, drama, simulations, and brainstorming. When approaching Bible study you ask the question, "What are the facts and content of this Bible passage?" For you, the Bible content (revelation) section of the Bible study is the most important. If the Bible study is worth your time, it will have a great section on Bible background and Scripture content.

Excavator: If you score the highest on "excavator," you are a practical, strategic thinker who problem-solves experientially. You value the kind of knowledge that skills produce. You learn best by being active and working things out for yourself. You prefer demonstrating rather than lecturing, being realistic rather than idealistic, being given questions rather than being given answers.

If given the opportunity, you excel at computer and technology. You hate sitting still, hearing or giving lectures, and working in groups. You like to work alone so that nothing interferes with the organized, sequential way you work through your projects.

When you participate in or teach Bible study, you value distilling the biblical principles for Christian living. For you, the value of Scripture is in the application of principles to today's world. The question you bring to Bible study is, "How does this passage apply to my contemporary world?" If a Bible study is worth "my time," it will not be just facts. What good is it to know all the content if none of it applies to today's here and now?

Activist: If you score the highest on "activist," you lead others to Christian action either literally or by example. You value creativity and humor. You are comfortable with ambiguity, and you value flexibility over sequence, people over projects, future over present, and intuition over logic. For you, there is never one right way.

You see many possibilities, and you value doing things differently. You prefer ideas to answers, different to same, abstract to concrete, people to projects, process to product, and you prefer not to have deadlines or time limits. You love being unique, having a hunch, drama, artistic interpretation, brainstorming, and group projects. You consider yourself a world changer. When you approach Bible study your question is, "What difference will this study make in my life? How can this study change my world?" The most important part of the Bible lesson for you is the challenge to action (results). You want to be different and to make a difference. You want to explore actions.

Styles assessments vary in what characteristics they test. Therefore, if you take a battery of inventories, you will find that some inventories fit you better than others. Also, when you take any inventory or assessment of learning styles, you are very likely not to fit exactly into any category. The categories are all man-made. People are God-made. God creates people with unique genetic construction and places them into unique learning environments. This nature/nurture combination gives infinite possibilities for characteristics and explains why no two of us are exactly alike. Imposing artificial categories fails because no one category fits exactly.

Why, then, do these exercises at all? It is because we can tell teachers that their students do not prefer learning the same way they do, and yet, teachers continue to teach the way they prefer to learn. In our experience, when teachers explore their learning styles, they begin to realize the variety of preferences represented in any classroom. It motivates them to teach to all learning styles. When you find the descriptor (discerner, constructor, excavator, or activist) that is closest to you, look at Table 9.3 and see how similar you are to others who chosen the same descriptor. As we have tested hundreds of students, we have noticed the tendency toward the characteristics displayed in Table 9.3. Most likely some of them will fit you.

In the table, the rows contain descriptors for different learning preferences. The first two rows describe preferences for people or tasks and process or product. The third row describes the degree of creativity. People with learning styles that focus on product tend to be less creative than those who focus on the process of discovery. The last row identifies preferred sensory modality. The correlations come strictly from testing our own students. Many Discerners and Excavators are visual (a few are kinesthetic), Constructors are often auditory, and many Activists (certainly not all) are kinesthetic. The patterns may not hold true for the learners in your Bible study classes, but wise teachers think about the implications of diversity as they write lesson plans, choose teaching methods, and facilitate learning.

So which style is the smartest or has the most genius? There is equal intelligence and genius in each style. For interest, examine the lives of the disciples.

What learning style do you think Peter preferred? How about the Sons of Thunder? What about John the Beloved? Obviously God loves variety. Christian teachers should seek to enhance the growth of all people by providing a learning environment conducive to each style.

Table 9.3

discerner	constructor	excavator	activist
prefer people	prefer tasks	prefer tasks	prefer people
process	product	product	process
very creative	not very creative	creative	very creative
visual	auditory	visual	kinesthetic

Take several of the instruments listed in appendix F, and you will know more about yourself as a learner/teacher. Reflect on the results of these indicators and decide what you think of the results. List what you consider to be your strengths and weaknesses. Compare the findings of the indicators with your teaching practice. Create a personal profile of your learning and teaching style. Make a list of things you could add to your teaching that would strengthen your communication with all learners.

LEARNING STYLES SYNTHESIS

The following model demonstrates visually one way to consider the relationships between the experiential teaching model, the neuroscientific transformative learning model, Kolb's learning styles, McCarthy's learning styles, and the star activity. It should be read from the outside toward the inside. The chart does not suggest that these approaches are parallel in every way. The model intends to picture certain patterns of similarities. For example, we are not saying that people who prefer theorizing only use the neuroscientific learning process that involves the back of the brain in grouping sensory input. Every healthy learner uses all of the brain processes. The "analytic learner" ALSO receives sensory input or creates new action. In the process of learning, we begin at the top of this graphic and move clockwise through the process. The correlations represent a comfort zone where certain learners excel. Even so, all learners must perform in all areas of learning.

Fig. 9.1 Relationships Visualized

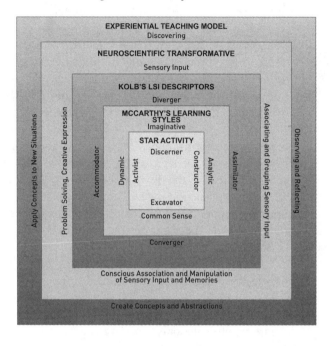

BENEFITS OF STUDYING LEARNING MODALITIES AND LEARNING STYLES

Learning styles inventories cannot be the magic remedy for bad teaching. If teachers struggle, however, with creating connections with some learners, learning styles inventories may help in understanding why certain learners are more difficult for some teachers to reach. Generally, the more alike the teacher and learner in learning preference, the easier it is for them to connect in the learning environment. Teaching practice informed by knowledge of learning styles has diversity of teaching methods and is inclusive of every learning preference. Inclusive teaching is teacher-led but learner-centered. It can make a difference in maximizing students' learning and retention.

Studying learning styles brings two lasting benefits. First, as teachers explore their own learning styles, they understand how they process information and why certain methods of teaching seem more comfortable to them. Second, as teachers realize that people are wired differently, they become more open to teaching outside their comfort zones—"teaching out of the box." They attempt to diversify their teaching methods so that they maximize learning and retention for all students.

How then should teachers teach? The answer to the dilemma of teaching/ learning preference is for teachers to teach to every preference. This is sup-ported by statistics on retention, and it is supported by current neuroscience research. Teaching with a variety of methods is difficult and time-consuming. At times it requires killing a sacred cow or two. The goal of teaching to all learning styles outweighs any teacher discomfort. The goal is transformactional learning: learning that acts.

The Star Method of Transformactional Teaching can meet the learning styles needs of many learners. By design, each component of the lesson has a focus that intentionally represents the diversity of learners. The introduction (relevance) can be designed to support the Discerner. The content (revelation) section of the lesson can support the Constructor. The application (responsibility) can support the Excavator. The action (results) can support the Activist.

In the next four Star points we describe the actual lesson plan with a chapter for each point. The lesson plan design accommodates learning styles by correlating the specific part of the lesson plan with a learning style preference from the activity. The correlation is to highlight the importance of directing at least some portion of the lesson to each learning style. It does not suggest, however, that the correlation is the only place for sensitivity to the diversity of learning styles.

Exercise 9.3

Teacher Check List

I have taken complete learning styles instruments from several categories.	
I have reflected on the results of these indicators	
I have created a personal profile of my teaching-learning style	
I have listed the changes I need to make in my teaching in order to connect with all learners.	

CONNECTING THROUGH UNDERSTANDING RELATIONSHIPS

The relationships between teacher and learner are very important to the learning environment. Before moving to the specific patterns for developing lesson plans, we feel it is important to express some guidelines in this area. They address both helpful and harmful concerns. The teacher and learner must treat the learners with respect using appropriate communication and providing tools for discovery. The teacher must work to empower students for self-actuation rather than manipulating students toward hidden agendas. The teacher/ learner relationship should be based on trust and exemplary *agapē* love.

The transformative neuroscience theory supports the importance of relationships between the mentor teacher and the learner.

> "The discovery that a trusting relationship with a mentor is connected to brain reorganization, growth, and learning underscores what adult educators have long held true: if the mentor creates a safe, trusting relationship and holding environment, learners are much more able to reorganize their thinking and move through the progressive stages of the developmental journey."[12]

RESPECT FOR CULTURE

Treating the student as a competent learner involves mutual respect with regard to culture, previous education, and learning preference. Differences in cultural background are embraced—not just tolerated. The teacher must realize that cultural differences, such as age, gender, disability, socioeconomic status, and ethnicity, can contribute to the richness of classroom dialog and perspective. Culture should be celebrated and shared. Bible teachers should recognize that the Bible was originally written to another culture. The cultural perspective of the teacher does not necessarily better equip one to understand the Bible. Multiple cultural perspectives also bring richness to the applications we make from the scripture. Teachers who listen to learners will also learn.

APPROPRIATE VOCABULARY

Educational differences must be acknowledged and accommodated in the class. It is important for the teacher to know the educational backgrounds of the students and to use appropriate vocabulary. Graduate school vocabulary may not be appropriate for a Bible study with students who have only high school diplomas. Jesus spoke the truth in simple terms that all people could understand. His followers did not always have the spiritual maturity to understand his teachings, but they did have the vocabulary to understand. Using an inappropriate level of vocabulary puts a barrier of mistrust between you and the learners. Speak on the level of the group God has given you. Work to create mutual respect and understanding.

Teachers should also avoid informal language that reflects a specific subculture in society. Words and language patterns often come from minorities and those who know English as a second language. They reflect an "inside" understanding of communication. Unless the teacher comes from "the inside" and naturally uses this speech, it is best to avoid it. An improper use of such proprietary language either makes one superficial (overly trying to relate) or

[12] S. Johnson and K. Taylor, eds., *The Neuroscience of Adult Learning,* New Directions for Adult and Continuing Education, no. 110, Summer 2006 (San Francisco: Jossey-Bass, 2006), 65.

irrelevant (completely miscommunicating). Great care must be taken to be on the wavelength of students but not superficial or incorrectly trendy.

PROVIDE EDUCATIONAL TOOLS

Teachers should not be condescending. Even though they will likely know more about the passage than the learners, if they have done proper preparation, they should never take the attitude of "helping the less fortunate learn." The research in discovery learning demonstrates the need to empower learners.

One way is to give them appropriate educational tools. Teachers should teach students how to discover truth for themselves. God speaks to each of us in light of and through our background of experiences. As we receive new knowledge through our senses, our brains combine that information with a backlog of experience and memory in order to interpret this new knowledge. Good teachers listen to their learners and respect their perspectives.

SHARE THE POWER

Teachers may choose to teach because it makes them feel powerful. They control the classroom, students, and the information provided. If they feel threatened, they may simply put learners in their place with sarcasm or criticism. This is never appropriate; Bible teaching should encourage student empowerment. Sarcasm and humiliation have no place in any classroom and can do permanent damage to learners.

There are several views of power. (1) Power is like a chocolate cake. If you give a piece away, you have less for yourself. People who view power in this way feel that if they empower another, they become less powerful. (2) Power is like a seed. If two birds fight over it, only one gets it. People who believe this model feel that empowering another leaves them impotent. (3) Power is like leading a flock of Canadian geese flying south for the winter. If you get tired you can pass the leadership to another and fall back in the flock. People who embrace this view feel that only one person can be empowered at a time. (4) Power is like candlelight. The more you share the light from your candle, the more the light grows. People who agree with this view believe that power multiplies when shared. They believe that when they empower another, they are enabling them, in turn, to empower. The Bible affirms this last view. Bible teachers should also affirm it and teach in accord with it.

NO HIDDEN AGENDAS

Why are you teaching? Is it because you hate being taught? You had to attend Herb's Bible study or teach your own? Is it because you want a church full of Christians who act and look exactly like you? Do you have a political agenda for social issues? You want to have a voting block for your position on the ballot? You have a political agenda for church issues? You really want to be on the finance committee and your Bible study class could vote you in?

The only reason that any teacher should teach Bible is to facilitate Christian growth toward Christlikeness, accompanied by the understanding that the Holy Spirit is the one who changes the heart and affects change in the life. If we believe that we, as Bible teachers, only have God's permission to relay what Scripture says and to help others learn to discover it for themselves, we must lay all other agendas aside and focus on our God-given task. We must learn, obey, and teach Scripture, while empowering others to learn. A clear focus on this task creates an environment of integrity and trust.

TRUST

Fowler's first stage of primal faith[13] points out the importance of initially learning to trust. Erikson's first psychosocial stage[14] is "trust verses mistrust." We are born with a need to trust. In a healthy family, when an infant cries, the mother or father goes to him, picks him up, and talks soothingly. If the baby is hungry, he is fed. If he is wet or cold, he is changed or swaddled. The baby learns that he can trust his caretakers, and he views the world as a safe and happy place.

Unfortunately, not all infants learn to trust. Some infants are born into dysfunctional families. Addicted parents, for example, may not have the capacity to meet the needs of their infant, and trust does not develop normally. The baby cries, and mom is unconscious from alcohol or dad is high on cocaine. The baby learns that he cannot count on his caretakers to meet his needs. The world becomes a frightening place. The baby learns he cannot trust anyone.

People do not generally outgrow difficulty with trust. Mistrust in infancy seems to haunt an individual throughout life. This is not to say a person who experienced mistrust in infancy cannot learn to trust, but it is almost certain that trust will be difficult.

---

[13] J. W. Fowler, *Stages of Faith: The Psychology of Human Development and the Quest for Meaning* (San Francisco: Harper & Row, 1981).119–121.

[14] L. E. Berk, *Exploring Lifespan Development* (San Francisco: Allyn and Bacon, 2008), 13.

Not only is a secure infancy important to developing trust, events in later life can also have an effect. Children and adults may suffer criticism or bullying that creates permanent scars. Often graduate students tell us that they still feel very insecure in the classroom because of memories of a teacher or parent who belittled or criticized them years ago. Humiliation leaves people wounded and struggling with self-esteem. A person can become an excellent student, perhaps a successful professional, and still struggle with the ability to trust others. Subsequent success does not completely erase previous negative experiences.

Although ultimately the Holy Spirit gives the learner the faith to believe, human response is shaped by human experience. The adults in our Bible studies or church congregations do not all have the same emotional "equipment" to respond in faith. Some find it extremely difficult to trust what can be seen, let alone to trust an invisible God. Biblical educators must be aware of the learner's perceptions and willing to wait as the learner navigates through fear and mistrust. The teacher must be sensitive to the learner's pain and ready to share it. The teacher must also be consistently trustworthy.

Learners' perceptions about the teacher may fluctuate between positive and negative, and they may be accurate or skewed. Learners may feed the ego of the teacher with great accolades, and, in the next breath, spew the venom of criticism or accusations. Teachers must answer the learner with humility even when misunderstood: must be slow to anger and radiating genuine love. First Thess 2:7–8 says:

> . . . we were gentle among you, as a nursing mother nurtures her own children. We cared so much for you that we were pleased to share with you not only the gospel of God but also our own lives, because you had become dear to us.

AGAPĒ

Agapē is biblical love, that which is first found in Scripture. It is the love of God as He gave His only Son to die for unworthy sinners. *Agapē* gives! It gives not because of who the recipient is, or what the recipient can do, but rather because of who the giver is.

Agapē comes from God and is revealed to others through us. If we are connected to God through our relationship with Christ, we are connected to the power source just like the pot was connected to the heat. Our connection with the power source generates a personal knowledge of *agapē* love and releases it from our lives.

God's love bubbles over to everyone around us. It cannot be contained. The pressures of the world pressing down on us cannot frustrate the love of Christ—it just keeps spilling over. Resistance from those who receive it does not affect love. Whether the receivers welcome or resist, love continues undiminished. The reason for prolific love is not the pot. The reason is the power source—the personal knowledge of the love of God.

The teacher knows God, walks with Him, and experiences God's undeserved *agapē*. Experientially for the learner, this phenomenon produces a consistent positive environment of love and acceptance for spiritual growth, regardless of the learner's perceptions or fluctuations. *Agapē* is the natural greenhouse where spiritual learning can flourish.

Both teachers and learners must choose to cooperate with God's plan and to become vehicles of His love. Christian educators will recognize that the holy task of teaching exceeds natural ability. In teaching, there is learning and developing spiritual maturity. The loving environment produces growth in both teachers and learners.

Yount says:

> *When I was small my mom shouted for me to run to the kitchen and turn off the pot of potatoes. As I arrived at the stove I saw a pot bubbling over, spilling the contents all over the stove with the lid rattling around on the top of the pot. My first response was to push down on the lid to secure it. All the pressure I could muster could not contain it. The contents continued to spill out and I was forced to turn off the source of the problem—the heat.*

> Maturity is the destination, the mountaintop, the masterpiece. Maturing is the journey, the climb, the fashioning. The challenge is to develop bifocal vision. Let us fix our eyes on both the destination and the journey, the mountaintop and the climb, the finished masterpiece and the fashioning.[15]

We are not only led by Christ to mature in our own lives, but as teachers and preachers of Scripture, we are responsible to lead others toward maturity. We are led to lead.

HANDLE MISPERCEPTIONS

Unfortunately, human perception often proves to be the enemy of truth. People, at times, misunderstand our intentions of demonstrating love. A teacher can make the ultimate effort to live worthy of the Lord and still have those efforts misunderstood by Christian brothers or sisters. It is also probable that the teacher will make mistakes. It is important, therefore, for the Christian teacher to be aware of the learner's perspective and to seek to build bridges.

---

[15] W. R. Yount, *Called to Teach* (Nashville: Broadman & Holman, 1999), 39.

The educator must make every effort to cultivate the vital elements of trust and *agapē* love—the foundation upon which learning occurs. Here are some suggestions for bridging the gap.

DON'T BE OBNOXIOUS!   Nothing is worse than deserving the negative perception. Many Christians strut around "suffering persecution for the Lord" when their perceived suffering is nothing more than people reacting to their truly obnoxious personalities. Understand that you are just as much under construction as the learners in your Bible study class. The part of your life that you think is most infallible is the part that Satan will target. You are never so holy that you are beyond a fall. Keep your eyes on "Jesus—the Perfect One," and stay updated in your walk with Him.

CONSISTENTLY CONNECT TO THE POWER SOURCE   Spend time in the Word of God daily and obey whatever God shows you to do. When a crisis comes and you are jostled, whatever is inside you will come out. If you harbor anger and bitterness, the fruit of anger and bitterness will gush forth. Christians should be full of the love of God so that no matter what the world does, you respond in love.

CHOOSE TO LOVE   *Agapē* is not based on emotion; it is a choice. Choose to love in everything you do, especially when you don't feel like it. Some people are easy to love. They are happy and pleasant, and they tell you how wonderful you are. Others are difficult and challenge you on everything you say. This second group is the real test of *agapē*. Ask God to help you choose to express acts of love that will impact their lives.

PRACTICE HUMILITY   If you have wronged someone, go and ask forgiveness—the sooner, the better. No matter how hard you try to be godly, you will at some time fail. Never fail on purpose. Choosing to wrong someone goes against everything God intends for you. When you do fail, however, do not let the wound you've inflicted fester. The infection will multiply until the whole group becomes infected. Go to the person and admit you're wrong. Ask God for forgiveness and ask the person you've wronged for forgiveness. Unforgiven sin stops *agapē*. Forgiveness opens the pathway for the flow of *agapē*. When we ask God for forgiveness, we experience *agapē* flowing from God to us. When we ask our brothers for forgiveness, it opens the flow of *agapē* between us. They will know we are Christians by our love (John 13:35).

PRACTICE LOVING CONFRONTATION   If a Christian brother wrongs you, talk with him in loving confrontation. Do not crawl to the corner and lick your wounds or tell everyone else about it. Do not fight to protect your reputation or to get revenge. If you are living a godly life, your reputation is God's business, and God's reputation is your business.

PRACTICE DISCERNMENT   Scripture tells us to turn the other cheek, not to lie down in front of a moving truck. If you love consistently, and the person responds by attacking you, first practice loving confrontation. If the abuse continues, however, don't become a punching bag. *Agapē* may mean to remove yourself and continue to pray for a loving resolution. Be discerning. You cannot fix everything. *Agapē* sometimes means knowing when to stop trying to fix things and exit.

Exercise 9.4

RATE YOURSELF (1 not really / 2 maybe / 3 yes, definitely)	1	2	3
Do I celebrate diversity of culture in my learning community?			
Do I use appropriate vocabulary when I teach?			
Do I empower learners?			
Do I have godly motives for teaching?			
Am I seeking learner feedback in order to improve my teaching methods?			
Am I regularly reviewing and evaluating my teaching methods in order to improve teaching practice?			
Am I trustworthy?			
When jostled by unexpected trauma does agapē bubble forth from my life?			

Place yourself on the continuum below:

Bull in a China Closet - Road Kill for a Mac Truck

SUMMARY

The first point of the Star Model of Transformactional Teaching is "Connecting Relationships." It begins with connecting to God through salvation and a life pattern of obedience and Christian growth. It includes connecting to Scripture through respect for God's Word and commitment to regular personal Bible study. Additionally, it includes connecting to the Bible lesson content by thoroughly studying the Bible passage and preparing to teach. Finally, it involves connecting to the learners through mutual trust, respect, and *agapē*. This environment of positive relationships enables the empowering of learners. It provides support for learners to move from teacher-dependent to learner-dependent learning. The teacher is a growing, godly Christian growing in love and showing love to all. To the degree that we can accomplish this, the learner perceives integrity, responding to a trustworthy teacher who consistently loves all learners.

CHAPTER TEN

CONNECTING RELEVANCE

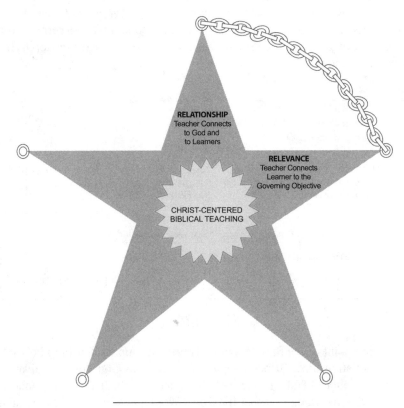

RELATIONSHIP
Teacher Connects
to God and
to Learners

RELEVANCE
Teacher Connects
Learner to the
Governing Objective

CHRIST-CENTERED
BIBLICAL TEACHING

Teacher Introduces—Learner Connects

THE RELEVANCE OF THE lesson occurs before the lesson begins. For that reason, our chapter on "Connecting Relevance" begins before the specific information in the Star lesson plan. Relevance begins at least when the learner enters the classroom. Relevance is as much an atmosphere as specific activities that draw the learner in. Learners must sense that the teacher knows how to relate the Bible lesson, but learners must also sense that the class and the classroom communicate to their needs and interests.

Connecting relevance answers two basic questions the learner may ask. First, "Is this place and are these people relevant to me?" Second, "Why is the Bible passage relevant to me?" This introduction part of the lesson plan has importance to every person. Adults all need to know how the Bible relates to them in real life.

This Chapter Covers

1. *The teacher's responsibility for the learning environment.* The classroom's atmosphere may communicate relevance, or its lack, more than the Bible lesson.
2. *The teacher's responsibility for understanding and using technology.* Without the use of technology, learners may prematurely determine that the class is out of date with modern concerns.
3. *The teacher's responsibility to construct an adequate lesson plan.* The chapter "Connecting Relationships" contains the Bible study, and it is the foundation for crafting the lesson plan. This chapter begins the Star lesson plan process. Without a prethought guide, the lesson will likely fail.
4. *The way learners can relate through the introduction to the lesson.* The lesson is introduced from the first moment a learner enters the classroom. In a broader sense, through the use of available technology, connecting relevance begins as much as a week ahead. It can produce a sense of anticipation about the lesson and a "must be there" attitude.

This Chapter Includes the Following Transformactional Principles

- *Transformactional Principle 6:* Adult learners are treated like adults, and the teacher recognizes that they are responsible for their own learning.
- *Transformactional Principle 7:* Motivation to learn is enhanced when adult learners know the purpose for learning.

This Chapter Provides Particular Support
for the Discerner Learner

Discerners appreciate and need connections. Their experiential learning type demands that the lesson has relevance to their lives. As teachers plan to create relevance with the learning environment and the lesson, they should think of ways to support Discerners. Key words to guide include: people, interactive, creative, sensitive, friendly, sociable, empathetic, noisy, ideas, feelings, talking, and colorful. Think of opportunities to create an atmosphere where those "words" belong.

This Chapter Addresses the Concerns of
Transformative Neuroscience

Transformative neuroscience theory supports the importance of creating relevance for learners. Relevance is established as new sensory experience connects with previous interest or need. Neuroscience proclaims the importance of multisensory impact in order to begin the learning process. It also supports the importance of positive emotions initiating the learning experience. For neuroscience, the initial stage of learning is receiving sensory input. The brain receives data from the body while experiencing seeing, hearing, touching, smelling, or tasting. The sensory data is sent to the back of the neocortex where it is collected and organized into coordinated chunks of related data. The brain sorts the chunks of information and discards any that do not seem important. Relevant data is sent on to the front of the brain for conscious thinking. Connecting the learner to the relevance of the lesson insures that learners engage cognitively in the Bible study session.

CONNECTING TO RELEVANCE IN THE
LEARNING ENVIRONMENT

PHYSICAL ENVIRONMENT

Adult learners need to be treated like adults. Too many churches value the carpet more than learning. Our priority should be to maximize learning, and our church budget should reflect that priority. A "no food or drink" policy helps the carpet last longer, but it does not support the kinesthetic learner who learns better when he can sip or chew. Folding chairs are cheaper, but they do not contribute to the fluid learning environment that maximizes experiential learning. Learners need to move easily from large group to small group, to table discussions, to peer pairs (see appendix G). Teachers need the freedom to move tables into configurations that support various learning activities. Classrooms need comfort and flexibility in order to treat adult learners as adults and to facilitate learning.

A comfortable physical environment includes appropriate temperature, never colder than 68 in the winter and never warmer than 72 in the summer. In older buildings with inadequate heat, purchase safe space heaters. In buildings without air conditioning, take a collection or have a fund-raiser and buy a unit for the classroom. Miserable learners have great difficulty learning. Abraham Maslow in his work on "hierarchy of needs"[1] says that our basic needs must be met before we are ready to learn. He describes the most basic level of need as physiological (see appendix H). If learners are hungry, hot, or their backs hurt from uncomfortable chairs, the "physiological body need" takes mental priority over learning. The focus becomes body distress, not new information.

A successful learning environment involves a sense of student ownership of the learning place. Students need pride in the place where they learn. They also need to feel they have contributed to its success and, therefore, they are responsible for their own learning. An occasional workday contributes to ownership. Students who clean and paint together, enjoy learning together. Rather than asking for donations, which can contribute to

We were visiting a new church one Sunday morning and were invited to an adult Bible study held after the morning worship service. We entered a large bright and inviting room and were immediately greeted by a friendly couple. The couple introduced themselves and led us to a coffee bar where people were visiting, casually helping themselves to coffee and refreshments. As we glanced down the length of the room, we noticed trees peeking in a pleasant wall of windows. We got a cup of coffee and went to find a chair. The chairs in our home church classroom were cold folding chairs that contributed to a miserable hour. These chairs were fabric, rocking, swivel, and on rollers. People were tilted at various angles turning easily to visit with each other. I noticed to my surprise that the eight-foot round tables scattered around the room were also on rollers. Before we could sit down, several people came up to introduce themselves. One couple asked us to share their table. By the time the study began, we felt relaxed, comfortable, and ready to participate.

---

[1] W. R. Yount, *Created to Learn* (Nashville: Broadman & Holman, 1996), 287.

cultural hierarchy, have a fund-raiser so that every member of the class has equal opportunity to contribute to buying the coffee pot or curtains for the windows.

HOSPITALITY AND FRIENDSHIP

Some futurists[2] predict our world will grow increasingly frightening. Wars, terrorism, pandemics, natural disasters, and fluctuations in world economy  fill people with a fear and flight mentality. Cocooning (protectively withdrawing into one's self) occurs because people have a need to feel safe and to lock out their fears. Some futurists feel that eventually people will not leave their homes at all. Any large grouping of people will be considered too dangerous. People will live in a virtual world locked away from their fears. Attending church, completing school, shopping, exercising, working, and attending meetings will all be done online. Although we sincerely hope that we never reach that extreme, we know that people are frightened and lonely. The twenty-first century is characterized by rampant dysfunctional relationships. Casual sex dehumanizes and emotionally isolates, leaving individuals raw and bleeding. Casualties of divorce are prevalent both inside and outside the church in equal numbers. Alcohol and drugs deadens the pain but also empties the person. Adults are looking for healthy relationships.

HOSPITAL/ADOPTION AGENCY

The church is not a "members only" club, but rather a hospital and adoption agency. The weary, wounded, empty, and frightened can be loved, receive God's healing forgiveness, and embrace a new life as adopted children of God. It is a place where sprouting new life is valued, and life is nurtured and encouraged to grow. In the church, mature brothers and sisters facilitate the maturing of newer members of God's family.

Unfortunately, we have visited so many churches that are happy "just the way they are." They not only do not "reach out"; they "shoo away." Are we not reading Scripture? As Christian educators, our job is to introduce people to the adopting Father, God. We should welcome them into God's family and facilitate Christian growth so that together the members of God's family will reflect

---

[2] F. Popcorn and A. Hanft, *Dictionary of the Future: The Words, Terms, and Trends that Define the Way We'll Live, Work and Talk* (New York: Hyperion, 2001). See also F. Popcorn, *The Popcorn Report on the Future of Your Company, Your World, Your Life.* (New York: HarperCollins, Inc., 1992), especially 27–33.

Christlikeness. As we grow together, we will draw the world to Christ. Bible teaching is nothing more grand and glorious—and nothing less awesome.

In 2005, Group Publishing in their publication "Friendship: Creating a Culture of Connectivity in Your Church"[3] shares the results of a Gallup Organization research that they sponsored in 2004. The national survey consisted of 1,002 respondents to phone interviews who were church members over 18. The findings indicate: "The most satisfied church members in America worship at places where they feel like they belong, where they are valued and appreciated, and where friendships flourish."[4] This study also demonstrates that caring spiritual leaders lead to spiritual growth. "Eighty-four percent of respondents who are very satisfied with their churches report 'the spiritual leaders of my congregation seem to care for me as a person.'"[5] Lindsay describes the value of relational teaching and learning as "The 'Silver Bullet' for Spiritual Depth"[6] and "loving relationships [that] produce members who are more satisfied with their relationship with God and who are more likely to describe their faith as a friendship with God."[7]

WELCOMING AND FRIENDLY

The Bible study should model a welcoming, friendly atmosphere. Even adult learners hesitate to enter a room where people avoid them, and they wonder what to expect. Train your Bible study group to practice what they are learning—*agapē*. Have designated door greeters who stand near the door to welcome newcomers. Do not stop there! Have the door greeter introduce new people to a coffee greeter who visits with them around the coffee bar and helps them get coffee. The coffee greeter then introduces them to a table greeter. Table greeters invite them to sit at their table, engages them in conversation, and introduces them to the other people sitting at the table. By the time Bible study begins, new people have met a number of people from the class and feel comfortable at the table.

EVERYONE CAN DO SOMETHING

Your Bible study group should not only invite new people and welcome them; it should also practice true friendship—*agapē*—as regular attendees

---

[3] M. Lindsay et al., *Friendship: Creating a Culture of Connectivity in Your Church* (Loveland, CO: Group Publishing, Inc., 2005).
[4] Ibid., 7.
[5] Ibid., 9.
[6] Ibid., 35.
[7] Ibid., 39. Insert is authors'.

Years ago we began a Sunday morning Bible study at a church in Tennessee, and the class had grown to about 100 people in the course of a year. We were studying the book of Philippians and had been discussing agapē when God taught us a lesson none of us would ever forget. We got a call on Friday morning: one of the men in our class was headed for work, and had pulled his car on to the freeway right in front of a semi-truck; the truck had run over his car, and he was killed instantly. The man and his wife had been coming to our class for several months, and we were all in shock. How could this happen to a man in his twenties? Then we realized our responsibility toward his wife and three small children. We were amazed to watch agapē in action under the leadership of our godly in-reach leaders Gary and Helen. Class members helped with funeral arrangements, cared for the children, brought food to the home, helped the young wife pay her bills, put a new roof on the house, and cared for the yard. Agapē in action provided support until this young woman could begin to function again, and the persons most blessed were those who served.

interface. This should be done not only by listening to each other in the face-to-face meetings, but also following each other's lives throughout the week. Continuing connections can be made by snail mail notes and cards, or with technology. Your class Web site can provide opportunities to post needs and resources. Regardless of the vehicle of communication, the needs of the individuals in the group should be important and addressed. It helps to have one individual who organizes the expressions of love, but every person who wants to be part should be included. Everyone can do something. Christ demonstrated service when He washed the disciples' feet. Your Bible study environment should be characterized by *agapē* in action.

CONNECTING RELEVANCE WITH TECHNOLOGY

Every adult classroom needs technology. We live in a technological world. Many colleges require students to own laptops in order to attend school. Computers are commonplace in school classrooms, and most children comfortably navigate the Internet. Elementary teachers have blogs where they answer parent questions daily, as well as a class Web site for posting weekly assignments and activities. Why, then, is the church without technology? Adults want to feel that they are learning in an "up-to-date" environment. Technology-supported adult learning environments should include convenience and flexibility, contextualization, collaboration and communication, and constructive feedback.[8]

Convenience and flexibility are essential in adult learning. The complexity of daily living often prohibits a weekly commitment to attend traditional classes. Churches can offer some Bible studies that take place totally online. This enables people, regardless of their work schedule, to participate in regular adult Bible Study. In addition, hybrid Bible studies can include both Internet and face-to-face class time. Hybrid classes can meet face-to-face once a month, with ongoing participation through the class Web site and chat room. Classes can also meet weekly face-to-face, with daily or weekly computer components that support the face-to-face classroom.

Allowing students to personalize learning through Internet exercises tailored to their spiritual maturity and experience base can effectively contextualize a Bible class. Advance study questions can be posted to build interest in an upcoming study. Persons have equal opportunity to offer ideas and evaluate contributions. Study questions posted after Bible study encourages reflection and, if offered in a threaded discussion format, give opportunity for reflective discourse. Individuals can each be heard and their cultural viewpoints expressed to the enrichment of the group and without class time constraints.

The Internet can enhance collaboration and communication whether a class is totally online, hybrid, or face to face. Chat rooms, blogs, Facebook, and MySpace illustrate the many opportunities for learners to interact on a personal level throughout the week. People tend to stay in a church or Bible study environment when they have good friends learning with them. Online collaboration also provides opportunity for students to get to know each other on a deeper level. Sharing pictures and information about family help form deeper friendships.

Bible study groups that involve older adults may not be as comfortable with forums such as Facebook because of reluctance to make personal information public. Most adults, however, are open to a secure class Web site so that their personal information is shared only with the class friends. Threaded discussion is a great opportunity for collaboration. It allows learners to log in at anytime and join an ongoing discussion. The teacher initiates a question or discussion topic, and the learners can respond to the original question or to the responses of the other class members. Chat rooms allow for open discussion in real time. Class news and prayer requests can be shared on the class Web site bulletin board.

[8] L. Webster and D. Murphy, "Enhancing Learning Through Technology: Challenges and Responses," in ed. R. Kwan, R. Fox, F. T. Chan, and P. Tsang *Enhancing Learning Through Technology: Research on Emerging Technologies and Pedagogies* (Hackensack, NJ: World Scientific Publishing Co., 2008), 11.

The teacher or an assistant must accept responsibility to monitor the on-line dialogue and maintain an emotionally safe environment, though it can be delegated. The class should post a set of rules that govern online discussion. Participants often forget that body language and facial expressions are absent when discussing online. On the next page you will find a few suggestions that you may want to post on your class Web site.

Technology can provide constructive feedback from learners. Online class surveys give the teacher opportunity to take the temperature of the class and respond with the appropriate prescription. Teaching methods can be evaluated through online surveys or questionnaires. Scripture passages can be selected considering every person's interest and needs. Surveys can be used as indica-tors of individual service interests. Post class evaluations indicate which needs were met and which needs should be addressed in further study.

TECHNOLOGICAL LITERACY

Contemporary teachers must have a comfort level with technology. Teachers should be computer literate and ei-ther have a laptop to bring into the classroom or have com-puters available in the classroom. Computers should be used in teaching and the images projected for all to see. PowerPoint or KeyNote should be used for adding visual images to regular class presentations. Television projection or LCD projected computer images allow learners to view the computer content from various vantage points in the room. An LCD projector is preferable because the im-age can be projected onto a wall or large screen. If a TV is used, a very large, flat-screen TV mounted on a wall increases visibility. Internet connections should also be available in every classroom for both small group research and for teacher presentations. Wireless Internet with a sufficient bandwidth for streaming video is advisable. Please note that the larger the number of people using the internet simultaneously, and the larger the files being used on the Internet, the larger the bandwidth needed. Movie clips and videos use a large amount of bandwidth. It is important to have DVD players or computer capa-bility to play and project DVDs.

Both teacher and learners should be made comfortable with the technology used in class. Explore the talents represented in your church and ask some-one who is comfortable with computers to teach Saturday sessions for learn-ers who are unfamiliar with current technology. This provides opportunity for them to expand their knowledge base and feel comfortable navigating the class Web site. There is no person too old to enter in.

Rules for Online Communication

1. **Avoid Offensive Language.** Sarcasm, strong words, profanity, or the excessive use of exclamation points may be misinterpreted or offensive. If you feel very emotional about your response, write a rough draft and read it carefully before posting it.

2. **Avoid Humor.** Humor usually is misunderstood online because of the absence of "environmental extras" that contribute to "being funny."

3. **Forgive Others.** Forgive others when you find something hurtful or offensive. Miscommunication is often caused by carelessness and the unfamiliarity of using the Internet. Encourage others to share any hurts or misunderstandings with you so that you can clear up differences.

4. **Avoid Saying Anything that You Might Want to Erase Later.** You cannot take back an online message. Be very careful. Think it through carefully and communicate clearly. Read your message out loud before sending it so that you can check it for clarity.

5. **Learn Netspeak.** Netspeak may be used by people who are used to communicating on the Internet. Here are a few expressions you may see:

DO NOT USE ALL CAPS. Caps communicate anger or shouting.

FYI = for your information

BTW= by the way

F2F= face to face

FAQ = frequently asked questions

:-) = smiley face

:-(= unhappy face

:-o =surprise face

:-/ =skepticism

Learners who do not have their own computers or Internet can access both for free at the local library. It is also advisable to have some donated computers in the church library so that people can access them during the week. Both teachers and learners can access online, self-paced instruction in many software programs for twenty-five dollars per month through lynda.com.[9] Lynda.com uses a programmed instruction approach to learning new software programs. Programs include simple word processing to Web authoring for the same monthly fee. Learners work at their own speed to assimilate new information and practice on their own computer in the privacy of their own homes. In addition, local community colleges and community centers offer simple computer courses for very reasonable fees. Check out availability in your area, and get the information to the participants in your study.

---

[9] http://www.lynda.com/home/otl_a.aspx?gclid=COOozo-wtZoCFQkzawodKBNJbg

Because personal data assistants (PDA) and mobile phone technology has multiplied recently, all computer programs used should be PDA/mobile phone compatible. Adults use PDAs and mobile phones to answer e-mails and access Web sites regularly. When designing your class Web site, it is possible to check the Web site for PDA/mobile phone compatibility.[10]

Teachers who are uncomfortable establishing a class Web site can access user-friendly programs. For example, through LifeWay Christian Resources "webmaster resources" is a link available for churches to help set up and manage a Web site. It is a LifeWay LINK and may be found at sbc.net/webmaster/default.asp. Extensive education class resources are available through *Moodle*.[11] *Moodle*[12] is an excellent resource, but it is not intuitive and requires more computer proficiency. *Blackboard*[13] is another program for online classroom instruction. *Moodle* and *Blackboard* are secular systems designed to support different levels of education and business. If Bible teachers choose to create their own Web sites, software such as *Dreamweaver*[14] or *Front Page*[15] are very helpful and can be transferred to a number of servers (Hostmonster, Godaddy, Google, etc.) with adequate space for about ten dollars per year.

My father always took pride in keeping up with contemporary living. When he turned 80, he decided that everyone else was doing computer so he would too. He purchased a desktop and launched into a new era. Before long he was using the Internet and e-mailing his friends. When he passed away, my mother decided she would learn. She now uses her computer every day, receiving the church newsletter, e-mailing friends, and receiving messages and pictures from friends all over the world. You are never too old to learn computer.

[10] This "PDA check" is a feature of Adobe's Dreamweaver and many other Web-authoring software packages.

[11] http://moodle.org (accessed May 4, 2009)

[12] J. Cole and H. Foster, *Using Moodle:* 2nd ed. (Sebastopol, CA: O'Reilly Media Inc., 2008); W. H. Rice IV, *Moodle: E-Learning Course Development-A complete guide to successful learning using Moodle* (Birmingham, AL: Packt, 2006).

[13] http://www.blackboard.com (accessed May 4, 2009).

[14] http://www.adobe.com/products/dreamweaver (accessed May 4, 2009). Betsy Bruce, *Sams Teach Yourself Adobe Dreamweaver CS3 in 24 Hours.* (Indianapolis: Sams Publishing, 2007).

[15] http://office.microsoft.com/en-us/frontpage/default.aspx (accessed May 4, 2009).

CONNECTING RELEVANCE IN THE STAR MODEL ADULT LESSON PLAN PART 1

There are many good ways to format a Bible study. The Star transformactional lesson plan is only one. If you learn this model, you will be able to take the essential components and include them if you choose to teach other formats. A lesson plan is like a skeletal structure for the lesson to be built upon. The muscle is the details of the plan, and the clothes are the methods, the appeal of the lesson to the learner.

Once you have learned the components of a skeleton and the usual muscle distribution, variety is possible. Ultimately it doesn't matter if you put on the arm of the skeleton before the leg, or the leg before the arm, but the skeleton is incomplete unless all parts are present. Similarly, the order or the density to the distribution of the muscle detail may change, but all parts of the skeleton must be covered. Finally, variety in clothes (methods) makes a more interesting and attractive presentation. Some colors and styles appeal to some individuals while other colors and styles appeal to others.

The Star Transformactional Lesson Plan comes from the personal transformactional Bible study (Star 1). The Bible study is the basis for setting the objectives for the lesson, establishing relevance, determining the content, selecting appropriate applications, and demonstrating choices for action. We have given the outline of the Star Model Adult Lesson Plan followed by instructions for developing Part 1 relevance. The remainder of the lesson plan will be covered in the chapters yet to come. We have used Rom 5:1–5 as an example so that you can follow the correlation between the Bible study and the progression of the lesson plan.

STAR MODEL ADULT LESSON PLAN

Passage and Reference:
Governing Objective: The overall objective of the passage is for the learner to . . . _____

I. Relevance:

Why is this passage relevant to your learners? (5 minutes)

Description: *Describe why this passage is relevant to contemporary adult learners.*

Methods: *Create an exciting introduction that connects the learner with the relevance of the Bible passage. Explain the methods you will use to introduce the passage.*

Evaluation: *I will know the learners have connected with the relevance of the passage by . . .*

Transition: *Write a sentence that will transition your learners from the introduction into the Bible content section.*

II. Revelation:

What will learners know/understand about the content of the biblical passage? (20–23 minutes)

Objective: *Learners will know/understand . . . (cognitive content of the passage).*

Description: *Create a guide for teaching the content of your lesson. This can be a comprehensive outline, narrative, or PowerPoint slide layout pages.*

Methods: *Describe your teaching methods for helping learners discover the Bible content of this passage.*

Evaluation: *I will know learners attain the content objective by . . . (the learner answering questions, filling in study sheet, restating, etc.).*

Transition: *Write a transition sentence that takes the learner from content to application.*

III. Responsibility:

How will learners apply the biblical principles of this passage to contemporary adults? (18–20 minutes)

Objective: *After applying (the Scripture principle) to today's adults, the learner will (desire, be convinced, appreciate, etc.) (describe a measurable conviction).*

Description: *List the principles in your passage that were true in Bible times that are still true today. Include the verse where you found them.*

Methods: *Methods in this section should focus on engaging students on a convictional level. Describe the methods you will use to lead the learners to explore the principles and why these principles are applicable to today's world.*

Evaluation: *I will know the learners engage convictionally with the contemporary application by learners (sharing, discussing, debating, reflecting, praying, expressing, dramatizing, etc. . . .What is it you will observe the learner doing that will indicate he accomplished the application objective?).*

Transition: *Write a transition sentence that takes the learner from application to personal action.*

IV. Results:

What will learners do to apply this passage to their own lives? How will their lives be different? (8–10 minutes)

Objective: *Learners will commit to . . . (an appropriate action of obedience).*

Description: *List some action responses you could suggest that would constitute personal obedience to the principles found in this passage?*

Methods: *What method will you use to challenge learners to take personal life-changing actions of obedience in response to the principles in this passage.*

Evaluation: *I will know the learners have committed to personal action by . . . _____*

Lesson Wrap-up: *Restate for your students in one or two sentences a summary of what you wanted them to learn. (1–2 minutes)*

Learner Evaluation for Governing Lesson Objective:

I know the learners accomplished my governing objective because they . . .

Materials: *Make a list of all materials and equipment you will need to teach this lesson. Include completed study sheets, scripts, PowerPoint layout pages, etc.*

DIRECTIONS FOR PART 1: RELEVANCE

PASSAGE AND REFERENCE

Always write the passage and reference on the lesson plan so that anyone could pick up your plan and teach your lesson and so that you can easily file it for future use. If it helps, you may write the verses in multiple versions. Whatever version or versions you used in teaching should be used consistently in other materials, such as PowerPoint slides, handouts, posters, white board, and resource tables. Consistency is less confusing and reduces learner stress. Remember that many learners do not bring Bibles with them. Always have the passage printed in the appropriate translation so that every learner can participate in reading and searching the passage.

LESSON OBJECTIVES

The Star lesson plan has four learning objectives: the governing objective and three component objectives: the revelation objective, the responsibility objective, and the results objective. The governing objective dominates. It provides the focus for the entire lesson. The section objectives are intermediate goals that incrementally build to accomplishing the governing objective. In this chapter we will discuss the definition of learning objectives, and we will explain how to write the governing lesson objective. In the next three chapters, each chapter will explain the component learning objective that goes with that particular section of the lesson.

Figure 10.6

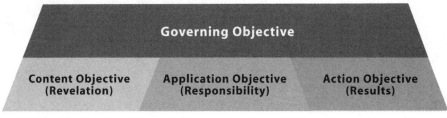

Learning objectives and learning goals are essentially the same. They define what you (the teacher) want your students (learners) to accomplish through the whole lesson (governing objective), or through a specific section of the lesson (component objective). Objectives are measurable. The teacher can give a test, ask for feedback, or observe the learners and discover whether or not the learners have accomplished the objectives. The teacher must create a learning environment and provide emotional support for the learner to accomplish the objective. The learner, however, is responsible for accomplishing the objective. Learning is life change based upon knowledge, conviction, and choices. Teachers cannot make students learn.

The governing lesson objective answers the question, "Do my students understand the focus of this passage, and are they willing to change their lives accordingly?" You can measure (evaluate) this goal by asking in the closing statement: "What was the one most important truth to remember in this passage, and how will it make a difference in your life?"

Review your Transformactional Personal Bible Study. Find section 7 that is telling you to: "In one sentence write the main point of the passage." From this main point write an overall governing lesson objective: "Upon completing this lesson the learner will understand that this passage teaches . . . and that they are willing to change their lives accordingly."

Example: Upon completing this lesson, the student will understand that this passage teaches that we can have peace with God through Jesus and that they are willing to change their lives accordingly (Rom 5:1–5).

> *There is a cartoon of an archer shooting arrows at a target. A* *second person has the target in his arms and is running around trying to catch the arrows with it.* The governing lesson objective is like this target. First, learners must hold the objective as their own. Second, like an archer shooting arrows, the teacher keeps every component of the lesson focused on and moving toward the governing objective. Third, unlike the archer in the cartoon, teachers need to focus the components of the lesson so effectively that the learner does not need to run all over the field to catch them. All component arrows should hit the governing target.*

* L. Ford, *Design for Teaching and Training: A Self-Study Guide to Lesson Planning* (Nashville: Broadman Press, 1978), 18.

INTRODUCTION/RELEVANCE DESCRIBED

It is difficult to connect your learners to the relevance of the passage unless you know why your passage is relevant. Before you write the introduction to your lesson, think through the connection between the main point of the passage and your adult learners. Why should your learners want to know the content of this passage? Write a sentence stating the relevance of the passage: "This passage is relevant to adult learners today because . . . ."

Transformactional principle 7 reminds us that adult learners need to know the purpose for learning the particular Scripture passage that the teacher presents. When adult learners can see the relevance or connectedness of the biblical passage to their own situations, they will be motivated to learn. With this in mind, the Bible teacher designs a dynamic, exciting, attention-grabbing introduction that connects the learners to the purpose of the passage.

INTRODUCTION/DELIVERY METHODS

Many different methods can introduce this passage in a captivating way, one that connects the learner to the relevance of the passage. Below is one example. For your further assistance, there is a collection of methods at the end of this book (see appendix G). Please feel free to use any of these suggested methods or add another of your own. Be cautious. It is easy to choose a method because it seems fun or because you think you have someone in the group who could lead it. Don't miss this opportunity to connect your learners to relevance. Keep your eye on the goal— maximize each learning opportunity.

Example: Brainstorming

Write in large letters on a grease board: "Peace with God?" Have learners sit in small groups with a recorder in each group. Invite learners to fire reactions to the phrase. Have the recorder write down each idea without comment for two minutes. At the end of two minutes have each group write responses on the grease board. The teacher or activity leader groups similar responses, leads in discussion, and summarizes.

> *Be a Dragon Slayer!*
> *"Centuries ago, when mapmakers ran out of known world before they ran out of parchment, they would sketch a dragon at the edge of the scroll. This was a sign to the explorer that he would be entering unknown territory at his own risk. Unfortunately some explorers took this symbol literally and were afraid to push on to new worlds. Other more adventuresome explorers saw the dragons as a sign of opportunity, a door to virgin territory."* As a teacher you can be too afraid to try new methods and hang on to the past OR you can be a dragon slayer.*
>
> * R. von Oech, *A Kick in the Seat of the Pants* (New York: Harper Perennial, 1986), 39.

EVALUATION

There is an evaluation for each section of the lesson plan. It measures whether or not the learner has understood the objective for that section of the plan. In

Part I Relevance the learner is to connect with the relevance of the passage and answer the question "Why should I study this passage?" The evaluation is the way that the teacher will know the learner has chosen to engage the learning experience. The evaluation should be written in terms of the learner.

Example: I will know the learner has connected with the relevance of the passage by the learner enthusiastically participating in the brainstorming session.

TRANSITIONS

Transitions are important for continuity. Although the Star model lesson plan has four distinct sections (relevance, revelation, responsibility, and results), your learners should see only a smoothly flowing whole lesson that moves along easily and builds to a life-changing action response from the learner. Consider a potter's task. A potter who throws a pot may wish to add a handle to the pot. The handle must be blended into the pot so that it appears seamless and contributes to the whole. Transition sentences smooth over the seams in the clay. They are the barely visible glue that holds the parts together.

Transitions are part of the Star model lesson plan because, while they happen very naturally for some teachers, other teachers struggle with moving from one part of the lesson to the next. Whether transitions are difficult for you or not, if you write out a transition sentence, you will help yourself easily move into the next section of the lesson. Transition statements are something like this: "We have just seen a video-clip of the terrorist attack on 9/11, and in our discussions we have determined that the world is a really scary place. Today our Bible study will give us practical tools for dealing with fear. Please turn with me to . . . ." Transitions are bridges. Without them, learners lose their way. Use them to help both you and the learners keep sight of your lesson objectives. Stay on track and remember where you are going.

Below you will see an example of the Star transformactional lesson plan part I, RELEVANCE, using Rom 5:1–5. The example expresses one of hundreds of ways you could teach the lesson. Put your own ideas and creativity to work and express yourself in your own plan.

STAR MODEL ADULT LESSON PLAN PART 1 SAMPLE

Passage and Reference: *Rom 5:1–5. "(1) Therefore, since we have been declared righteous by faith, we have peace with God through our Lord Jesus Christ. (2) Also through Him, we have obtained access by faith into this grace in which we stand, and we rejoice in the hope of the glory of God. (3) And not only that, but we also rejoice in our afflictions, because we know that affliction produces* *endurance, (4) endurance produces proven character, and proven character produces hope. (5) This hope does not disappoint, because God's love has been poured out in our hearts through the Holy Spirit who was given to us."*

Governing Objective: The overall objective of the passage for the learner: Upon completing this lesson, the student will remember that this passage teaches "that we have peace with God through our Lord Jesus Christ," when we have been declared righteous by faith.

I. Relevance:

Why is this passage relevant to your learners? (5 minutes)

Description: *Describe why this passage is relevant to contemporary adult learners.* Romans 5:1–5 is relevant to adult learners today because every adult must die, and only making peace with God will give a person eternal peace.

Methods: *Create an exciting introduction that connects the learner with the relevance of the Bible passage. Explain the methods you will use to introduce the passage.* Drama/Testimony: Get the book *Joni* [16] from Amazon.com or from Joni and Friends.[17] One week ahead, ask a woman or teenage girl to dramatize the testimony of Joni Eareckson Tada, using the material in the book (3–5 minutes). Ask the actress to come in a wheelchair. You can borrow a wheelchair or rent one from a medical supply store. (Most medical supply stores will rent one for 24 hours for a nominal fee.) On the day of the study, have the words, "Peace with God" in huge letters on the wall of the classroom. Begin the lesson time by wheeling in the actress playing Joni Eareckson Tada, a quadriplegic. Have the actress share Joni's testimony. She will tell (in first person) about how she broke her neck diving when she was a teenager. Have the actress tell how she felt lying there unable even to kill herself. Have the actress explain how she was afraid to die because

---

[16] J. E. Tada, *Joni.* (Grand Rapids: Zondervan, 2001).
[17] http://www.joniandfriends.org

she was afraid of God and she was afraid to live because she couldn't move anything. After the actress has thoroughly explained Joni's desperate need to find peace with God, STOP! Have learners discuss her dilemma and how it relates to the words "Peace with God" on the board. Do not resolve the dilemma. (You will bring Joni back later in the lesson.)

Evaluation: *I will know the learners have connected with the relevance of the passage by . . .* facial expressions, body language, and participation in the discussion about Joni's dilemma.

Transition: *Write a sentence that will transition your learners from the introduction into the Bible content section.* "Thanks for sharing that with us, Joni. What a dilemma! Today we are going to study a Bible passage that will address the problem Joni experienced, how do we find peace with God? Please look together at Rom 5:1–5."

SUMMARY

Star model point 2 is connecting relevance. The teacher, having studied the passage carefully, creates the learning environment helping adult learners to feel ownership of their own learning. The teacher begins the lesson plan creating the structure and organization of the lesson. A carefully constructed, exciting introduction establishes the purpose of studying the passage and connects the learner to the relevance of the passage.

Exercise 10.1

RATE YOURSELF: 1 being poor, 5 being terrific	1	2	3	4	5
1. My Bible study learning environment makes my learners feel that they are more important than the facility.					
2. A new person visiting my Bible study would find it warm and friendly.					
3. My use of technology in teaching is ...					
4. I have support in place for my students to feel comfortable with participating in class computer activities.					
5. I have selected a passage, completed my Bible study and Part I of the Star Lesson Plan.					
6. I have considered the diversity of learners in my Bible study as I have selected methods for my Introduction.					
7. I have committed to dragon slaying and have planned to use a new method.					

Chapter Eleven

CONNECTING REVELATION

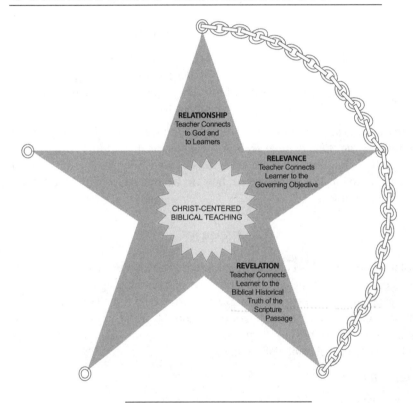

Teacher Reveals Historical Scripture
Content—Learner Understands

IN THIS CHAPTER THE teacher facilitates connections between the historical biblical material and the learner. The teacher has prepared thoroughly by completing the Transformactional Bible Study (Star Point 1, Chapter 9) and has prepared, in the Star Lesson Plan "Relevance" section, an exciting introduction to the lesson. This connected the learners to the purpose for the Bible Study. Now, in the "Revelation" section, the learner experiences the scripture passage content. This does not mean memorizing a piece of history. "Connecting

Revelation" involves understanding the original author of the passage and his context. It involves understanding the original recipients and their contexts. It also involves understanding the content of the biblical passage by observing grammatical structure of the language in the passage. Which sentences in the passage take primary importance and which are secondary? What do the unfamiliar terms mean? How does the original culture influence the meaning of the passage? In Star 3 we visit the historical biblical world, try to put ourselves in the place of the recipients of the original text, and try to understand the meaning in its original cultural context.

"Connecting Revelation" is also the place where the teacher may present material in a more formal way. Teaching methodology is more conducive to a lecture or other teacher-directed approach. For that reason, we believe this is the place to discuss communication skills. If the teacher cannot communicate effectively, the content portion of the Bible study is seriously hindered. Thus we will discuss communication skills and techniques first, and then address Star lesson plan "Revelation."

This Chapter Covers

1. *The teacher's responsibility to communicate as accurately and clearly as possible.* There is little value in having something to say if it cannot be said in a dynamic way.
2. *The teacher's responsibility to connect the learner with the biblical passage through understanding the passage in its original context.* The basic question of this section is "What did the original hearers of the passage understand the passage to mean?"
3. *The teacher's responsibility to construct the Revelation section of the Star lesson plan as the format for connecting learners with the biblical/historical content of the passage.* This part of the lesson plan pays special attention to the Constructor learner.

This Chapter Includes the Following Transformactional Principles

*   *Transformactional Principle 8:* Retention of learning increases when learners have multisensory experiences gathering new information through discovery and experience.

- *Transformactional Principle 9:* Retention of learning increases when, through reflection, the learner connects new learning to memories of previous experiences.
- *Transformactional Principle 10:* Bible learning is a lifelong process that should move from teacher-directed to self-directed as the teacher changes roles to match the learner's needs.

This Chapter Provides Particular Support for Constructor Learners

When crafting the Revelation section of the lesson plan, teachers should remember the Constructors. Constructors love the rich content of the passage and accurate historical facts. They enjoy logic and sequential lecture presentations, assuming the presenter is well prepared. When engaging in self-discovery, Constructors prefer to have clear, concise questions presented in an organized way with excellent resources available. Key words to guide preparation are: facts, logic, accurate, history, background, culture, grammatical structure, geography, historical events, historical people, and definitions. Although teachers can stroke learners who prefer the Constructor style when teaching the Revelation section of the lesson, they cannot teach people with these styles exclusively. All learners need to know the content of the passage. Teachers must include methods that engage all learners while satisfying the hunger of the Constructors for the facts. A well-prepared teacher can do both.

This Chapter Addresses the Concerns of Transformative Neuroscience

From neuroscience we understand that adult information processing requires four basic elements. They are: learning experiences for gathering sensory information, time for reflection, a positive emotional learning environment, and opportunity for conscious associations of past and new information. In the Revelation section of the lesson, students gather information both from what is said and what is discovered. Teachers give opportunity for reflection in class activities that encourage reflective dialogue or ongoing Internet opportunities for reflection and discussion. Small group and Peer Pair sharing can support learners in consciously associating memories with related information. By the end of the content section of the lesson, learners should own the content of the passage and be ready to use the information they have discovered.

Learning creates physical changes in the brain. Areas of the brain associated with specific types of learning actually increase in density as the neurons develop intricate networks of connections. When specific neurons repeatedly fire because they are engaged in specific learning experiences, and positive emotion chemicals surround those neurons, neuron density occurs. These neuron density changes occur only in the parts of the brain that are used. "Connections with relatively high activity are stabilized and strengthened, while connections with relatively low activity are weakened and, eventually, eliminated. As connections between neurons are modified, the brain is gradually shaped to reflect experience."[1] The changes can be observed with brain imaging techniques from medical science. Therefore, we can say that a brain given to regular Bible study that results in life change can actually look physically different from what it did before studying God's Word.

CONNECTING REVELATION THROUGH COMMUNICATION SKILLS

Teachers should consider the question, "Should you teach the lesson or the student?" Can you teach the lesson without teaching the student? Absolutely! You can talk your heart out and speak the truth about the lesson content without ever engaging and teaching the student. Conversely, can you teach the student without teaching the lesson? Absolutely! We have heard many great communicators entertain a group of students without saying anything worthwhile. The big question again is: do we teach the lesson or the student? The answer is YES. The only valid reason for teaching a Bible study is giving students the opportunity to learn the content of God's Word and experiencing changed lives as a result. Without a doubt, this content section is the most important part of the lesson. It helps people understand what God says! We must be certain we are communicating the best that we can, so that students have the best possible learning opportunity.

Whatever your limitations, you can improve communication by maximizing your available resources and sharpening your skills. Improving oral communication skills comes from improving your use of words, using voice inflection, varying speed, and adding other sounds and voices to your presentation. Visual communication skills can also be improved as you work on facial expressions, eye contact, hand gestures, and graphic visual support to your presentations. Finally, your interactive communication skills will be improved as

---

[1] C. Hinton, K. Miyamoto, and B. Della-Chiesa, "Brain Research, Learning and Emotions: implications for education research, policy and practice," *European Journal of Education,* vol. 43, no. 1 (Oxford, UK: Blackwell Publishing Lts., 2008), 89.

you practice interactive dialogue with students.

> Mobile Oil Company studies support the importance of "display devices" in teaching. They found that from hearing alone, 70 percent of material taught was recalled three hours later and 10 percent was recalled three days later. Seeing alone produced a 72 percent recall rate three hours later and 20 percent recall three days later. But the combination of both seeing and hearing had a dramatic impact on recall. Participants in the study recalled 85 percent of what they both saw and heard three hours later and obtained a 65 percent rate of recall three days later.[2]

The Mobile Oil Company study motivates us to sharpen our communication skills and use multiple methods of communication to increase our ability to communicate the truth of Scripture effectively.

One Sunday I went into the church service knowing that we were having a guest speaker. Because I enjoyed our pastor, I was fussing to myself as I found a seat and joined in the singing. When it was time for preaching, an assistant wheeled David Miller onto the platform, physically lifted him out of his wheelchair, propped him against the pulpit, and locked his leg braces into place. Leaning on the pulpit precariously, unable to move his arms or legs, David Miller opened his mouth, recited the long passage that was his text, and began the most eloquent narrative I have ever heard. He created word pictures and colorful descriptions that captivated his audience, and his piercing eye contact engaged every listener. Learners' eyes were glued to him, ears were listening to every word, and hearts were open to the conviction of the Holy Spirit.

ORAL COMMUNICATION

Language is the primary form of communication in teaching. It consists of both the words used in communicating, and the manner of using your voice. Oral language at the most basic level is composed of phonemes, the smallest vocal unit of language. The phonetic alphabet consists of 45 sounds. Children sometimes learn to read through phonics. Both reading and listening, however, involve more than simply identifying sounds and blending them to make words. The meaning of words changes by adding morphemes: "units of meaning" such as "ing" or "ed." What is it we are really trying to convey by using these words? Semantics is the definition of words, sentences, phrases, and paragraphs. Syntax is the relationships of words to each other that are

[2] L. O. Richards and G. J. Bredfeldt, *Creative Bible Teaching* (Chicago: Moody Press, 1998), 223–24.

often represented through punctuation and grammar. Pragmatics is the use of language in context: knowledge of when to speak and how to use intonation, accents, and voice inflection to make meaning. These components work together to communicate meaning. Effective communicators understand how to make these elements of language work for them as they present their ideas.

CORRECT LANGUAGE Many Bible teachers struggle with one or more of the components of language. English may be a second or third language, in which case phonemes and morphemes may bring challenges. Regional grammatical nuances or childhood environments may make standard semantics or syntax difficult. People have great difficulty correcting language that sounds acceptable to them. Common slang may violate acceptable pragmatics. Whatever the challenge, it is important to work at speaking correct English.

Rehearsing through recording or having someone else read and correct your notes or PowerPoint slides may help. When typing the lesson plan or preparing study sheets and slides, always use the spell and grammar correction tools. Avoid using slang or sarcastic expressions. They are easily misunderstood. Never use swear words—not even for a shock effect. Learners may mentally turn off your voice if it offends their sense of language or their personal commitments. Everyone can improve oral communication with practice. We recommend the following exercises for all communicators.

PICTURESQUE WORDS When teaching the content section of the lesson, work at creating picturesque images with your words. Descriptions should bring pictures to the eyes of the vision impaired. Here are several exercises to improve this skill.

Exercise 1: Find a simple color drawing in a children's picture book. Give a friend colored markers and a pad of paper. Sitting back to back, look at the picture and describe it in detail to your friend. Have your friend draw what you are describing. When you have finished, look at the drawing and discuss with your friend how you could have done a better job of describing the picture.

Exercise 2: Blindfold a friend and lead him to an unknown place such as a garden or zoo. Try to describe every detail of the setting so that your friend can see it through your words. Then take the blindfold off of your friend and have him tell you how you could have helped him visualize it better.

Exercise 3: Invite five to seven people to sit in a circle, sitting on their hands so they cannot use hand gestures. Ask each person in turn to tell the story of the most frightening thing that ever happened to them. Ask them to think about describing it in such a way that all of you become frightened. Discuss the best word pictures used by individuals in your group. Discuss what would have made each story more vivid.

VARIATION IN VOICE 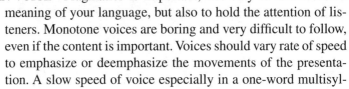 Pragmatics is important, not only to reinforce the meaning of your language, but also to hold the attention of listeners. Monotone voices are boring and very difficult to follow, even if the content is important. Voices should vary rate of speed to emphasize or deemphasize the movements of the presentation. A slow speed of voice especially in a one-word multisyllable response can convey disapproval or hesitation (O——Kay), whereas a faster speed between syllables can convey approval or enthusiasm. (O-KAY).

Notice that the inflection and emphasis on the syllables also affects the meaning. High-pitch voice tone and low pitch tones should also convey the meaning of the story. If you have a small pitch range with very little variation, your words will sound similar. If your pitch variation is greater, learners catch transitions and follow progressions more easily. Too much volume can make your voice sound angry or tire both speaker and listener. Speaking too softly makes listening a strain. Variation in volume both stimulates and rests the listener.

Exercise 1: Record a voice presentation of yourself and listen to it. Is your voice interesting or boring? Do you vary the speed of your words? Do you vary the tone of your voice?

Exercise 2: Get a group of five to seven friends and sit in a circle. Sit on your hands so that you cannot depend on hand gestures. Take turns going around the circle and telling the most exciting thing that has ever happened to you. Concentrate on voice variation. Try to make the story exciting by using the tones and speed of your voice. Have each member of the group answer the following questions after each presentation.

On a scale of 1 to 5 (1 being poor, 5 being terrific), rate the following:

- The use of variation in the speed of the voice really contributed to the excitement of the story.
- The variation in high pitch and low pitch carried the listeners with the ups and downs of the story.
- The use of sounds and noises really set the mood and created images that contributed to the meaning of the presentation.

AUDIO RECORDINGS AND SOUNDS   The use of audio recordings can be very helpful in creating a mood or reinforcing oral language. Learners get tired of hearing the same voice no matter how interesting. It is helpful occasionally to use an audio recording of an interesting voice reading Scripture. Listen to people as you talk with them. Choose some interesting voices and ask them to record small segments of information or a Scripture passage. For example, when you are giving content on the apostle Paul, it is vocally interesting to have a recorded "voice of Paul" tell part of his story or interject a truth that you particularly want the learners to remember. Background noises, such as wind or crashing waves can be very helpful as you describe a storm at sea or Jesus calming the waves. Background music also helps in setting the mood before class, during a search and discover session, or during a reflective period of the lesson.

VISUAL COMMUNICATION

Studies like the one from Mobile Oil motivate us to include visual communication in all teaching sessions. Visual communication includes facial expressions, eye contact, hand gestures, and graphic visual supports. Visual communication not only reaches students with visual modality preference; it improves information retention for all learners.

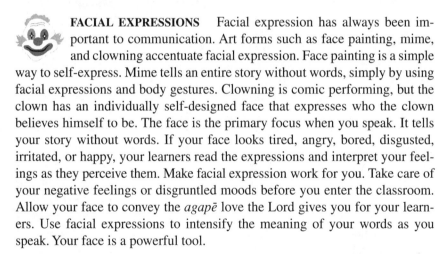

FACIAL EXPRESSIONS Facial expression has always been important to communication. Art forms such as face painting, mime, and clowning accentuate facial expression. Face painting is a simple way to self-express. Mime tells an entire story without words, simply by using facial expressions and body gestures. Clowning is comic performing, but the clown has an individually self-designed face that expresses who the clown believes himself to be. The face is the primary focus when you speak. It tells your story without words. If your face looks tired, angry, bored, disgusted, irritated, or happy, your learners read the expressions and interpret your feelings as they perceive them. Make facial expression work for you. Take care of your negative feelings or disgruntled moods before you enter the classroom. Allow your face to convey the *agapē* love the Lord gives you for your learners. Use facial expressions to intensify the meaning of your words as you speak. Your face is a powerful tool.

EYE CONTACT Teachers often develop bad habits and are totally unaware of them. Even as the speaker at the medical technology conference disenfranchised half of his audience, we also alienate our students by connecting with only certain students or speaking to part of the room. It is important for the teacher to engage every learner. Eyes convey emotion and give the individual who receives "the look" a positive or negative perception of the "looker." Be aware of your habits. Where do you look when you teach/speak? Do you favor one side of the room over the other? Do you leave out the people who sit in the back because you feel they are not really there to learn? If you have too much eye contact with certain persons in the study group, it may be perceived as aggression or flirtation. If you have too little, it may be understood as having no interest in that person. Use your eyes to make every learner feel part of the learning group. Use them to convey your interest in each learner.

Exercise 1: Video one of your teaching sessions. Watch the video, looking for eye connections with learners. Identify the learners you connect with most and least. Make a plan to connect with the learners that you have been neglecting. Watch the tape again. This time look for the parts of the room you connect with most and least. See if you can identify a section of the room that you need to focus on more.

Exercise 2: Ask your group of five to seven friends to help you once again. Have them sit in a circle. Have each member of the group hold up five fingers. Instruct the individuals in the group to put down one finger each time you have eye contact with them. Rule number one is you cannot move from one to the next in a clockwise or counterclockwise fashion. The eye contact must be random and as natural as possible. Rule number two is you cannot look at any individual two times in a row. Do this eye-contact exercise while you describe to your friends a person from your past who you truly love.

One Spring I went to a half-day seminar on nanotechnology and was eagerly anticipating an update on the latest research. I was a highly motivated learner and looked forward to three hours of hearing from a leading medical technology researcher. About 20 minutes into the first session I began to have difficulty feeling part of the seminar. The speaker, although fascinating and extremely knowledgeable, was speaking to the left side of the room. I was sitting on the right. I began squirming and clearing my throat, trying to attract attention to my side of the room. I was unable to budge the speaker who had now moved physically toward the left. I spent a miserable morning, feeling like an intruder and totally disgruntled, having paid good money to be on the outside of the party.

HAND AND BODY GESTURES   Hand and body gestures are amazing tools. There are said to be between 6,000 and 7,000 different motions possible using just the arms, hands, and wrists. Hand gestures are so powerful we have a language for the deaf that is composed totally of hand gestures. In sign language, the signer uses an area of space in front of him, a body box, in order to perform the hand gestures that convey the meaning of language to the deaf. "When one signs inside a small body box, the signs are constricted and convey less power. Increase the size of the body box, and you increase the power of the signed message."[3] Both the gesture and the size of the gesture are significant. The larger the gestures you make, the more power you convey. Here are a few other gestures that convey meaning:

- Hands on hips: Impatience or disapproval
- Crossed arms: barrier between you and the listener—defensive
- Holding yourself erect: confidence
- Slouching or bad posture: lack of confidence
- Pointing the index finger: directing to a location or speaking with emphasis
- Touching or rubbing the nose: thinking, doubting, or lying
- Rubbing the eye: not believing
- Eyes downcast: feeling bored or tired
- Pulling the ear: Unable to decide
- Clenched fist: anger or strong emphasis
- Rubbing hands: anticipating good things ahead
- Hands in pockets: dejection or discouragement
- Hands clasped behind back: frustration or anger
- Open palms: no barriers, openness and acceptance,
- Raised open palms: asking for response, imploring
- Pacing: restlessness or nervousness
- Fiddling with hands, buttons, zipper, hair, glasses: nervousness
- Rubbing chin: indecision
- Tapping your fingers on the table or podium: impatience

I have a vivid memory of a Christmas church service. A choir of 200 voices sang "O Holy Night" in beautiful melody while a woman who was dressed in a filmy white, long-sleeved, floor-length dress used hands and arms and body, signing the song as it was sung. It was beautiful, graceful, rhythmic, dynamic, and moving. I could feel the music as I viewed the motion.

Gestures require appropriate timing. Use gestures in concert with the part of the sentence you wish to emphasize. Random gestures are confusing and misleading. Be aware of habits that include annoying gestures, such as fiddling with your hair or glasses. Annoying habits can distract from the content of your lesson. Improving your gesture skill is well worth the time. Here are some exercises.

[3] W. R. Yount, *Called to Teach* (Nashville: Broadman & Holman, 1999), 114.

Exercise 1: Video one of your teaching sessions. Review the video and evaluate your hand and body language. What gestures were effective at enhancing communication? What gestures might have been misunderstood? What body movement habits do you have that might annoy your listeners?

Exercise 2: Read Psalm 100 and prepare a mime to interpret the meaning of the Psalm. Video your mime. Watch it and evaluate your gestures. How could you improve your nonverbal communication? Play the tape for another person. Ask that person to identify the Psalm you were miming. Ask for suggestions as to how you could improve your gestures.

Exercise 3: Collect your group of five to seven friends sitting in a circle. Take turns describing the most exciting adventure you ever had. At the end of each person's presentation, evaluate the hand and body gestures used by the speaker. What was most effective and least effective?

GRAPHIC VISUAL SUPPORT   In this age of technology, there is no excuse for any teacher omitting visuals in any presentation. The omission of visuals is either blatant egotism, without regard for research, or laziness on the part of the speaker. Because we have positive evidence from learning preferences and from neuroscientific research, we have no excuse for not including visuals in every presentation whether preaching or teaching. Visual support can include simple objects.

PowerPoint and Keynote are available to every speaker and can be a tremendous visual stimulus to support and expand any oral presentation. These are simple to use and can not only provide visuals, but also serve to keep the teacher on task. Usually people who have the most difficulty using PowerPoint to teach are those who are random in their thinking rather than sequential. Sequential thinkers approach life by creating steps to get from A to Z. They are comfortable building a logical and sequential approach. PowerPoint

> *Our son was preaching on the subject of hearing and obeying God's voice instead of others. While preaching, he called his dog Mak to the platform and asked him to lie down. After a few minutes, with Mak obediently lying, he introduced the dog to the congregation and asked them to call him. Multiple voices called "Mak," with all the usual incentives for dogs to respond. Mak lay quietly on the platform, unimpressed with their attempts to seduce him to disobedience. While the congregation continued to call, our son asked his wife to call Mak. She was sitting on the fourth row. Mak heard her voice, rose and ran to her chair. It effectively illustrated our response to God's voice instead of the crowds around.*

is easy for them to create and to use because they can design visual steps that help learners visualize how to complete the process.

Random abstract[4] thinkers see the world in chunks. They do not consider progressive steps to be particularly useful. They collect environmental sensory chunks until the big picture comes into view. For random thinkers PowerPoint can be very frustrating and confining. A chunk may occur to them that they wish to explore, but it isn't in the PowerPoint. Random abstract thinkers are often colorful, interesting, and imaginative public speakers. It is easy for them to keep the attention of the audience but difficult for them to communicate a defined body of information. If you are a random abstract thinker, we suggest that PowerPoint can be even more helpful for you than for sequential thinkers because it will encourage you to map out the content in a way that helps the learners. It will be more work than "flying by the seat of your pants," but your learners will be grateful for your effort. You can then maximize your creative giftedness and still communicate content.

Here are a few suggestions that will make PowerPoint a more useful tool:
1. *Use at least 28-point font so that print can be easily seen.* It is difficult to read small print from the back of the room. Vary the font size but keep the same font type throughout the presentation.
2. *Limit print so that there is plenty of white space.* Clutter discourages learners from attending to the slide.
3. *Include pictures and clip art.* Every slide should have some interesting visual to capture the attention of the viewers. Subscribe to a clip art Web site[5] or purchase appropriate clip art. Be careful not to download images from the Internet that are copyrighted. (We take a camera in the car wherever we go. When we see something interesting, we take a picture and file it away for future use. Be careful, however, to get written permission if you are taking pictures of people.)
4. *Check each slide for appropriate grammar and spelling.*
5. *Use pleasing color combinations and be consistent with a set of colors throughout the presentation.*
6. *Use graphs and builds to picture relationships.*
7. *Background templates are helpful to use.* If you use them, do not use multiple sets of templates in one presentation. Keep the same theme.

[4] You can explore your thinking style by taking the Gregorc Style Delineator, Gregorc Associates, Inc., 15 Doubleday Rd., Box 351, Columbia, CT 06237–0351, (860)–228–0093, www.gregorc.com
[5] For example, we often use Animation Factory, http://www.animationfactory.com

Do not use the same favorite set of templates for every teaching session. Templates get monotonous. Break up the templates by inserting plain background slides with complimenting colors. There are many resources for accessing new backgrounds.[6] Explore the possibilities of creating your own set of templates. You can use the fade feature to fade photographs for backgrounds, or superimpose a large light shape in the middle of a photo where you can create text. You can also select similar color and texture backgrounds and form your own templates. Be careful when using texture backgrounds because they can reduce readability.

8. *Use contrasting colors for font and background.* Dark text on a light background is more restful to the eye (navy on light blue). However, using a black text on yellow background with an occasional yellow on black slide can produce an eye-catching startling effect.
9. *Do not overuse flashy transitions or special effects because they can get old fast and can distract from your presentation.*
10. *Practice your presentation using a projection screen.* Check your colors and images for readability. Make sure your cables are new. Old cables can diminish color and acuity.
11. *Practice moving slides forward and backward in your presentation. Learners often ask to see a slide again.*
12. *Insert video clips into PowerPoint when appropriate.*
13. *Practice showing your video.* Be sure it is set correctly and comes on when you click on the prompt.
14. *Use PowerPoint to connect to Internet Web sites or "YouTube."* Check your streaming to be sure your download does not keep pausing. You need an adequate bandwidth to connect to videos and online contributions. Students also accessing the Internet on their computers during the presentation may overload the bandwidth and affect the streaming of your video.
15. *Do not read from your slides or face your PowerPoint.* Always face the audience. Never apologize for your slides. No matter how great your presentations, always work to make them even better next time.

As you become more familiar with PowerPoint, you will come up with your own guidelines as to what you feel maximizes or hinders your presentation.

---

[6] http://www.sermonspice.com

Whatever you do, jump in, and try it. It is never too late to add this important dimension to your teaching.

INTERACTIVE COMMUNICATION

All good teaching involves interactive communication. In the Revelation section of the lesson, the teacher shares the content of the passage. If lecture is to be used anywhere in the lesson, this is the section it fits most comfortably. However, lecture must be interactive to be effective. Interactive communication dictates two-way communication. Some of us easily spend 30 minutes talking because we think our learners need to hear what we have to say. The question is, "What is learning?" If learning is distributing knowledge, then one-way communication might be more justified. If learning, however, is "life change" because of receiving, understanding, and applying new knowledge, communication can never be just one way.

Transformactional learning is interactive. It is a discovery experience that demands participation on the part of the learner. Even if the teacher shares knowledge in a lecture format, the transformactional lecture format includes interaction. Teachers must know what learners actually hear, and they must allow learners to process information through discovery, reflection, and dialogue. There are hundreds of techniques for interactive communication. We will mention a few. It is helpful to remember that kinesthetic learners prefer to assimilate information through sensory motion. Don't be afraid to include activity as a teaching component.

QUESTIONS AND ANSWERS   It is important to get feedback from learners in order to measure understanding during an information-sharing session. Very often people do not hear what we say, and people hear what we do not say. Good teachers ask for responses to determine if the learner accurately receives the intended message.

WRITTEN RESPONSE   Writing a response helps many students assimilate and understand information. The teacher may say to the learners, "We have been talking about redemption. Take a piece of paper and write down a definition of redemption." The teacher gives the students a few minutes to reflect on the meaning of redemption and write a definition. Then the students share in small groups what they have written. Finally, the teacher restates in a concise definition the meaning of redemption. Writing demands that the learners engage the information and reflect on its meaning. Sharing the information promotes interaction and allows the learner to negotiate meaning.

PEER PAIRS   Using peer pairs as an interactive communication technique allows the learner to pair with another learner and discuss their understandings of a concept. Usually the teacher says something like, "Share your understanding of the word 'salvation' with the person next to you." This technique builds relationships within the group, allows the learner to negotiate meaning in a small nonthreatening environment, and encourages clarification of understanding.

METAPHORS   One of the difficulties of teaching Bible is helping learners to comprehend difficult words used in Scripture. Words like "propitiation," "redemption," and "justification" are just a few. Having students create metaphors promotes understanding of word meanings. The teacher says, "Let's break into groups of 5. Create a metaphor that describes the meaning of redemption. If you wish, you can begin with, "Redemption is like a . . . ." We have used this technique many times in classes and have been very pleased with the shared insight it creates.

QUIZZES   Quizzes sometimes help during information sharing. Be careful that the learners do not perceive a quiz as threatening. We usually say, "Here are five questions that review the content of the passage. You may answer them alone or with two or three friends." When students have answered the questions, have them gather in groups of five to seven to share and discuss their answers. The teacher reinforces the correct information by giving a concise recap at the end of the discussion.

HUMOR   When teachers perceive that a barrier exists between them and the learners, sometimes the tasteful use of humor reduces or eliminates the barrier. Laughing together is healthy and promotes relationships. Humor, however, should never be directed toward anyone in the class. Never make fun of a learner or allow anyone else to make fun of a peer. Creating a learning environment where everyone feels safe is essential to the learning process. Good humor is never harmful.

VULNERABILITY   Interactive communication is facilitated by vulnerability. The teacher should be "real" with learners and expect to learn with them. When teachers place themselves above students, perhaps talking down to them, interactive communication is hindered. When teachers are open and vulnerable, students also feel free to be vulnerable.

One way for a teacher to be vulnerable with students is to share real stories from their lives. For example, Sunday morning our pastor reported an event from his week. It was the true story of a woman who mistook him for her ex-husband. It was tasteful, humorous, and made him vulnerable. He presented himself as a very real person to the learners in the congregation. Barriers came down. Mutual acceptance prevailed.

INTERCULTURAL COMMUNICATION

Communication is complicated by diversity of culture. Culture can be defined as the values and customs of a particular social group. Culture is not tied to ethnicity. It can be related to such things as generation, gender, physical challenges, and regional social expectations. In America, like almost every other nation, we have difficulty communicating effectively with the myriad of cultures that come into play in any given group of people. Frequently these are described as "subcultures."

Every group of learners brings cultural bias. The bias may come from the different mixes of ethnic, regional, socioeconomic, physical, gender, and educational factors. This makes creating a learning environment extremely difficult. The teacher teaches from a cultural perspective, and the learners listen from their cultural perspectives. Additionally, in studying the Bible, teachers lead learners to understand a third culture that is regionally, generationally, and ethnically different, the cultures in which the Bible was written. This was discussed in the hermeneutics section of part 1.

God cares about cultural diversity. He could have created everyone in uniformity. How boring this world would be if everyone looked alike, talked alike, and had the same background experiences. God created diversity and He loves it. Diversity within any group has the potential to deepen perspective and enrich the lives of the participants. We should not simply "tolerate" diversity. We should celebrate diversity!

CONNECTING REVELATION THROUGH THE STAR MODEL ADULT LESSON PLAN PART 2

Part 2 of the Star lesson plan creates the blueprint for the content portion of the lesson. This section focuses on understanding what the biblical author said to the original audience. It relies on the transformactional personal Bible study items 2 through 8. The goal is to use the information gleaned on grammar, structure, background, history, culture, literary patterns, and word definitions, to format a plan for teaching the highlights of this Scripture passage, so that students understand what God said and why God inspired the author to write this passage.

II. Revelation:

What will learners know/understand about the content of the biblical passage? (20–23 minutes)

> Objective: *Learners will know/understand . . . (cognitive content of the passage).*
>
> Description: *Create a guide for teaching the content of your lesson. This can be a comprehensive outline, narrative, or PowerPoint slide layout pages.*
>
> Methods: *Describe your teaching methods for helping learners discover the Bible content of this passage.*
>
> Evaluation: *I will know learners attain the content objective by . . . (the learner answering questions, filling in study sheet, restating, etc.).*

Transition: *Write a transition sentence that takes the learner from content to application.*

DIRECTIONS FOR PART 2: REVELATION

CONTENT LESSON OBJECTIVE

The Bible content section is the most important part of the lesson. The teacher may easily teach the content of the lesson without teaching the learner. We can love waxing eloquent and forget that the only validation of our teaching is the learner's changed life. Alternatively, we can also teach learners without teaching anything worth experiencing. The content section demands worthy preparation. Teachers teach both Scripture and learners. The question answered in the Revelation section of the lesson is: What did God say to the original audience through the original author? Without this part of the lesson, there is no Bible study.

When writing the content objective, remember that it makes a contribution to the governing objective. The content objective furnishes the factual information that supports the governing objective. Write the content objective according to the guidelines in the previous chapter. Write it in terms of measurable learner behavior. Because you are dealing with content (facts), the verbs you will use in writing the content objective are usually "know" or "understand."

Objective Example: Learners will know by studying Rom 5:1–5 that we can have peace with God through Jesus Christ, and that the resulting right relationship with God brings the peace of God. (Notice that this content objective contributes to the governing objective.)

DESCRIPTION

When completing the content description for the lesson plan, outline the passage content that you wish to share with the learners regardless of the method you use for teaching this section. Refer to the transformactional Bible study. The steps should include the following:

1. Read the passage.
2. Background and/or author information that is helpful to the content
3. Outline what will be said about the passage.

   - Make main points with contributing information.
   - Include details and/or clues to remember details.
   - Connect every point to the verses in the passage.

Example: See example in Star Model Adult Lesson Plan Part 2 Sample.

METHODS FOR TEACHING THE CONTENT

Many methods can be used to teach the content portion of the lesson effectively. Methods include: lecture, Bible character impersonation, drama, video, rewriting, study sheets, search and discover, among others. The Collection of Methods section at the end of the book (see appendix G) describes these and others.

In selecting methods, keep in mind that the learner needs encouragement to connect this new content information with past knowledge and experiences. Offer ample opportunity for learners to share ideas from previous Bible knowledge. Learning exercises should encourage learners to share other passages that are similar in content. Teachers need to give opportunity for learners to reflect, remember, and connect old and new knowledge. Remember that the Internet can be used easily and effectively for reflection and sharing ideas both before and after the Bible study.

Example: Search and Discover

Although this section of the lesson is the best place for teacher-directed learning, it is also a proper place to teach learners to be self-directed. Methods for teaching content should teach the learner the tools for learning as well as the content. Because an important teaching goal is for adults to move progressively toward being self-directed learners, the teacher encourages independent study skills. The teacher introduces new tools intermittently and mentors as needed.

Learners need to feel safe. They migrate toward familiar activities. When teaching the Bible, the teacher must create an emotionally safe learning environment where learners climb out of their comfort zone and choose to learn new Bible study tools. Learners should become proficient using different versions of the Scripture text, commentaries, Bible dictionaries, Bible atlases, and Bible study software such as *Logos* and *BibleWorks*. We are not suggesting that every session be used to teach tools, but in the scope of the study, the teacher should regularly introduce opportunities for learning new Bible study tools. An example of this method is found in Star Model Adult Lesson Plan Part 2 sample.

> *As students came into class I told them that I was introducing important new material. I invited them to choose a table. I explained each table as: music table with keyboard and score paper, math table with calculators and manipulatives, art table with paper and paint, engineer table with an erector set and simple motors, plumbing table with connectable plastic pipes and water, and science table with microscopes and petri dishes. I watched as students selected their tables. Then I asked, "Who is sitting at a table that offers them a brand new experience?" No one raised a hand. Every student had selected a table that held familiar items that they knew how to use.*

Example: Bible Character Impersonation

Another effective method of presenting content is Bible character impersonation or dramatic monologue. The teacher comes into class dressed in a Bible character costume. Although full costume is usually most effective, a headpiece or bathrobe can serve as a partial costume. The Bible character should appear suddenly and without warning in full costume and remain in character for the entire presentation. Appropriate props should be used. If the teacher prepares thoroughly, this can be a very effective method of sharing facts/story from the passage.

Example: If teaching Rom 5:1–5, the leader could impersonate the apostle Paul. Paul would explain who he is, whom he is writing to, and his message. It is helpful to use props throughout the presentation (scroll, background maps and pictures of Rome, a legal balance scale for example). Learners are encouraged to interact with Paul at frequent points in the presentation. Paul teaches the content of the passage.

One Christmas, our daughter and son-in-law invited us to a special Sunday at their church. When it was time for the sermon, the pastor appeared suddenly in full Bible costume and introduced himself as Joseph. Never leaving character, he told the Christmas story from his perspective in a 30-minute dramatic monologue that captured the attention of every listener. We saw the birth of Christ from a whole new perspective that day.

EVALUATION

Consider the content objective for this section of the lesson plan. Determine how the learners will demonstrate that they are accomplishing the objective.

It became a yearly tradition at that church. Each year a different Nativity character shared the story from his/her perspective. We were thrilled the year we were invited to hear our daughter tell Mary's story in drama and song.

Example: I will know that my learners understand how to have peace with God because of their participation in the dialog with the apostle Paul (drama) and in their ability to restate the plan of salvation.

TRANSITION

Write a transition sentence that will help your learners move from their focus on the Bible content to contemporary application of the principles of the passage.

Example: "Now that we understand that God wants us to have peace with Him, we need to talk about what that means for adults today."

STAR MODEL ADULT LESSON PLAN PART 2 SAMPLE

Example

II. Revelation:

What will learners know/understand about the content of the biblical passage? (20–23 minutes)

        Objective: *Learners will know/understand . . . (cognitive content of the passage).* Learners will know that we can have peace with God through Jesus Christ, and that this right relationship   with God brings the peace of God.

        Description: *Create a guide for teaching the content of your lesson. This can be a comprehensive outline, narrative, or PowerPoint slide layout pages.*

Read the Passage Rom 5:1–5

Author and Background:
- Paul is the author.
- Written from Corinth to the church at Rome
- Rome was the center of the known world.
- People in Rome were in turmoil from political and cultural unrest, and controversy was in the church between Jews and Greeks.
- People in Rome needed peace with God. People in the church needed the Peace of God.

Passage Content:
I.   Peace <u>with</u> God (Romans 5:1–2a)

    1.   People need peace with God because they are sinners. God is perfect and He cannot by His nature tolerate sin.

    2.   The prerequisite for peace is Justification (Rom 5:1a) —justification means God sees me "just as if I never sinned" because of Jesus' death

    3. The Path to Peace (Rom 5:1b-2a) is trusting Jesus. God sent Jesus to die for our sins so that when we receive what Jesus did for us, God justifies us.

—We are seen by God as pure because when He looks at us, He sees Christ.

    4. God's grace + our faith = Peace with God.

II. Peace of God (Rom 5:2b-4)

    1. Foundation for Joy (Rom 5:2b)

When we have peace with God, we bring glory to God and that gives us the peace of God and a life full of joy.

    2. Triumph of Joy (Rom 5:3–4)

We rejoice in tribulation because we can still bring glory to God.

Suffering produces hope, character, and perseverance.

III. Presence of Love (Rom 5:5)

    1. God gave us love when he gave us Jesus (Rom 5:5a).

    2. God gives us the Holy Spirit when we trust Jesus for salvation.

    3. God's love is continually revealed in our lives through the Holy Spirit (Rom 5:5b).

Methods: *Describe your teaching methods for helping learners discover the Bible content of this passage.*

SEARCH AND DISCOVER After the introduction and transition (Part 1) the teacher will have learners read the passage from study sheet provided from each student. The teacher will explain that today we will work together to search and discover what Rom 5:1–5 says about peace with God. The teacher explains that there are (five to seven) centers for discovery at tables around the room. The teacher gives a brief explanation of each table and learners are invited to choose a table that interests them and spend the next 20 minutes working with the materials at the tables and answering the questions at the tables.

We stated earlier in this chapter that this section of the lesson is a good place for lecture. However, we are choosing to demonstrate Search and Discover because the "content" section of the lesson is also the best place to teach tools for self-directed Bible study. Search and discover should be used at least every five to six weeks in order to move learners toward self-directed learning.

Table 1.	Background on Author
Materials:	Bibles, commentaries
Questions:	Who was the **author** of the book of Romans?

List everything you know about the author.
- Where was the author writing from?
- Who was the author writing to?
- Why was the author writing this book?

Table 2.	Background on Readers of the letter Romans
Materials:	Bibles, commentaries, atlas
Questions:	Describe the church at Rome.

- Where was Rome located?
- Describe any historical or cultural issues that would affect the writing or receiving of this letter to the church at Rome.

Table 3.	Passage Structure:
Materials:	Bibles, commentaries, computer with Logos
Questions:	What is the main point of this passage?

- List the truths the author is saying about the main point.
- Why did God include this passage in the Bible?

Table 4.	Metaphors
Materials:	Bibles, paper, pencils, and commentaries
Questions:	Find words in the passage that may be difficult to understand.

- Create metaphors for each word. Justification is like . . .
- Select your favorites to share.

Table 5.	Rewrite
Materials:	Bibles in several translations, paper, pencils, and commentaries

Qu*estions:*	Read Rom 5:1–5 in several translations.
	• Discuss what you think the passage means.
	• Rewrite the passage in modern language so that anyone could understand.
Table 6.	Compose a Song
Materials:	Bibles, staff paper, pencils, keyboard, and commentaries
Questions:	Read Rom 5:1–5 in several translations.
	• Discuss what you think the passage means.
	• Compose a song that tells the meaning of the passage.
Table 7.	Artistic Expression
Materials:	Bibles, paper, markers, paint, and commentaries
Questions:	Read Rom 5:1–5 in several translations
	• Discuss what the passage means
	• Create a collective or individual art that expresses the content of the passage. Be prepared to share with the group.

During "Search and Discover" the teacher circulates and facilitates. The teacher makes certain the learners know how to use the resource materials. Students are encouraged to consult with students at other tables and with the teacher to make sure they are able to find the correct Bible content as they work on their individual projects. At the end of the "Search and Discover" session, the teacher has the learners share their discoveries. The teacher supports and encourages the students as they share, and the teacher contributes information when appropriate. The teacher gives a wrap-up of the main points of the content:

Example:	This passage teaches:
	We can have peace with God by accepting Christ's death for our sin.
	We can have the peace of God in our lives when we have made peace with God and we live for God's glory.
	We can know the love of God daily in the midst of any circumstances as we live with the presence of the Holy Spirit.

Evaluation: *I will know learners attain the content objective by . . . (the learner answering questions, filling in study sheet, restating, etc.).*

I will know learners attained the content objective by actively participating in the discovery session and having accurate information to report to the groups.

Transition: *Write a transition sentence that takes the learner from content to application.*

Now that we understand what Paul was trying to tell us, let's think together about how these truths apply to our world today.

SUMMARY

In the star lesson plan point 3, "Connecting Revelation," the teacher leads the learners to discover the meaning of the Scripture passage content. The learners discover what God communicated to the original readers of the passage. Cultural diversity enriches the learning environment through valuing each learner's input. The teacher sharpens skills in oral, visual, and interactive communication so that the learning environment surrounds the learners with sensory learning opportunity. The teacher supports the learner's processing information by providing for reflection and reflective discourse.

*Teacher Reveals Historical Scripture
Content—Learner Understands*

Exercise 11

"Teacher Rate . . . "

Rate the following: 1 poor, 2 working on it, 3 excellent	1	2	3
1. I have set up my Bible study learning environment to celebrate diversity.			
2. I have completed at least one of the exercises to improve my oral communication.			
3. I have completed at least one of the exercises to improve my visual communication.			
4. Rate your Bible study learning environment for interactive communication effectiveness.			
5. Rate your Bible study learning environment for variety in interactive communication.			
6. Even when lecturing I am concerned with using multisensory techniques.			
7. I have written Part II of the Star Lesson Plan.			
8. I included a method that is unusual for me. (I am planning to get out of my box.)			

CHAPTER TWELVE

CONNECTING RESPONSIBILITY

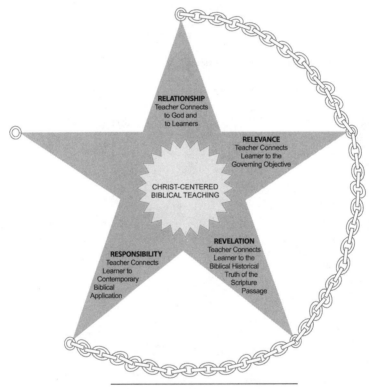

Teacher Bridges the Historical to the
Contemporary—Learner Engages Convictionally

IN THE REVELATION SECTION of the lesson, the learner studied the historical background, the structure of the passage, and the content from the original author to the historical audience, and discovered the principles (truths) in the text. In this chapter, the teacher and learners select the biblical principles that transcend history and apply them to contemporary life.

Principles are the fundamental truths of the text: they are self-evident and supported by other passages. A biblical principle is a strand of truth from the Scripture text that reaches to contemporary learners. The "Responsibility" section of the lesson does not include a challenge to obey. It is an intermediate phase allowing the learner to attain deeper understanding of the general application of the passage.

In the "Results" section of the lesson (next chapter) the passage principles are directed to personal application and action. Usually the connection happens in a gradual progression: understanding the passage content in biblical context, discovering the transcending principles, applying the principles to contemporary life, applying the principles to one's personal life, and personally choosing to act out life change.

Figure 12.1

Progress of Learning

This Chapter Covers

1. *The teacher's responsibility of understanding emotion leading to conviction.*
2. *The teacher's responsibility to engage learners in activities that promote involvement.* This is done by a discussion of reflective dialogue and problem-solving as examples of effective methods leading to retention.
3. *The teacher's responsibility to lead the learners to discover biblical principles that transcend time and culture.*
4. *The teacher's responsibility to construct this portion of the lesson plan to accommodate Connecting Responsibility.*

This Chapter Includes the Following Transformactional Principles

- *Transformactional Principle 11:* Retention of learning increases when learning is accompanied by emotion.
- *Transformactional Principle 12:* Retention of learning increases through collaboration and reflective dialogue.

- *Transformactional Principle 13:* Learning and retention is enhanced when problem-solving is employed.

This Chapter Provides Particular
Support for Excavator Learners

Teachers should thoughtfully include Excavators in constructing part 3 of the lesson plan, "Responsibility." Excavators are practical, strategic thinkers who love to solve problems experientially. Teachers should make Excavators feel included. Methods that pose problem-solving opportunities will give Excavators opportunity to excel—using their natural skills. Although Excavators prefer working alone, working in small groups in an area of strength will stretch Excavators and support them in building relationships. Key words for Excavators are: organized, sequential, task completion, efficient, hands-on, logical consequences, skilled, goal-oriented, strategic, problem-solver, and mechanical. Excavators usually rise to recognition during this section of the lesson. They easily discover the biblical principles and apply them to modern scenarios, ensuring the practicality of the Bible study. For Excavators, the worth of the Bible study depends on whether or not it works in today's world.

This Chapter Addresses the Concerns of
Transformative Neuroscience

Emotion plays an important role in the application of Bible principles. It is also important to the physiological process of learning. The role of emotion in learning is connected to the limbic system in the brain. As discussed in earlier sections, emotion releases chemicals from the limbic system that bathe the "sensory association" area in the back of the brain and the "conscious association" area in the front of the brain. These emotion chemicals, if positive, facilitate the process of learning as well as the retention of learning. This has definite implications for the learning environment.

Teachers must be aware that negative emotions associated with learning can inhibit learning. When a person feels threatened the brain emits a chemical response. A frightened person focuses attention on the causative signals coming from his environment. The more frightened a person, the less capable he is of learning. The physical response is characterized by, and increases in, sympathetic nervous system response: "increased heart rate, blood pressure, and respiration, a release of glucose stored in muscle, and increased muscle tone."[1] The person focuses only on critical information and tunes out all other. The body is tense, ready to ward off the danger.

Learning can also be inhibited by previous traumatic learning experiences. "A traumatized person in a state of alarm (for example, thinking about an earlier trauma) is less capable of concentrating, more anxious, and more attentive to non-verbal cues such as tone of voice, body posture, and facial expressions—and may, in fact, misinterpret such cues because of anxiety-induced hypervigilance."[2] A common reaction to fright is dissociation. The learner appears bored, often staring off into space, daydreaming.

Brain research demonstrates that severe psychological trauma causes elevation in a chemical, cortisol, that causes cell damage and even death among the neurons in the hippocampus located in the limbic area of the brain. Psychological trauma physically damages the brain.

However, there is hope for learners who have had distressing experiences with educators. Recent discoveries reveal that the brain is capable of repairing itself. Examining old memories and learning to think about them in new ways (psychotherapy and transformative learning) can repair and restructure neurons. "Certain aspects of education—those that correspond to tools used in psychotherapy (creating a trusting environment, narrative, reflection, and insight)—are interventions capable of repairing damaged adult brains."[3]

Although learning must maintain a positive emotional environment for the entire learning session, from our experience the application of biblical principles to contemporary life can place learners in a vulnerable position. In this area of the lesson, particularly, personal opinions are shared freely and learners may become disenfranchised even when it is not intended. Teachers must proactively work to include all learners, to support them with positive emotion, and to assist them in working through negative past experiences. Remember the goal of biblical application is becoming more Christlike.

CONNECTING RESPONSIBILITY THROUGH CONVICTION

Application of Scripture truth requires emotion. The application of Scripture calls for the learner to respond convictionally. We have often been taught in American culture to think of emotion as negative. Emotion creates vulnerability, and today's adult aspires to self-sufficiency and independence emotionally. In Christian settings, emotion often produces mental images of tear-jerking

[1] B. D. Perry, "Fear and Learning," 23.
[2] Ibid., 24.
[3] C. A. Ross. "Brain Self-Repair in Psychotherapy: Implications for Education," in *The Neuroscience of Adult Learning,* ed. S. Johnson and K. Taylor, New Directions for Adult and Continuing Education, no. 110, Summer 2006 (San Francisco: Jossey-Bass, 2006), 32.

altar call stories that equate emotion with sometimes shallow decision-making. We have been taught that as children approach adulthood they should outgrow emotional responses. Adults think of emotion as the antithesis to logic and thought. From our recent review of brain research, however, we understand that the chemical neurological reactions that take place in the brain during learning require emotion. They can have positive or negative impact.

Think back to the most memorable things that you have experienced. Do they involve emotion? Yes, they do! The more emotion involved in the activity, the more memorable the moment (a bike for Christmas, graduation, engagement, marriage, a baby's birth). Positive emotions can be a tremendous tool for information retention.

I was five years old, and it was Halloween. I was at a Christian conference center in California. My dad and I were walking to a friend's cabin together hand in hand. As we walked down the narrow winding road with thick, looming redwood trees on either side, I realized it was pitch black with no moon, no stars, no street lights. I couldn't see my hand in front of my face. The hair on the back of my neck stood up, and my heart began to pound as I remembered the scary stories I heard about Halloween at school that day. I clung to my daddy's hand and walked so close that my body bumped his with each step. That frightening event happened quite a few years ago, but I still feel the emotion when I remember that night.

Negative emotions, however, are also memorable. People who survived the tragic sinking of the *Titanic* never forgot the incident or the associated emotion. When they remember their terror and horror, they also remember the strong hands that rescued them.

When people experience severe negative emotion with no rescue, or when negative emotion overpowers them, their brains can shut down. If emotions are overwhelmingly negative, the person can repress rather than remember because the mind cannot cope with the volume or severity of negative emotion (for example: adults, who at 30 years old remember for the first time being molested at 8). The horror, and lack of rescue, was more than their minds could process, so they blocked the memories. Negative emotions associated with learning can incapacitate the learner. Depending on the severity of the negative experience or memory, the person can withdraw from all formal learning experiences—temporarily or permanently.

The teacher needs to monitor the interactions and perceptions in the learning environment in order to avoid the psychological trauma created by negative emotions. Teachers should never belittle a learner or respond to a learner with sarcasm. A good teacher constantly monitors the responses of students and measures their perceptions. It is not enough, however, to monitor only the teacher-learner relationship. It is very important to be aware of peer relationships between learners. Teachers should monitor the dialogue to perceive any arguing or stress evident in the learning environment.

The Golden Rule still works in the classroom. If your learners argue during class or online discussions, the teacher should have a few well-understood rules. Appendix K has a list of rules for healthy discussion or debate. The rule that rules, however, is always separate what a person says or does from the value of the person. Learners may object to what a person says but may not attack the person. Think of how God treats us. He hates our sins but loves us. He doesn't agree with everything we do or say, but He treats us with love and acceptance and forgiveness. He listens to us with respect—even when we are dead wrong. He preserves our self-esteem as we rest in His love. We are to love others the same way.

Some learners come into your Bible study already traumatized from having been shamed or humiliated by former teachers, peers, or parents. They immediately have a fight or flight reaction. They need friendship, predictability, and structure. They also need reassurance that they will not be shamed or humiliated in this new learning experience. Teachers need to protect and nurture. Teachers should never call on people to read or do an activity. Invite people to participate and ask for volunteers. Participation should always be a choice. When you notice marginalized learners, encourage them verbally and with positive body language. Often God places persons in a class that have the gift of discernment. Those individuals may recognize a struggling person before the teacher does. The discerner may come to the teacher and report the problem.

I had been teaching an adult ladies Bible study for several weeks and noticed that one lady seemed unengaged. She did not enter discussions or volunteer for any of the learning activities. Wanting to help her feel included, I asked if she would read the next verse of Scripture we were studying. She flushed and stumbled agonizingly over the two or three sentences. I was immediately overwhelmed with regret. It took me weeks of working with her one on one before she was comfortable enough to come back to class. As I got to know her better, I found that she was a high-school drop out with a severe learning disability and very damaged self-esteem. I learned my lesson at her expense.

The wise teacher encourages the discerner to become a friend to strugglers and quietly give the support and encouragement they need.

Aside from the issues of trauma, emotions play an important role in Bible study for every learner. As the teacher introduces the lesson, the learner's interest is aroused. The Holy Spirit prompts the Christian to realize the relevance of this Scripture passage. In the Revelation section of the lesson, the Scripture text is studied, and the Holy Spirit confirms truth and convicts of sin. In the Responsibility section, the Holy Spirit leads the believer to understand the biblical principles and their relationship to contemporary living. Finally, in the Results section of the lesson, the Holy Spirit personally convicts—an emotion—and the learner responds by choosing to act differently. God gives us the Holy Spirit who moves us to emotion. In the next two sections we discuss opportunities to create positive emotion in the Responsibility section of the lesson.

CONNECTING RESPONSIBILITY THROUGH COLLABORATION AND REFLECTIVE DIALOGUE

Collaboration simply means working in harmony with others to create something. The Responsibility section of the lesson is the ideal place to encourage collaboration. Collaboration builds relationships within the learning environment, allows learners to share the responsibility of creating, encourages learners to view things from different perspectives, and gives learners the opportunity to support each other with positive emotion. As you read the methods section in this chapter, you will see several small group activities that require collaboration. They may include such activities as artistic interpretation, case study, chat rooms, drama, peer pairs, reflective dialogue, simulation, threaded discussion, games, and teach to teach. (Descriptions are found in appendix G.)

Reflective dialogue includes two important components of learning: reflection and dialogue. It is important to take time for reflection. It gives the brain time to process information and allows the learner to examine paradigms in light of new information. Reflection is important for Christians because it is in prayer and reflection that the Holy Spirit guides, convicts, and corrects our thinking. Dialogue allows the learner to verbalize thinking and to receive responses from both other learners and the teacher. It strengthens Christians as peers share together. If conducted amicably, it creates friendship and empathy. Reflective dialogue can be accomplished during class time, through reflective journaling, or through online activities.

The Responsibility section lends itself to reflective dialogue as learners contemplate biblical principles applicable to adults today. Learners evaluate how contemporary living aligns or does not align with Scripture. Dialoging with other learners, they are forced to engage other perspectives that differ from their own. As learners collectively compare their views to Scripture, they confront stark differences between the Bible and modern life. It reveals areas that need to be corrected in their world. At this stage the interchange is safe because the discussion concerns "contemporary adults." While they share personal opinions, they can verbalize in general. In the next chapter the lesson progresses to internalization and personal response.

Here are some activities you can use to increase reflection and reflective dialogue:

1. Talk about the importance of reflection and reflective dialogue with your learners. Discuss the importance of supporting peers even when disagreeing.
2. When asking learners questions, wait three to five seconds before allowing a volunteer to voice an answer. This gives students the opportunity to formulate thoughts of their own.
3. When asking a question, invite students to indicate their response with thumbs up or thumbs down on the count of three. Tell them to look around the room and realize that we all have different perspectives. This encourages them to share their thoughts without fear of being different.
4. Give learners three cards, one with a happy face, one with a sad face, and one with an indifferent face. After you have completed a learning experience, ask the students to, on the count of three, raise the face that shows the way they felt about this particular learning exercise. Ask learners to view the variety of responses. Students need to understand that it is safe to think their own thoughts and have their own opinions.
5. When posing a question, sometimes have students write their answers. (A written answer usually involves more thought than a spontaneous verbal answer.) Then ask students to participate in small groups and, if they wish, share their ideas.
6. After introducing some new information, ask students to discuss it with the friends sitting next to them.

7. Use small groups as a nonthreatening way to share ideas.
8. On the class Web site offer a new threaded discussion topic each week that explores thoughts about the lesson. Students can respond to each other and read and consider other ideas.
9. E-mail students and dialogue about the lesson.
10. Encourage reflective journaling. Give students a notebook and ask them to write in their book their thoughts about the Bible study after you meet each week. Make yourself available to read and respond to any person's journal if they so desire.
11. Phone or meet with Bible study participants individually on a regular basis, making yourself an available friend for questions or discussion.

Reflective dialogue is a process for developing and verbalizing one's beliefs in a safe environment. In the process, the learner considers other views and experiences and adjusts personal views. In the Christian setting, this is not a process of searching for a relative, adjustable truth. Christian reflective dialogue focuses on discovering the ultimate truths of the Bible through *koinonia*—fellowship with other believers. The Holy Spirit operates in both the individual and the group as Christians share their spiritual insights and personal applications.

CONNECTING RESPONSIBILITY THROUGH PROBLEM SOLVING

 Since the beginning of adult learning theory in andragogy, educators have recognized the importance of problem-solving as a component of enhancing adult learning and retention. Recently, neuroscience has identified the anterior neocortex of the brain as the physiological location for problem-solving. Scientists can view the chemical and neurological changes that take place during problem-solving.

Educational psychologist, Benjamin Bloom, is known for recognizing progressive strata in thinking. His levels move from very simplistic to very complex. (See appendix J.) Problem-solving is higher thinking. Problem-solving puts the learner into a disorienting dilemma that requires synthesizing past and present knowledge and constructing new meaning. Mezirow identified "disorienting dilemmas" as triggers that begin transformative learning.

Methods that encourage problem-solving should be used in the Responsibility section of the lesson where new information from Scripture is applied to contemporary learners. Methods that provide a learning environment for problem-solving include: case studies, storytelling, drama, simulations, video clips, and testimony. These methods allow learners to place themselves in an imagined situation where they are safe to explore the dilemma and to apply the truth of Scripture. Through this vicarious journey, the Holy Spirit helps them to see their own dilemmas and the needs in their own lives for the principles they are applying to the imaginary scenario.

CONNECTING RESPONSIBILITY THROUGH THE STAR MODEL ADULT LESSON PLAN PART 3

How will learners apply the biblical principles of this passage to contemporary adults? (18–20 minutes)

    Objective: *After applying (the Scripture principle) to today's adults, the learner will (desire, be convinced, appreciate, etc.). (describe a measurable conviction).*

    Description: *List the principles in your passage that were true in Bible times that are still true today. Include the verse where you found them.*

    Methods: *Methods in this section should focus on engaging students on a convictional level. Describe the methods you will use to lead the learners to explore the principles and why these principles are applicable to today's world.*

    Evaluation: *I will know the learners engage convictionally with the contemporary application by (sharing, discussing, debating, reflecting, praying, expressing, dramatizing, etc . . .What is it you will observe the learner doing that will indicate he accomplished the application objective?)*

Transition: *Write a transition sentence that takes the learner from application to personal action.*

DIRECTIONS FOR PART 3: RESPONSIBILITY

LESSON OBJECTIVE FOR RESPONSIBILITY

The contemporary application section takes the learner from knowing Bible facts to identifying the biblical principles for the contemporary world. These principles light our way as we strive to be more like Christ. The question this section answers is, "What Bible truths is God saying to adults today through this Bible passage?" If the learner really understands the Bible passage and can identify the principles that apply to today's adult, there will be emotion (conviction).

When writing the application objective, remember that it makes a contribution to the governing objective. Follow the guidelines for writing objectives. Remember to write a measurable goal in terms of the learner—not the teacher. The verbs you will use in writing the application objective should indicate emotion. Here are a few you might use: be convicted, be convinced, desire, be committed to, rate, appreciate, have confidence in, internalize, be sensitive to, sympathize, be enthusiastic, care, pray about, value, and evaluate.

Application Objective Example: After applying the scripture principles found in 1 John 1:9, learners will be convinced that adults today should confess their sins and find God's forgiveness.

DESCRIPTION

Find number 8 in your transformactional personal Bible study (list the principles [biblical truths] in this passage that were true for the biblical world and are true for our contemporary world). List the answer to number 8 as the principles that were true in Bible times that are still true today, including the verses that apply.

Example: (See Star Model Adult Lesson Plan Part 3 Sample).

METHODS FOR TEACHING APPLICATION

The teacher should select methods to facilitate the application portion of the lesson while keeping in mind the learner's need to associate the knowledge they learned in the content section with the needs of the contemporary world. This association requires the learner to be actively involved, negotiating concepts and engaging in reflective dialogue. Usual methods for Responsibility are collaborative and convictional. (Please see appendix G for a more complete collection of methods.)

Avoid adopting a method that becomes a sacred genie lamp—one that you just love to use four out of every five lessons. People begin to hate the lamp and the genie. Keep the magic; use it occasionally. Change your methods regularly. Try something new. Here is an example of a method that can be used in application:

Example: Artistic Expression: There are times when artistic expression is especially helpful in applying the principles of the Scripture passage. Many people consider themselves unartistic and, therefore, this can be a threatening activity. Always allow people to choose to work individually or as part of a team. Always offer art as an open-ended item on a menu. It can be one option at a table, or there can be a plethora of materials and students can express themselves in any way they wish.

For example, we know that our world like the biblical world needs salvation. The teacher says, "You have been studying Romans 10:9–10, on how to be saved. Tables around the room have different art media. Select any table you wish and either work alone or with others to create a tool for sharing your faith. Use the content that we have just studied in Rom 10:9–10."

Table 1: Sample bracelet with colored beads, each representing a different step to faith in Christ. All of the materials for making a bracelet are at the table, along with written directions.

Table 2: Sample booklet of colored blank pages. Each page represents a step in trusting Christ. All of the materials for making the book and the written directions are at the table.

Table 3: Keyboard and score paper and written steps to becoming a believer. Directions say to create a very simple song you could share to teach someone how to be saved.

Table 4: Paints and paper. Instructions say to create a picture that you could use to explain to a person how to be saved.

Table 5: Variety of art media and computer. Instructions say to create anything you wish to use as a tool to share your faith.

Table 6: New Bibles and colored marking pens for writing in Bibles. The directions are: " We have been studying for several weeks some verses from

Romans that help us understand how to be saved. The verses are: Rom 3:23; 6:23; 5:8; 10:9–10; 12:1–2. Select from these verses or add others that are helpful to you. Write the steps and verses in the front of your Bible. Underline verses in your Bible that will help you share your faith. Use colors, if you wish, to picture the steps."

By creating a tool for sharing salvation in Part 3 Responsibility, the learner is applying the principles (truths) found in Rom 10:9–10. In Part 4 Results, students might use this tool to practice sharing salvation with peers, and then make a commitment to share the plan of salvation with an unbeliever during the following week.

EVALUATION

The learners will accomplish the application objective during the Responsibility section of the lesson. The evaluation for the Contemporary Application Objective enables the teacher to know that learners attained the objective. An evaluation tool includes any feedback activity that is an indicator that learners "got it."

> **Example:**   I will know the learners engage convictionally with the contemporary application by seeing them peer pair and discuss ways people today can manage their money according to heavenly values.

TRANSITION

The transition sentence carries the learner from the general contemporary application into the personal application and action.

> **Example:**   Now that we understand how God expects Christians to use money, let's consider what God may want us personally to do with our own money.

STAR MODEL ADULT LESSON PLAN PART 3 SAMPLE

Example

III. Responsibility:

How will learners apply the biblical principles of this passage to contemporary adults? (18–20 minutes)

> **O**bjective: *After applying (the Scripture principle) to today's adults, the learner will (desire, be convinced, appreciate, etc.). (describe a measurable conviction.)*
>
> After applying the Scripture principles found in Rom 5:1–5, learners will be convicted that adults today should have peace with God through receiving God's gift, Jesus, and that they should glorify God no matter what happens so that they will know real joy and love.
>
> **D**escription: *List the principles in your passage that were true in Bible times that are still true today. Include the verse where you found them.*
>
> 1. True righteousness is something God gives, not something we earn ("declared righteous," 5:1).
>
> 2. True righteousness alone brings us into the relationship with God that we all desire ("peace," 5:1).
>
> 3. The person and work of Jesus Christ is God's way of granting us righteousness (through Jesus, 5:1).
>
> 4. Once converted, the believer identifies and longs for God to be glorified. This has both immediate aspects and refers to the second coming of Christ when God will be glorified before all the earth ("we rejoice," 5:2–3).

5. God is able to use difficult circumstances to promote our good character so that all situations help Him accomplish His work in us ("afflictions," 5:3).

6. The presence of a living hope enables us to remain steadfast and confident regardless of the circumstances of life ("hope," 5:4–5).

7. The Holy Spirit brings a conscious realization of hope in our lives by applying to our lives the implications of our relationship with Christ ("Holy Spirit," 5:5).

8. We consciously feel and understand the love of God as we walk with the Holy Spirit ("God's love poured out in our hearts," 5:5).

Methods: *Methods in this section should focus on engaging students on a convictional level. Describe the methods you will use to lead the learners to explore the principles and why these principles are applicable to today's world.*

Peer Pair: The teacher gives each student a written list of the Scripture principles from Rom 5:1–5 as listed above. Included in this list are 3 principles that are true but are not found in this passage. The teacher explains that the list of principles has 3 that are not in this passage. The learners are asked to use their Bible to compare the list and identify those principles that don't belong. The students are told to work independently or get help from their neighbor. When they have identified the three that are incorrect, they check answers with a friend sitting nearby (peer pairs). The teacher then has student volunteers orally share the correct principles.

Drama/Interview: The teacher invites the actor playing Joni to come back into the classroom. Joni, in her wheelchair, goes to the front and the teacher sits in a chair beside her.

Teacher: "Joni, you were so kind to tell us at the beginning of class all about your diving accident and about your suicidal depression. We have been studying Rom 5:1–5 about having peace with God and knowing the peace of God. Would you mind telling us how you feel about what God did to you?"

Joni: Explains how she came to make peace with God through accepting Jesus as her Savior.

- She explains how God sees her as righteous because of Jesus even when she makes mistakes.
- She explains that when she received her new life in Christ, her desire became wanting to glorify God with her life.
- She talks about her daily struggles with her physical disability and her many trials and how she learned to glorify God through every circumstance no matter how difficult.
- She describes realizing that she could glorify God if she served Him regardless of what happened to her.
- She describes the joy she experiences daily in the midst of trials.
- She explains to the class that when she received the gift of Jesus, she was given the Holy Spirit who dwells within her and helps her know the love of God more and more as she lives each day for Jesus.

The teacher invites the learners to divide into small groups and share about friends they know who need Jesus in their life. This takes two to three minutes. The teacher transitions to the Results section.

(See the accompanying study sheet in the Complete Lesson Plan Sample)

Evaluation: *I will know the learners engage convictionally with the contemporary application by (sharing, discussing, debating, reflecting, praying, expressing, dramatizing, etc. What is it you will observe the learner doing that will indicate he accomplished the application objective?)*

"I will know the learners engage convictionally with the contemporary application by seeing them participate in the discussion."

Transition: *Write a transition sentence that takes the learner from application to personal action.* "We've seen how this scripture actually happened in Joni's life. Now let's talk about how it can happen in your life."

SUMMARY

In Star Point 4 the teacher understands the value of positive emotions in the learning process. The teacher learns to facilitate reflective dialog and problem-solving as methods of supporting information processing. In Star Model Lesson Plan development, the teacher plans to support the learners as they discover the contemporary significance of the Bible principles found in the Scripture passage. The teacher leads learners to apply Scripture truths to contemporary scenarios, understanding the difference this application of truth can make in adults' lives. The teacher facilitates learning experiences that bridge the historical to the contemporary. The learners are moved affectively as they understand the application of Scripture truths to today's needs.

Exercise 12.1

Rate the following: 1 being poor, 5 being terrific	1	2	3	4	5
1. I intentionally craft learning activities to facilitate collaboration.					
2. I am sensitive to traumatized learners.					
3. I meet with my Bible study participants individually on a regular basis.					
4. I use reflective dialog in my teaching.					
5. I use problem-solving to support my students in information processing.					

CHAPTER THIRTEEN

CONNECTING RESULTS

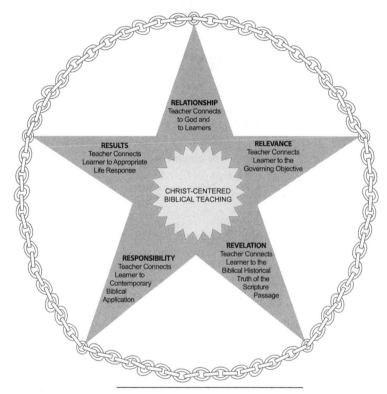

Teacher Challenges—Learner Acts

MANY PEOPLE SIT UNDER Bible studies each week at church or elsewhere. They know many facts about Christianity, but many show no evidence that their thinking has changed. Their lives seem no different.

Teachers may teach Bible to the same learners year after year and nothing happens. We hear and see but do not act. Education is not as much about knowing as it is about learning. Learning is measured by life-change. Teaching is quantifiable. Learning is qualifiable.

God's primary concern is not the amount of material we have been taught, but rather, in our progress toward becoming more like Christ. Christians are concerned about life-change. Are we any more like Christ today than we were a year ago? James describes our faith as faith that acts (Jas 2:14). Saving faith results in obeying God. The Results section of the Star Bible study plan is about obeying Scripture and making choices that enable us to be more like Christ. In this section learners should realize that God wants them to obey what they understand. Obedience takes action.

This Chapter Covers

1. *The teacher's responsibility to encourage learners to think in a deeper way.*
2. *The teacher's opportunity to learn through evaluation. Wise teachers profit from evaluations of students as well as themselves.*
3. *The teacher's responsibility to emphasize life-change by challenging learners to act appropriately and personally on the knowledge they gained through the lesson.*

This Chapter Includes the Following Transformactional Principle

- *Transformactional Principle 14:* Learning the negotiation of one's reality in light of new insight, resulting in change.

This Chapter Provides Particular Support for Activist Learners

Because of a natural preference for action the Activist naturally excels in the Star lesson plan Part 4: Results. Activists' preference for people over projects makes them very interested in the effect of the Bible study on individuals.

In the Results section, learners focus the principles of the Bible study on their own lives. They choose to act differently because of what they now know. Activists have been asking throughout the Bible study, "So, what difference does all of this make?" Now they see the culmination and purpose. Activists may lead other learners to act—either by enthusiastic example or by taking other learners with them as they collectively act. God often uses the convictions and purpose of the activist to lead others to make right choices. The teacher, however, monitors enthusiasm to prevent it from becoming coercion.

Some words that help us recognize the activist are: humor, flexibility, options, experiment, student-directed, curious, creative, insightful, future-directed, people persons, intuitive, dramatic, skilled communicator, risk-taker, multiperspective, and improver.

This Chapter Addresses the Concerns of Transformative Neuroscience

Brain function is hierarchical. It moves from the initial sensory input experience into more and more complex association, such as emotion, memory retrieval, sorting out and discarding the trivial, conscious association, and creative planning. It moves simultaneously because every part of the brain functions at once, handling different input at different stages.

Sooner or later all of these processes need a supervisor. That job is called executive functions, and it is located behind the forehead at the frontal cortex of the brain. Some have compared this area of the brain to the conductor of an orchestra. The conductor controls how the music comes together. He directs and synthesizes the individual effects into a new sound.[1] The executive functions area of the brain is "associated with coordination and synthesis of emotions, thinking, memory, and body or physical movement."[2] It integrates many processes including problem-solving. The problem-solving function is more than "here and now." It is the ability to create a plan and retain it until the right time for execution or to move to a more appropriate plan B.

When adult learners enter the Results section of the Bible study, they should be engaging executive functions. They apply Scripture principles personally, deciding on a future course of action, making personal commitments, and executing action. This takes personal reflection, commitment, and action.

CONNECTING TO RESULTS THROUGH HIGHER THINKING

The question the deceased asked the congregation was, "Have you really learned? Are you ready to put your life actions where your mouth is?" It was time for the church who *knew* about the body of Christ to *be* the body of Christ. We are not as Christian as we want to be. We are as Christian as we choose to be.

Connecting results requires the learner to connect to Scripture on a deeper level than simply knowing facts or understanding meaning. Educators have

---

[1] G. Caine & R. N. Caine. "Meaningful Learning and the Executive Functions of the Brain," in *The Neuroscience of Adult Learning,* ed. S. Johnson and K. Taylor, New Directions for Adult and Continuing Education, no. 110, Summer 2006 (San Francisco: Jossey-Bass, 2006), 56.

[2] Ibid.

long understood that there are levels of learning. In the late 1950s Benjamin Bloom, with a group of psychologists, studied different learning behaviors and classified them according to increasing intellectual activity. The result was Bloom's Taxonomy[3] (see appendix J).

In 2001, Bloom's Taxonomy was revised. The steps in ascending order are now: remember, understand, apply, analyze, evaluate, and create.[4] The new Bloom's suggests sequence, but does not confine learners to an exclusive pattern. It understands that learners move with flexibility among the levels. However, the ascending levels indicate increasing complexity.

Neuroscience tells us that the more complex the thinking process, the more searching, sorting, and integrating among complex neural pathways, and the more opportunity for learning to result in change. This challenges Christian educators to facilitate learning at all levels. Many Bible studies only emphasize the remembering and understanding levels, with teacher-directed information giving. Christian educators should encourage learners toward self-directed learning. One of the challenges of this chapter is to facilitate all levels of learning,

The most gripping funeral we have attended was that of our dentist's brother. Chuck, also a dentist, was a young man in his early thirties, the father of three children. He was a godly man, active in his church, and a good husband and father. One day he had minor outpatient surgery for a small lump on his back. When the surgeon tried to remove it, he could not find the end of the tumor. It had tentacles in every direction. It was a rare aggressive form of cancer, and within a very short time, Chuck was dead. The funeral was packed with over 1,000 people. There was standing room only. The funeral was moving and God-honoring, but the real heart-stopper was an audiotape played without warning. It was Chuck's voice. He said something like this: "If you are listening to this, I have gone on to be with the Lord. The wife and children I have left behind are very precious to me. I have served God and this church with all my heart, and now I am asking you to care for the ones I love. Men, be the father to my children. Love them and guide them. Teach them the ways of the Lord. Support my wife and be certain she has whatever she needs. . . ." Everyone in the church was weeping. We all prayed that we would not just hear the words, but also act. Real learning is knowledge in action.

---

[3] D. A. Sousa, *How the Brain Learns,* 3rd ed. (Thousand Oaks, CA: Corwin Press, 2006), 249.
[4] Ibid., 250–51.

recognizing that learners must apply, analyze, evaluate, create, and act if we are to see Christian growth.

Using the Star Model of Transformactional Teaching, as it is intended, includes all of these levels of learning. Star 1-Relationship establishes the emotional connections (neuroscience) to the teacher. Star 2-Relevance establishes connections to the learning environment, learning peers, and the purpose of the study (neuroscience, andragogy). Star 3-Revelation calls for learners to remember and understand (Bloom's) the Scripture text. Star 4 -Responsibility challenges the learners to apply and analyze (Bloom's). Now, in Star 5-Results, learners evaluate their own needs in light of the truths of the Scripture passage and create (Bloom's) more Christlike lives by acting (transformactional) differently in obedience to new understanding.

CONNECTING TO RESULTS THROUGH EVALUATION

Connecting to results through evaluation views evaluation from both the learner's perspective and from the teacher's. The learner asks, "Who is this teacher? Is this information important to me? Do I understand? Can it make a difference? Do I choose to become different because of it?" The teacher asks, "Is the learner actually learning what I think I am teaching?" For the learner and the teacher, evaluation is both spontaneous and constructed.

LEARNER EVALUATIONS

SPONTANEOUS LEARNER EVALUATION Learners evaluate the teacher throughout the lesson. Their evaluations include dress, body language, credibility, and communication. The learner may think, "Not that dress again! Looks like he's in a bad mood. I wish she would keep her hands out of her hair! Enough of your talking! Stop and let us discuss! He is quoting a really old commentary. I wonder if he knows what he's talking about? She is boring, boring, boring!" The teacher rarely receives this feedback. When it comes, it often takes the form of a critical comment. Spontaneous learner evaluation does affect learning, especially if the evaluation is negative, and if there is no vehicle for the learner to express frustration.

Teachers should provide a way for students to express both frustration and accolades. An anonymous suggestion box is always a good addition to the classroom. Teachers should prepare a closed, opaque box with a slit in the top, labeled "Suggestions and Comments." Teachers should regularly mention suggestions and comments that have been made and provide a response. Too often learners make suggestions, but nothing ever changes. For example, if someone complains about the heat, the teacher should never ignore the comment. If there is a reason it is too hot (the class is saving for a portable air conditioner and needs 53 more dollars) the class should know it. Value the complaint as well as the encouragement. Consider what you can do to improve the learning environment, which includes you, and verbalize your response. Realize that you are teaching because God has called you. Even the apostle Paul had complaints.

CONSTRUCTED LEARNER EVALUATION   Learners should have regular opportunities for more constructed evaluations. Constructed evaluation should be directed at the learning experience for the purpose of correction and improvement. Remember that the teacher's perception of the learning experience may only be part of the picture. Constructed evaluation can clear up misperception and close the gap between teacher perceptions and learner perceptions. Many sources provide tools to use for evaluations. Here is an example of a constructed learner's evaluation tool.

Exercise 13.1

Star Model Learner's Evaluation of the Learning Experience: (Learners complete this evaluation after completing the learning experience. Rate 1-5, 1 very poor and 5 very well done)	1	2	3	4	5
1. The introduction was exciting and established relevance.					
2. There was quality Bible content.					
3. Passage principles were clearly defined.					
4. Clear application of Bible principles to contemporary daily living					
5. Clear and appropriate challenge to personal action					
6. Clear and concise lesson wrap-up					
7 Provided opportunity for experiential (hands on) learning					
8. Provided opportunity for peer collaboration					
9. Allowed time for personal reflection					
10. Encouraged peer discussion					
11. Maintained supportive emotional environment					
12. Facilitated personal friendships among learners					
13. Used creativity in teaching					
14. Moved learners toward being more self-directed					
15. Used teaching methods supporting auditory learners					
16. Used teaching methods supporting visual learners					
17. Used teaching methods supporting kinesthetic/tactile learners					
18. Overall rating for effectiveness of lesson					

TEACHER EVALUATIONS

SPONTANEOUS TEACHER EVALUATION

 Teachers automatically conduct informal evaluations of their own teaching during and after every teaching session. The teacher senses the effectiveness of teaching methods by observing the signals sent by learners through body language and verbal feedback. Responding to these signals, a good teacher changes an approach or modifies the delivery method as the lesson progresses. Questions and answers, discussion, and group participation assist the teacher in measuring the quantity and quality of the learning that is taking place. Along with the immediate evaluation that goes on during the lesson, the teacher usually evaluates the lesson immediately following the lesson. Most teachers think about failures, successes, and projections for "do overs." Teaching can always be improved. We never "arrive." The question should always be "How could I do this more effectively next time?"

CONSTRUCTED TEACHER EVALUATION There are two types of constructed teacher evaluation instruments. The first is used during the teaching of the lesson. It is demonstrated in the Star Model Adult Lesson Plan. Each section of the lesson plan has an "evaluation" component so that teachers are aware of whether or not the section objectives are being met. By observing the learner's response to specific learning exercises, teachers can evaluate and use flexibility in meeting the learning needs of students.

The second type of constructed teacher evaluation is a meta-evaluation tool that is constructed to evaluate the whole lesson after teaching it. An example of this is Robert Stack's Model. This model is demonstrated by Richards and Bredfeldt in their book *Creative Bible Teaching*[5]. This type of instrument answers the questions, "What worked?" "What didn't work?" "How could I have improved the lesson?" By using an instrument that reflects on the completed teaching session, teachers can learn from both success and failure. They can adapt future lessons for more effective communication. Flexibility and adaptation are keys to negotiating effective teaching. The following is a constructed teacher evaluation for the Star Model Adult Lesson Plan.

---

[5] Richards and Bredfeldt, *Creative Bible Teaching* (Chicago: Moody Press, 1998), 317 (table 18).

Exercise 13.2

Teacher Self Evaluation

Rate yourself by checking the columns or making a comment.	Yes	Not sure	No
1. The governing goal of my lesson was accomplished.			
2. The introduction I planned connected my students with the relevance of the Scripture passage.			
3. The Bible content was clear, and I presented it in an interesting way.			
4. I made sure my students understood the principles in the passage.			
5. I helped my students really understand the contemporary application of the passage.			
6. I made a clear challenge to obedience while not dictating or using coercion.			
7. I used smooth transitions throughout the lesson.			
8. I used methods for every modality and learning style.			
9. My lesson was interesting and creative.			
10. The best part of this lesson was . . .			
11. The worst part of this lesson was . . .			
12. One thing that would have made this lesson better is . . .			
13. If I was a student in this Bible study, I would rate it . . .			
14. Extenuating circumstances that affected the lesson were . . .			

CONNECTING RESULTS THROUGH THE STAR MODEL ADULT LESSON PLAN PART 4

The learner has applied the Scripture principles to contemporary adults and is convicted that adults need to apply these principles. As the learner moves into the Results section of the lesson, the focus becomes personal. The learner turns attention inward. The teacher gives opportunity for personal reflection and personal application. The teacher shares several ways to apply the passage personally. The teacher does not impose change or pressure the student in any way. Instead, the teacher provides opportunity to hear the urging of the Holy Spirit and to decide how to act in obedience.

IV. Results:

What will learners do to apply this passage to their own lives? How will their lives be different? (8–10 minutes)

Objective: *Learners will commit to . . . (an appropriate action of obedience).*

Description: *List some action responses you could suggest that would constitute personal obedience to the principles found in this passage.*

Methods: *What method will you use to challenge learners to take personal life-changing actions of obedience in response to the principles in this passage?*

Evaluation: *I will know the learners have committed to personal action by . . .*

Lesson Wrap-up: *Restate for your students in one or two sentences a summary of what you wanted them to learn.*

Learner Evaluation for Governing Lesson Objective:

I know the learners accomplished my governing objective because they . . .

Materials: *Make a list of all materials and equipment you will need to teach this lesson. Include completed study sheets, scripts, PowerPoint layout pages, etc.*

DIRECTION FOR PART 4: RESULTS

LESSON OBJECTIVE FOR ACTION

Objective for Results: The teacher offers suggestions or leads learners to discover ways they can respond in obedience to the text. The teacher gives the learner time for personal reflection and decision. The learner seeks the guidance of the Holy Spirit to illuminate needs in his life and to decide on an action of obedience. The learner chooses to obey and makes a commitment to obey the Scripture text. This is not a response to the teacher. This is a response to God.

The teacher writes a learning objective for personal action. The objective must make a contribution to the governing objective. The teacher uses action verbs to describe what the learner will do to respond in obedience to the text. The objective is learner-centered and measurable.

Action Objective Example: Learners will commit to "pray without ceasing" this week by signing a commitment card.

DESCRIPTION

Make a list of possible actions for each of the principles listed in the text (Transformactional Bible Study #9). Select several responses that are appropriate and suggest them to the students during this last section of the Bible study. Understand that this is the learner's choice. Learners may choose a teacher's suggestions, create their own response, or choose no response.

Examples: Gal 5:14 (love your neighbor as yourself).

1. List on a piece of paper all the things you hate about your appearance. Put the open paper in front of you and pray. Ask God to forgive you for hating yourself. Tell God that you understand He made you in His image just the way He wanted you. Tell God you realize that He loves you just the way you are. Ask God to help you to love and accept yourself as He does. Tear up the paper in little pieces and throw it away. Thank God for His love and for making you just the way you are.

2. Choose a person in your life who you really don't like. Ask God to help you love this person. Choose one thing you can do this week to show this person God's love. (Take him/her a gift. Ask them for dinner. Do their lawn.)

3. Write on a card: I will love others as I love me! Put it on your dash or on your refrigerator. Do random acts of kindness to random people in your life. Keep reminding yourself that God wants you to love others as you want to be loved.

METHODS FOR TEACHING ACTION

The methods in this section are designed to encourage students to act on the principles found in the Scripture passage. Some methods are used immediately in the class session and some are used as the learner goes out into a personal life routine.

Apprentice: Many times people feel that God is calling them to serve, but they have no idea what the service looks like. It helps to have godly men and women who are available to mentor and teach the learners in your class as they show interest. Service areas where learners may apprentice may include: pastor, pastoral staff, women's ministry coordinator, Sunday school teacher, Bible study leader, children's worker, clothes closet manager, food bank facilitator, and soup kitchen worker. Consider this frequent scenario:

Learner says, "I think God may want me to help with the children's ministry."

Teacher says, "Great, you have a class of four-year-olds next Sunday."

Frequently the learner decides that he is not called to serve children or he leaves the church. Instead, we need to offer opportunities to apprentice with veteran workers without stress or pressure. The learner works alongside the veteran until the learner feels comfortable to take the lead. Find a resource person who is willing to mentor. Set up a meeting and keep in touch with the learner throughout the process.

Example: John 13 (Jesus washes the disciples' feet—serving). As the teacher enters the Results section of the lesson, the teacher says, "In our Bible study, God is telling us that He wants us to serve others just as Jesus did. What is God telling you to do? Here are some opportunities coming up at church. As I share them with you, write down the one that you think God might want you to do or write down something God brings to mind that you can do, to serve Him. If you wish, you will be assigned to a person who will guide you through this new activity of service. You will not be expected to serve alone until you are ready. Here is the list: vacation Bible school workers, vacation Bible school kitchen helpers, widow's helpers (fixing roofs, yards, painting), church garage sale worker, retirement home visitation team . . ."

EVALUATION

Consider the lesson action objective. How does the teacher know that the learner accomplished this objective? The teacher must be careful not to invade privacy because this transaction is between the learner and the Lord. However, the teacher can observe whether or not it appears the learner committed to an action.

Example: I will know the learner is committed to personal action by observing that the learners are (1) writing on a piece of paper the traits in their appearance that they hate, (2) having prayer, and (3) tearing up the paper.

LESSON WRAP-UP

The lesson wrap-up is one to two minutes of restating what you hope the students have learned.

Example: Today we have discovered that God wants us to love others as we love ourselves. We learned that we must first love ourselves as God loves us and then pour out His love on everyone around us. We have committed to love others this week by proactively doing acts of love as we go through our daily routines. Let's pray together and ask the Lord to help us as we go.

LEARNER EVALUATION FOR THE GOVERNING LESSON OBJECTIVE

The teacher looks back at the governing lesson objective found in part 1 of the lesson plan. All of the lesson objectives were subordinate to this governing objective. The teacher may have taught many aspects of the passage, but this is the one most important point that everyone needed to understand. Now, at the end of the lesson, the teacher looks back at what was accomplished and selects at least one indicator demonstrating that the learner really understood the focus of the lesson.

Example: The learners each share on the class Web site one of the acts of love they have given to their neighbors.

MATERIALS

The teacher reviews the lesson plan and makes a list of materials and preparation needed for the lesson. A comprehensive list includes everything from paper and pencils to volunteers. Creativity takes time and preparation. The lesson plan includes every written prop, such as the study sheet or drama script. It also includes Power Point layout and notes. Nothing is left until the last minute.

STAR MODEL ADULT LESSON PLAN PART 4 SAMPLE

IV. Results:

What will learners do to apply this passage to their own lives? How will their lives be different? (8–10 minutes)

Objective: *Learners will commit to . . . (an appropriate action of obedience).* Romans 5:1–5. The learner will commit to know peace with God through receiving His provision, to tell others, and to glorify God in the midst of difficulty.

Description: *List some action responses you could suggest that would constitute personal obedience to the principles found in this passage?*

1. The learner could accept Christ as Savior.

2. The learner could learn to share his faith.

3. The learner could learn to glorify God in the midst of difficulty.

Methods: *What method will you use to challenge learners to take personal life-changing actions of obedience in response to the principles in this passage?*

1. The teacher gives the learners a **study sheet** with the steps to having peace with God, salvation.

2. The learner and **peer pairs** partner practice sharing the steps to salvation with each other.

3. The learners have a time of personal prayer and **reflection**, and the teacher invites students to do whatever God is telling them to do:

—To believe that God sent Jesus to die for your sin and to accept his gift of salvation as the only way to make peace with God.

—Show them a person with whom they can share this good news—salvation—and begin to pray for

Peace with God

¹Therefore, since we have been declared righteous by faith, we have peace with God through our Lord Jesus Christ. ²Also through Him, we have obtained access by faith into this grace in which we stand, and we rejoice in the hope of the glory of God. ³And not only that, but we also rejoice in our afflictions, because we know that affliction produces endurance, ⁴endurance produces proven character, and proven character produces hope. ⁵This hope does not disappoint, because God's love has been poured out in our hearts through the Holy Spirit who was given to us.

Compare the following true principles to the text above. Select the three principles that are not found in this passage and cross them out. Check your answers with a friend.

1. True righteousness is something God gives: not something we earn ("declared righteous," 5:1)
2. Prayer is the key to peace with God ("be prayerful," 5:1).
3. True righteousness alone brings us into the relationship with God that we all desire ("peace," 5:1).
4. The person and work of Jesus Christ is God's way of granting us righteousness (through Jesus, 5:1).
5. Once converted, the believer identifies and longs for God to be glorified. This has both immediate aspects and refers to the second coming of Christ when God will be glorified before all the earth ("we rejoice," 5:2–3).
6. God wants us to pray that we will have afflictions ("afflictions," 5:3)
7. God is able to use difficult circumstances to promote our good character so that all situations help His accomplish His work in us ("afflictions," 5:3).
8. Hope produces endurance ("hope," 5:4).
9. The presence of a living hope enables us to remain steadfast and confident regardless of the circumstances of life ("hope," 5:4–5).
10. The Holy Spirit brings a conscious realization of hope in our lives by applying to our lives the implications of our relationship with Christ (Holy Spirit," 5:5).
11. We consciously feel and understand the love of God as we walk with the Holy Spirit ("God's love poured out in our hearts," 5:5).

Steps to Salvation[1]

1. Confess that you are a sinner and that you are sorry for your sins. (Rom 3:23)
2. The payment for sin is eternal death. (Rom 6:23)
3. God is holy and cannot tolerate sin, but he loves us so much that He sent His son Jesus to die in our place and pay for our sin. (Rom 5:8)
4. We need to receive God's gift of Jesus as the only way we can have peace with God. (John 1:12)
5. We need to give God our life and try to be more and more like Jesus. (Eph 4:24)
6. We need to thank God and tell others what God has done for us. (Rom 10:9–10)

Today I have promised God _____

Share what God is doing in your life. Read what God is doing in your friends' lives.   Class Web address

---

[1] http://www.fprespa.org/userfiles/image/footprints(1).jpg

an opportunity and for the Holy Spirit to prepare their heart.

If learners are experiencing difficulty in their lives and they already have made peace with God, pray for them to glorify God and have joy in the midst of difficulty.

4. The learners are invited to respond on the class Web site during the week what God is doing in their lives.

5. The teacher will contact every learner personally and invite him to share how he made peace with God.

Evaluation: *I will know the learners have committed to personal action by . . .*

I will know the learners commit to personal action by the learners participating in the rehearsal of the plan of salvation, in the reflective prayer time, and in the class Web site response.

Lesson Wrap-up: *Restate for your students in one or two sentences a summary of what you wanted them to learn.* Today we have found that we can have peace with God through accepting Jesus' death for our sin and trusting Him alone for our salvation. We have learned the steps to share our faith. We have learned that we need to glorify God even in the midst of difficulty.

Learner Evaluation for Governing Lesson Objective:
I know the learners accomplished my governing objective because they . . .
The teacher will know that learners have made peace with God by personally contacting each and having them share how they came to salvation through Jesus.

Materials: *Make a list of all materials and equipment you will need to teach this lesson. Include completed study sheets, scripts, PowerPoint layout pages, etc.*

- The book *Joni*, contact a person to do the drama, read and approve the script, wheelchair.
- Grease board and pens
- Study sheet

SUMMARY

This last point of the Star focuses on results. This chapter encourages teachers to challenge learners to think in deeper ways. It discusses opportunities for teachers to improve themselves through various evaluation venues. Finally, in this section the lesson plan is completed. In part 4 of the Star Model lesson plan, learners prayerfully select their response of obedience to the Scripture passage after prayerful reflection. The result is life-change—step by step becoming more like Christ, obeying whatever is understood. Change involves progressively making choices to take off the old and put on the new. The teacher challenges and the learner acts.

Exercise 13.3

Rate yourself: 1 being poor and 5 being terrific	1	2	3	4	5
1. I am intentionally facilitating learning at all levels.					
2. I created a suggestion box for my learners to anonymously express their concerns.					
3. I monitor suggestions and respond so that my learners know their concerns matter to me.					
4. I use a constructed learners evaluation tool periodically in order to receive helpful feedback.					
5. I modify my teaching in response to learner evaluations.					
6. I use a formal teacher evaluation tool periodically in order to self-evaluate my teaching sessions.					
7. I modify my teaching in response to my self-evaluation.					
8. I have completed the Star Model lesson plan part 4.					

CONCLUSION

THE STAR TRANSFORMACTIONAL TEACHING model is a way of thinking about teaching. Building on recent adult learning theory, it emphasizes teaching the way adults learn. Learning differs from knowledge. Knowledge may be abstract, filed away in the brain until ready to be called into service. Learning involves change. It involves putting knowledge into action so that the learner lives differently. We believe the word transformactional captures this dynamic.

Teaching the Bible challenges us. We are handling "the words of life." We have been called to be agents of reconciliation between God and man, and have been charged with facilitating growth to Christlikeness. The calling deserves our best effort. We must take advantage of every opportunity to sharpen both our understanding and our skills. It is not enough to "wing it." God expects thorough preparation: thoroughness in Bible study and thoroughness in teaching methodologies. Our best, blessed with the Holy Spirit's power, can meet people in the intersections of life and lead them down a better path.

In this book we have taken you through the Star transformactional teaching method. We emphasized relationship by introducing our credentials and ourselves. Although reading a book is more artificial than face-to-face interaction, we have attempted to share ourselves through personal examples from our ministries. We tried to demonstrate relevance by sharing the importance of facilitating Christian growth through excellent Bible teaching. We shared revelation as we discussed facts about the Bible, hermeneutics, Christian living, and adult learning theory. The foundation of the method is the 14 principles we gleaned from the vast materials relating to adult teaching and learning.

We connected you with responsibility as we applied the principles to the Star transformactional Bible study and lesson plan models. We encouraged you toward becoming self-directed learners by sharing tools for teaching in the ideas and methods we presented. Now we have come to results.

The choice is yours. You can continue teaching as you always have, or you can ask the Lord if there is something in this book that will help you better facilitate Christian growth in your learners. If there is, we pray you will take action. May God bless you as you strive to communicate clearly His Word and encourage His children toward salvation and Christlikeness.

"Therefore, brothers, by the mercies of God, I urge you to present your bodies as a living sacrifice, holy and pleasing to God; this is your spiritual worship. Do not be conformed to this age, but be transformed by the renewing of your mind so that you may discern what is the good, pleasing, and perfect will of God."

The apostle Paul
Romans 12:1–2

BIBLIOGRAPHY

Entries listed by author where author is in a multiauthored volume.

Accordance (Altamonte Springs, FL) www.accordancebible.com

Aland, Kurt and Barbara. *The Text of the New Testament: an Introduction to the Critical Editions and to the Theory and Practice of Modern Textual Criticism.* Grand Rapids: Eerdmans, 1995.

Alfred, Mary V. "Philosophical foundations of andragogy and self directed learning: A critical analysis from an Africentric feminist perspective." In *Proceedings of the 19th Annual Midwest Research to Practice Conference in Adult, Continuing, and Community Education.* Edited by M. Glowacki-Dudka, (pp. 21–26). Madison: University of Wisconsin, 1993.

"Andragogy," *Wikipedia, Wikimedia Foundation, Inc.*, January 18, 2009,

Animation Factory, www.animationfactory.com

Arndt, William F., and Wilbur F. Gingrich. *A Greek-English Lexicon of the New Testament.* Chicago: University of Chicago Press, 1957.

Baker Exegetical Commentary on the New Testament. Grand Rapids: Baker Publishing Group.

Bandura, Albert. *Social Learning Theory.* Englewood Cliffs, NJ: Prentice-Hall, 1977.

The Baptist Faith and Message. Nashville: LifeWay Christian Resources, 2000.

Bauer, David R. *An Annotated Guide to Biblical Resources for Ministry.* Peabody, MA: Hendrickson, 2003.

Baumgartner, Lisa, Ming-Yeh Lee, Susan Birden, and Doris Flowers. *Adult Learning Theory: A Primer.* Center on Education and Training for Employment, College of Education, the Ohio State University, Information Series No. 392. Columbus, OH: 2003.

Baumgartner, Lisa M. "An Update on Transformational Learning." In *The New Update on Adult Learning Theory.* Edited by Sharan B. Merriam. New Directions for Adult and Continuing Education, no. 89, Spring 2001. San Francisco: Jossey-Bass, 2001.

Berk, Laura E. *Exploring Lifespan Development.* San Francisco: Allyn and Bacon, 2008.

BibleWorks LLC (Norfolk, VA*), www.bibleworks.com*

Blomberg, Craig L. *Interpreting the Parables.* Downer's Grove: InterVarsity, 1990.

Boa, Kenneth. *Conformed to His Image: Biblical and Practical Approaches to Spiritual Formation.* Grand Rapids: Zondervan, 2001.

Brisco, Thomas V., ed. *Holman Bible Atlas: A Complete Guide to the Expansive Geography of Biblical History.* Nashville: B & H Publishing Group, 1999.

Brockett, Ralph G., and Roger Hiemstra. *Self-Direction in Adult Learning: Perspectives on Theory, Research, and Practice.* New York: Routledge, 1991.

Brockett, Ralph, et al. "Two decades of literature on SDL: A content analysis." Boynton Beach, FL: International SDL Symposium, 2000.

Brookfield, Stephen. "Self-Directed Learning, Political Clarity, and the Critical Practice of Adult Education," *Adult Education Quarterly* 43, no. 4 (Summer 1993).

Brooks, Arthur C. *Who Really Cares?* New York: Basic Books, 2006.

Bruce, Betsy. *Sams Teach Yourself Adobe Dreamweaver CS3 in 24 hours.* Indianapolis: Sams Publishing, 2007.

Bruner, Jerome. *The Process of Education.* Boston: Harvard University Press, 1962.

Bruner, Jerome S., Jacqueline J. Goodnow, and George A. Austin. *A Study of Thinking.* New York: John Wiley & Sons, Inc., 1956.

Butler, Trent C., Chad Brand, Charles Draper, and Archie England eds. *Holman Illustrated Bible Dictionary.* Nashville: B & H Publishing Group, 2003.

Caine, Geoffrey, and Nummela Caine. "Meaningful Learning and the Executive Functions of the Brain." In *The Neuroscience of Adult Learning.* Edited by Sandra Johnson and Kathleen Taylor. New Directions for Adult and Continuing Education, no. 110, Summer 2006. San Francisco: Jossey-Bass, 2006.

Carson, D. A. *New Testament Commentary Survey.* 6th ed. Grand Rapids: Baker, 2007.

Carter, T. J. "The Importance of Talk to Midcareer Women's Development:
A Collaborative Inquiry." *Journal of Business Communication* (2002): 39,
55–91.

Cole, Jason, and Helen Foster. *Using Moodle: Second Edition.* Sebastopol, CA:
O'Reilly Media Inc., 2008.

Corley, Bruce, Steve W. Lempke, and Grant I. Lovejoy. *Biblical Hermeneutics:
A Comprehensive Introduction to Interpreting Scripture.* Nashville: Broadman
and Holman Publishers, 2002.

Cozolino, Louis, and Susan Sprokay. "Neuroscience and Adult Learning." In
The Neuroscience of Adult Learning. Edited by Sandra Johnson and Kathleen
Taylor. New Directions for Adult and Continuing Education, no. 110, Summer
2006. San Francisco: Jossey-Bass, 2006.

Daloz, Laurent. *Effective Teaching and Mentoring: Realizing the
Transformational Power of Adult Learning Experiences.* San Francisco:
Jossey-Bass, 1986.

Davenport, J., and J. Davenport. "A Chronology and Analysis of the Andragogy
Debate," *Adult Education Quarterly* 35(3) (1985): 152–59.

Dirkx, John." Engaging Emotions in Adult Learning: A Jungian Perspective on
Emotion and Transformative Learning." In *Teaching for Change: Fostering
Transformative Learning in the Classroom.* Edited by E. W. Taylor. New
Directions for Adult and Continuing Education, no. 109, Spring 2006. San
Francisco: Jossey-Bass, 2006.

———. "Transformative Learning Theory in the Practice of Adult Education:
An Overview," *PAACE Journal of Lifelong Learning* 7:1–14.

Dockery, David. "The Divine-Human Authorship of Inspired Scripture." In
Authority and Interpretation: A Baptist Perspective. Duane Garrett and
Richard Melick, 13–43. Grand Rapids: Baker Book House, 1987.

Dockery, David S. *Biblical Interpretation Then and Now: Contemporary
Hermeneutics in Light of the Early Church.* Grand Rapids: Baker Academic,
1992.

Edwards, David L. "6. An Evaluation of Contemporary Learning Theories." In
*The Christian Educator's Handbook on Teaching: A Comprehensive Resource
on the Distinctiveness of True Christian Teaching,* Edited by Kenneth O.
Gangel and Howard G. Hendricks. Grand Rapids: Baker Books, 1988.

English, L. M., ed. *International Encyclopedia of Adult Education.* London:
Palgrave, 2005.

The English Standard Version. Wheaton: Crossway Books/Good News
Publishers, 2001.

Erickson, Millard. *Christian Theology.* Grand Rapids: Baker Book House, 1983.

Fee, Gordon D., and Douglas Stuart. *How to Read the Bible for All Its Worth.*
Grand Rapids: Zondervan, 2005.

————. *How to Read the Bible Book by Book: A Guided Tour.* Grand Rapids: Zondervan, 2002.

Ford, Leroy. *Design for Teaching and Training: A Self-Study Guide to Lesson Planning.* Nashville: Broadman Press, 1978.

Fowler, James W. *Becoming Adult, Becoming Christian: Adult Development & Christian Faith.* San Francisco: Jossey-Bass Publishers, 2000.

Fowler, James W. *Stages of Faith: The Psychology of Human Development and the Quest for Meaning.* San Francisco: Harper & Row, 1981.

Gangel, Kenneth O., and Howard H. Hendricks, eds. *The Christian Educator's Handbook on Teaching: A Comprehensive Resource on the Distinctiveness of True Christian Teaching.* Grand Rapids: Baker Books, 1988.

Garrison, D. R., "Self-Directed Learning: Toward a Comprehensive Model." *Adult Education Quarterly* 48, no. 1 (Fall 1997). *Education Research Complete, EBSCO host* (accessed February 24, 2009).

Glenn, John. *Commentary and Reference Survey.* 9th ed., Grand Rapids: Kregel Publishers, 2003.

Glowacki-Dulka, M. *Proceedings of the 19th Annual Midwest Research to Practice Conference in Adult, Continuing, and Community Education,* 21–26. Madison: University of Wisconsin, 1993.

Godtube. www.GodTube.com

Goleman, Daniel. *Working with Emotional Intelligence.* New York: Bantam Books, 1998.

Greenlee, Harold J. *The Text of the New Testament: From Manuscript to Modern Edition.* Peabody, MA: Hendrickson Publishers, 2008.

Grow, Gerald. "Teaching Learners to Be Self-Directed," *Adult Education Quarterly* 41, no. 3 (Spring 1991).

Healy, Mike. "East Meets West: Transformational Learning and Buddhist Meditation," in *AERC 2000 An International Conference: Proceedings from the 41st Annual Adult Education Research Conference.* Edited by T. Sork, V. Lee, and R. St. Claire. Vancouver, Canada: University of British Columbia, 2000.

Hill, Lillian H. "The Brain and Consciousness: Sources of Information for Understanding Adult Learning." In *The New Update on Adult Learning Theory.* Edited by Sharan B. Merriam. New Directions for Adult and Continuing Education, no. 89, Spring 2001. San Francisco: Jossey-Bass, 2001.

Hinton, Christina, Koji Miyamoto, and Bruno Della-Chiesa. "Brain Research, Learning and Emotions: implications for education research, policy and practice," *European Journal of Education. Vol. 43, no. 1.* Oxford, UK: Blackwell Publishing Lts., 2008.

Holman Christian Standard Bible, Nashville: Holman Bible Publishers, 2004.

Holman New Testament Commentary series, 12 volumes. Nashville: B&H
Publishing Group, 1998–2000.

Holman Old Testament Commentary series, 20 volumes. Nashville: B&H
Publishing Group, 2001–2009.

Holy Bible: The New International Version. Grand Rapids: Zondervan
Publishing Co.

Houle, Cyril O. *The Inquiring Mind.* Madison, WI: University of Wisconsin
Press, 1961.

James, Waynne, and Patricia Maher. "Understanding and Using Learning Styles."
in *Adult Learning Methods: A Guide for Effective Instruction.* 3rd ed. Edited
by Michael Galbraith. Malabar, FL: Krieger Publishing Company, 2004.

Janik, Daniel S. *Unlock the Genius Within: Neurobiological Trauma, Teaching,
and Transformative Learning.* Lanham, MD: Rowman & Littlefield
Education, 2005.

Johnson, Sandra. "The Neuroscience of the Mentor-Learner Relationship." In
The Neuroscience of Adult Learning. Edited by Sandra Johnson and Kathleen
Taylor. New Directions for Adult and Continuing Education, no. 110, Summer
2006. San Francisco: Jossey-Bass, 2006.

Julicher, Adolph. *Die Gleichnisreden Jesu.* Tubingen: J.C.B. Mohr, 1910.

Kaiser, Walter C., and Moises Silva. *An Introduction to Biblical Hermeneutics: The
Search for Meaning.* Revised and expanded. Grand Rapids: Zondervan, 2007.

Keefe, James W., and Barbara G. Ferrell, "Developing a Defensible Learning
Style Paradigm," *Educational Leadership* vol. 48, issue 2 (October 1990): 57.

Kilgore, Deborah. "Critical and Postmodern Perspectives on Adult Learning."
In *The New Update on Adult Learning Theory.* Edited by Sharan B. Merriam.
New Directions for Adult and Continuing Education, no. 89, Spring 2001. San
Francisco: Jossey-Bass, 2001.

King, Patricia M., and Karen Strohm Kitchener. *Developing Reflective
Judgment: Understanding and Promoting Intellectual Growth and Critical
Thinking in Adolescents and Adults.* San Francisco: Jossey-Bass Publishers,
1994.

Kitchener, Karen. "Cognition, Metacognition and Epistemic Cognition," *Human
Development,* no. 26 (1983).

Knowles, Malcolm S. *The Adult Learner: A Neglected Species.* 4th ed. Houston,
TX: Gulf Publishing, 1990.

————. *The Modern Practice of Adult Education.* Chicago: Association Press,
1980.

————. "Andragogy, not Pedagogy," *Adult Leadership* 16 (10): 350–352, 386.

Lang, E. "Transformative and Restorative Learning: A Vital Dialectic for
Sustainable Societies," *Adult Education Quarterly,* 2004: 54, 121–39.

LeFever, Marlene. *Learning Styles: Reaching Everyone God Gave You to Teach.*
Colorado Springs: David C. Cook Publishing Co., 1995.

Liefeld, Walter L. *New Testament Exposition.* Grand Rapids: Zondervan Publishing House, 1989.

Lindsay, Michael, et al. *Friendship: Creating a Culture of Connectivity in Your Church.* Loveland, CO: Group Publishing, Inc., 2005.

The Living Bible Paraphrased. Guideposts Associates, 1971.

Logos Bible Software (Bellingham, WA), www.logos.com.

Long, Huey B., and associates. *Self-Directed Learning: Application and Theory.* Athens, GA: Department of Adult Education, University of Georgia, 1988.

Longman, Tremper, III. *Old Testament Commentary Survey.* 4th ed. Grand Rapids: Baker, 2007.

Lucado, Max. *You Are Special (Max Lucado's Wemmicks).* Wheaton, IL: Crossway, 2007.

Melick, Rick. *Called to Be Holy.* Nashville: LifeWay, 2000.

———. "Preaching and Apocalyptic Literature." In Michael Duduit, *Handbook of Contemporary Preaching.* Nashville: Broadman Press, 1992.

Merriam, Sharon B., ed. *The New Update on Adult Learning Theory.* Edited by Sharan B. Merriam. New Directions for Adult and Continuing Education, no. 89, Spring 2001. San Francisco: Jossey-Bass, 2001.

———. *Third Update on Adult Learning Theory.* New Directions for Adult and Continuing Education, no. 119, Fall 2008. San Francisco: Jossey-Bass, 2008.

Metzger, Bruce M., and Bart D. Ehrman. *The Text of the New Testament: Its Transmission, Corruption, and Restoration.* Oxford, MA: Oxford University Press, 2005.

Mezirow, Jack. "Contemporary Paradigms of Learning," *Adult Education Quarterly* 46, no. 3 (1996).

———. *Transformative Learning: Theory to Practice.* San Francisco: Jossey-Bass, 1991.

Mezirow, Jack, et al. *Learning as Transformation: Critical Perspectives on a Theory in Progress.* San Francisco: Jossey-Bass, 2000.

The New American Commentary: An Exegetical and Theological Exposition of Holy Scripture. Nashville: Broadman Press.

New International Commentary on the New Testament. Grand Rapids: Eerdmans.

New International Commentary on the Old Testament. Grand Rapids: Eerdmans.

New International Greek Commentary on the New Testament. Grand Rapids: Eerdmans.

The New Living Translation. Carol Stream, IL: Tyndale House Publishers, 2004; we recommend the 2nd ed.

Osborne, Grant. *The Hermeneutical Spiral: A Comprehensive Introduction to Biblical Interpretation.* Downer's Grove: InterVarsity, 1991.

Perry, Bruce D. "Fear and Learning: Trauma-Related Factors in the Adult Education Process." In *The Neuroscience of Adult Learning*. Edited by Sandra Johnson and Kathleen Taylor. New Directions for Adult and Continuing Education, no. 110, Summer 2006. San Francisco: Jossey-Bass, 2006.

Peterson, Eugene H. *The Message: The Bible in Contemporary Language*. Colorado Springs: NavPress, 2005.

Popcorn, Faith. *The Popcorn Report on the Future of Your Company, Your World, Your Life*. New York: Harper Collins Publishers, Inc., 1992.

Popcorn, Faith, and Adam Hanft. *Dictionary of the Future: The words, terms, and trends that define the way we'll live, work and talk*. New York: Hyperion, 2001.

Rachal, John R. "Andragogy's Detectives: A Critique of the Present and a Proposal for the Future," *Adult Education Quarterly* 52, no. 3 (May 2002): 211.

Rice, William H., IV. *Moodle: E-Learning Course Development—A complete guide to successful learning using Moodle*. Birmingham, AL: Packt Publishing, 2006.

Richards, Lawrence O., and Gary J. Bredfeldt. *Creative Bible Teaching*. Chicago: Moody Press, 1998.

Ross, Colin A. *Creative Bible Teaching*. Chicago: Moody Press, 1998.

Salkind, Neil J. *Theories of Human Development*. 2nd ed. New York: John Wiley & Sons, 1985.

Sandlin, James A. "Andragogy and Its Discontents: An Analysis of Andragogy from Three Critical Perspectives," *PAACE Journal of Lifelong Learning* 14 (2005): 27.

Shor, Ira, and Caroline Pari, eds. *Education Is Politics: Critical Teaching Across Differences, Postsecondary*. Portsmouth, NH: Boynton/Cook Publishers, Inc., 2000.

Smith, Mark K. "Eduard Lindeman and the Meaning of Adult Education," *The Encyclopaedia of Informal Education*, January 30, 2005 (1997, 2004).

Snodgrass, Klyne R. *Stories with Intent: A Comprehensive Guide to the Parables of Jesus*. Grand Rapids: Wm. B. Eerdman's Publishing Co., 2008.

Solorzano, Daniel. "Teaching and Social Change." In *Education Is Politics: Critical Teaching across Differences, Postsecondary*, Edited by Ira Shor and Caroline Pari. Portsmouth, NH: Boynton/Cook Publishers, Inc., 2000.

Sork, T., V. Lee, and R. St. Claire. *AERC 2000 An International Conference: Proceedings from the 41st Annual Adult Education Research Conference*, Vancouver, Canada: University of British Columbia, 2000.

Sousa, David. *How the Brain Learns*. 3rd ed. Thousand Oaks, CA: Corwin Press, 2006.

Spear, George E. "Beyond the Organizing Circumstance: A search for methodology for the study of Self-Directed Learning." In Huey B. Long et al., *Self-Directed Learning: Application and Theory.* Athens, GA: Department of Adult Education, University of Georgia, 1988.

Straughn, Harold Kent. "James Fowler," *The Mind Spiral.* www.lifespirals.com/TheMindSpiral/Fowler?fowler.html (accessed August 23, 2006).

Strong, James H. *Strong's Exhaustive Concordance of the Bible with CD* Peabody: Hendrickson Publishers, 2007.

Tada, Joni Eareckson. *Joni.* Grand Rapids: Zondervan, 2001.

Taylor, Edward W. "Transformative Learning Theory." In *Third Update on Adult Learning Theory.* Edited by Sharan B. Merriam. New Directions for Adult and Continuing Education, no. 119, Fall 2008. San Francisco: Jossey-Bass, 2008.

———, ed. *Teaching for Change: Fostering Transformative Learning in the Classroom.* New Directions for Adult and Continuing Education, no. 109, Spring 2006. San Francisco: Jossey-Bass, 2006.

Taylor, Kathleen, and Annalee Lamoreaux. "Teaching with the Brain in Mind." In *Third Update on Adult Learning Theory.* Edited by Sharan B. Merriam. New Directions for Adult and Continuing Education, no. 119, Fall 2008. San Francisco: Jossey-Bass, 2008.

Tisdell, Elizabeth J. *Exploring Spirituality and Culture in Adult and Higher Education.* San Francisco: Jossey-Bass, 2003.

———. "Feminism." In L. M. English. ed. *International Encyclopedia of Adult Education.* London: Palgrave, 2005.

———. "Spirituality and Adult Learning" in *New Directions for Adult and Continuing Education: Third Update on Adult Learning Theory,* ed. Sharan B. Merriam. San Francisco: Jossey-Bass, 2008.

Tough, Allen. *The Adult's Learning Projects: A Fresh Approach to Theory and Practice in Adult Learning.* 2nd ed. Research in Education Series No. 1, The Ontario Institute for Studies in Education. Toronto, Canada: The Ontario Institute for Studies in Education, 1979.

Vischer, Phil. *Sidney & Norman: a tale of two pigs.* China: Tommy Nelson—a division of Thomas Nelson Publishers, 2006.

von Oech, Roger. *A Kick in the Seat of the Pants.* New York: Harper Perennial, 1986.

Watson, John B. *Behaviorism.* New York: W.W. Norton & Company, Inc. Publishers, 1930.

Webster, Leonard, and David Murphy. "Enhancing Learning Through Technology: Challenges and Responses." In Reggie Kwan, Robert Fox, F. T. Chan, and Philip Tsang, eds. *Enhancing Learning Through Technology: Research on Emerging Technologies and Pedagogies.* Hackensack, NJ: World Scientific Publishing Co., 2008.

The Westminster Shorter Catechism, 1674. *Center for Reformed Theology and Apologetics,* www.reformed.org

Wiessner, C. A., S. R. Meyer, H. L. Pfhal, and P. G. Neaman, Peds. *Proceedings of the Fifth International Conference on Transformative Learning,* 2003.

Williams, S. H. "Black Mama Sauce: Integrating the Theatre of the Oppressed and Afrocentricity in Transformative Learning." In C. A. Wiessner, S. R. Meyer, H. L. Pfhal, and P. G. Neaman, eds., *Proceedings of the Fifth International Conference on Transformative Learning,* 2003.

Worley, Karla. *Growing Weary Doing Good: Encouragement for Exhausted Women.* Birmingham, AL: New Hope Publishing, 2001.

Young, James. *Young's Analytical Concordance to the Bible.* Peabody: Hendrickson Publishers, 1984.

Yount, Rick. "Jesus the Master Teacher." In *The Teaching Ministry of the Church: Integrating Biblical Truth with Contemporary Application.* Edited by Daryl Eldridge. Nashville: Broadman & Holman, 1995.

Yount, William R. *Created to Learn.* Nashville: Broadman & Holman Publishers, 1996.

Youtube, www.youtube.com

Zondervan Exegetical Commentary on the New Testament. Grand Rapids: Zondervan Publishing.

Zuck, Roy. *Spirit-Filled Teaching: The Power of the Holy Spirit in Your Ministry.* Edited by Charles Swindoll. Nashville: Word Publishing, 1998.

Zull, James E. "Key Aspects of How the Brain Learns." In *The Neuroscience of Adult Learning.* New Directions for Adult and Continuing Education, no. 110. Edited by Sandra Johnson & Kathleen Taylor. San Francisco: Jossey-Bass, 2006.

APPENDICES

APPENDIX A

Piaget's Stages of Cognitive Development[1]

Stage	Period of Development
Sensorimotor	Birth–2 years
Preoperational	2–7 years
Concrete Operational	7–11 years
Formal Operational	11 years on

APPENDIX B

King and Kitchener's Reflective Judgment Stages[2]

Prereflective Thinking (Stages 1, 2, and 3)

Stage 1

View of knowledge: Knowledge is assumed to exist absolutely and concretely; it is not understood as an abstraction. It can be obtained with certainty by direct observation.

Concept of justification: beliefs need no justification since there is assumed to be an absolute correspondence between what is believed to be true and what is true.

> *"I know what I have seen."*

Stage 2

View of knowledge: Knowledge is assumed to be absolutely certain or certain but not immediately

> *"If it is on the news, it has to be true."*

---

[1] L. E. Berk, *Exploring Lifespan Development* (San Francisco: Allyn and Bacon, 2008), 16.

[2] P. M. King and K. S. Kitchener, *Developing Reflective Judgment: Understanding and Promoting Intellectual Growth and Critical Thinking in Adolescents and Adults* (San Francisco: Jossey-Bass, 1994), 14–16.

available. Knowledge can be obtained directly through the senses (as in direct observation) or via authority figures.

Concept of justification: Beliefs are unexamined and unjustified or justified by their correspondence with the beliefs of an authority figure (such as a teacher or parent). Most issues are assumed to have a right answer, so there is little or no conflict in making decisions about disputed issues.

Stage 3

View of knowledge: Knowledge is assumed to be absolutely certain or temporarily uncertain. In areas of temporary uncertainty, only personal beliefs can be known until absolute knowledge is obtained. In areas of absolute certainty, knowledge is obtained from authorities.

> *"When there is evidence that people can give to convince everybody one way or another, then it will be knowledge; until then, it's just a guess."*

Concept of justification: In areas in which certain answers exist, beliefs are justified by reference to authorities' views. In areas in which answers do not exist, beliefs are defended as personal opinion since the link between evidence and beliefs is unclear.

Quasireflective Thinking (Stages 4 and 5)

Stage 4

View of knowledge: Knowledge is uncertain and knowledge claims are idiosyncratic to the individual since situational variables (such as incorrect reporting of data, data lost over time, or disparities in access to information) dictate that knowing always involves an element of ambiguity.

> *"I'd be more inclined to believe evolution if they had proof. It's just like the pyramids: I don't think we'll ever know. Who are you going to ask? No one was there."*

Concept of justification: Beliefs are justified by giving reasons and using evidence, but the arguments and choice of evidence are idiosyncratic (for example, choosing evidence that fits an established belief).

Stage 5

View of knowledge: Knowledge is contextual and subjective since it is filtered through a person's perceptions and criteria for judgment. Only interpretations of evidence, events, or issues may be known.

> *"People think differently and so they attack the problem differently. Other theories could be as true as my own but based on different evidence."*

Concept of justification: Beliefs are justified within a particular context by means of the rules of inquiry for that context and by context-specific interpretations of evidence. Specific beliefs are assumed to be context specific or are balanced against other interpretations, which complicate (and sometimes delay) conclusions.

Reflective Thinking (Stages 6 and 7)

Stage 6

View of knowledge: Knowledge is constructed into individual conclusions about ill-structured problems on the basis of information from a variety of sources. Interpretations that are based on evaluations of evidence across contexts and on the evaluated opinions of reputable others can be known.

> *"It's very difficult in this life to be sure. There are degrees of sureness. You come to a point at which you are sure enough for a personal stance on the issue."*

Concept of justification: Beliefs are justified by comparing evidence and opinion from different perspectives on an issue or across different contexts and by constructing solutions that are evaluated by criteria such as the weight of the evidence, the utility of the solution, or the pragmatic need for action.

Stage 7

View of knowledge: Knowledge is the outcome of a process of reasonable inquiry in which solutions to ill-structured problems are constructed. The adequacy of those solutions is evaluated in terms of what is most reasonable or probable according to the current evidence, and

> *"One can judge an argument by how well thought out the positions are, what kind of reasoning and evidence are used to support it, and how consistent the way one argues on this topic is as compared with other topics."*

it is reevaluated when relevant new evidence, perspectives, or tools of inquiry become available.

Concept of justification: Beliefs are justified probabilistically on the basis of a variety of interpretive considerations, such as the weight of the evidence, the explanatory value of the interpretations, the risk of erroneous conclusions, consequences of alternative judgments, and the interrelationships of these factors. Conclusions are defended as representing the most complete, plausible, or compelling understanding of an issue on the basis of the available evidence.

APPENDIX C

Fowler's Stages of Faith[3]

Stage 1: Primal Faith

Usually is evident in infants and toddlers birth to two years of age. The young child develops a rudimentary understanding of trust as his caretakers meet his needs. This learning of trust or mistrust is basic to the understanding of a God who can be trusted.

Stage 2: Intuitive/Projective Faith

Usually is evident in children two through six or seven (although it can be seen in adult of any age). It's a changing and growing and dynamic faith characterized by a growth in knowing through one's perceptions, feelings, and imagination.

Stage 3: Mythic/Literal Faith

The child or (adult) can tell the story of his faith that explains the meaning. Literal meaning is dealt with inside of the story but not externally as abstract concept. This stage is characterized by linear order, rules, and predictability.

Stage 4: Synthetic/Conventional Faith

This stage is typical of 12- or 13-year-olds, although it is also true in adults. The individual can now think about their thinking. Abstract thought takes the place of concrete. This stage is characterized by a relationship with a God who knows me and values me but faith has not developed to the point of critical reflection.

---

[3] H. K. Straughn, "James Fowler," *The Mind Spiral.* www.lifespirals.com/TheMindSpiral/Fowler?fowler.html (accessed August 23, 2006).

Stage 5: Individuative/Protective Faith

This stage is a 17-to-adult stage that is characterized by stepping out of one's group identity and engaging in self-reflection. This stage is characterized by a concern for authenticity. What group can I belong to, and what relationships can I have and have them fit my ideological commitments? Many adults do not enter this stage until the late twenties or thirties if ever. This is problematic because early relational choices may not fit this new concern for authenticity.

Stage 6: Conjunctive Faith

Usually occurs between midlife and beyond. This stage is characterized by the recognition that conscious self is not all there is of me. Much of my responses come from a deeper unconscious self. It is an acknowledgment that we can engage in relationships with people who have a different view of truth. It is also an acceptance that God is not just available and close, but He is also unavailable and strange and there is still a desire to have a relationship with him.

Stage 7: Universalizing Faith

In this stage the focus changes from just me and mine to participation in God's reality. It is negating self for the sake of affirming.

APPENDIX D

Zuck's 14 Propositions: The Holy Spirit and Biblical Interpretation[4]

1. The Holy Spirit's work is always through the written Word of God, not beyond or in addition to it.
2. The role of the Holy Spirit in interpreting the Bible does not mean that one's interpretations are infallible.
3. The Holy Spirit reveals the normal literal meaning of the Scripture passage—not hidden divergent meaning.
4. Although the unregenerate may be able to comprehend some of the Bible's statements, they are not able to apply God's truth to their lives.
5. The work of the Holy Spirit means that biblical truth can be understood by all.

---

[4] R. Zuck, *Spirit-Filled Teaching: The Power of the Holy Spirit in Your Ministry*, ed. C. Swindoll (Nashville: Word Publishing, 1998), 102–8. (Condensed and Paraphrased)

6. Spiritual devotion, depth, and spiritual sensitivity make correct interpretations of Scripture more possible.
7. The Holy Spirit's work in interpretation means that lack of spiritual preparedness hinders accurate interpretation.
8. The role of the Spirit in interpretation is not a substitute for diligent study. With a heart sensitive to the Spirit, the interpreter must study the Word intensely.
9. The Spirit's work in biblical interpretation does not rule out the use of study helps such as Bible commentaries, dictionaries, encyclopedias, and concordances.
10. The ministry of the Holy Spirit in Bible interpretation does not mean interpreters can ignore common sense and logic.
11. The place of the Holy Spirit in interpreting the Bible means that He does not normally give sudden intuitive flashes of insight.
12. The Spirit's ministry in interpreting the Bible is included in but is not identical with illumination. Interpretation involves perception; illumination includes interpretation, but it also involves reception.
13. The role of the Spirit in scriptural interpretation does not mean that all parts of the Bible are equally clear in meaning.
14. The Spirit's work in interpretation does not result in believers having a comprehensive or complete understanding of the entire Scripture.

APPENDIX E

Star Model Adult Lesson Plan

Passage and Reference:

Governing Objective: The overall objective of the passage is for the learner to . . . _____

I. RELEVANCE:

Why is this passage relevant to your learners? (5 minutes)

Description: *Describe why this passage is relevant to contemporary adult learners.*

Methods: *Create an exciting introduction that connects the learner with the relevance of the Bible passage. Explain the methods you will use to introduce the passage.*

Evaluation: *I will know the learners have connected with the relevance of the passage by . . .*

Transition: *Write a sentence that will transition your learners from the introduction into the Bible content section.*

II. REVELATION:

What will learners know/understand about the content of the biblical passage? (20–23 minutes)

Objective: *Learners will know/understand . . . (cognitive content of the passage).*

Description: *Create a guide for teaching the content of your lesson. This can be a comprehensive outline, narrative, or PowerPoint slide layout pages.*

Methods: *Describe your teaching methods for help-
                ing learners discover the Bible content of this
                passage.*

Evaluation: *I will know learners attain the content objective
                by . . . (the learner answering questions, filling
                in study sheet, restating, etc.).*

Transition: *Write a transition sentence that takes the learn-
                er from content to application.*

III. RESPONSIBILITY:

*How will learners apply the biblical principles of this passage to contem-
porary adults? (18–20 minutes)*

Objective: *After applying (the Scripture principle) to to-
                day's adults, the learner will (desire, be con-
                vinced, appreciate, etc.) (describe a measurable
                conviction).*

Description: *List the principles in your passage that were
                true in Bible times and are still true today. In-
                clude the verse where you found them.*

Methods: *Methods in this section should focus on engag-
                ing students on a convictional level. Describe
                the methods you will use to lead the learners to
                explore the principles and why these principles
                are applicable to today's world.*

Evaluation: *I will know the learners engage convictionally
                with the contemporary application by (shar-
                ing, discussing, debating, reflecting, praying,
                expressing, dramatizing, etc.What is it you will
                observe the learner doing that will indicate he
                accomplished the application objective?)*

Transition: *Write a transition sentence that takes the learn-
                er from application to personal action.*

IV. RESULTS:

What will learners do to apply this passage to their own lives? How will their lives be different? (8–10 minutes)

Objective: *Learners will commit to . . . (an appropriate action of obedience).*

Description: *List some action responses you could suggest that would constitute personal obedience to the principles found in this passage.*

Methods: *What method will you use to challenge learners to take personal life-changing actions of obedience in response to the principles in this passage?*

Evaluation: *I will know the learners have committed to personal action by . . .*

Lesson Wrap-up: *Restate for your students in one or two sentences a summary of what you wanted them to learn. (1–2 minutes)*

Learner Evaluation for Governing Lesson Objective:

I know the learners accomplished my governing objective because they . . .

Materials: *Make a list of all materials and equipment you will need to teach this lesson. Include completed study sheets, scripts, PowerPoint layout pages, etc.*

APPENDIX F

Learning Styles/Modalities Inventories[5]

Cognitive

- Gregorc Style Delineator— Order online (fee) http://gregorc.com /instrume.html
- Learning Style Inventory 3 (Kolb)— Available online (fee) http://www.haygroup.com/tl/Questionnaires_Workbooks/Kolb _Learning_Style_Inventory
- Sternberg-Wagner Thinking Styles Inventory— Available online (no fee) http://www.ldrc.ca/projects/tscale/

Affective

- Kolb— Available online (no fee) http://www.haygroup.com/tl/EI/Quiz .aspx
- Myers-Briggs Type Indicator— Available online (fee) http://www .discoveryourpersonality.com/MBTI.html?source=Google

Physiological and Perceptual Modalities Indicators

- DVC Learning Style for College— Available online (no fee) http:// www.metamath.com/multiple/multiple_choice_questions.html
- Kaleidoscope Profile— Available online (fee) http://www.plsweb.com /learningstyles_ca/
- The Temperament Sorter II— Available online (no fee) http://keirsey .com/

Multiple Intelligence Inventory

- Learning Disability Resource Community— Available online (no fee) http://www.ldrc.ca/projects/miinventory/miinventory.php

APPENDIX G

Collection of Methods
(parenthetical word indicates a likely place to use the method)

1. **Apprentice: (Results)** There are times when the "action of obedience" that a passage requires brings conviction for vocational change

---

[5] For a more complete list see W. James and P. Maher, "Understanding and Using Learning Styles," in *Adult Learning Methods: A Guide for Effective Instruction,* 3rd ed., ed. M. Galbraith (Malabar, FL: Krieger Publishing Company, 2004), 130–31.

or to take on a new area of service. Apprenticing can help in two ways. First, it takes the anxiety out of being in a new situation. Second, it gives the learner the opportunity to try it on and see if it fits. The mentor helps the learner know what the job entails, allows him to observe, and gradually encourages the learner to try out the tasks and see if they are a comfortable fit. Many times people feel that God is calling them to full-time Christian service, but they have no idea what the service looks like. Pastors, staff members, missionaries, and Bible study leaders can all mentor. We have seen so many students who feel called to pastor but have no experience whatsoever. We have seen students called into missions who have never been on a mission trip. God calls us to areas that fit our gifts and talents. When we can apprentice, God can confirm His calling or redirect us.

Example: (Results) Matthew 28:18–20 (Great Commission) As the teacher challenges students to share Christ with their neighborhoods, their city, and their world, learners share that they think God might be calling them to be a career missionary. The teacher responds by asking them if they would like to go on the summer mission trip to Brazil. The teacher links the learner with a person in the class who has been on summer mission trips several times. The teacher links the learner with the leader of the trip (a career missionary) and shares that the learner is possibly considering career missions. The learner is mentored by both the veteran summer missions traveler and the career missionary. He has the opportunity to apprentice and either move into career missions or have God redirect into another avenue of service.

2. **Artistic Expression: (Relevance, Responsibility)** Remember the fun in kindergarten manipulating clay and creating with Legos? Adults can benefit from hands-on manipulation of materials that allow them to express or interpret meaning. Not only does this stroke kinesthetic learners, but it also adds another sensory dimension for all learners.

    Example: (Relevance) Put five tables around the room with chairs at each table. At Table 1 have clay or play dough in various colors, pipe cleaners, etc. At table 2 have large Manila paper and paints or markers. At table 3 place writing paper and pencils or pens, and at table 4 place a tub of Legos. On table 5 place old magazines, scissors, Manila paper, and glue. Write in large letters on the grease board

at the side of the room, "People I know need peace with God because . . . " As adult learners come in to Bible study, ask them to
choose any table and create a response to the words on the grease
board. Encourage discussion and collaboration, but allow learners to
work by themselves or contribute to a group response. Learners who
do not wish to express with art media may write a response.

3. **Bible Character Impersonation: (Revelation)** Bible character impersonation takes place when a person "becomes" a Bible character
and tells the story of the Bible passage from a personal perspective. It
is most effective when done with appropriate costume. Costumes can
be a simple bathrobe and sweatband. The storytelling can be a monologue or interactive dialogue with the audience. It is a very effective
way of communicating the content of a passage if the impersonator
prepares ahead and presents the first part of the content section of the
Bible study. It can also be done in review of the content portion of the
lesson as a learner becomes a character from the Bible story and retell
the events of the passage.

   Example: (Revelation) Our special guest for today is the apostle
Paul. He is here to tell you about what happened to him on the road
to Damascus. Paul enters and tells his story.

4. **Brain Storming: (Relevance, Responsibility)** Brainstorming is a
great way to introduce a lesson (Relevance) or to create possible applications (Responsibility) of the passage's principles. It can be done
in a large group with everyone participating or in small groups of five
through seven learners with a "share session" to pool the ideas from
every group. Brainstorming usually begins with the introduction of a
word, picture, or question. Every person throws out ideas as rapidly
as possible. No judgments are passed against any ideas. A recorder
writes down all ideas so that everyone can view them. At the end of a
specific time limit the group goes through a process of grouping ideas
that are alike and selecting the most relevant ideas, finally deciding on
one idea (or a couple of ideas) that most encapsulates what they are
considering. The purpose of this activity is to stimulate creativity in
considering a concept. It helps individuals within the group interact
with and examine other ways of thinking.

   Example: (Relevance) Learners sit at round tables in groups of
five through seven. On each table is the word "love" and a large piece

of paper with markers. A preselected facilitator for each table explains to the learners that they are to say anything that comes into their mind when they think of love. The facilitator writes down all ideas without comment. Learners speak out their ideas for three minutes. Then the facilitator stops the time for input, and the group discusses the concepts that have been recorded. They group together the ideas that are similar, coming up with three or four main ideas that express what the group associates with the word "love." Each table shares their ideas with the other tables, and the teacher keeps a composite list of all new ideas on the white board at the front of the room. When the session is over, the teacher says, "The word 'love' makes us think of many interesting concepts. Love can be self-giving or self-seeking. It can involve payback or pleasure. The passage we are studying today explains God's concept of love. Let's see which of our concepts of love are similar to God's. Our study passage is . . . "

5. **Captivating Questions: (Relevance, Revelation, Responsibility, Results)** This method uses a question posted on the grease board or on a PowerPoint slide that grabs the attention of the learner and produces thought-provoking images. Captivating questions can be used in any section of the lesson.

   Example: (Responsibility) You have just studied 1 Tim 6:17–19, instructions to the rich. One of the principles in this passage is "God wants us to store up a good foundation for the age to come" (6:19). Learners sit in groups of five through seven. The question is: "How do you think God wants your best friend to spend the $500,000 he just won?" The discussion brings the dilemma into the contemporary world close to the learner, but does not yet force the learner to apply the passage personally. As the teacher moves the learner into the Results section of the lesson, the focus for the learner will become— What does God want me personally to do with my finances?

6. **Case Study: (Relevance, Responsibility)** A case study poses a problem that the Scripture passage will answer (Relevance) or to apply the Scripture passage to a scenario in the contemporary world (Responsibility). It can involve real people and circumstances, or it can be totally fictitious.

   Example 1: (Relevance and Responsibility) The teacher introduces the Bible study on 1 Tim 6:17–19 with the following case study. Jason, a 58-year-old financial planner, was very successful. He had a large house with a swimming pool, a vacation cabin on a beautiful lake, two BMWs, a ski boat, and $800,000 in his 401(K). As he looked forward to retirement he felt very good about the future. He attended church regularly and gave several hundred dollars a month. He thought God was very happy with him. Then the bottom dropped out of the economy. In two months' time he found himself without a job and unable to make the payments on his two homes, two cars, and boat. His $800,000 was now $450,000, and he had to make some very hard decisions—and fast. He wondered what happened to God. Why had God let this happen to him? (Relevance) The teacher then leads the learners in discovering the content of 1 Tim 6:17–19 and reflecting on what God meant by this passage. During the application section of the lesson the teacher asked the students to continue Jason's story, applying what they learned from the Scripture passage (Responsibility). Case studies can be carried from the introduction into the application like in the example above, or they can be used only in the introduction to establish relevance, or only in the application to apply the Bible passage and help the learners move from the meaning of the passage in Bible times to the application of the passage in the contemporary world.

Example 2 (Relevance): Learners take their coffee to a round table and sit in comfortable chairs. There is a prepared case study at each place. Each table group reads a case study and discusses the scenario. The table facilitator distills the discussion and responds to the question (include the written question on the handout with the case study), "How does peace with God relate to your case study?"

Table 1: "Bill is in shock as he leaves the doctor's office. He can't quite comprehend the life-ending pronouncement he has just heard. How could he be dying? What should he do? What good would his financial security do now? What was he going to do about God? Is there a heaven and a hell?"

Table 2: "Carol and John are 45. They are very successful in their careers and have enjoyed beautiful things. They have been very careful to invest money and plan to retire at 50 with a financially secure future. However, the stock market has taken a nose dive, and their 401(K) has diminished significantly. They feel very insecure and worried. For the first time in their lives they realize they cannot handle the situation. If life isn't about money—what is it about? As fear grips their hearts, they wonder if going to church might help. They have always felt God was the enemy. Maybe if they went to church God would be on their side and they would get their money back."

Table 3: "Sue and Fred wanted a baby for 15 years. They tried everything. When Fred found out they were finally pregnant and that they were having a boy, he began a college savings fund and went out and bought that boy a football. Finally, the long await-ed day arrived and the baby was born. The pediatrician has just left the hospital room after sharing the news that their precious baby has Downs Syndrome and that he has a lifelong sentence of mental and physical challenges ahead. How could God do this to them? God must be paying them back for leaving God out of their life. Maybe if they could apologize to God He would take this away."

Table 4: "Cynthia is a 35-year-old mother of a two-year-old and a newborn. When she tried to breast feed her new infant, she discovered a small lump in her breast. Immediately her obstetri-cian sent her to a surgeon for a biopsy. She has just finished a conversation with the surgeon who told her that her cancer is a rare type and is deadly. She must have radical surgery and ag-gressive chemo if she is to have a chance. Cynthia is panicked. Why would God do this to her? She is afraid to die. Who will take care of her baby?"

Table 5: "Jemmy and Franco have three teenagers. On Friday evening, they went to the door and a policeman informed them that their 16-year-old has been killed in a car accident. They have been through so much with this kid! He was just beginning to get it together. He just started going to church and was baptized last Sunday. He seemed so happy. What did he call it? —being in God's family? Why would God take him now? Jemmy and Fran-co had been thinking their son might have the right idea about becoming a church member. Maybe God was punishing them for not believing."

The large group leader puts the question on the board: "Peace WITH God?" After the learners at each table discuss the scenario and answer how their scenario relates to peace with God, the large group leader has each table leader share their ideas. The large group leader then points out that although peace with God differs from feelings of peace from God, making peace with God is a prerequisite to having peace from God. The leader then says, "Today we will be studying how to get peace with God that produces the peace of God."

Example 3: (Responsibility) The learners have just studied James 2:1–12 about the sin of favoritism. There are multiple principles in this passage. We will use one as an example. The learners have learned the principle, "God does not want Christians to show favoritism (2:1)." The teacher asks the learners to sit in groups of five through seven and create a case study (scenario) where a contemporary adult demonstrates obeying this biblical principle. The learners work in their groups for 10 minutes and then share their case studies, pointing out how the character in this story obeyed the Scripture principle. The teacher then transitions to the Results section of the lesson.

Example 4: (Responsibility) The teacher invites the learners to sit at tables in groups of five through seven. The table leader leads a discussion about this scenario. "Susan is growing in Christ and trying to follow the new things she is learning in Scripture. Last week a lady, Delilah, came to Bible study for the first time. Delilah cried as she shared that she had just given her life to Christ, and she asked the class to pray that she could stay off drugs. The class prayed with her. The Bible study was James 2:1–12. Susan felt that God was urging her to be a friend to Delilah. Susan asked Delilah to meet her for coffee on Friday morning. Tuesday, Katherine called Susan and invited her to go with her to a new spa. Katherine had two free gift cards that were for Friday morning. Susan's heart fell to her toes. She wanted so much to go with Katherine. Katherine was pretty and had so many friends. Katherine had never invited Susan to do anything. How could she get out of taking Delilah to coffee? Delilah didn't even have a phone. Susan remembered James 2:1. She prayed and asked God what to do. If she applies the principles from James 2:1–12, what do you think she will do and why?" After the learners have discussed applying the Scripture principles to the scenario, they share their ideas with the other groups. The teacher summarizes.

7. **Chat Rooms: (Relevance, Revelation, Responsibility, Results)** Today's adults live in a world of computer dating, computer shopping, computer directions for travel, computer gaming, and Facebook. The computer is a wonderful tool for communicating with learners before, during, and after class. Every Bible study group should have a chat room to use as a catalyst for Christian growth. Chat rooms are easy to set up and easy to use. They create opportunity for introducing the lesson (Relevance), continuing Reflective Dialogue regarding a passage (Revelation), expanding possible applications of a passage (Responsibility), or creating accountability for promised actions (Results).

   Example 1: (Relevance) E-mail all class members and visitors and invite them to enter the class chat room at a certain day and time. At the appointed time begin the chat with the words "Peace with God—what is it and why do we need it?" After participants discuss this issue online, ask them to ask at least three other random adults face-to-face what it means to have peace with God. Ask them to be prepared to share responses during the next Bible study.

   Example 2: (Results) The teacher posts, "We studied Paul's instructions that we should pray for one another, and we committed to pray for our class members this week. We are halfway through the week. How are we doing? Let's share something that has been a challenge or a blessing." The learners then post responses to the teacher's inquiry.

8. **Creative Reminders: (Results)** Remembering our promises to God can be very difficult in our busy lives. It sometimes helps to take a reminder home. The reminder might be things like a crucifixion nail, a Bible verse to post, a share your faith bracelet, a tiny glass heart, and a get out of jail free card.

   Example: (Results) Luke 21:1–4 (the Widow's Mite). The teacher shares the difference between the rich giving a little from their wealth and the widow giving all she had. During the Results section of the lesson, the teacher challenges the students to give themselves to God so that He controls every part of their lives. After reflection and a prayer of commitment, the teacher gives each learner a replica of a "widow's mite," an ancient coin that would have been worth very little. The learner keeps the coin as a reminder that all our possessions belong to God.

9. **Debate: (Responsibility)** Debate is an effective method for expressing opposing views and examining the arguments on each side of the issue. Debate should be lively and fun but also purposeful. It is important to protect emotions because a debate can become heated if personal feelings are involved. The key to protecting participants is to randomly select the teams. This ensures that teams do not have ownership of the issue and can be more objective in their preparation and expression.

   Example: (Responsibility) 1 Timothy 3:1–12 (Role of Leaders in the Church) After studying the role of leaders in the church in 1 Timothy, teams prepare and debate whether or not this is a pattern for churches today. Give students opportunity to prepare arguments. It may be helpful to ask one week ahead for volunteers to participate. Randomly select the debate teams from the volunteers, give them the rules for debate, and give them the week to prepare. Debate question is: "Does 1 Tim 3:1–12 apply to the church today?" After the teacher leads the class in learning the content of the passage, the debate teams are invited to debate. One team takes the affirmative, yes; the passage applies to today's churches. The other team takes the negative, no; the passage refers to that historical culture.

10. **Drama: (Relevance, Revelation, Responsibility)** Drama is a great tool to use for all ages in most parts of the lesson. Drama is acting out a story. In the Relevance section the drama portrays a contemporary scenario that connects the learner to the relevance of the Bible passage. In the Revelation section, actors represent the characters in the Scripture passage, and they dramatize the content of the passage. In the Responsibility section of the lesson, drama should be a contemporary scenario that applies the Bible passage. Drama should only be used when a passage can be more effectively taught by visualizing the events through dramatization. The overuse of drama makes it irritating and ineffective.

    Example 1: (Relevance) In the Relevance section of the lesson, drama can be used in either Bible character or contemporary form. If a Bible character introduces the story, he does not give all the facts; he catches the attention of the learners and gives a few interesting details from the Bible passage that connects the learners with a contemporary need. If contemporary drama is used, the actors set up a modern scenario that peeks the interest of the learners in the lesson because they identify with the scenario that presents the relevance. The setting is a husband (George) and wife (Martha) drinking coffee across the table from each other. George says, "Honey, you realize I might get laid off—right?" Martha responds, "I know. I'm trying not to think about it." George says, "We need to put some money away in a hurry. We don't even have enough to make it one month without my salary." Martha responds, "I know, and the only extra money we have is the few dollars we give to the church. Do you think God would care if we stop giving temporarily and save that money?" They both sit there looking off into the air thoughtfully. The teacher says, "Today we are going to look at a passage of Scripture that talks about how we should think about material things. After we study the Scripture passage, we will talk about what kind of decision God might want George and Martha to make."

Example 2: (Revelation) Since Scripture contains so many stories in narrative form, much of the Bible lends itself to drama, such as Ananias and Saphira, Paul and Silas in prison, the widow and the mite, Abraham and Isaac, and the disciples fishing. For explaining content it is important for actors to include all of the facts as they tell the story. A script can be very helpful in making sure that the important information is conveyed.

Example 3: (Responsibility) Because the purpose of the Responsibility section is to apply Bible principles to the contemporary world, contemporary drama is helpful. Scenarios apply the Scripture principles found in the text to contemporary problems in today's world. The scripture passage is 1 Tim 6:17–19, Instructions to the rich. One of the principles is: "God wants us to set our hope on him, not on the uncertainty of wealth" (6:17).

Frank:	"Hey Joy, the Martins are going on a European cruise in July. I think we should do a cruise this summer."
Joy:	"It sounds great but not INSTEAD of our new ski boat. I have been waiting all year for you to buy that boat. I want to go water skiing. AND remember, it needs to match my blue convertible."

Frank:	"I am brilliant when it comes to making money. I am soooo good at it."
Joy:	"I'm really glad you are. I love spending it! We are going to have a great retirement. We already have almost $600,000 in our 401K. Our house will be paid for by the time we're 50. We'll be able to take trips and buy whatever we want. "

Phone Rings.

Joy answers the phone: "Dr Silver? You have my test results. It's what? That can't be right. I feel fine. Chemo? You can't be serious."

Joy puts down the phone crying. Frank comes over and puts his arms around her.

The teacher invites the class to participate in discussing the implications of applying 1 Tim 6:17–19. Small discussion groups are asked to write three ways adults today could *do* verse 18. After discussion, the class shares their deliberations. The teacher summarizes and transitions into the Results section of the lesson. Drama can be creatively done with costumes, with partial costumes (such as hats or signs), or without costumes. Costumes can be elaborate professional costumes that are purchased and kept in a church costume closet, they can be made by volunteers in the church, or they can be impromptu—created by the performers out of their own home closets. Bathrobes make great Bible time costumes. A hand towel and a sweatband make an inexpensive headdress. Flip-flops or sandals are also appropriate.

11. **E-mail a Partner: (Results)** E-mailing a partner is a personal way to create accountability for commitment to action. Learners pick a partner during the Bible study and exchange e-mail addresses. Learners who do not have e-mail can do the same with "snail mail." The peer partners share their promise to action and agree to connect midweek and check on each other. The peers then connect through e-mail. They report and encourage each other to stay with the action.

Example: (Results) Matthew 28:18–20 (Great Commission) Learners commit to share their faith with one person during the week. Peer partners commit to pray for each other and to hold the other accountable for the commitment. Midweek they e-mail each other and report attempts or lack of attempts. They renew their commitments and check with each other at the next Bible study.

12. **Games: (Relevance, Revelation, Responsibility)** Games can be used both to learn new information (creating the game) and to recall learned information. In the Revelation section of the lesson, teams of learners can create a game by studying the passage and using the information to form questions or matches. Teams can swap games and play the other team's game in order to review and remember the information. In the Responsibility section of the lesson, teams of learners can create games to apply the principles of Scripture to the contemporary world. There are hundreds of ways to use games in learning. When using games, select ideas that match the learners in your class. Usually, individual competition is not appreciated, but team competition is viewed as nonthreatening and more fun. Be aware of cultural differences and learners who are not proficient in English. It may be difficult for them to understand a game or know the vocabulary.

Example Matching: (Responsibility) Create a matching game. Give a team of learners (3–5) a large square piece of cardboard with a large square drawn on it and the square divided into 16 equal squares, four vertical rows and four horizontal rows. This is the game board. Create 16 cards out of light-colored posterboard. Each card should be the same size as one of the 16 small squares. Write questions on each of eight cards that will guide the students toward discovering the content of the Bible passage. Give the students Bibles and commentaries. Encourage the students to find the answers to each of the questions and write the answer on a blank card. The team should end with eight question cards and eight answer cards. The teacher should be available to check information and guide in the use of the resources. After 10–15 minutes of preparing the game, learners play the game together—reviewing the material. Mix the 16 cards and place them face down on the cardboard game board. Players take turns uncovering two cards. If they match (a question and matching answer), the player gets to keep the cards. If they do not match, the cards are turned back over face down. The person with the most matches wins. Variation 1: Have teams play the game and have the matches agreed upon by the teams. This reduces the stress of individuals knowing or not knowing answers. Variation 2: Give different teams different games to create.

Have the teams swap with another team and play the other team's game. Variation 3: Have each team contribute questions and answers for a collective game. Have team play against team.

13. **Habit Sacrifice: (Results)** Sometimes during the Results section of the lesson, God moves learners to release something in their lives that is keeping them from being more Christlike. A habit can be anything from TV soaps to drug addiction. A "Habit Sacrifice" is a visual expression of giving up the habit.

> **Example 1: (Results)** The learners write a habit on a piece of paper and throw it in a trashcan. The learners then pray together for strength to break the habit and burn the contents of the can. (Be careful not to violate a fire code. It may be possible to do this in the parking lot.)

> **Example 2: (Results)** The teacher brings a paper shredder to class and places a sign on it: "GONE FOREVER." The learners have a time of reflection, then write the habit on a piece of paper. They then pray with an accountability partner for the strength to break the habit and together the partners shred their habits.

> **Example 3: (Results)** The Scripture is Rom 12:1–2. The students have learned that every part of them belongs to God. During the Revelation section of the lesson the learners in the biblical-historical group created a simple replica of an Old Testament altar. During the Responsibility section learners discussed what it means to give your body to God. They identified areas of the lives of contemporary adults that might hinder God's being in control of their lives. During the Results section of the lesson the learners have a time of personal reflection. They ask God to bring to mind something in their lives that might be hindering them from growing in Christ. They are directed to write the habits on pieces of paper and fold them over. The learners with papers in hand gather around the altar. They pray for each other and for strength to give these habits to God. They lay the papers on the altar and light it. The habits are consumed. (Build the altar in a large aluminum foil roasting pan. Have a fire extinguisher available. Use the parking lot, if possible.)

14. **Interviews: (Relevance, Revelation, Responsibility)** Interviews can be used in a multitude of ways. Usually the teacher poses the question and the person interviewed answers. However, any learner(s) can

be the interviewer(s). The persons interviewed are usually resource people from the congregation or from the church staff or community. Resource people from the congregation might be mature Christians suffering from disability or recent widows. A pastor or Christian education director or youth minister might be great resources. Christians from your community such as a ballplayer, singer, or artist can offer interesting perspectives in an interview.

Example: (Responsibility) The teacher thanks the pastor for coming today for the interview. The teacher explains to the pastor in front of the learners, "Today we have been studying 1 Tim 6:17–19, instructions to the rich. One of the things we have learned is that God wants us to depend on Him rather than our money."

Question 1: "Has there ever been a time in your life when you trusted your money more than in God? If so, tell us about it."

Question 2: "Can you share one time you depended on God rather than money?"

Question 3: "In our Bible study we learned that we should be using our money so that it counts when we get to heaven. Can you tell us some ways you use your money so that it has eternal value?"

The teacher may encourage the learners to ask further questions or to discuss how the answers from the person interviewed related to the principles in the text. The teacher then transitions the learners into the Results section for personal application.

15. **Journaling: (Responsibility, Results)** Journaling is an opportunity for learners to put into words newly acquired concepts connecting new ideas with old experiences. This gives deeper meaning and more significance to new concepts. With journaling they can be retrieved from memory more easily when needed for creative thinking or problem-solving. It is appropriate for times of reflection during the application phase of Bible study (Responsibility) or to record progress when a learner desires to monitor action responses following Bible study. (Results)

Example 1: (Responsibility) Today we've been studying Job's response to God even through difficult times. Think of someone in your life that reminds you of Job. Tell their story and describe how they behaved in similar ways to Job.

Example 2: (Results) Describe something in your life that is a Job-like struggle. What can you do to respond to your circumstances, as Job did? Continue to write in your journal this week describing the actions/attitudes you are taking daily that are similar to the actions/attitudes of Job.

Example 3: (Results) The Bible study focuses on learning to pray. After studying the Lord's Prayer, in the Results portion of the lesson the teacher challenges the students to pray following God's pattern. The learners commit to their new prayer habits. The teacher gives each of the learners a journal and encourages them to record how often they are praying, what they are praying for, and how prayers are being answered. The learners take home their journals as tools for recording progress and for self-accountability.

16. **Lecture: (Revelation)** Lecture is the most widely used method of teaching the Bible. It can be very effective, especially in the "Bible Content" section of the lesson. It is an opportunity for the teacher to share facts found in the personal Bible study. Effective lecture is organized and orderly. It tells a story or shares content. Lecture should never be done without visual and kinesthetic support.

17. **Mail a Reminder (Results)** Mail a Reminder is to help learners remember the commitment they made during the Results section of the Bible study. The teacher provides postcards, and the learner writes anything they wish that will remind them of their commitment. They address the card to themselves, and the teacher collects them and mails them in a day or two. Learners receive the card during the week between Bible studies and are reminded of their commitment.

18. **Mesmerizing Pictures: (Relevance, Revelation, Responsibility, Results)** Mesmerizing pictures are not images that put people to sleep but rather pictures that plunge people into deep thought. The teacher puts the mesmerizing picture on the PowerPoint screen or uncovers a prepared picture. The picture should be related to the contemporary life if it is used in the Relevance, Responsibility or Results section of the lesson. It should be from Bible times if used during the Revelation

section. Pictures can be found in newspapers, magazines, Internet,[6] and paintings. Pictures must be large enough for every person in the class to see when projected. If you do not wish to project the picture, each person or each study group needs a personal copy. Pictures can also be included in a study sheet so that students can take them home.

Example: (Responsibility) The learners have just completed the content section of a Bible study on Psalm 46, God is our Refuge. After the learners reflect on the learning principles that were gleaned from the passage, the teacher puts up a PowerPoint picture of the September 11th Twin Tower tragedy. The class goes to personal reflection for two minutes, followed by group discussion. The discussion question is "What does Psalm 46 have to do with September 11th?"

19. **Metaphors: (Revelation)** Learners can create metaphors to help them understand the meaning of difficult words in the Bible passage. Metaphors engage the brain on a creative level and require the learner to experiment with the meaning of language. This technique is usually used during the content section of the lesson.

Example: (Revelation) As the teacher shares the Bible passage Eph 1:3–9, a learner expresses confusion regarding the word "redemption" in verse 7. The teacher leads the learners to experiment with creating metaphors that explain the meaning of redemption. The teacher puts up on the wall "Redemption is like a . . ." The learners are to complete the metaphor. Here is one that some learners created. "Redemption is like a governor pardoning a prisoner on death row."

20. **Mime: (Relevance, Responsibility)** Mime is drama without words. Faces can be painted to accentuate expressions. The advantage to mime is that learners must focus on action and emotion. It can be a very effective way of presenting an introduction or an application.

Example: (Relevance) The passage is Rom 6:23 (The gift of God). Two mimes introduce the Bible study. Mime 1 brings mime 2 a gift. Mime 2 refuses. Mime 1 tries everything to get mime 2 to take it. Mime 2 refuses. Mime 1 leaves with the gift. Mime 2 thinks about the

---

[6] For ideas, put a word that relates to the application of the Scripture passage into an Internet search engine. When the list of addresses comes up, click on images at the top of the page and it will change your pages to images from multiple Web sites. Be careful to use only images that are free and do not have copyright.

gift and gets very sad. Mime 2 paces and pouts, finally sitting down in dejection. Mime 1 comes back and offers the gift again, and Mime 2 takes it and expresses elation. The teacher asks the learners to verbalize the mime. They discuss what happened. The teacher tells the learners that today's Bible study is about a gift. The teacher invites the learners to look at Rom 6:23.

21. **Mission Trips: (Results)** Going on a mission trip is a great action that should come out of a challenge to share Christ and to serve God. Mission trips can be local or international. Whenever the teacher shares passages of Scripture that teach service or sharing the gospel, the teacher should challenge learners in the Results section of the lesson with opportunities to go.

Example 1: (Results) Matthew 20:26–28 (The greatest is one who serves, not one who is served.) A deacon in our church taught a men's Sunday school class. One morning the class had been studying about God wanting us to serve in His name. He told his class that his wife had prepared a picnic lunch for them and their wives if they would go on a Sunday afternoon mission trip. They agreed, and after enjoying the picnic at the church, they got in their cars and followed him out into the country. They arrived at a little shack miles from civilization. They all got out of their cars, and the teacher said, "God led me to this woman yesterday. She needs us." He led the way into the shack. The shack had dirt floors and a huge hole in the roof. There was no bathroom, and the woman had been using the fireplace. Her hair was matted and filthy. Her clothes were tattered, and her mind was dull. There were remnants of foul food here and there. The teacher went to work immediately. He poured clean water from a container that he had brought with him. He knelt in the dirt and washed her hands, arms, and feet. His wife fed her some soup she had brought. The class members began to look for things they could do to help. They tried to clean and patch holes. As they left, they planned to come again with tools and dishes and food. They contacted social services and tried to get the woman help. They took turns going to her house and helping until they could get her professional care. They served. This was impacting and life-changing. I know because I was a seminary student and I was in that group that went that day.

22. Music: (Relevance, Revelation, Responsibility, Results) Music is very helpful during any section of the lesson. It can add to drama, provide a background for group activities, contribute to reflection, and more. It can also restate the impact of the lesson. The teacher can play a DVD player, a person can sing, or someone can play an instrument live. Music can also involve learners singing together a song of commitment. Music during a time of decision and commitment must support dialogue with God. Music should never be distracting or self-serving.

Example 1: (Results) The lesson has been Psalm 23. During the personal reflection time, the teacher plays a DVD of the New 23rd quietly in the background.

23. Panel Discussions: (Responsibility) Panel discussions can be a very effective method of applying a Bible passage to contemporary life. After the principles of the passage have been reviewed, the teacher introduces a panel of guests. Guests should be persons who have personal experiences that make them experts in applying the principles of the passage. Guest panelists might represent different generations or different cultures. Guest panels might have some unbelievers, some new believers, and some old believers. Guest panels might represent different vocations or different life experiences. The teacher should carefully select the panel, choosing guests who are going to help students understand the contemporary application of the passage. Panels should be three to five people. The teacher should prepare some questions that lead the panel to share helpful information. The panel usually answers questions from the learners, with the teacher supplying questions if needed. Questions can be directed to a specific panel member, or the question can be offered for anyone on the panel to answer.

Example 1: (Responsibility) The learners have just completed the study of James 2:1–12. (Favoritism) The panel is:

> Guest 1:   The first guest is a Hispanic male, 35 years old, who has just come back from a business trip to Belgium where he visited the International Baptist Church in Brussels. He experienced a church where there was no majority culture. The church was a blend of people representing at least 35

different cultures. People conversed in multiple languages, and they also sang in multiple languages simultaneously.

Guest 2:   This guest is a 29-year-old white woman covered in tattoos and piercings. She has been coming to your church for five months and was saved three weeks ago. She was baptized and joined your church last Sunday.

Guest 3:   This guest is a 44-year-old black male who is a deacon in your church. He is a bank manager in your city and is well respected in the community. Most people do not realize that he was homeless during most of his childhood.

The teacher gives the learners the written list of principles that they uncovered in James 2:1–12, and the list of guests with a brief introductory sketch. The teacher asks the learners to select a table and, with a small group of five students, create three to five questions that will help them understand how to apply James 2 to contemporary life. The students are given five minutes before they join the large group. The panel guests introduce themselves and the learning groups take turns sharing questions with panel members. The teacher has not only selected guests strategically; he has also prepared questions if needed. When the interview is over, the teacher thanks the guests, summarizes, and then transitions to Results.

24. **Peer Pairs: (Relevance, Revelation, Responsibility, Results)** Peer pairs encourage learners to discuss in pairs something being taught or discovered in the lesson. It gives opportunity for self-expression and to receive and reflect upon peer reaction. It also gives opportunity for learners to hear another's perspective, negotiate ideas, or become more convinced of one's own opinion. It can be effectively used during any part of the lesson.

Example 1: (Relevance) At the beginning of the Bible study session the teacher tells the learners to pick a partner and together write down one attitude that they think Christ has and they don't. Then the teacher says, "In Philippians 2:5 the Scripture tells us that we should have the same attitude as Christ. Today we are studying Philippians

2:1–11 so that we will understand what Christ's attitude is and how we can have it."

Example 2: (Revelation) Peer pairs can also be used during the content section by the teacher saying, "Pick a partner and study Philippians 2:1–11. Together make a list of the attitudes of Christ."

Example 3: (Responsibility) Peer pairs can also be used in application. The teacher says, "From the list of Christ's attitudes that we discovered while studying the content, discuss with a partner how adults today can live with those Christlike attitudes."

Example 4: (Results) Peer pairs can also be used in the action section of the lesson. The teacher says, "Now that we understand that God wants us to have attitudes like Christ, choose a partner and share one attitude that you would like to work on this week. Pray for each other now in class and promise to pray for each other every day this week. Next week when we meet again, you can share your experience."

25. **Personal Reflection: (Relevance, Revelation, Responsibility, Results)** Personal reflection is taking time to rehearse mentally and process new information and concepts while relating them to existing experience. This can take place any time during the lesson, but is most often used during the challenge to action (Results). This allows learners the time to consider alternative responses to the challenges of the Bible study and to select an appropriate action.

Example: (Results) Today we have studied the plan of salvation from Rom 10:9–10. We have studied Christ's provision for our redemption. We have learned the steps we must take to give our lives to God. God may be asking you to give your life to him. He may be asking you to share with a friend how to be saved. Bow your heads and think about what God wants you to do. After a time of reflection, the teacher asks learners to pray and make their commitment to God.

26. **Pictures of History Locations and Culture: (Revelation)** Graphic images have tremendous impact on retention. It is important for teachers to include pictures of history, culture, locations, and anything else that will help the learner understand the biblical setting of the passage. Pictures should be large enough to be easily seen. They can be projected on a wall or included on study sheets to increase visibility.

27. Prayer of Commitment: (Results) The teacher should include time for prayer during the Result section of the lesson. Reflection is meditation. It is thinking through your life, the new information, and how God wants you to respond. Prayer accompanies reflection because, whether silently or aloud, it verbalizes your feelings, your commitment, your promises to God. It is essential to Christian action. It connects the learner with the Source of power needed to carry out the action.

   Example: (Results) 1 Peter 1:13–16. After studying about holy living in 1 Peter, the teacher leads the learners to reflect on a choice they could make that would improve their personal holiness. They are encouraged to talk with God, meditate, and respond to whatever He is telling them to do. After several minutes of reflection and prayer, they pray with a partner for strength to obey God.

28. Promise Ring: (Results) A promise ring reminds you of your promise to God. It can be made from things like rubber bands, paper, paper clips, soda can lids, etc. It can be worn on your little finger, your toe, or just carried with your change. The point of it is to remind you that you have made God a promise.

   Example: James 5:12. The lesson was on truthful speech from James, and the challenge to commitment was to be known as a person who tells the truth. After the reflection and prayer time, the teacher passes out little aluminum rings that have the word "truth" engraved on them. The learners wear the promise rings (or put them with their coins), reminding them that their tongue has been given to God and that they have promised it will always tell the truth.

29. Puppets: (Relevance, Revelation, Responsibility) Although puppets are usually used in children's ministry, adults also enjoy puppets occasionally.

   Option 1: If you have a puppet team at the church, three months ahead explain to them the kind of scenario you want them to dramatize to apply a particular passage of Scripture. Get a commitment for a particular Sunday. One month ahead check on them to read and approve the script. The drama team will come on the appointed Sunday and use five to ten minutes to present a story that portrays the contemporary application of your text.

Option 2: Set up learning tables. Include clean old socks, glue, yarn, buttons, and permanent markers. Give each table a written list of principles that they discovered during the Revelation section of the Bible study. Ask students to create a contemporary story applying the principles of the Scripture text (10 mins.). Tell students they may use puppet props if they wish. The sock puppets are so simple that they are less threatening. If the teacher makes it clear that they can share the application story with or without puppets, and that puppets can mean a plain or decorated sock, adults feel more relaxed about the learning experience. The teacher then leads the learners to share their applications with each other (10 mins.). The teacher summarizes and transitions to the Results section of the lesson.

Option 3: Another simple puppet that adults may be more comfortable using is a nylon stocking over a coat hanger. Turn the coat hanger upside-down. Bend the two lateral edges of the coat hanger toward the center so that the coat hanger forms a diamond shape with the crook of the hanger at the bottom. Thread a clean nylon over the coat hanger and cut and tie both ends. The entire diamond shape should be covered with nylon front and back. This forms the puppet face. The face can be simply decorated with permanent marker, construction paper and glue, or buttons for eyes.

Option 4 Buy paper lunch bags either in white or brown. Use the paper bags to create puppets. Turn the bags upside down so that the bottom is at the top. The folded bottom becomes a moving mouth when your hand is inserted. Bag puppets can be decorated simply with bright colored markers. Remember, the application story is the point of this exercise. The puppets are just tools.

Example: (Responsibility) The learners have just studied Phil 2:12–18 about being lights in the world. The learners are invited to participate in small groups. Each learning table has a list of the principles of the passage, but each table has its own highlighted principle. Each table writes a two-minute puppet presentation demonstrating the contemporary application of their principle. For example: Principle (2:14) God wants us to do everything without arguing and complaining.

> Husband and wife puppets come in arguing about who has to drive carpool.

Wife :	*(in a whiny voice)* "James, I know it's your turn to drive carpool. You always try to get out of it."
Husband:	"Dorothy, it's your turn. I'm sick and tired of driving your turn as well as mine!"
	Puppets leave and come back arguing about who should take out the garbage.
Wife:	"I asked you to take out the garbage. Why is that always so hard?"
Husband:	"Dorothy, I'll do it in just a minute—just leave it!"
Wife:	Grumbling to herself as she takes out the garbage. "Well, I might as well do it myself! Later means never!"
	Puppets leave
	They come back and the wife starts complaining
Wife:	"Oh! I'm soooo tired. I work all day and then come home and have to cook. I hate cooking! Why can't we just eat out?"
	Door bell rings.
Wife:	"Hi Madge. What's up?"
Madge:	"I just came by to pick up that book I wanted to borrow. Hey, do you know the Bible study we had this week about how God wants us to stop grumbling and complaining? Well Steve and I promised each other that we would try it for a week. Wow! It's really hard. We are praying about it every day and God is helping us. I've only messed up one time. It sure makes a difference in our home. No fussing. I never realized what a bad habit I have gotten into —griping all the time. Anyway—God's working on us and we need it! See you, Dorothy. Thanks for the book!"

Dorothy leaves.

Husband and wife puppet look at each other. They look down.

Husband: "I'm willing to try it if you are."

Wife: "Yeah. I guess I am."

The other tables each share their puppet story applying the other principles from the passage. The teacher summarizes and transitions to the Results section of the lesson.

30. **Puzzles (crossword and others): (Revelation)** Puzzles are a great thing to include on a study sheet to review Bible facts. Crossword puzzles are easy to make with a very inexpensive software program such as http://www.crosswordweaver.com.

31. **Reflective Dialogue: (Relevance, Responsibility)** Reflective dialogue is the process of allowing our thinking to evolve through dialogue. It is interactive conversation with the purpose of thinking through, adjusting, and rethinking ideas. It involves putting your ideas on the table, listening to the perception of others, adjusting and clarifying your ideas, applying them to different scenarios, listening to and restating feedback, adjusting and clarifying your ideas again while understanding that your ideas may change permanently.

    Example: (Relevance, Responsibility) As the learners enter the Bible study, the teacher has a large poster on the wall with the statement, "God blesses men and women of faith." Learners are encouraged to sit in small groups of five, and they are challenged to agree upon an explanation of this statement. Then the groups share their explanations, and the teacher shares that the passage being studied today may change their explanation (Relevance). The teacher then facilitates the study on Heb 11:32–40. Following the study, the learners are asked to return to their small groups and discuss their previous explanations. Because the Bible study talks about men and women of faith who experiences death and persecution, learners will be challenged to talk about a broader view of "blessed faith" (Responsibility).

32. **Rewriting: (Revelation)** This method is useful for clarifying facts and is used most effectively when teaching the content of the Bible passage. When learners receive or uncover new information, the

meaning of the new information can be clarified by putting it in their own words in a few simple sentences.

Example: (Revelation) We have been talking about the background and content of Psalm 100. Please rewrite Psalm 100 expressing the meaning of the psalm in your own words.

33. **Role Play: (Relevance, Responsibility)** This is a variation of drama. Learners volunteer to play a role in a situation. The roles may or may not be scripted. The purpose is to help learners see a situation from different perspectives.

34. **Search and Discover: (Revelation)** Adult learners might believe a teacher when told facts. However, learners will not only believe, they will also remember facts that they discover for themselves. Search and discover activities are a great addition to a rich learning environment. It encourages learners to move from teacher-directed to self-directed learning because it introduces tools for discovery. Search and Discover is especially effective during the content portion of the lesson. It should be done at least every month to six weeks.

Example: (Revelation) The learners have had the lesson introduced and are ready to explore the content of the Bible passage. The teacher has prepared (before the class begins) five tables and placed them around the room. Each table has casual comfortable chairs placed around, and the tables hold learning materials. The teacher explains the content and challenge of each table, and learners are encouraged to choose a table of interest. It is best to limit the number of learners per table so that there is a variety of input for the lesson.

Table 1 has different versions of the Bible, different commentaries, and a computer with Bible software. The content challenge for table 1 is: Find out about the author and date of the writing of Psalm 100 and be ready to share your findings. List information about the author and date that could be significant in the writing of this psalm.

Table 2 has Bibles, commentaries, and a computer with Bible software. The content challenge is: Find and list the Bible truths (principles) in this psalm.

Table 3 has Bibles, commentaries, and a computer with Bible software. The content challenge is: Examine the genre and grammatical structure of Psalm 100. What can you find (cause-effect, metaphors, progressions in time or place, connecting words, etc.) that would help someone understand what the author meant when he wrote this psalm?

Table 4 has a keyboard and blank music paper and different versions of the Bible and a commentary. The table 4 content challenge is: Read and discuss the content and meaning of Psalm 100. Create a song or a poem that expresses the meaning of Psalm 100.

Table 5 has art supplies paper and colored chalk, spray fix, a Bible, and a commentary. The table 5 content challenge is: Read and discuss the meaning of Psalm 100. Pretend that you are the author. Give an artistic interpretation of what the author is trying to convey through this psalm.

The search and discover session should be about 15 minutes followed by 5 minutes of sharing. The teacher then summarizes the learning (3 mins.) by clarifying and adding necessary information to the reports from the groups at the tables. Search and Discover never takes the place of teacher preparation. The teacher must have in-depth knowledge that can be shared or added if search and discover proves to be weak or incomplete. The teacher moves among tables helping learners use the tools and facilitating learning. The teacher invites the learners to share their findings and then summarizes, making sure all learners understand the truths in the passage. The teacher then transitions the learners to application.

35. **Simulation: (Relevance, Responsibility)** In a simulation each learner participates in an artificial experience that is similar to a real-life experience. In some cases learners are assigned to play a role in the simulation. In other cases the learner plays himself and reacts to the circumstances confronting him. The purpose of a simulation is to allow the learner to identify with persons who are actually experiencing the circumstances represented in the simulation.

Example: (Relevance) Learners in an adult Bible study receive an e-mail telling them that they are being watched because they are Christians. Police have arrested 13 from their church already, and 3 have been killed. Every Christian is now in danger and must go into hiding. They are instructed not to go to the church on Sunday morning but to meet in the basement of the building across from the church. They are told to bring some food and money and approach with extreme caution and not to talk to anyone. They are warned that when a sentry stops them, they should bend down and draw a fish in the dirt without saying a word. On Sunday morning the simulation is acted out. The class follows the instructions, approaching with caution and drawing the sign of the fish. Entering the dark building they are taken by a sentry with a candle through the dark hallway into a candle-lit basement room. As they come in they are asked to put whatever they have on the "share table" in the center of the room. The teacher shares a lesson on the early church from 1 Pet 3:13–17. Before they leave the teacher asks them to take what they need from the share table. The simulation is similar to an experience believers in Peter's time may have had. It helps learners think through what it would be like to live in times or places of persecution. Experiencing the simulation helps learners to personalize the Scripture learning and appreciate it on a deeper level.

36. Stories/Parables: (Relevance, Revelation, Responsibility, Results) Stories and parables are a great way to apply Scripture to everyday living. Be on the watch for short stories that can be used effectively. Keep a story file. Divide your file into the four sections of the lesson. Relevance stories will connect the learner with the theme of the Bible passage. Revelation stories will be paraphrased Bible stories with accurate content. Responsibility stories will apply the Bible principles to the contemporary world. Results stories will challenge the learner to act. Stories can be shorts from magazines, newspapers, or books. Stories can sometimes be found in good children's books. When you are using a story as a teaching method, it is best to tell it rather than read it. You can use the story in large group and project the pictures on the wall, or you can get multiple copies and have learning groups read and discuss it together. Stories should not take more than two to five minutes.

Example 1: (Responsibility) James 4:6, *Sidney & Norman: A Tale of Two Pigs* by Phil Vischer.[7] We have used this story in an adult class. Students were moved—some to tears. This is a powerful

---

[7] P. Vischer, *Sidney & Norman: A Tale of Two Pigs* (China: Tommy Nelson—a division of Thomas Nelson Publishers, 2006).

illustration of God's acceptance and the need for us to view ourselves with humility and honesty.

Example 2: (Responsibility) Galatians 6:1–10, *You Are Special* by Max Lucado.[8] We have seen this book read, told, and acted out. It is a powerful story of how we cannot create and maintain our own righteousness. and we cannot make other people view us as we really are. We need to come to God, our Maker, for forgiveness and healing.

Example 3: (Results) Philippians 3:17, a story found in Karla Worley's *Growing Weary Doing Good: Encouragement for Exhausted Women*.[9] This story is about a dog that was run over by a car and lost her two back legs. The vet wanted to put the dog to sleep, but the owner begged for her life and nursed the dog back to health. The dog could only walk precariously on her front legs with her back arched holding her bottom over her head, but was able to get around and became very proficient walking that way. In several months, the owner incredulously realized that the dog was going to have puppies. The worried owner fussed over the pregnant dog, and the dog was amazingly healthy throughout her pregnancy. In due time she delivered eight cute little pups. The owner came in a few days later to find all eight puppies following their mother, walking on their front paws, bottoms over heads. The question is, "What do your followers look like?"

37. **Study Sheets:** (Relevance, Revelation, Responsibility, Results) A Study Sheet is a visual that supports multiple activities throughout the lesson. It is an excellent way to include both visual and kinesthetic learning activities. There are infinite ways to design a Study Sheet in format and shape. Graphic images, word art, colored paper and colored ink enhance the appeal and please your visual learners. Leave white space between sections so that important points are emphasized. Check for grammar, spelling and clarity. Study Sheets can contain questions, puzzles, games, activities, instructions, and case studies. Make a practice of using Study Sheets to write instructions for learning exercises. Writing instructions lowers the anxiety level in the classroom. Consider using both sides of one page rather than

---

[8] M. Lucado, *You Are Special (Max Lucado's Wemmicks)* (Wheaton, IL: Crossway, 2007).

[9] K. Worley, *Growing Weary Doing Good: Encouragement for Exhausted Women* (Birmingham, AL: New Hope Publishing, 2001), 113.

multiple pages. Concise is usually better than prolific. Remember, students often take a Study Sheet home to help them remember the lesson. It needs to be worthy of their attention.

Example Relevance: Students are handed a Study Sheet as they enter the classroom. The instructions are: Find a table and discuss the following question: "Why does God let bad things happen to good people?" After about 5 minutes of discussion, the teacher transitions the class into a Bible study on Gen 50:19-21.

Example Revelation: The Scripture passage is written on the Study Sheet so that every learner has the Bible translation that is being used in the study. The instructions are for students to work in small groups and answer the following questions about the content of the Bible passage: Who? What? When? Where? Why? On the Study Sheet the questions are listed with space for answering after each question.

Example Responsibility: The teacher has included in the Study Sheets a case study with a modern day scenario. The students are asked to apply the principles they have learned from the study of the Bible passage to the contemporary scenario.

Example Results: The teacher says, "Today we have been studying the power of praying for each other. Choose a prayer partner for this week. Talk with your partner about prayer requests. Write down the requests in the prayer box on your Study Sheet. This week use your Study Sheet to remind you to pray for your prayer partner's requests."

38. **Teach to Teach: (Revelation, Responsibility, Results)** A method of supporting learners in any section of the lesson is Teach to Teach. When learners teach what they learned, they attain deeper levels of understanding and a higher capacity for retention.

Example: (Results) The learner has learned from the lesson on Rom 10:9–10 how to share his faith. The challenge is to teach another person in the coming week how to share their faith. The learners develop the materials for sharing their faith during the lesson. They rehearse how they will teach. They practice with a partner. They commit to teaching someone during the week.

Call to Holy Living

¹³Therefore, get your minds ready for action, being self-disciplined, and set your hope completely on the grace to be brought to you at the revelation of Jesus Christ. ¹⁴As obedient children, do not be conformed to the desires of your former ignorance ¹⁵but, as the One who called you is holy, you also are to be holy in all your conduct; ¹⁶for it is written, Be holy, because I am holy. (1 Pet 1:13–16)

Principles for Christian Living

List at least one principle for Christian living that is found in each of the following verses.

v. 13

v. 14

v. 15

Small Group Activity

Please read the following scenario; reflect on how 1 Pet 1:13–16 might be applicable. Answer the di*scussion* questions and be prepared to share your answers.

(Case Study) Herb wants a promotion. He works very hard and he is good at his job, but he always gets passed over. He notices that the guys who hang around with his boss and share shady jokes, go to the bar after work, and brag about their sexual exploits, are the ones who seem to move up in the company. Herb has never participated because of his Christian convictions. But, he was not chosen again this week, and it was at least the fifth pass over. Herb thinks he may need to change his tactics.

After studying this passage, what advice would you give Herb? (1:16)

What does verse 13 say about Herb's hope?

What does it mean to get your mind ready for action? Decide on 3 things that could help Herb get his mind ready for action.

1.

2.

3.

Be prepared to share your answers with the large group.

39. **Time-Lines: (Revelation)** Time-lines can be teacher- or student-created visual support to Bible learning. Butcher paper spread across a wall and magic markers are all you need to create a great visual image.

   Example: (Revelation) While studying the book of Acts, the learners create a time-line of the missionary journeys of the apostle Paul.

40. **Testimony: (Relevance, Responsibility)** The teacher or learner shares a personal experience that is relevant to the Bible study. When used as an introduction to a passage, it stimulates interest and helps the learners see the relevance of the Bible passage to be studied. When used for application, testimonies share a failure or a success in applying the principles of the passage.

   Example 1: (Relevance) Marjorie shares about her recent bout with cancer. She tells how devastated she was when she found out and how scared she was about having surgery. She then says, "As I found myself in the depths of despair, the Lord kept bringing to mind Psalm 27:1 and it made all of the difference." Today we are going to study Psalm 27:1–6. What is happening in your life that makes you afraid? This psalm can help you too.

   Example 2: (Responsibility) The principles of Rom 12:1–2 are discovered and discussed by learners. A man stands and shares: "Five years ago I had a great job, a wife, and two little girls. But I loved myself and wanted my freedom. I started hanging around the bars and doing some drugs. I met a woman who thought I was great. She was enjoying the same life. I left my wife and children to hang out with her. Eventually I lost my job. My wife divorced me. My friend went back east. I lost everything that mattered to me, and I was really feeling alone. One day, about a year ago, I met a guy at the gym. He told me about Jesus, and he told me how to belong to God's family through trusting Jesus as my Savior. God began to change my thinking. I started reading and studying the Bible, and I realized that I needed to change my life. I started hanging out with other Christians. I didn't really care about the bar or the drugs. I realized that I had new values and a new outlook. The more I learned about what Jesus has done for me, the more I wanted to stop sinning. Now I want to grow more and more like Christ, but it's not easy. Some days I make mistakes. When I blow it, I read the Bible and pray a lot. Everything God shows me to do, I try to obey. When I fail, I tell God I am sorry, and I remind myself that God isn't finished with me yet. I am a new person. It's amazing!"

The teacher says to the learners. Let's peer pair and do this activity. Take the piece of paper in front of you. Put on the left top "BEFORE" and on the right top "AFTER." On the left side of the paper, list the things that characterized Pete's life before Christ. On the right list the things that characterized Pete's life after he gave his life to Christ. When you are finished, discuss with your partner some things Pete does as a Christian that helped his life change.

41. **Threaded Discussion: (Relevance, Revelation, Responsibility, Results)** Online threaded discussion is an electronic discussion via e-mail or Web site that is visually structured in a hierarchical fashion so that responders can address any participant's contribution by clicking on the contribution and typing a response. The participants can easily see who has responded to each piece of information and how many responses each question or comment has. Often teachers will begin with a thought-provoking question posed online and instruct students to respond over a particular time period. This is a great method to use for a preclass activity to connect learners to the passage and point out the relevance of the passage (Relevance). It is great to continue a discussion of the Bible content presented in a lesson (Revelation). It is helpful for continuing the application discussion that began in class (Responsibility). Threaded discussion can encourage follow-up and accountability as students share the ongoing results of their personal commitment (Results).

   Example 1: (Relevance) Learners are e-mailed and asked to watch for frightening things that happen during the week. Personal experiences, newscasts, newspapers, etc.—may all be used. Ask the learners to share the events as they occur and discuss how God relates to the negative events in the world. Encourage learners to contribute new ideas as well as respond to each other. At the beginning of the face-to-face Bible study, read a few highlights from the threaded discussion and explain that today's Bible study focus passage answers the question, "How does God relate to the bad things that happen in the world?" Then begin studying Isaiah 12.

   Example 2: (Results) At the end of class the teacher says, "Today we have been studying Isaiah 12, and we have committed to carry the

Bible verse Isaiah 12:2 with us this week and when things happen to us that cause us to fear, we will read the verse and trust in God. Please join our online discussion by [suggest a day] and share what God is teaching you through this passage this week."

42. Video Clips: (Relevance, Revelation, Responsibility, Results) Video clips can be used effectively in any section of a Bible study. Video clips should usually be two to five minutes and be used only when they accomplish the teaching objective for that section of the lesson. Sources include both commercial and amateur. Sample sources for both commercial and personal downloadable video clips include: Sermon Spice,[10] Point of Power,[11] Worship House,[12] Bluefish TV,[13] God Tube,[14] and Visual Bible.[15] All sources have both good and poor videos, and each video must be carefully considered for its biblical accuracy and appropriate contemporary content. Personal videos can also be very effective, especially with personal interviews on specific topics or videotaping a personal testimony.

Example 1: (Relevance) Interview people on the street (with their permission) and videotape their responses to the question, "How do you get peace with God?" Either post your resulting video (3–4 mins.) on YouTube and send the address to your class participants asking them to view it before class, or play the video in the first few minutes of class. Have a class discussion about the responses and come to the collective conclusion that people need to know the answer to this question and that is why you are studying Rom 5:1–5.

Example 2: (Revelation) In the content section of a lesson on Paul and Silas in Jail (Acts 16), the teacher shows a video from "The Visual Bible,"[16] dramatizing the Bible scene as the Scripture passage is read. This is a creative way to read Scripture, and it helps learners visualize the passage. The teacher then proceeds with facilitating the learning of the Bible content.

Example 3: (Responsibility) After the learners have studied 2 Cor 9:7 and have determined the principles in the passage on giving, the

---

[10] http://www.sermonspice.com
[11] http://www.pointofpower.com
[12] http://www.worshiphousemedia.com
[13] http://www.bluefishtv.com/Store/downloadable_video_illustrations
[14] www.GodTube.com
[15] www.visualbible.com
[16] www.visualbible.com

teacher plays "The Offering Plate,"[17] which is a very short video clip that tells what people might be thinking as they put money in the offering plate at church. The teacher then invites learners to discuss in small groups how the Scripture text applies to the people in the video.

43. Workdays: (Results) Workdays are planned opportunities to serve others. Workdays should not just involve parishioners cleaning the church. The teacher should investigate needs in the church family: widows who need a roof or yard work, people who need transportation to doctors, single mothers who need a break, people who have cancer and need their house cleaned. It is also great to plan trips to nursing homes or jails for the purpose of serving. It is helpful to have available in the class an ongoing list of work needs in the class and in the church.

Example: (Results) Matthew 25:37–40. The learners have just completed a lesson on "Whatever you did for one of the least of these brothers of mine, you did for me." The teacher provides the learners with a list of things that their brothers and sisters need. They plan work teams and select a day to go. They pray about ways they can share their faith as they serve.

---

[17]http://www.bluefishtv.com/Store/Downloadable_Video_Illustrations/1573/The_Offering _Plate__Lesson_Available_

APPENDIX H[18]

Maslow's Hierarchy of Needs

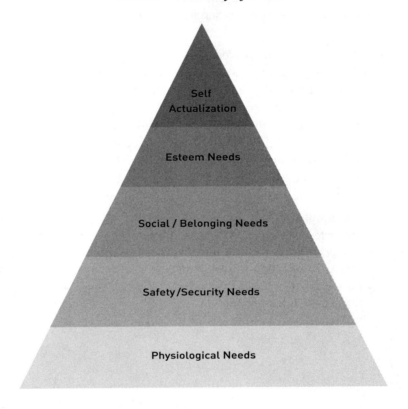

Self Actualization

Esteem Needs

Social / Belonging Needs

Safety /Security Needs

Physiological Needs

---

[18] L. E. Berk, *Exploring Lifespan Development* (San Francisco: Allyn and Bacon, 2008), 13.

APPENDIX I

Debate Rules and Suggestions, [19]
Advice on Debating with Others

1. Avoid the use of "never."
2. Avoid the use of "always."
3. Refrain from saying you are wrong.
4. You can say your idea is mistaken.
5. Don't disagree with obvious truths.
6. Attack the idea, not the person.
7. Use "many" rather than "most."
8. Avoid exaggeration.
9. Use "some" rather than "many."
10. The use of "often" allows for exceptions.
11. The use of "generally" allows for exceptions.
12. Quote sources and numbers.
13. If it is just an opinion, admit it.
14. Do not present opinion as facts.
15. Smile when disagreeing.
16. Stress the positive.
17. You do not need to win every battle to win the war.
18. Concede minor or trivial points.
19. Avoid bickering, quarreling, and wrangling.
20. Watch your tone of voice.
21. Don't win a debate and lose a friend.
22. Keep your perspective—you're just debating.

---

[19] http://www.paulnoll.com/Books/Clear-English/debate-advice.html (accessed on June 2, 2009).

APPENDIX J

Bloom's Taxonomy Early Version

Knowledge: arrange, define, duplicate, label, list, memorize, name, order, recognize, relate, recall, repeat, reproduce, state.

Comprehension: classify, describe, discuss, explain, express, identify, indicate, locate, recognize, report, restate, review, select, translate.

Application: apply, choose, demonstrate, dramatize, employ, illustrate, interpret, operate, practice, schedule, sketch, solve, use, write.

Analysis: analyze, appraise, calculate, categorize, compare, contrast, criticize, differentiate, discriminate, distinguish, examine, experiment, question, test.

Synthesis: arrange, assemble, collect, compose, construct, create, design, develop, formulate, manage, organize, plan, prepare, propose, set up, write.

Evaluation: appraise, argue, assess, attach, choose, compare, defend, estimate, judge, predict, rate, core, select, support, value, evaluate.[20]

---

[20] http://www.officeport.com/edu/blooms.htm (accessed on June 8, 2009).

NAME INDEX

SCRIPTURE INDEX